Governing Cities

This book presents the latest research on three issues of crucial importance to Asian cities: governance, livability, and sustainability. Together, these issues canvass the salient trends defining Asian urbanization and are explored through an eclectic compendium of studies that represent the many voices of this diverse region. Examining the processes and implications of Asian urbanization, the book interweaves practical cases with theories and empirical rigor while lending insight and complexity into the towering challenges of urban governance. The book targets a broad audience including thinkers, practitioners, and students.

Kris Hartley is Assistant Professor in the Department of Asian and Policy Studies at The Education University of Hong Kong. His research interests include public policy and administration in Asia with a focus on environment and technology.

Glen Kuecker is Professor of Latin American history and Director of City Lab at DePauw University. His recent work explores the role of cities in the perfect storm of 21st-century systemic crises.

Michael Waschak is Assistant Professor in Public Policy at Nazarbayev University in Kazakhstan. He received his doctorate in public policy in 2009 from the Georgia Institute of Technology in Atlanta, Georgia, USA. Prior to Joining Nazarbayev University Dr. Waschak worked for eight years at the Rochester Institute of Technology (RIT) in Rochester, New York (USA) and for the RIT Kosovo campus in Pristina, Kosovo.

Jun Jie Woo is Assistant Professor in the Department of Asian and Policy Studies at The Education University of Hong Kong. His research interests include policy design, education governance, technology and urban governance, and the political economy of development in Asia.

Charles Chao Rong Phua researched comparative problem-solving approaches of US, China, and Singapore for his PhD at the National University of Singapore and was Fulbright Fellow at Brookings Institution. Formerly the deputy director of a state think-tank on cities and head research trainer (defence), he now heads Solaris Strategies Singapore, chairs the Association for Public Affairs (Singapore) and is adjunct faculty for the Smart City programme at Singapore Management University.

Routledge Advances in Regional Economics, Science and Policy

Gastronomy and Local Development
The Quality of Products, Places and Experiences
Edited by Nicola Bellini, Cécile Clergeau and Olivier Etcheverria

The Geography of Scientific Collaboration
Agnieszka Olechnicka, Adam Ploszaj and Dorota Celińska-Janowicz

The Canada-U.S. Border in the 21st Century
Trade, Immigration and Security in the Age of Trump
John B. Sutcliffe and William P. Anderson

Economic Clusters and Globalization
Diversity and Resilience
Edited by Francisco Puig and Berrbizne Urzelai

Transnational Regions in Historical Perspective
Edited by Marten Boon, Hein A.M. Klemann and Ben Wubs

Urban Development in China under the Institution of Land Rights
Jieming Zhu

The Geography of Mobility, Wellbeing and Development in China
Understanding Transformations Through Big Data
Edited by Wenjie Wu and Yiming Wang

Traveling Expertise and Regional Development
Andreas Öjehag-Pettersson and Tomas Mitander

Governing Cities
Asia's Urban Transformation
Edited by Kris Hartley, Glen Kuecker, Michael Waschak, Jun Jie Woo, and Charles Chao Rong Phua

For more information about this series, please visit: www.routledge.com/series/ RAIRESP

Governing Cities
Asia's Urban Transformation

**Edited by Kris Hartley,
Glen Kuecker, Michael Waschak,
Jun Jie Woo, and
Charles Chao Rong Phua**

Foreword by Tommy Koh

Routledge
Taylor & Francis Group

LONDON AND NEW YORK

First published 2020 by Routledge

2 Park Square, Milton Park, Abingdon, Oxon OX14 4RN
605 Third Avenue, New York, NY 10017

Routledge is an imprint of the Taylor & Francis Group, an informa business

First issued in paperback 2022

Publisher's Note

The publisher has gone to great lengths to ensure the quality of this reprint but points out that some imperfections in the original copies may be apparent.

British Library Cataloguing-in-Publication Data
A catalogue record for this book is available from the British Library

Library of Congress Cataloging-in-Publication Data
A catalog record for this book has been requested

ISBN: 978-1-138-34188-3 (hbk)
ISBN: 978-1-03-233692-3 (pbk)
DOI: 10.4324/9780429439940

Typeset in Galliard
by Apex CoVantage, LLC

Contents

Figures

Tables

Foreword

I commend the editors for having taken the initiative to bring together this timely book. Why is this an important book?

First, the book is important because it addresses a paradigm shift that has taken place recently. The shift is from a world in which most of its population lives in the rural areas to a world in which the majority lives in the cities. We have become an urban world, and this trend will accelerate in the coming years. By the year, 2050, two-thirds of the world's population will live in cities.

Second, the book is important because it focuses on the future of cities in Asia. More than half of the world's urban population will be in Asia. The future of humanity will therefore be decided by how well or how badly the cities of Asia will be governed. Will they enjoy good governance? Will they be sustainable? Will they be able to fulfil the aspirations of their citizens? Will they be successful in achieving the UN's Sustainable Development Goals?

Third, Asia is a vast continent of great diversity and sharp contrasts. For example, at one end of the spectrum, we have the cities of Japan. They are close to being heaven on earth. At the other end of the spectrum, we have some cities in some other parts of Asia, which are closer to being hell on earth. The question is, can all the cities of Asia emulate the cities of Japan and, in time, approximate the quality of life that Japanese cities offer to their citizens?

Fourth, the cities of Asia face many challenges. It is a very sad reality that many Asian cities do not provide their citizens with clean drinking water. It is an even sadder fact that so many Asians do not have access to a toilet. It has been said that the great country, India, has more mobile phones than toilets. Prime Minister Modi has decided to put an end to open defecation in India. Housing, education, jobs, transportation, healthcare, safety, order, justice, social harmony, and a clean and healthy environment are some of the other challenges.

Fifth, the future of Asia and, therefore, of Asian cities, is confronted by three new challenges. Until recently, Asia was able to make progress because of free trade, the international division of labour, and globalization. We see, in some parts of the West, a new wave of protectionism, anti-globalization, and xenophobia. This is a threat to Asia. The second challenge is climate change and sea level rise. The third challenge is the Fourth Industrial Revolution. Asians, who are well-educated and skilled, will be able to harness the new opportunities that the revolution will bring. However, the revolution will also bring destruction and job losses.

In closing, I thank the editors of this volume and my friend Charles Chao Rong Phua for inviting me to contribute the foreword of this important book.

Tommy Koh
Professor of Law, NUS
Ambassador-At-Large, MFA

Contributors

Mulya Amri is an urban planning and public policy specialist based in Jakarta, Indonesia. He is the program director of Jakarta Property Institute and the senior consultant at the World Bank. Prior to that he was Research Fellow and Deputy Director at the Asia Competitiveness Institute, Lee Kuan Yew School of Public Policy, Singapore. Mulya has a PhD in Public Policy from the National University of Singapore. His research interests are planning, governance, and economic development of cities and sub-national regions.

Donna Doan Anderson is a PhD student in the Department of History at the University of California – Santa Barbara. Her research uses a cultural history approach to engage with the translocal and transnational connections of Asian American communities in the Midwest.

Elva Sagita Cindra is a Political Science graduate from the Faculty of Social and Political Science Universitas Indonesia (FISIP UI) with specialization in comparative politics. She is interested in research about human rights, public policy, and women's empowerment issues. She has served on a researcher team for WikiDPR and Sandya Institute.

Daixin Dai is an associate professor in the College of Architecture & Urban Planning at Tongji University. His research interest is creative and sustainable planning and design methodologies focused on the ecological and cultural context of sites. He also practices as a registered architect and urban planner in China.

George Frantz is an associate professor in the College of Architecture Art & Planning at Cornell University, where he teaches urban and regional planning. Trained as both landscape architect and urban planner, he has over 30 years of experience in teaching and professional practice in the USA and China.

Kris Hartley is Assistant Professor in the Department of Asian and Policy Studies at The Education University of Hong Kong. His research interests include public policy and administration in Asia with a focus on environment and technology.

Vishnu Juwono is an Assistant Professor (Lektor) in Public Administration and a researcher both in Collaborative Governance and Dynamic Public Service

(CG-DPS) and Politics of Taxation, Welfare and National Resilience (PolTax) research cluster at the Faculty of Administrative Science at Universitas Indonesia (FIA UI). He has been a Coordinator for International Cooperation in FIA UI since July 2017.

Rumit Singh Kakar is Assistant Professor in the School of Rehabilitation Sciences, Old Dominion University (USA). His research focuses on biomechanics, injury prevention, and human factors/ergonomics. He also has research interests in health care systems and public health issues as they relate to public policy and planning, with a focus on southeast Asia.

Tommy Koh is Ambassador-at-Large at Singapore's Ministry of Foreign Affairs. He was Singapore's Permanent Representative to the United Nations from 1968 to 1971 and again from 1974 to 1984. He was Ambassador to the United States of America from 1984 to 1990. He has also served as the UN Secretary-General's Special Envoy on a peace mission to Russia, Estonia, Latvia, and Lithuania in 1993.

Glen Kuecker is Professor of Latin American history and Director of City Lab at DePauw University. His recent work explores the role of cities in the perfect storm of 21st-century systemic crises.

Seunghyun Lee is a PhD candidate in Public Administration and Policy at the Graduate School of Public and International Affairs at the University of Pittsburgh. Her research interests include inter-organizational networks and collaborative governance in the context of public health, environment, and emergency management. Prior to her doctoral work, she was a Korea Foundation Think Tank intern at the RAND Corporation.

Lili Li is currently a PhD candidate at Lee Kuan Yew School of Public Policy, National University of Singapore. She holds a master's degree in science from Peking University. Her PhD thesis is about policy design and implementation for accelerating the low-carbon energy transition in China.

Charles Chao Rong Phua researched comparative problem-solving approaches of US, China, and Singapore for his PhD at the National University of Singapore and was Fulbright Fellow at Brookings Institution. Formerly the deputy director of a state think-tank on cities and head research trainer (defence), he now heads Solaris Strategies Singapore, chairs the Association for Public Affairs (Singapore) and is adjunct faculty for the Smart City programme at Singapore Management University.

Farukh Sarkulov majors in urban studies and mathematics at DePauw University. He is originally from Kyrgyzstan and now calls Chicago home. In addition to field research about smart cities in Delhi, Bangalore, and Jaipur, Farukh has done research with the Center for Financial Accountability in Delhi and Bhopal.

Tristan Stamets is a 2018 graduate of DePauw University. After majoring in energy & urban studies, he currently works to bring energy efficiency to underserved populations. Born to an Indian mother and an American father, he grew up in Singapore, Bangalore, and New Delhi. He is fascinated by global urban development and the way technology, social issues, and cultural identity intersect within Smart Cities.

Si Ying Tan is Postdoctoral Fellow at the Lee Kuan Yew School of Public Policy at National University of Singapore. Her research interests encompass health policy reforms in Asia, long-term care policies, social work interventions, and governance of disruptive technology in healthcare.

Hung Vo is an urban planner at the United States Agency for International Development. He was a GEO-6 Fellow at UN Environment and a Negotiation Research Fellow at the Bloomberg Harvard City Leadership Initiative. He has paneled in many high-level UN panels and been a member of Expert Working Groups related to urban development.

Michael Waschak is an assistant professor in public policy at Nazarbayev University in Kazakhstan. He received his doctorate in public policy in 2009 from the Georgia Institute of Technology in Atlanta, Georgia, USA. Prior to Joining Nazarbayev University Dr. Waschak worked for eight years at the Rochester Institute of Technology (RIT) in Rochester, New York (USA) and for the RIT Kosovo campus in Pristina, Kosovo.

Jun Jie Woo is Assistant Professor in the Department of Asian and Policy Studies at The Education University of Hong Kong. His research interests include policy design, education governance, technology and urban governance, and the political economy of development in Asia.

Yifei Yan is a fellow at the Department of Social Policy of the London School of Economics. Specializing in comparative public policy and administration, her research interests are at the intersection of policy and governance, education and development, and China and India.

Wei Yang is a lecturer in Global Health at King's College London. Her research focuses on measuring the impacts of social health insurance on inequities in access to care and fairness in financing and on identifying factors that drive inequities using longitudinal survey datasets.

Jingru Zhang received her PhD from the Lee Kuan Yew School of Public Policy, National University of Singapore. After earning her undergraduate degree from Shanghai Jiao Tong University, she joined the Energy and Environmental Sustainable Solutions for Megacities (E2S2) project, where her research focuses on urban municipal solid waste management.

Introduction

Globalization is facing uncertain headwinds in the 21st century, and cities are at the eye of the storm. After decades of increased global economic interconnectivity, many national governments appear to have soured on globalization, turning inwards amidst a political torrent of populist nativism. As nodes for trade and the exchange of ideas, cities can remain bastions of global engagement in the coming era of possible isolationism. However, the pursuit of cities in maintaining global economic and political connectivity is tempered by concurrent and often competing concerns about social equality, political representation, and cultural identity. At the same time, the heightened autonomy of local government and increasing importance of urban policy to national development agendas places cities at the center of debates about "good" governance and other normative growth models, shaping a policy legacy that must reconcile the convergence of an array of conflicting trends. This volume contributes to a deeper understanding of these forces by examining Asian urbanization in three analytical contexts: governance, social development, and sustainability.

In many ways, the 21st century will be the age of the Asian city, with transformative implications for the health, livelihoods, and happiness of the region's four billion inhabitants. According to the United Nations, two thirds of the global population will reside in cities by 2050. Half of that urban population will be in Asia, already home to 16 megacities (cities with more than 10 million inhabitants). Despite these gathering trends, Asia's recent urbanization has often been poorly managed and understood. Further, Asian cities are now becoming petri dishes for overlapping trends and colliding ideologies – generating opportunities for cultural hybridization but also testing the already fragile capacities of newly developed democratic and participatory governance systems. Against this backdrop, there is an increasingly urgent imperative for governments to address the challenges and opportunities of urbanization.

A lingering question provides the motivation behind the creation of this volume: what are the dominant trends in Asian urbanization that help scholars and practitioners to understand how well-prepared the region is to absorb systemic change and enter an age of uncertainty and instability? Asia's urban transformation calls for continual revisions in how we understand cities at a time when the role of cities as actors on the global stage is growing. The three analytical contexts of this volume – governance, social development, and sustainability – encompass many of the salient issues defining Asian urbanization and are explored through an eclectic compendium of studies representing the rich diversity of voices characterizing the region.

The notion of an uncertain future or "age of disruption" (with reference to social, political, and economic systems) is explored by the volume's three parts, which fit together to form a narrative about Asian urbanization. That narrative suggests that neoliberalism has precipitated changes in governance (Part I) that stimulated social contestations and concern for the public (Part II), with both shaping the policy values and epistemological frames guiding Asian cities as they face an uncertain future (Part III). Neoliberal economic transformation has re-worked the governance of Asian cities, resulting in contestation over the role and meaning of the "public" – aspects of civil society not in official service to corporate or government interests. This contestation remains unresolved as Asian cities enter an age of uncertainty that threatens their sustainability. Indeed, it is the marginalization of the public as a concept and agent of change – precipitated by particular manifestations of neoliberalism – that has arguably compromised sustainability at a critical juncture when the public is needed the most. As the conclusion of this volume argues, these problems are poorly recognized because policymaking remains stuck in a legacy framework of neoliberal transformation while failing to mediate the consequent tensions in social development and public life.

Part I

Part I of this volume examines these and other dynamics within a rapidly evolving governance environment disrupted by globalization and democratization, focusing on the role of actors, the flow of ideas, and the power of institutions to precipitate or obstruct policy change. Part I is informed by the idea that Asia is experiencing an historic evolution from statist-developmentalism and top-down planning to more distributed and polycentric forms of governance, as manifest through decentralization, democratization, and political liberalization. This trend predictably elevates the role and importance of cities. This phenomenon is propelled both by the now decades-long spread of new public management as a public sector reform model and by situational imperatives to improve service delivery and government responsiveness at ground-level. As such, Part I establishes a crucial theoretical basis for the volume's remaining parts by exploring the role of governments, policy, and governance models. It begins with an exploration of governance trends in the Philippines and Indonesia, two countries carrying the banner of decentralization and local autonomy in Asia. It continues with chapters about Singapore's governance efforts to be a "smart" nation, governance reform and corruption in Indonesia, ideology and pragmatism in Singapore's governance, urban master-planning in Central Asia, and a call for a new theoretical approach to understanding urban governance in Asia. This mix spans developmental contexts while capturing the evolutionary dynamics of power and policy change in urbanizing settings.

In Chapter 1, Mulya Amri examines the performance of city governance amidst decentralization, with a comparative focus on Indonesia and the Philippines. According to Amri, cities are increasingly occupying the attention of scholars and commentators, but there is little understanding about how they are governed. Amri considers salient questions of urban governance, including what motivates city mayors and how they are held accountable. He also considers how urban leaders balance the interests of citizens, central governments, and their own personal ambitions. City governance throughout most of Asia since the late 20th century has been characterized by decentralization, where mayors and city-level administrations have varying degrees of autonomy to decide the fate of their jurisdictions. This chapter explores the mechanisms of local governance in Indonesia and the Philippines – the largest countries in Southeast Asia – in the era of local autonomy. These two countries have been at the forefront of devolution for the past 20 years, and during that time there has been growing interest in ensuring that decentralization leads to better city government performance. A further similarity between the two countries is the adoption of both top-down (administrative) and bottom-up (political) incentives to ensure local government performance. The top-down decentralization measures include the central governments setting minimum service standards, conducting annual performance assessments, and presenting prestigious awards to local governments. When coupled with local democracy, these measures have triggered a competitive environment among city leaders to be recognized for their performance and gain political capital to boost their position in subsequent elections. Amri's chapter provides a window onto the mechanisms of city governance in the Asian Century, which has been much influenced by the discourse on decentralization.

In Chapter 2, Jun Jie Woo examines the governance dimensions of an increasingly common urban policy project: smart cities. The growing application of advanced information and communications technology (ICT) to urban governance and policymaking has led to the emergence of the "smart city" as an urban policy innovation capable of addressing the increasingly complex policy issues faced by city governments. More than simply applying new technological tools and solutions to urban problems, smart cities have given rise to novel and more responsive modes of urban governance. This chapter takes a policy design approach to understanding urban governance in a smart city. Focusing on Singapore's Smart Nation initiative, the chapter identifies the various design components and dynamics of the initiative that have influenced Singapore's development as a smart city. Woo argues that the Smart Nation initiative constitutes an act of policy layering, where new policy elements that are related to the smart city are layered upon Singapore's existing developmental approach to governance and policymaking. The result of this is an increasingly complex urban policy mix that features interconnections between new policy instruments and old policy goals.

In Chapter 3, Vishnu Juwono and Elva Sagita Cindra examine the issue of policy reform to address corruption in Indonesia's capital city, Jakarta. Having served as the mayor of a small Indonesian town, Solo, Joko Widodo (Jokowi) was elected as Governor of Jakarta in 2012. There were high hopes that he and his Deputy Governor, Ahok, would champion significant change toward more accountable, free, and transparent governance in a city that was famously riddled with systemic corruption. The two were elected on their credible track records of running smaller towns and regions. Not connected to the political elite of Jakarta, Jokowi and Ahok offered a promising new vision for governance, including a humbler and more accommodating leadership style representing the poor and confronting an established and corrupt patronage network. This chapter applies the lens of political pluralism to analyze the motivations of proponents and opponents of governance reform and anti-corruption initiatives in Jakarta during the period 2012–2017. In so doing, the chapter provides a comprehensive review of the progress and regress of governance reform under the leadership of Jokowi and Ahok. During his short tenure, Jokowi projected a style of governance, with the help of mass media, that aimed to be receptive to the needs of the poor. His healthcare and education programs boosted his popularity among Jakartans and elevated him to national prominence and a successful bid for the Indonesian presidency in 2014. Ahok become Governor of Jakarta through succession, adopting his own responsive leadership style – but not without controversy. Against this backdrop, this chapter focuses on the degree to which Jokowi and Ahok delivered on promises for more accountable, transparent, and responsive governance – an instructive case for similarly situated cities across Asia.

In Chapter 4, Charles Chao Rong Phua examines the role of pragmatism in the development of prevailing governance values in Singapore. Singapore's economic growth story provides a potentially useful model for closing the development gap between rich and poor countries. While Singapore enjoyed certain advantages such as a strategic location, the country in its infancy also had to overcome the challenge of natural resource scarcity and small size. One characteristic of its highly effective governance model, which has drawn attention from both scholars and practitioners, has been the country's unwavering commitment to the concept of pragmatism. Singapore's government has historically been focused on the efficient pursuit of development outcomes and the establishment of durable institutions to ensure consistency and resolve in development policies. This chapter examines the concept of Singaporean pragmatism as a force behind the formation and implementation of domestic social, economic, and infrastructure policies. The chapter takes a comparative historical perspective, examining the evolution of pragmatism across the leadership of the country's three prime ministers: Lee Kuan Yew, Goh Chok Tong, and Lee Hsien Loong. Historical and governmental documents are examined, along with interview data and other research and press materials.

In Chapter 5, Michael Waschak examines the issue of urban development through the lens of master-planning. In this chapter several important themes of urban planning are elaborated and combined to tell the story of the growth of Kazakhstan's new city of Astana/Nur-Sultan, which received national capital designation in 1997 and underwent a name-change in 2019. A capital city serves many purposes. First, it provides physical spaces with unique security, transportation, and logistical burdens for the operations of government. Second, it serves as a center of national culture and education, providing landmarks that reflect the goals, aspirations, and history of a people. Finally, it provides a livable and sustainable community for the diverse populations that typically accumulate in and around a capital city. The development of Astana encompasses all these elements, offering an instructive case to observe the formation and furtherance of national identity even as physical infrastructure continues to be built. Notably, many of the difficulties in planning and governing Astana's built environment parallel the challenges of building a cultural identity that has been evolving since the breakup of the Soviet Union. This chapter provides a broad review of the many forces shaping a new capital city and thereby has application to the study of similarly situated cities in both the developing and developed worlds.

In Chapter 6, the final chapter in Part I, Kris Hartley examines the potential for a new framework to explain urban governance and competitiveness in the 21st century. Against the backdrop of strong state intervention in the development of industrial capacity throughout the mid to late 20th century, Asian countries are now facing the prospect of a second-generation growth model in which the market plays a significant role in steering productive resources and thus determining urban and national economic competitiveness. This chapter introduces an analytical model that seeks to systematize the study of a new Asian growth reality, one in which the forces of global markets and the attendant reform pressures come up squarely against industrial systems that have been shaped by – and indeed are deeply embedded within – a dominant state. In what the chapter describes as a "New Asian Statism", legacy development policies are having to reconcile these two forces while at the same time accommodating a third – civil society. The framework introduced (the "RICE" framework) considers the roles of resilience, innovation, and civic enterprise as a confluence of dynamics shaping urban growth. More specifically, resilience is defined as the structural capacity of governance institutions to adapt to exogenous change, innovation as creative processes within government as opposed to the private sector, and civic enterprise as entrepreneurial behavior arising from multi-sectoral collaboration engaging government, private sector, and non-market civil society. The chapter argues that a fully realized version of market liberalization is not necessarily the fate of Asian countries, as the practices of historically wealthy non-Asian countries are not only being received but also reinterpreted to suit context in the interest of stability and welfare provision. As such, this chapter contributes not only to studies of evolving political economy in the region but also to understandings about how the market, state, and citizens interact within legacy institutional structures to shape cities and their growth paths.

Part II

Part II of this volume examines social development from a variety of perspectives on policy, inclusion, and livability, with cities as a setting for interactive, complementary, and conflicting ideas. According to Lefebvre and Enders (1976: 31), "space has been shaped and molded from historical and natural elements, but this has been a political process. Space is political and ideological. It is a product literally filled with ideologies". Any exploration of urbanization in Asia requires a thorough understanding of contestation around urban society and social development. As an expression of the rich tapestry of overlapping histories, cultures, and ideas, Asian cities provide an ideal setting for studies about the transformation of society and the plight of the individual. This relates to the theme of governance in Part I by underscoring the implicit contestation and messiness associated with societal challenges and transformation. A city's social environment is a literal expression of competing ideologies. From Seoul to Jakarta, urban settings are being continually reshaped by the inflow of global and domestic capital. Yet, tensions have long centered on the loss of vernacular authenticity in the face of modern development fueled by the neoliberal pursuit of capital returns. The struggle to keep cities "public" (see Lefebvre's 1970 "right to the city" thesis) is now at the forefront of many policy debates about Asian cities, particularly as the magnetic effect of urban economies attracts low-income migrants, compounds the wealth of economic and political elites, and creates greater competition for space. The embodiment of this dynamic can be seen in the geography of unequal adjacency: swathes of deprivation interrupted by pockets of extreme wealth, evident particularly in cities such as Manila, Bangkok, and Kuala Lumpur. A convergence of policies – from land use and infrastructure investment on the planning side to education, health, and labor on the social policy side – has created conditions in which the growth of cities is marked by this patchwork inequality.

At the same time, an emerging urban growth strategy claims to ensure the happiness of the individual within a mix of lifestyle amenities. One example of this next-generation urban scene is the art district. Even in creating stimulating urban environments, forceful solutions can fail to have desired effects: art districts designated and protected by local governments often become isolated spaces of cultural instrumentalization. In the creation of such amenity spaces, civil society is an increasingly engaged stakeholder. At the opposite end of the engagement spectrum, the migration of rural and low-income workers into cities is placing a strain on housing and infrastructure systems and highlighting a growing crisis of weak policy effort to address the needs of the poor. The pursuit of upper-class livability risks monopolizing the attention of urban policymakers in Asia, at the risk of further marginalizing an increasingly voiceless group in society.

Public health is another emerging concern for urban governments, as the environmental pathologies of cities are implicated in the degradation of health among urban residents. Providing proper healthcare under increasingly constrained budgetary environments, for increasingly complicated illnesses, is testing the capacity of public health systems and related policies. Demographic shifts are also a rising concern; the aging population of many Asian cities will test the ability of governments to finance adequate care at a time when some societies appear to be facing a fiscal crisis related to population aging. These and other themes are explored in Part II through examinations of citizen participation in planning, healthcare, education, and urban morphology, among other topics related to individual empowerment and state–society relations in the context of urbanization.

In Chapter 7, Si Ying Tan and Wei Yang examine the political economy of social health insurance (SHI) expansion in two of the largest and most populous developing countries in the world: Indonesia and China. Achieving universal health coverage (UHC) is positioned as an important political agenda that signals a government's effectiveness in health policy. SHI is one of the most popular financing tools implemented to achieve this goal. Early this century, Indonesia and China introduced two of the largest state-controlled SHI schemes in the world. Governments from both countries were ambitious in expanding the financing and coverage of these schemes to rural populations and informal sector workers in their respective pledges to achieve universal health coverage by 2020. At the point when these two schemes were rolled out in both countries, less than a quarter of the population was covered. After more than a decade, the performance of SHI in the two countries, in terms of coverage, shows considerable divergence. While China managed to achieve universal health coverage in 2011, by 2017 Indonesia still had significantly lower coverage. Given that they are both large and highly decentralized countries with similar policy intents, introducing similar policies around the same time and at similar scale, it is useful to consider why China achieved its target while Indonesia did not. While it is often understood that health reforms are highly context-specific and have shown different outcomes under different jurisdictions, despite similar starting points, key factors that could explain such divergence are less well-understood. Examining the SHI reform trajectories of both countries, this chapter analyzes the importance of policy tools and policy experiments – ushered in by bold central governments and flexibly endowed to local governments in terms of design and implementation – in the expansion of SHI schemes. Using a comparative case study approach, the authors dissect the implementation process at various stages of reform and analyze the different mechanisms that led to diverging reform outcomes in the two countries by using a policy capacity framework that comprises six capacity domains. The chapter shows that the Chinese central government effectively mobilized its sub-national counterparts with performance incentives, endowing local government with the flexibility and nimbleness to leverage capacities in adjusting design through policy experiments. Indonesia's central government, on the other hand, lacks the capacity to exert a strong command-and-control position in policy implementation. Regional autonomy enacted under the decentralization law enabled varying interpretations of centralized regulations. Despite the presence of some flourishing social health insurance schemes across Indonesia, heterogeneities in local government capacities have resulted in substantial differences in population coverage and fragmentations of design. The chapter concludes with policy implications for both countries.

In Chapter 8, Hung Vo and Donna Doan Anderson examine public space in Vietnam as an expression of social agency. Political and economic reforms throughout Vietnam's *Doi Moi* ("Renovation Era") led to dramatic transformation in Saigon. Embedded in the state's strategy to incorporate its populace as a newly unified nation are its efforts to control public space. Even as Vietnam continues to privatize state-owned enterprises and allow for the inheriting, transferring, exchanging, leasing, and mortgaging of land use rights, the state retains full ownership of land. With business and government often in collaboration, urban space becomes a site of political, economic, and social contestation. This chapter draws on historical and contemporary analyses and ethnographic studies to elucidate ways in which urban dwellers' appropriation of and interaction with public space have changed in contemporary settings. The authors discuss broader implications for lived social experience, planning, and politics in the city. They argue that capitalist development under the guise of neoliberal economic policy has resulted in the global image of a "new metropolitan mainstream" that has compromised the lives of those at the margins of urban society. To contribute to existing understandings of public space and its policing, the authors explore the emerging impacts of Vietnamese returnees on the built environment, around which a call for further research is made.

In Chapter 9, Daixin Dai and George Frantz explore the physical layout of China's cities and its impact on the experience of urban dwellers. The large city blocks that dominate Chinese cities create urban residential enclaves nested within the matrix of arterial streets. They form islands of livability within the metropolis, buffering residents from heavy traffic, incompatible land uses, and other undesirable aspects of the urban environment, providing a relatively high-quality living environment within the city. As cities in China grapple with unprecedented population growth and development, a new debate has erupted about the merits of the larger city block relative to the advantages, perceived or otherwise, of the American New Urbanist concept of small city blocks. This debate is framed against the backdrop of China's deep history with large city blocks, a foundation of the country's cities for over 3,000 years since the work of Zhou Li (Duke of Zhou) around 1030 BCE. This chapter reviews planning in Shanghai since the early 20th century, revisiting several debates over block size during this period, as well as the supersession of the historic *lilong* housing with Garden City-inspired residential designs, particularly in the context of the creation of *xincun* residential communities in the 1950s. It overlays empirical analysis of the contemporary urban fabric onto this historical review to derive policy insights relevant for maintaining and improving the urban experience for citizens.

In Chapter 10, Seunghyun Lee examines healthcare in South Korea with a focus on the metropolitan and urban scale and imbalances between these across the country. Universal health *insurance* in South Korea has developed over several decades. Any person can walk into any primary care hospital and receive treatment at a low cost. As a result of good access to healthcare, Koreans' life expectancy reached 82.3 years in 2015, ranking 11th among 201 countries, according to the World Health Organization. When examining the healthcare network, universal health*care* is a somewhat different story, reflecting both positives and negatives. On one hand, the concentrated healthcare network in Seoul, which offers low healthcare costs and high-quality care, attracts people from outside Korea and promotes medical tourism. On the other hand, if a citizen outside Seoul contracts a serious and acute disease, treatment options are limited. Rural areas lack quality healthcare facilities, and physicians have only limited resources. National hospitals and national university-affiliated hospitals exist in rural areas, but trust in those hospitals is low. Instead, patients seek treatment at the small number of large hospitals in Seoul. This concentration of healthcare networks in Seoul and their relative absence in smaller cities and rural areas means that prominent hospitals in the capital face shortages of beds, and patients endure long waiting times to see a physician. Thus, patients and families often pursue informal networks to accelerate treatment. This chapter examines these issues in-depth through an analysis of historical and current trends, arguing that a national healthcare network with one strong urban hub is not enough to serve an entire nation of patients. The chapter concludes with a proposal for developing health-care networks at local levels to improve the quality of healthcare and to narrow geographic gaps in health outcomes.

In Chapter 11, Yifei Yan explores the issue of education governance in Beijing and Delhi – capital cities of the world's two most populous countries. Account-ability has been highlighted both in the literature on education governance and in the reforms guided by it. Nevertheless, current literature is focused overwhelm-ingly on short-term interventions, mostly on student discipline and control. This chapter complements and extends the literature by exploring the roles of two institutionalized supportive mechanisms, namely teachers' in-service training and career development, in China and India, whose public education systems – despite being among the world's largest – are relatively under-explored. Govern-ment middle schools in the two capital cities, less constrained by resources than by how those resources are managed and utilized (i.e., governance), are also sites in which these mechanisms can be meaningfully scrutinized. For this chap-ter's empirical analysis, school and teacher questionnaires are complemented by semi-structured interviews with education officials, experts, and NGO workers to understand various aspects of the two mechanisms mentioned. The analysis focuses on the match between supportive mechanisms and stakeholder incen-tives. Preliminary results highlight several specific structural rigidities while also identifying some common problems. To the extent that problems such as seniority-based career path or top-down training delivery are common to other developing countries, these exploratory efforts can generate broader policy impli-cations relevant to education and human capital development in Asian cities.

Part III

As cities look toward an uncertain future, issues around sustainability demand the attention of urban policymakers. Climate change is a challenge that tran-scends political boundaries and is arguably a threat to global economic, social, and political stability; it also has serious implications for urban growth. Envi-ronmental management and resilience are issues that local governments must address with urgency, and recent episodes underscore this need: air pollution in Delhi and flooding in Bangkok and urban China are examples. Predictions about sea level change are also raising concerns for coastal cities such as Ho Chi

Minh City and Jakarta, while continental weather patterns can disrupt agriculture and water resources in ways that impact inland cities in places like Central
Asia. Despite global multilateral efforts to reduce emissions, rapid economic
growth in developing countries is likely to keep emissions levels high for the
foreseeable future. Furthermore, the increasing degradation of environmental
resources associated with urban sprawl and the wider spillover effects of resource
depletion are underscoring the urgency for urban governments to understand
the broader interactions between cities and nature in establishing longer-term
sustainability.

Urban policymakers have looked to a variety of solutions to the sustainability
challenge. Efforts to curb emissions outputs through demand management (e.g.,
compact development) and restructuring of the energy mix have been commonly
discussed measures. At the same time, technology presents its own transformative
potential in how to address resource usage and lifestyle change (along with many
other disruptive impacts to employment and broader society). While advance-
ments in automation and ICT are facilitating industrial upgrading and structural transformation, the use of "big data" is providing city governments with
increasing capabilities in monitoring and analyzing environmental conditions and
urban behavior patterns to improve services and address intractable challenges
such as traffic, crime, and pollution. The push for cities to be global leaders in
the application of technologies, including so-called smart city systems, is opening new pathways for public – private partnerships and other hybrid forms of
service delivery. The crucial task will be to maintain the sovereignty of the public
amidst a technology push that is driven, on the innovation and marketization
side, by private interests. Part III addresses the issue of environmental sustainability, its multiple policy pathways, and the technological forces shaping future
urban growth, through chapters focused on waste management, new town planning, and smart cities, among others.

In Chapter 12, Jingru Zhang and Kris Hartley explore the policy challenges
of incentivizing residents to adopt voluntary recycling programs through cases in
Singapore and Shanghai. In both cities, rising incomes and modernizing lifestyles
have created an environment of growing consumer demand, leading to increasing amounts of waste generated in the course of daily living. This chapter examines the challenges of managing household waste. In both cities, governments
have experimented for many years with programs to encourage more sustainable behaviour regarding waste management. These initiatives, including various
education, information, and communications campaigns about how to properly
deal with disposables, have produced only middling results. Even the effort to
improve infrastructure access to make recycling more convenient, such as the
placement of receptacles around neighborhoods, has not guaranteed widespread
uptake of recycling efforts. The chapter considers explanations for this lag in
uptake and makes policy proposals to address it. The chapter examines the issue
through the tension between individual and collective rationality, arguing that
governments have had trouble achieving a balance between policies that reward

and those that punish. The chapter concludes by arguing that the optimization of recycling programs themselves risks distracting governments from the more difficult work of fundamentally restructuring the production and consumption systems; moving from a linear economy (which recycling, well-intentioned as it is, can further institutionalize) to a circular economy is a more strategic policy goal in the pursuit of sustainability.

In Chapter 13, Lili Li examines central–local relationships in environmental governance in China. This chapter proceeds from the argument that anthropogenic activities in urban areas are a major source of greenhouse gas (GHG) emissions. At the same time, cities are threatened by the very problem they are helping to create: climate change. Local policy is crucial for making substantive progress on climate change mitigation and adaptation. This chapter addresses the question by investigating the cases of three policy instruments in China: pollutant discharge fee (*pai wu fei*), environmental target system (*mu biao ze ren zhi*), and policy experimentation of CO_2 emissions trading schemes (CO_2 ETSs, *tan pai fang quan jiao yi*). The implementation of the three policy instruments faces various obstacles and reflects different dynamics of central–local government interactions. The chapter addresses how each policy instrument functions, how it has been established, and what implementation issues it has encountered. The final section summarizes the three policy instruments and provides an in-depth discussion.

In Chapter 14, Rumit Singh Kakar and Kris Hartley examine urban public health in India, with a focus on the effectiveness of service delivery and the relationship between sustainability and human well-being. India boasts one of the largest public healthcare systems in the world but has failed to provide basic healthcare to a majority of its population. Minimal access to clean water and sanitation, along with high levels of exposure to atmospheric and environmental pollutants, are factors contributing to the nation's declining public health outcomes. While environmental pollution is a challenge for nearly all of India's residents, rural populations and families living below the poverty line are the most affected by poor access to healthcare. There are numerous explanations beyond geographic isolation: daily-wage workers unable to miss work for health check-ups, financial disparities between private and government hospitals, and health insurance systems offering inadequate coverage. The chapter argues that healthcare programs instituted by the central government are further contributing to the decline of general health in the country as a whole, while a variety of peripheral factors related to social and economic marginalization exacerbate the problem. This chapter analyzes factors that are most responsible for declining public health outcomes in India, utilizing existing research, government documents, and other published materials. Broad statistics are complemented with in-depth case studies. The general finding is that the prevailing narrative about the health pathologies of urban life fail to recognize systemic problems that are also compromising public health in rural areas. This has important implications for the distribution of resources, the urgency of policies

addressing environmental sustainability, and core–periphery governance relationships within India.

In Chapter 15, Glen Kuecker, Tristan Stamets, and Farukh Sarkulov explore
the embrace by India of the smart cities development paradigm, focusing on its
ability to deliver promises about sustainability and on broader questions about
the underlying policy logic. Indian Prime Minister Modi has an ambitious plan to
build 100 smart cities. The plan is the centerpiece for India's great transformation, which finds the convergence of population growth and urbanization driving
the nation toward a bifurcating tipping point of realizing the promise of modernity or a dystopian reality of inequity, inequality, and environmental catastrophe.
Understanding the 100 smart cities agenda and everything at stake invites consideration of key questions about 21st-century Asian cities, especially an analysis
of how the intersections between policy formulation, the place of cities within
national development agendas, and the underlying systems of thought within
grand, "winning the future" mega-projects reproduce modernist approaches to
social problems. In exploring this line of inquiry, this chapter makes use of critical urban theory to unpack Modi's 100 smart cities agenda, reveal the limitations
of the development agenda, and expose the false premises of its utopian vision.
The chapter argues that smart cities are a mechanism of capitalist reproduction in
the 21st century that retain technocratic approaches to social and environmental
problems derived from instrumentalist reasoning. Far from being the bridge to a
utopian urban future, they promise to reproduce inequity and inequality, exacerbate the urban–rural divide, and devastate the environment.

Conclusion

This volume addresses the dominant trends in Asian urbanization to consider the
degree to which the region is prepared to absorb systemic change and negotiate the uncertainty and instability that will likely define the coming era. Taken
together, the diverse set of chapters in this volume illustrates key themes for
thinking about Asian urbanization. First, governance at all levels has been shaped
by the sweeping development ideas of the late 20th century, namely neoliberalism, the hollowing-out of the state, the managerialization of the public sector,
and the pre-eminence of markets. This revolution sits in stark contrast with Asia's
legacy of state intervention but has resulted in the evolution of a mindset in
policymaking that has precipitated an increasing alignment with Western models.
Second, this revolution has led to new frameworks for how markets, the state,
and the public are viewed in relation to one another and how their respective
roles and power balances are determined. The marginalization of the public has
led to contestation and tension as manifest in a variety of domains, including
urban space, social welfare, and popular expression. Third, the result is a set of
understandings, assumptions, and practices that are defining whether and how
Asian cities are prepared to meet the challenges of complex, "wicked" problems
such as climate change and systemic disruption. These three themes illustrate
how transformations in urban governance driven by neoliberal economic reforms

have generated contestations that redefine the role and meaning of "public" within the governance of Asian cities. As transformed governance has stimulated a deep yet incomplete reconstitution of the public, Asian cities have entered a period of uncertainty marked by significant disruptions to the abilities of society, politics, economics, and culture to remain sustainable. As such, the practical contribution of this volume is to provide a critical barometer for understanding the prospects of progress for Asian cities in an age of disruption. It also serves as a call for researchers to discern what is likely to occur under steady-state versus disruptive scenarios.

References

Lefebvre, H. (1970). *La revolution urbaine*. Paris: Editions Gallimard.
Lefebvre, H., and M.J. Enders (1976). "Reflections on the Politics of Space." *Antipode* 8 (2): 30–37.

Part 1

Transitions in governance

1 Improving city government performance in the era of decentralization

The experiences of Indonesia and the Philippines

Mulya Amri

Introduction

Increasing awareness of urbanization and the important role that cities play in a nation's economy (Dobbs et al., 2011; Glaeser, 2011) has shifted the spotlight onto city governments and city leaders (Barber, 2013). Issues related to "managing fast growing cities" have been well-documented (see, e.g., Devas and Rakodi, 1993). Central to tackling these challenges is the capacity of city governments to plan for, finance, and manage change. In the developed and developing worlds alike, city governments and leaders are expected to deliver not just performance but also innovations to deal with new problems and/or old problems of unprecedented scale.

Decentralization leads to more efficient allocation of resources, more responsive public service, and improved economic development at the local level, proponents claim (Oates, 1972; Tiebout, 1956). Local governments are considered to be better at identifying and serving local needs and more easily held accountable to the public. Different configurations of offers by the local government will keep existing firms and residents while attracting new ones, thus creating a situation where city governments compete with each other by offering the most desirable social and business environments.

The Philippines and Indonesia are notable for their adoption of direct democracy and extensive decentralization within a short period of time. This transformation started with the Philippines' "people power revolution" in 1986 and Indonesia's *Reformasi* in 1998. Along with this phenomenon came a drastic change in the way governance takes place at the local level. Mayors are increasingly taking center stage, and local democracy is gradually institutionalized, albeit to various extents and at different speeds. Despite claims of association between decentralization and improvement in local public services, the link between the two is not a direct one. After more than 25 years of decentralization in the Philippines and 15 years in Indonesia, improvement in local government performance has been debatable (Lewis 2010) and economic growth at the local level remains disputable (McCulloch and Malesky 2011). But as Indonesia and the Philippines slowly tinker with their incentive systems and implement more measures to encourage or incentivize local governments to deliver quality public services, we are seeing some positive changes in the way such incentive systems are utilized.

This chapter highlights the presence of two types of incentives to improve city government performance in the context of decentralization. The first is top-down incentives in the form of administrative measurements and rankings conducted by the central government; the second is bottom-up incentives in the form of citizens' political support (votes) for local leaders who perform well and deliver quality public services. The remainder of the chapter will be presented as a case study comparing the Philippines and Indonesia, exploring decentralization, top-down incentives, and bottom-up incentives for local performance first in the Philippines and then in Indonesia. The final section provides a conclusion and agenda for future research.

Decentralization and local public performance incentives in the Philippines

Decentralization

The Philippines' "people power revolution" toppled Ferdinand Marcos' authoritarian regime in 1986 and brought forth a new era of democracy at both the national and the local level. The country's new 1987 Constitution institutionalized reforms that limit the power of the executive and mandated Congress to enact a code that gave more autonomy to local government units (LGUs). This code was later enacted as Republic Act No. 7160, also known as the Local Government Code (LGC) of 1991.

Decentralization in the Philippines has been taking place since 1992 according to the provisions of LGC 1991. It has taken the form of devolution, whereby LGUs (provinces, cities, and municipalities) are given considerable autonomy to decide their development priorities and implement relevant programs. The sectors that are now within the purview of the LGUs are wide-ranging: agriculture, industrial development, environmental protection, health services, social welfare, local infrastructure, land use, and tourism. For cities, specifically, communications, transportation, education, and civil defense are also included in the LGU remit.

The transfer of authority from the national government to LGUs is supported by transfer of personnel and fiscal resources. In 1992, at the onset of decentralization, about 60% of staff from the Department of Agriculture, Department of Health, and Department of Social Welfare and Development were transferred from the national government to various local governments (Wallich et al., 2007). In the period 1992–2003, the average yearly expenditure of the Philippines' LGUs was about 23% of the country's total public expenditure. This is a substantial increase compared to the yearly average of 11% before decentralization (1985–1991). By 2009, the proportion had risen even further to 25% (Martinez-Vazquez and Vaillancourt, 2011).

Despite having more resources to spend, LGUs' authority to generate revenue remains limited. Most of the substantial taxes (i.e., personal and corporate income tax, consumption tax) are collected by the national government as part of the Philippines' internal revenue. LGUs, on the other hand, collect real property tax, property transfer tax, and amusement tax. LGUs are also able to impose fees for services (e.g., yearly renewal of business permits), as well as charge for the public utilities that they provide.

Of the internal revenue collected by the national government, 40% is redistributed to LGUs according to a simple formula based on each LGU's land area and population. This is called the Internal Revenue Allotment (IRA). For the most part, LGUs have the autonomy to plan and decide what to do with their IRA. The IRA is large enough to enable LGUs to pay staff salary costs and provide very basic services but not enough to carry out substantial development schemes or programs. As a result, LGUs that lack motivation or pressure may just be able to survive, providing a minimal level of service, while those that are more motivated would be encouraged to generate additional revenue to complement the IRA.

Devolution as assigned by LGC 1991 follows a hierarchy in which provinces are identified as first-tier LGUs, municipalities and component cities are second-tier, and *barangays* – the smallest administrative unit in the Philippines – are third-tier. Cities fall into one of three possible legal classes: "component", "independent component", or "highly urbanized".[1] Component cities, together with municipalities, occupy the second-tier hierarchy under the provincial government. However, highly urbanized and independent component cities occupy the first-tier hierarchy, on a par with provinces. These higher-tiered cities do not report or share any of their tax revenues with the provincial government (neither do their citizens vote for provincial government officials). Instead, independent component and highly urbanized cities report directly to the national government and coordinate with their respective provinces.

Based on the 2015 census, there are 17 regions, 81 provinces, 145 cities, and 1,488 municipalities in the Philippines.[2] Of the 145 cities, 35 are "highly urbanized" and five are "independent component" cities. In terms of population, four cities had more than 1 million inhabitants in 2015 (three of which are in the National Capital Region, NCR), 16 cities had between 500,000 and 1 million, 94 cities had between 100,000 and 500,000, and 31 cities had a population under 100,000. The average population of Philippine cities was 282,240 and the median 168,110.

Top-down administrative incentives

It is generally acknowledged that decentralization in the Philippines has worked to a certain extent in enabling civic involvement in local public affairs and innovations in the ways that local public services can be financed and delivered (Brillantes, 2003). However, at the same time there is a sense that much more could be achieved and improved. Local government performance remains uneven, and there are at least as many or more bad practices as there are good ones. Possible explanations for variation in local government performance have been explored.

Some also argue that economic development level may play a role in determining the quality of public services – as much as we would like to acknowledge that better public services are likely to trigger local development (Capuno, 2005).

From the central government's point of view, a performance management system is needed to ensure that LGUs deliver quality public services at the local level. The Philippines had already established the Local Productivity and Performance Management System (LPPMS) in the 1980s, but when decentralization began much of the focus was on local government capacity building rather than performance monitoring. The LPPMS was revived in 1998, and since then it has been further developed and supplemented with other systems. One of these is the Local Government Performance Management System (LGPMS), which helps LGUs to conduct self-assessment of how they are performing in their functions. Other systems include the Citizens' Satisfaction Index, the Seal of Good Housekeeping, and Seal of Good Local Governance (Adriano and Estimada, 2014; Medina-Guce, 2016). A list of the tools to measure and improve LGU performance that have been implemented in the Philippines has been compiled by Capuno (2005).

The Seal of Good Local Governance (SGLG), which expands on the earlier Seal of Good Financial Housekeeping (SGFH), is awarded to LGUs that show satisfactory performance in three "core components" (good financial housekeeping, disaster preparedness, and social protection) and three "essential components" (business friendliness and competitiveness, peace and order, and environmental management) (Medina-Guce, 2016). The more comprehensive SGLG has raised the bar for performance: while as many as 1,535 LGUs passed the Seal of Good Financial Housekeeping in 2016, only 306 LGUs passed the SGLG that year.[3]

Aside from the standard, compliance-related performance management system described previously, the Philippines is also implementing the Performance Challenge Fund (PCF). This is a fiscal incentive for LGUs that initially pass the SGFH and ultimately the SGLG by providing a maximum of 50% "counterpart funding" for larger-scale local development projects that otherwise do not have sufficient resources for implementation.[4] There are four categories of PCF-eligible projects: those that aim to improve the achievement of (1) the Millennium Development Goals, (2) local economic development, (3) disaster risk reduction and management, and (4) ecological solid waste management. The PCF started small in 2010 with a budget of P 30 million for 30 municipalities. In financial year 2015, as much as P 982 million was budgeted to 254 LGUs that qualified. As of May 2017, PCF had recorded a total of 2,698 encoded projects, of which 2,585 had been completed.[5]

A good performance management system does not reward only compliance but also innovations. In the developing world, the Philippines is among the first to acknowledge local public-sector innovations through awards. Started in 1993, not long after the country embarked on decentralization, the Galing Pook (GP) Awards were launched to "recognize innovation and excellence in local governance" (Brillantes, 2003). This started as a joint initiative of the Department of Interior and Local Government, with support from the Ford Foundation and other high-profile national and local figures. Four judging criteria were used to determine the award winners: positive results and impact, promotion of people's participation and empowerment, innovativeness, and efforts to ensure transferability and sustainability of the program. Now in its 24th year, the award organizers hold a wealth of data on innovative city governments and programs in the Philippines. Every year, the GP Awards are given to 16–20 local programs, reaching a total of 338 awardees as of 2015.[6] These 338 local programs are spread over multiple sectors, ranging from economics/livelihoods to environmental protection and to community involvement in public affairs. The awarded programs have come from various regions of the Philippines, conducted by barangays, cities, municipalities, and provinces alike.

Some LGUs have won more awards than others. As many as 35 out of 81 provinces (43.2%), 59 out of 145 cities (40.9%), and 99 out of 1,488 municipalities (6.6%) have won a GP award at least once. Between 1993 and 2015, 14 cities won an award three or more times, and eight cities won at least four times: Naga City in Camarines Sur (ten times), Marikina City in the NCR (eight), Quezon City in the NCR (seven), Cebu City in Cebu (six), San Carlos City in Negros Occidental (six), Puerto Princessa in Palawan (five), Mandaluyong in the NCR (four), and Muntinlupa in the NCR (four).

Bottom-up political incentives

While national directives and incentives to improve local performance are indeed helpful, they address only one of the two characteristics that make the concepts of federalism and decentralization as argued by Tiebout (1956) so attractive. The other is the role of citizens in putting pressure on local governments to deliver the services that they require.

Decentralization in the Philippines has taken place simultaneously with democratization, whereby the autonomy of local government leaders from the central government is balanced by their accountability to the citizens who voted for them. Provinces, cities, municipalities, and barangays conduct local elections every three years. The mayor, vice mayor, and city councilors each serve a three-year term and can serve a maximum of three consecutive terms (nine years). The LGC 1991 provides the legal and institutional means for the people to participate in local government affairs beyond elections. These include joint ventures between the LGU and NGOs, people's organizations, and the private sector. Members of the public are also eligible to participate as members in special committees or councils that govern how public services are to be delivered, such as the local school board, the local development council, etc. (Alinio, 2008).

Even in the presence of a democratic system of governance, decentralization in the Philippines has not resulted in better public services and more responsive local governments. Some authors have explored deep-rooted institutional factors to explain why this is so. One of the often-cited issues is elite capture of local institutions due to the existence of strong patronage systems (Shair-Rosenfield, 2016; Yilmaz and Venugopal, 2013). Political parties at the local level are arguably weak, and politics tends to be dominated by personalities (Kasuya, 2009); thus it is not uncommon to find political leadership at the local level dominated by strong families ("clans" or "dynasties") and even alliances of corrupt bureaucrats, clan leaders, business interests, and criminals (Lacaba, 1995; Sidel, 2004). The 1987 Constitution discourages political dynasties by stating that: "The State shall guarantee equal access to opportunities for public service and prohibit political dynasties as may be defined by law".[7] However, to date there has been no legal definition of a "dynasty", and thus the phenomenon has persisted (Querubin, 2012).

Despite this pessimistic note, society is not static, and the relationship between elites and citizens is constantly changing – although perhaps not as fast as regulations can change. Institutions can be tweaked, and, with the right form of intervention, voters can become more demanding and elites more accommodative. For example, one study found that when the performance rating of a local government was publicly announced to the people through accessible media and language, mayors and barangay captains showed signs of being more responsive to their citizens (Capuno and Garcia, 2010). Another study found that higher government spending on economic development projects tends to help an incumbent governor to win re-election (Solon et al., 2009). These seem to indicate that democracy and voter pressure can have an effect, even after controlling for the presence of clans.

This exploration of decentralization, top-down incentives, and bottom-up incentives of local government performance in the Philippines demonstrates, I would argue, that there has been an evolution in how decentralization is being managed, including small improvements in both top-down and bottom-up incentives. The Philippine case shows that progress is possible, though slow. Next, we turn to Indonesia, where the experience of decentralization is about 10 years younger than the Philippines.

Decentralization and local public performance incentives in Indonesia

Decentralization

Indonesia's "people power" moment took place in 1998, ending Suharto's 32 years of authoritarian rule. The movement, called *Reformasi*, promised to bring a new era of democracy and decentralization. Within a few years of Suharto stepping down, the original 1945 Constitution was amended to curb the powers of the executive, strengthen the legislature, adopt direct elections, acknowledge human rights, and enable a larger governing role for sub-national governments. The 1998 reform mandated decentralization through an increase in regional autonomy by way of devolution. Indonesia's "big bang" decentralization started in 1999 with the passing of two laws that devolved authority and responsibility – and distributed monetary resources – from the central to regional governments.[8] The extent of responsibilities being redistributed covered almost everything except foreign affairs, defense, justice, finance, religion, and natural resources, which remain in the hands of the central government.

Immediately prior to decentralization, transfers of funds from central government to sub-national governments (provinces, cities or *kota*, and regencies or *kabupaten*) made up 14.9% of total central government expenditure. By 2001, that figure had jumped to 23.7%.[9] The average annual proportion of transfers to regional governments for the period 1990–2000 was 19.6%; this increased to 30.9% for the period 2000–2010. The central government also shifted many staff to local government payrolls, with the percentage of civil servants at the local level increasing from 12.2% to 66.7% between 1999 and 2001 (World Bank, 2003).

Transfers from central to regional governments consist of three types of funds: unconditional, general-purpose grant (*Dana Alokasi Umum* or DAU); special-purpose grant (*Dana Alokasi Khusus*); and revenue sharing (*Dana Bagi Hasil*). Each regional government receives transfers directly from the central government. The amount of DAU that each regional government receives is determined by the region's land area and population. The DAU is noteworthy because it accounts for a large proportion of funds: it made up 64.1% of total regional government revenue in 2003 but decreased to 46.9% in 2008 and to 42.4% in 2013.[10] It is also "unconditional", which means that regional governments can use it as they see fit, with no link between the entitlement to receive the grant and the performance of the region (Ahmad and Mansoor 2002, Lewis 2010).

Meanwhile, the power of regional governments to raise their own revenue remains limited. Income tax and value-added tax and revenue from natural resources are collected by the central government. Part of the natural resource revenue is redistributed to provincial and local governments according to a formula that favors the locality where the resource is found. Other than that, taxes collected by local governments include hotel and restaurant tax, entertainment tax, and advertising tax. Local governments could also collect fees from the public and businesses, but there is no requirement for businesses to register with the local government on a regular basis.

Under the new decentralization framework, Indonesia has adopted a flat rather than a hierarchical structure, whereby provinces, as well as the cities and regencies therein, are all called "autonomous regions". Politically, each regional government is accountable to the people, but administratively, they receive money from and report to the national government. Cities and regencies are at the forefront of regional autonomy, while provinces – which were considered superior in the former hierarchy – now hold a lesser coordinating role. The sudden increase in authority in the regions has presented some challenges, such as failures of coordination, an increase in the number and types of predatory local taxes, and local regulations that tend to discriminate against people from other regions. There has also been a rise of local "dynasties". In response to these challenges, the original 1999 decentralization laws have been gradually revised to better clarify the authority and responsibility of the provincial and local governments, to re-strengthen the role of the province in coordinating and ensuring local government performance, and to facilitate more democratic local elections.[11]

Based on the latest Ministry of Home Affairs Regulation issued in 2017, there are 508 autonomous local governments (415 rural regencies or *kabupaten* and 93 cities or *kota*).[12] Local governments are further broken down into sub-districts (*kecamatan* – 6,994 in total) and villages (urban *kelurahan* or rural *desa* – 72,944 in all). The 93 cities vary greatly in size. Following the Ministry of Public Works' city size classification, 12 cities had a population of larger than one million, 14 cities had between 500,000 and one million inhabitants, 58 cities had between 100,000 and 500,000, and nine had a population of less than 100,000. The average population of Indonesia's 93 autonomous cities is 486,235, while the median is 235,305 (based on the 2015 inter-census survey).

Top-down incentives

Indonesia's post-1998 political reforms mandated the development of a cleaner, more effective and more responsive government.[13] However, progress has been slow. In the context of decentralization, the national government faces the daunting task of overseeing not only bureaucracy reform at the national level but also that which is taking place in more than 500 regional (sub-national) governments.

Indonesia's decentralization started with the hope that bringing power closer to the people would lead to better public services, but various concerns have been raised about regional governments' performance. There are issues related to the use of regional finances – including the large proportion of the local budget used for staff salaries (Jaweng, 2011) – and substantial amounts spent on constructing lavish new government offices (Lewis and Oosterman, 2011). Other concerns include territorial splits to create new regional government entities (Firman, 2009) and a general sense that public services have not improved (Lewis, 2010).

To expedite the achievement of a "world class government" by 2025, President Yudhoyono issued a Presidential Regulation in 2010 that outlined a "grand design" for bureaucracy reform.[14] According to this document, bureaucracy reform aimed to achieve three major goals: (1) a clean government, free of corruption, collusion, and nepotism; (2) improvements in the quality of public services; and (3) increases in performance and accountability of the public sector. At the individual level, the word "performance" only entered the civil service lexicon in 1999, when it was stated that promotions would be determined through "performance evaluations".[15] However, details of the operationalization of this measure were only issued in 2011, whereby every government staff member was to be evaluated and receive a "performance score".[16]

Regulations to enable monitoring of government performance both at the national and local levels were established in 1999, in the requirement to implement a performance accountability system and prepare annual performance accountability reports (Jurnali and Siti-Nabiha, 2015).[17] Over time, efforts have been mobilized to better regulate local governance and incentivize local public performance (Lewis and Smoke, 2012). Laws on decentralization were updated and operationalized with regulations, and complementary laws on local elections, local councils, taxation, etc. were also passed. Among such regulations were those that require minimum public service standards and the evaluation of regional governments, passed in 2005 and 2008, respectively.[18]

It was only after the passing of these regulations that the central government started to conduct regular assessments of regional governments. Since 2009, evaluations on the public management aspects of regional government performance (*Evaluasi Kinerja Penyelenggaraan Pemerintahan Daerah* or EKPPD) have been conducted by the Ministry of Home Affairs on an annual basis, covering aspects such as compliance to law, human resource management, fiscal management, asset management, development planning, provisions for people's participation, and achievement of minimum service standards. Results of these evaluations are ranked, and the top three provinces, as well as the top ten cities and regencies, are announced and receive awards.

Along with this initiative, other ministries and national level agencies have also presented awards to regional governments for good performance in their respective sectors or fields, such as waste management (the *Adipura* award),[19] traffic management (*Wahana Tata Nugraha* award), investment (BKPM Investment Award), housing (*Adiupaya Puritama* award), health (public health development index), information and communications technology (*ICT-Pura* award), and e-government (Indonesia e-government ranking). Many of these are presented based on satisfactory implementation of national directives by sub-national governments.

Three awards in particular have recognized public innovation at the regional level. First, the Urban Management Innovation (*Inovasi Manajemen Perkotaan* or IMP) Award was established in 2008 and is awarded biannually for innovative programs in the fields of urban planning and management. Second, the Innovative Government Award (IGA) began in 2010 and is presented annually to acknowledge innovative programs of city and regency governments in the fields of public administration, public service, community empowerment, and regional competitiveness. Both the IMP and IGA are awarded by the Ministry of Home Affairs and presented by the Minister. The third, the Public Service Innovation Competition (*Kompetisi Inovasi Pelayanan Publik* or Sinovik), is a more recent effort to encourage public innovation that was initiated in 2014 by the Ministry of State Apparatus and Bureaucratic Reform.

Looking at a combination of awards,[20] we find that 124 regional governments have won at least one award since 2006. Of these, 75 are regency governments, making up 60% of the award winners, but just 18% of the total number of regency governments. Meanwhile, 49 are city governments, which represents 52% of all the cities in the country. As many as fifteen local governments have won five or more awards over the years. Seven cities stand out especially for winning multiple awards: Surabaya in East Java (seventeen awards), Surakarta or "Solo" in Central Java (twelve), Palembang in South Sumatra (eleven), Cimahi City in West Java (ten), Balikpapan in East Kalimantan (nine), Yogyakarta (eight), and Bandung City in West Java (eight).

Bottom-up incentives

Similar to the case of the Philippines, decentralization in Indonesia has been implemented hand-in-hand with democratization. The second amendment of the Indonesian Constitution states that heads of province, city, and regency are to be "democratically" elected. Until 2004, governors, mayors, and regents were appointed by their respective representative councils, but since 2005 regional leaders have been directly elected by citizens.[21] A law on rural villages (*desa*) was passed in 2014, extending some autonomy to these villages in the form of direct election of village heads and councilors, direct transfer of funds, and autonomy to utilize such funds.

Candidates for local leadership roles (city mayor, regency regent, provincial governor) typically run in the local election with support from one or more political parties, although independent candidacy is also possible. The local leader is elected together with his or her vice leader as a pair, and they both serve a five-year term; one subsequent term is permissible, giving a maximum of ten years in office. Many of the pairings of leader and vice leader are the result of political considerations, with political parties forming coalitions and matching one popular candidate with another to win the election. Such coalitions often disintegrate after the pair assumes power; five years down the line, many chief executives would run for their second term against their current vice chief executives.

The sub-national councils (*Dewan Perwakilan Rakyat Daerah* or DPRD) pass regional regulations (*Peraturan Daerah* or Perda), approve the regional budget, and watch over the executive. For cities and regencies, the DPRD will have between 20 and 50 councilors elected in their legislative districts. For the 93 Indonesian cities, the average number of councilors is 33.65, and the median is 30. Regional councilors serve a five-year term and can be re-elected with no term limits. The political composition of Indonesia's legislative councils, be it at national or regional level, is rarely dominated by one or two political parties alone.

Before the implementation of direct local elections, democracy and decentralization in Indonesia were often viewed negatively. For example, some have argued that local autonomy has resulted in the proliferation of "little kings" (Firman, 2009), local elections are flush with money politics (Choi, 2004; Mietzner, 2013), and decision-making is dominated by elites and their interest (Hadiz, 2004). Interestingly, a number of surveys found a high level of satisfaction among households regarding the quality of public services (Lewis and Pattinasarany, 2009). This may indicate a lack of awareness of public service standards among the citizens leading to a lack of demand for better public performance, or it may indicate actual improvement – albeit perhaps slow.

There are no formal mechanisms whereby civil society groups or business interests have a say in the legislation of the region. Each councilor exercises political accountability to his or her constituents by actively seeking, receiving, and following up on their inputs and aspirations. However, it is quite rare to find regional councils conducting meetings that are open to the public and media. It was only recently (starting in 2014) that the former governor of Jakarta, Basuki T. Purnama, ordered his departments to record meetings that they conduct with the provincial council and to upload them on social media. Theoretically, the general public has an opportunity to voice their aspirations in a process of participatory planning and budgeting (*musyawarah perencanaan pembangunan* or *musrenbang*), where plans and proposed budgets from lower-tier governments (villages, sub-districts) are aggregated and trimmed at the city or regency level. There is, however, much divergence in how actively the local governments seek participation from their citizens or in how actively the citizens pursue this participation.

Regardless of the people's "readiness" to participate in democracy, direct local elections (*Pilkada*) are argued to act as a trigger for more responsive regional governments. For example, in Indonesian cities and regencies, Fossati (2016) found that there was more accurate targeting of low-income households for a public health program in the year that direct elections were to take place. Additionally, local governments that are facing direct elections tend to spend more on public works projects (Skoufias et al., 2011), which bring visible and tangible benefits for the people. Mayors who know they are "successful" also capitalize on this by making sure that their "success" is publicized (Bunnell et al., 2018) and aim to contest on a higher political level as governor – or even president, as in the case of Mr. Joko Widodo, former mayor of Surakarta, Central Java.

Conclusion

Indonesia and the Philippines have undergone very similar experiences in terms of ending authoritarian regimes and adopting large-scale decentralization and democratization in a short time period. The Philippines leads this process by about ten years, but as both countries experiment with systems and incentives to ensure better local government performance, various lessons could be drawn, compared, and contrasted.

This chapter has explored two types of incentives for local performance: one is top-down and directed by the central government through administrative requirements, the other is bottom-up and based on the political demands of the citizen. I argue that the publication of a local government's performance measurement, ranking, or awards is a good link between the top-down and bottom-up incentives. The performance ranking is conducted based on central government standards, but once it is announced to the public and shared and re-shared in mainstream and social media it affects citizens' perceptions of their incumbent leader.

There are examples showing good performance of local governments being rewarded politically and local leaders capitalizing on the fact that their "success" is well-publicized. This chapter has noted cases in which the expectation of direct elections tends to result in better targeting of beneficiaries in Indonesian cities and regencies (Fossati, 2016) and in which the publication of a local government's performance rating in appropriate ways leads to local leaders being more responsive to citizens' needs in the Philippines (Capuno and Garcia, 2010). Meanwhile, incumbent leaders who spend more on development projects increase their chances of winning their re-election bid (Solon et al., 2009), while some have capitalized on their perceived success at the local level to contest for higher political positions (Bunnell et al., 2018).

The presence of top-down and bottom-up incentives applies pressure on mayors and city governments to improve public performance and to deliver better services. However, this only works if the central government and citizens are strong. Top-down incentives are less effective without a capable and committed central government, and the benefits of bottom-up incentives are similarly dependent on the presence of organized, informed, and meritocratic societies. To enable decentralization to have greater benefits, improving the capacity of local governments is not enough. A strengthening of civil society, as well as capacity building for the central government, are just as important, as they keep local governments in check.

Notes

1 Highly urbanized cities have a population of at least 200,000 and an annual income of at least 50 million pesos (1991 constant prices). Independent component cities are independent of the province as they have charters that prohibit voters from voting for provincial elective officials. Component cities are those that do not meet the previous requirements and are thus considered a component of the province in which they are geographically located. Source: National Statistical Coordination Board, Philippine Standard Geographic Code (www.nscb.gov.ph/activestats/psgc/articles/con_cityclass.asp)

2 National Statistical Coordination Board, Philippines Standard Geographic Code (www.nscb.gov.ph/activestats/psgc/); accessed December 2014.

3 The lists of SGLG and SGFH awardees are available at the Department of the Interior and Local Government (DILG) website: http://dilg.gov.ph/reports-and-resources/seal-of-good-local-governance/12/ (accessed June 2017).

4 See the PCF website: http://pcf.dilg.gov.ph/ (accessed June 2017).

5 Ibid.

6 The GP Awards have been held every year since 1994, except 2001, 2006, and 2011.

7 1987 Constitution, Article II, Section 26.

8 The first post-reform decentralization laws were Law No. 22/1999 on Regional Government and Law No. 25/1999 on Fiscal Balance between Central and Regional Governments. Prior to that, Indonesia followed a largely centralistic law on regional government (Law No. 5/1974).

9 Indonesia's national budget (APBN), 1990–2012, from *Statistik Ekonomi dan Keuangan Indonesia*, Bank Indonesia (www.bi.go.id/id/statistik/seki/terkini/keuangan-pemerintah/).

10 Indonesia's sub-national budget (APBD), 1994–2014, from Directorate General of Fiscal Balance, Ministry of Finance (www.djpk.kemenkeu.go.id/data-series/data-keuangan-daerah).

11 There have been numerous updates to the original 1999 decentralization laws, including Laws No. 32/2004, 33/2004, 12/2008, and 23/2014. Other legislation, such as Laws No. 8/2005, 22/2014, 1/2015, 2/2015, and 8/2015 specifically address issues related to regional elections and the roles of regional chief executives and vice chief executives.

12 These do not include five cities and one regency in the Jakarta Special Capital Region, which are "administrative" rather than "autonomous". Data from Ministry of Home Affairs (www.kemendagri.go.id/) – Daerah Otonom (Provinsi, Kabupaten, dan Kota) di Indonesia per December 2013.
13 See, for example, measures such as Tap MPR RI No. XI/MPR/1998 and Law No. 28/1999 on state management that is free of corruption, collusion, and nepotism; Tap MPR RI No. VI/MPR/2001 on national ethics; Tap MPR RI No. VII/MPR/2001 on policy directions to eradicate and prevent corruption, collusion, and nepotism; and Tap MPR RI No. VI/MPR/2002 on bureaucracy reform with emphasis on transparent, accountable, clean, and responsible bureaucratic culture.
14 Presidential Regulation No. 81/2010 on Grand Design of Bureaucracy Reform: 2010–2025.
15 Law No. 43/1999 on Principles of Civil Service, article 20.
16 Government Regulation No. 46/2011 on Civil Servants Performance Evaluation.
17 The Performance Accountability System of Government Institutions (SAKIP) and corresponding Performance Accountability Report (LAKIP) were first mentioned in the Presidential Instruction No. 7/1999. This instruction was later revised as Presidential Regulation No. 29/2014.
18 Government Regulations No. 65/2005 on minimum service standards and No. 6/2008 on evaluation of regional governments.
19 The Adipura award for city cleanliness actually started much earlier, in 1986.
20 This is a count that combines data on winners of ten awards between 2006 and 2015: (1) urban management innovation, (2) innovative government award, (3) public innovation competition, (4) solid waste management, (5) traffic and transportation, (6) investment, (7) housing, (8) public health, (9) ICT, and (10) e-government.
21 Direct election of regional leaders started in 2005 as per Law No. 32/2004, but Law No. 22/2014 returned the authority to elect regional leaders to the regional councils. However, due to the widespread negative response, the government annulled this law after just two days.

References

Adriano, Ma Nina I., and Diosdado P. Estimada (2014). "The Effectiveness of the Local Governance Performance Management System (LGPMS) in Improving Governance in the Municipality of San Rafael." *Asia Pacific Journal of Education, Arts and Sciences* 1 (5): 29–38.
Ahmad, Ehtisham, and Ali Mansoor (2002). "Indonesia: Managing Decentralization." Working Paper WP/02/136, IMF.
Alinio, Buenafe F. (2008). "Philippine Local Government Officials' Perceptions of Decentralization and Its Effects on Local Governments' Administrative Capabilities." Ph.D. Thesis, Washington, DC: The Trachtenberg School of Public Policy and Public Administration of The George Washington University.
Barber, Benjamin R. (2013). *If Mayors Ruled the World: Dysfunctional Nations, Rising Cities.* New Haven, CT: Yale University Press.
Brillantes, Alex B. (2003). *Innovations and Excellence: Understanding Local Governments in the Philippines.* Quezon City: Center for Local and Regional Governance, National College of Public Administration and Governance, University of the Philippines.
Bunnell, Tim, Rita Padawangi, and Eric C. Thompson (2018). "The Politics of Learning From a Small City: Solo as Translocal Model and Political Launch Pad."

Regional Studies 52 (8): 1065–1074. https://doi.org/10.1080/00343404.2017. 1298087.

Capuno, Joseph J. (2005). "The Quality of Local Governance and Development Under Decentralization in the Philippines." Working Paper 2005/06. Quezon City: School of Economics, University of the Philippines. www.econstor.eu/handle/ 10419/46627.

Capuno, Joseph J., and Ma M. Garcia (2010). "Can Information About Local Government Performance Induce Civic Participation? Evidence From the Philippines." *The Journal of Development Studies* 46 (4): 624–643. https://doi.org/ 10.1080/00220380903023521.

Choi, Nankyung (2004). "Local Elections and Party Politics in Post-Reformasi Indonesia: A View From Yogyakarta." *Contemporary Southeast Asia* 26 (2): 280–301.

Devas, Nick, and Carole Rakodi (1993). *Managing Fast Growing Cities: New Approaches to Urban Planning and Management in the Developing World.* New York: Longman Scientific and Technical.

Dobbs, Richard, Sven Smit, Jaana Remes, James Manyika, Charles Roxburgh, and Alejandra Restrepo (2011). *Urban World: Mapping the Economic Power of Cities.* New York: McKinsey Global Institute.

Firman, Tommy (2009). "Decentralization Reform and Local-Government Proliferation in Indonesia: Towards a Fragmentation of Regional Development." *Review of Urban & Regional Development Studies* 21 (2–3): 143–157. https://doi. org/10.1111/j.1467-940X.2010.00165.x.

Fossati, Diego (2016). "Is Indonesian Local Government Accountable to the Poor? Evidence From Health Policy Implementation." *Journal of East Asian Studies* 16 (3): 307–330.

Glaeser, Edward L. (2011). *Triumph of the City: How Our Greatest Invention Makes us Richer, Smarter, Greener, Healthier, and Happier.* New York: Penguin Press.

Hadiz, Vedi R. (2004). "Decentralization and Democracy in Indonesia: A Critique of Neo-Institutionalist Perspectives." *Development and Change* 35 (4): 697–718.

Jaweng, Robert Endi (2011). "Reformasi Birokrasi Bagi Efisiensi APBD." *Suara Pembaruan*, 5 August.

Jurnali, Teddy, and A.K. Siti-Nabiha (2015). "Performance Management System for Local Government: The Indonesian Experience." *Global Business Review* 16 (3): 351–363. https://doi.org/10.1177/0972150915569923.

Kasuya, Yuko (2009). *Presidential Bandwagon: Parties and Party Systems in the Philippines.* Pasig City, Philippines: Exclusively Distributed by Anvil Pub.

Lacaba, Jose F. (Ed.) (1995). *Boss: 5 Case Studies of Local Politics in the Philippines.* Pasig, Metro Manila: Philippine Center for Investigative Journalism and Institute for Popular Democracy.

Lewis, Blane D. (2010). "Indonesian Decentralization: Accountability Deferred." *International Journal of Public Administration* 33 (12–13): 648–657.

Lewis, Blane D., and Andre Oosterman (2011). "Subnational Government Spending in Indonesia: Level, Structure, and Financing." *Public Administration and Development* 31 (3): 149–158.

Lewis, Blane D., and Daan Pattinasarany (2009). "Determining Citizen Satisfaction With Local Public Education in Indonesia: The Significance of Actual Service Quality and Governance Conditions." *Growth and Change* 40 (1): 85–115.

Lewis, Blane D., and Paul Smoke (2012). "Incentives for Better Local Service Delivery." In *Fiscal Decentralization in Indonesia a Decade After Big Bang*, edited by Ministry of Finance, 255–288. Jakarta: Ministry of Finance, Republic of Indonesia.

Martinez-Vazquez, Jorge, and François Vaillancourt (2011). *Decentralization in Developing Countries: Global Perspectives on the Obstacles to Fiscal Devolution.* Northampton, MA and Cheltenham: Edward Elgar.

McCulloch, Neil, and Edmund Malesky (2011). "Does Better Local Governance Improve District Growth Performance in Indonesia?" Working Paper series 17–2001. Brighton: University of Sussex Economics Department.

Medina-Guce, Czarina (2016). "Good Housekeeping: Local Governance Performance Measures in the Philippines." *Open Government Partnership*, 23 November. www.opengovpartnership.org/stories/good-housekeeping-local-governance-performance-measures-philippines.

Mietzner, Marcus (2013). *Money, Power, and Ideology: Political Parties in Post-Authoritarian Indonesia.* Singapore: NUS Press.

Oates, Wallace E. (1972). *Fiscal Federalism.* New York: Harcourt Brace Jovanovich.

Querubin, Pablo (2012). "Political Reform and Elite Persistence: Term Limits and Political Dynasties in the Philippines." Paper presented at APSA 2012 Annual Meeting. https://ssrn.com/abstract=2108036.

Shair-Rosenfield, Sarah (2016). "The Causes and Effects of the Local Government Code in the Philippines: Locked in a Status Quo of Weakly Decentralized Authority?" *Journal of Southeast Asian Economies* 33 (2): 157–171. http://doi.org.lib proxy1.nus.edu.sg/10.1355/ae33-2c.

Sidel, John T. (2004). "Bossism and Democracy in the Philippines, Thailand and Indonesia: Towards an Alternative Framework for the Study of 'Local Strongmen'." In *Politicising Democracy: The New Local Politics and Democratisation*, edited by John Harriss, Kristian Stokke, and Olle Törnquist, 51–74. Basingstoke and New York: Palgrave Macmillan.

Skoufias, Emmanuel, Ambar Narayan, Basab Dasgupta, and Kai Kaiser (2011). "Electoral Accountability, Fiscal Decentralization and Service Delivery in Indonesia." SSRN Scholarly Paper ID 1799161. Rochester, NY: Social Science Research Network. https://papers.ssrn.com/abstract=1799161.

Solon, Jose Orville C., Raul V. Fabella, and Joseph J. Capuno (2009). "Is Local Development Good Politics? Local Development Expenditures and the Re-election of Governors in the Philippines in the 1990s." *Asian Journal of Political Science* 17 (3): 265–284. https://doi.org/10.1080/02185370903403475.

Tiebout, Charles M. (1956). "A Pure Theory of Local Expenditures." *The Journal of Political Economy* 64 (5): 416–424. https://doi.org/10.1086/257839.

Wallich, Christine, Rosario G. Manasan, and Saloua Sehili (2007). "Subsidiarity and Solidarity: Fiscal Decentralization in the Philippines." In *Fiscal Fragmentation in Decentralized Countries: Subsidiarity, Solidarity and Asymmetry*, edited by Richard M. Bird and Robert D. Ebel, 363–397. Cheltenham: Edward Elgar.

World Bank (2003). "Decentralizing Indonesia: A Regional Public Expenditure Review Report." Report No. 26191-IND, 2003. Washington, DC: World Bank.

Yilmaz, Serdar, and Varsha Venugopal (2013). "Local Government Discretion and Accountability in Philippines." *Journal of International Development* 25 (2): 227–250. https://doi.org/10.1002/jid.1687.

2 The smart city as layered policy design
Singapore's Smart Nation initiative

Jun Jie Woo

The growing application of advanced information and communications technology (ICT) to urban governance and policymaking has led to the emergence of the "smart city" as an urban policy innovation capable of addressing the increasingly complex policy issues faced by city governments. More than simply applying new technological tools and solutions to urban problems, smart cities have given rise to new and more responsive modes of urban governance. This chapter will take a policy design approach to understanding urban governance in a smart city. Focusing on Singapore's Smart Nation initiative, the chapter identifies the various design components and dynamics of the initiative that have influenced Singapore's development as a smart city. I argue that the Smart Nation initiative constitutes an act of "policy layering", where new policy elements that are related to the smart city are layered upon Singapore's existing developmental approach to governance and policymaking. The result of this is an increasingly complex urban policy mix that features new interconnections between novel policy instruments and old policy goals.

Introduction

The advent of advanced information and communications technology (ICT) and the growing prominence of data analytics as a possible tool for policymaking have led to the emergence of the "smart city" as an urban innovation deemed capable of addressing increasingly complex policy issues through the application of advanced ICT and digital technologies (Batty, 2013; Crivello, 2015; Gil-Garcia et al., 2016; Goldsmith and Crawford, 2014; Goodspeed, 2015; Townsend, 2014). Indeed, urban policymakers are increasingly focused on establishing the infrastructure necessary for smart city formation (Bakıcı et al., 2012; Crivello, 2015; Lee et al., 2013; Zygiaris, 2013), with the "smartness" of a city seen as part of a broader set of urban strategic agendas aimed at addressing emerging and increasingly complex urban issues and problems (Gil-Garcia et al., 2016: 2). As Gil-Garcia et al. further point out, a city's "smartness" tends to be determined by the extent to which it uses ICT in urban policy and governance.

Beyond this focus on the application of ICT and digital technology, however, smart cities continue to be plagued by a lack of definitional precision and universality, with understandings of the socio-political and policy processes underlying smart city formation particularly fuzzy (Albino et al., 2015; Hollands, 2008; Neirotti et al., 2014). Nonetheless, there is emerging interest in the various "smart governance" mechanisms and institutions that determine the emergence and success of smart cities (Calder, 2016; Gil-Garcia et al., 2016).

This chapter aims to continue on this trajectory by taking a policy design approach to understanding the policy initiatives and dynamics that have driven the formation and governance of Singapore as a smart city. In doing so, it seeks to provide a design-centric approach to understanding urban governance in a smart city. More than simply a case study of smart city formation in Singapore, the findings of this chapter have significant implications for other emerging smart cities in Asia.

The choice of Singapore as a case study is by no means arbitrary. First, Singapore is known to be a leading proponent of the smart city movement (Infocomm Development Authority of Singapore, 2014; Mahizhnan, 1999; Watts and Purnell, 2016; Woodhouse, 2016), beginning with its early efforts at implementing e-government initiatives (Chan et al., 2008; Sriramesh and Rivera-Sánchez, 2006). In 2016, Juniper Research named Singapore the top smart city of the world, ahead of Barcelona, London, San Francisco, and Oslo (Juniper Research, 2016).

Furthermore, Singapore's status as one of the world's few functioning city-states also suggests that its approach to transforming itself into a smart city differs from those of other cities. Unlike other cities that exist under the aegis of a larger nation-state, smart city initiatives in Singapore tend to be elevated to the national level. As Calder (2016: 3) notes, Singapore's dual identity as city and state allows for the "pragmatic, flexible, nonideological domestic politics characteristic of cities", even as "national standing provides the legitimacy and resources required to play credibly on the international scene". Evidence of this can be found in its Smart Nation initiative, a suite of smart city policies that were introduced in 2014 as part of the government's efforts to address complex urban issues through technological means. While the initiative is centrally developed and administered by a Smart Nation Programme Office (SNPO) situated within the Prime Minister's Office, it also involves public agencies that deal with citizens at the grassroots level, such as the Housing Development Board or Municipal Services Office (Ministry of National Development, 2015; SNPO, 2017a).

This chapter will discuss Singapore's Smart Nation initiative as policy design, identifying the various design components of the initiative as well as the design dynamics that have influenced its development. In so doing, I argue that the Smart Nation initiative constitutes an act of "policy layering", where new policy elements that are related to the smart city are layered upon Singapore's existing developmental approach to governance and policymaking. The result of this is an increasingly complex urban policy mix that features new interconnections between novel policy instruments and old policy goals.

The findings of this chapter suggest that there is much scope for taking a policy design-centric approach to understanding urban governance. While the policy design approach has often been applied to policy domains such as economic development, healthcare, and climate change, efforts to draw on the insights of policy design in urban policy are much harder to come by. Conversely, smart city governance tends to emphasize the incorporation of smart technologies in decision-making and policy implementation (Meijer and Bolívar, 2016) without sufficiently addressing the macro-level policy design processes.

The following section will provide a brief overview of the existing literature on smart cities and, at the same time, provide a broad introduction to Singapore's Smart Nation initiative. I will then discuss the Smart Nation initiative in the context of policy design. This is followed by a discussion of the design dynamics that underpin the initiative, before concluding with theoretical implications and potential avenues for future research.

Of (smart) cities and (smart) nations

As a concept and in practice, smart cities emerged from and continue to exist at the intersection of advanced ICT and data technology with increasingly complex urban problems. Fundamental to the concept of a smart city is the assumption that complex "wicked" problems – urban transport, crime, healthcare, and education, among others – can be addressed through the use of data analytics and sensors that allow for more effective information collection and management (Batty, 2013; Goodspeed, 2015; Kitchin, 2014; Perera et al., 2014; Stimmel, 2015).

This notion of a smart city as source of policy solutions has become increasingly prominent over the past decade, with cities across the world seeking to utilize data analytics to address urban and municipal issues (Batty, 2013; Goodspeed, 2015; Kitchin, 2014; Stimmel, 2015; Townsend, 2014). This often involves the use of data-sharing platforms (Goldsmith and Crawford, 2014; Misuraca et al., 2014; Noveck, 2015), "city dashboards" (Dameri, 2017; Kitchin and McArdle, 2016), as well as networks of sensors and the "internet of things" (Bakıcı et al., 2012; Filipponi et al., 2010; Gubbi et al., 2013; Perera et al., 2014; Zanella et al., 2014).

More than simply a matter of establishing the necessary ICT infrastructure, however, smart cities have also been associated with new approaches to urban governance. While initial understandings of such smart governance focused on governments' ability to "cope with the conditions and exigencies of the knowledge society" (Willke, 2007: 165), the increasing application of data analytics and "sensible" technologies to policymaking has led to a stronger focus on responsive urban governance, through the effective collection of policy feedback and data (Goldsmith and Crawford, 2014; Greco and Bencardino, 2014; Perera et al., 2014; Resch et al., 2012). More importantly, this emphasis on "responsiveness" places a stronger focus on citizens and communities, with new digital tools and platforms facilitating civic engagement and policy collaboration with industry and societal actors (Bakıcı et al., 2012; Goldsmith and Crawford, 2014; Townsend, 2014). As Meijer and Bolivar point out, "smart city governance is about crafting new forms of human collaboration through the use of ICTs to obtain better outcomes and more open governance processes" (Meijer and Bolívar, 2016: 392).

Indeed, it is this focus on open collaboration and civic engagement that separates these studies of smart cities from a pre-existing e-government literature that emphasizes a one-way delivery of public services through online mechanisms and platforms, with limited scope for interactivity (Meijer and Bolívar, 2016; Norris and Reddick, 2013). Furthermore, e-government is associated with incremental changes in policy processes and outcomes (Norris and Reddick, 2013). In contrast, smart cities tend to be associated with more integrated approaches to urban governance that emphasize the responsiveness and transparency of a city's policy processes (Gil-Garcia, 2012; Goldsmith and Crawford, 2014; Meijer and Bolívar, 2016; Noveck, 2015).

As the world's only "fully-functioning city-state" (Long, 2015), Singapore's approach to establishing itself as a smart city differs from that of other cities. In particular, the conflation of city and state in Singapore suggests the convergence of a national–local divide in smart city strategies (Angelidou, 2014) and an elevation of urban and municipal issues to the national policy agenda, allowing for greater policy expediency when compared to countries with more layers of government (Balakrishnan, 2016; Lim, 2016). As a consequence, its smart city initiatives tend to be more centralized and far more extensive that those implemented in other cities (Watts and Purnell, 2016). This is further encouraged by the relatively high level of political and administrative centralization in Singapore,[1] which allows for swift decision-making and hence the ability to quickly implement large-scale policy changes (Low, 2006; Tan, 2012; Woo, 2016a). The following section will take a policy design approach to understanding Singapore's smart city policies, which are collectively known as the Smart Nation initiative.

The Smart Nation initiative as policy design

Originating from the seminal work of Harold Lasswell, the fundamental precept of policy design is that the policy process comprises policy means (instruments) and ends (goals) (Lasswell, 1951, 1971). Under this design orientation, policy instruments are essentially the tools, techniques, or mechanisms that governments use to achieve policy goals, usually by giving effect to public policies (Bressers and Klok, 1988; Howlett, 2011; Howlett and Rayner, 2007; Woodside, 1986).

While early policy design studies had sought to build up comprehensive typologies of policy instruments and their varied functions and effects (Bemelmans-Videc et al., 1998; Elmore, 1987; Grabosky, 1995; Hood, 1986; Howlett, 2000; Woodside, 1986), subsequent efforts would seek to develop a deeper understanding of how instruments tend to be "packaged" within larger "policy mixes" (Doelen, 1998; Gunningham et al., 1998; Howlett, 2004) or "new governance arrangements" (Howlett and Rayner, 2007; Rayner and Howlett, 2009). Often taking a portfolio approach to understanding policy mixes, these studies seek to understand the relationships between policy instruments within a given policy mix, paying particular attention to the dynamics that arise when new instruments are added to a mix or existing instruments omitted or changed (Howlett and Rayner, 2013a, 2013b). This has allowed for the identification and categorization of the different

		Instrument Mixes	
		Consistent	Inconsistent
Multiple Goals	**Coherent**	Integration	Drift
	Incoherent	Conversion	Layering

Figure 2.1 Policy Mix Dynamics

dynamics that emerge when new instruments and goals interact with existing ones within a given policy mix. Four main dynamics have been identified in the literature, with each dynamic associated with the extent of policy goal coherence and policy instrument consistency within a policy mix, as illustrated in Figure 2.1.

While "policy layering" has been taken to mean the adding of new policy goals and policy instruments onto an existing regime without removing previous ones, "conversion" involves changes to policy instrument mixes without any change to policy goals (Béland, 2007; Rayner and Howlett, 2009; Thelen, 2004). "Policy drift" occurs when policy goals are changed but not the instruments used to attain them (Hacker, 2004; Rayner and Howlett, 2009: 103). Dynamics of layering, conversion, and drift are fundamentally rooted in the assumption that policy mixes ought to be designed in such a way that policy instruments support, rather than undermine, each other, i.e., to ensure *coherence* in policy goals and *consistency* among policy instruments (Howlett and Rayner, 2007: 7). As Figure 2.1 shows, an ideal situation of integration occurs when instrument mixes are consistent and policy goals are coherent. In contrast, the addition of new instruments and goals without sufficient consideration of existing ones may result in mismatches between goals and instruments. Lastly, conversion reflects a more systematic attempt to change the policy instrument mix in order to meet new policy goals. These dynamics of policy design can provide a useful framework for understanding new policy initiatives such as the Smart Nation initiative and interactions between components of these new initiatives and the existing urban policy milieu.

Launched in 2014, the Smart Nation initiative aims to harness data and technological solutions to address urban policy issues (Lee, 2014). According to the SNPO, the Smart Nation initiative aims to "support better living, stronger communities, and create more opportunities, for all", with a focus on "how well a society uses technology to solve its problems and address existential challenges" (SNPO, 2016). The initiative places a strong emphasis on five key domains: transport, home and environment, business productivity, health and enabled aging, and public sector services.

In terms of policy instruments, the Smart Nation initiative relies on a set of "enablers" (SNPO, 2016), which include:

- Test-bedding and collaboration with industry and research institutions
- An open data portal and a Smart Nation Platform that allow for the consolidation and sharing of government data
- Investments in Research and Development (R&D)

- Laboratories for the development and piloting of technological solutions
- Start-up accelerators to nurture creative start-ups and innovations
- Cybersecurity measures for the safeguarding of data, systems, and networks
- Building computational capabilities among citizens through educational programs at various levels, including young children, secondary school students, and working professionals.

The policy goals and instruments that the Smart Nation initiative has articulated differ from those of Singapore's hitherto development-oriented approach to governance or the Asian "developmental state" model (Huff, 1995; Low, 2001; Perry, 1997). The developmental state model generally emphasizes policy goals of economic growth and industry development, with policy instruments typically including subsidies, incentives, government investments in economic and physical infrastructure, and direct market interventions by the state, most notably through state-owned industries and other quasi-governmental organizations.

Although developmental goals are also emphasized in the Smart Nation initiative, there appears to be a clear focus on citizens and communities in the initiative's policy goals, with these goals broadly emphasizing stronger communities, greater policy collaboration with businesses and citizens, and the nurturing of a culture of innovation and experimentation. As the SNPO emphasizes: "(c)itizens are ultimately at the heart of our Smart Nation vision, not technology!" (SNPO, 2016). By providing a list of the policy goals and instruments that are associated with the development state model and the Smart Nation initiative, Figure 2.2 highlights the significant differences between the two approaches.

	Developmental State	**Smart Nation**
Policy Goals	Development-driven • Economic growth • Industry development	Citizen-centric • Stronger communities • Policy collaboration • Innovation and Experimentation Development-driven • Creation of new opportunities
Policy Instruments	Developmental • Subsidies • Incentives • Government investments • Market interventions	Enabling • Test-bedding • Open Data Portal & Smart Nation Platform • Laboratories • Start-up Accelerators • Cyber Security • Computational Capabilities Developmental • Investments in R&D

Figure 2.2 Policy Design Elements

These differences are particularly distinct in terms of policy instruments. In thinking about the policy instruments employed by the two approaches, it is useful to think about "developmental" versus "enabling" instruments (Woo, 2015, 2016b). Where the former involves the allocation of state and societal resources toward the attainment of developmental goals (Chang and Grabel, 2004; Murinde and Mlambo, 2011; Stiglitz et al., 1993), the latter is associated with "the creation not merely of incentives but of those conditions that allow activities to take place" (Baldwin et al., 1998: 4). As Figure 2.2 shows, the developmental state model emphasizes developmental instruments that involve the mobilization of resources toward the stimulation of economic growth and industrial development. In contrast, the Smart Nation initiative favors instruments that establish the enabling conditions and infrastructure necessary for the development and operations of innovation start-ups. Calder (2016: 61) describes this as "minimalist, enabling governance".

However, it is important to note that the design of Smart Nation policies – or any instance of policy design for that matter – is not a static process. As discussed earlier, policy design tends to be an iterative process that involves the inclusion (or exclusion) of policy instruments from an existing policy mix or portfolio over an extended period of time. There is, in other words, no tabula rasa in policy design – but legacies of urban policies and design processes past. What then, are the dominant design dynamics – whether layering, conversion, drift, or integration – involved in the Smart Nation initiative?

Layered hybridity: a developmental smart city?

Despite its focus on citizen- and community-centric policy goals, as articulated in official documents and reports, the Smart Nation initiative retains a strong emphasis on goals and objectives associated with economic development. These range from ensuring greater efficiency in its ports to exporting data-related products and services or smart city solutions as potential streams of trade revenue (Bhandari, 2017). Indeed, the Smart Nation initiative has often been evaluated in economic terms, such as its ability to generate employment, create new business opportunities for firms, and create value for consumers (Chng, 2016).

As Prime Minister Lee noted in a speech in 2014, the advanced data and IT technologies that may emerge from the Smart Nation initiative can contribute to greater economic productivity and generate business opportunities (Lee, 2014). This linkage between the Smart Nation initiative and economic development is further emphasized by Vivian Balakrishnan, the initiative's Minister-in-Charge:

> It is technological advancement that leads to economic development, and ultimately economics determines political outcomes. In other words, it is technology first, then economics, and finally politics. If you get it wrong and put the cart before the horse, you get a very confused world that is unable to solve the existential challenges. And more importantly, a world unable to capitalise on the opportunities that these technological advancements present.
>
> (Balakrishnan, 2016)

Fundamental to the Smart Nation initiative, therefore, is the primacy of economic policy goals and the assumption that the various technological tools and innovations associated with the Smart Nation initiative should be geared toward the attainment of these economic goals. The Smart Nation initiative's direct predecessor, the "Intelligent Nation 2015", had already placed a strong emphasis on the transformation of key economic sectors (Angelidou, 2014: S8).

As Minister Balakrishnan has pointed out, the government's investments in data-related R&D aim to "improve the quality of life and to enhance economic opportunities and provide good jobs for our people" (Balakrishnan, 2016). The economic value of such R&D activities is underscored by the Minister's assertion that:

> data (and nowadays the term big data is in fashion) is the new currency, but raw data is commoditised, everyone has access to it. The real value is in insight and the ability to synthesise and generate new perspectives and the ability to exercise judgement and wisdom to create new ideas, products and services.
>
> (Balakrishnan, 2016)

Perhaps most tellingly, the Economic Development Board (EDB), which has been Singapore's de facto "pilot agency" under its developmental state approach, remains the lead agency for the development of the various smart or knowledge sectors associated with the Smart Nation, such as real-time data solutions (Calder, 2016: 92–97; Economic Policy Board, 2016). Furthermore, the EDB's role often extends beyond economic or sectoral development to include other aspects of the smart city. For instance, the EDB has recently signed a memorandum of understanding with MasterCard to develop new technological solutions for both business development and urban mobility, with a further aim of potentially exporting these solutions (MasterCard, 2016). The Smart Nation initiative therefore continues to emphasize economic development goals, whether in terms of enhancing business and economic activity through technological solutions or even potentially exporting these urban-technological solutions. As Angelidou (2014: S8) has noted, Singapore's smart city initiatives tend to be economic sector-based rather than geographically or spatially based.

This addition of new policy instruments (smart city policies) and policy goals (citizen and community development) to an existing mix of development-oriented policy instruments and goals suggests a significant degree of policy layering. Indeed, as the previous discussion has shown, there are numerous cross-linkages among these new policy instruments and old policy goals, with new Smart Nation initiatives emphasizing the attainment of economic policy goals. While the Smart Nation initiative has sought to recast Singapore as a 21st century smart nation, vestiges of its old developmental state persona remain. Rather than a transformation into a smart city or smart nation, Singapore's efforts have culminated in the hybrid form of a "developmental smart city".

Where collaborative opportunities are discussed, these tend to be top-down and state-centric, with potential collaborations taking place on state-owned platforms and institutions such as the Smart Nation platform or government-owned start-up accelerators. Furthermore, many of the smart city solutions that aim to improve the quality of life of citizens, such as the introduction of smart home technologies, tend to be associated with or developed by public agencies, in this case, the Housing Development Board (SNPO, 2017b). There is, in short, a continued prevalence of both developmental policy goals and state-driven solutions in Singapore's approach to developing a smart city, with new smart city initiatives layered upon an existing legacy of development-oriented policy instruments, goals, and logics.

While the conventional wisdom in policy design would suggest that such policy layering may give rise to incoherent policy goals and inconsistent policy instruments (Rayner and Howlett, 2009), the policy outcome of the Smart Nation initiative remains to be seen. All we can say at this point is that the Smart Nation initiative is either a bold act of policy innovation, with the possibility of achieving both economic and societal policy goals through one set of policy instruments, or a potential risk, with linkages between policy instruments and policy goals not clearly explicated (or, indeed, explicable) and hence leading to some degree of confusion and complexity.

Conclusion

This chapter has sought to understand Singapore's Smart Nation initiative through the lens of policy design. In doing so, it has found that the initiative constitutes an act of policy layering, with new policy instruments and goals associated with smart city formation layered onto an existing legacy of development-oriented policy instruments and goals. What has emerged, as a result, are cross-linkages between new policy instruments (smart city initiatives and solutions) and old policy goals (new economic opportunities and sectors associated with the application of smart technologies).

While the rhetoric in many smart cities, Singapore included, has been the need for a transformation into a 21st-century smart city that not only relies on advanced digital and data technologies for the development of urban policy solutions but also involves new collaborative approaches to urban governance, the case of Singapore's Smart Nation initiative suggests that such a transformation may not necessarily give rise to a state of tabula rasa for urban policymakers and designers. The reality is that new urban policies and interventions tend to be layered upon existing policy legacies. In other words, the emergence of a smart city depends not so much on a large-scale transformation but on an ongoing process of incremental layering and policy adaptation.

As Shelton et al. (2015: 14) have noted, "smart city interventions are always the outcomes of, and awkwardly integrated into, existing social and spatial constellations of urban governance and the built environment", with "greenfield smart cities . . . the exception rather than the rule". The successful formation of a smart city therefore hinges upon urban policymakers' ability to successfully integrate new policy measures, goals, and models with existing ones. As the policy design literature has pointed out, an inability to do so can result in incoherent policy goals and inconsistent policy instruments.

In framing Singapore's Smart Nation initiative as policy design, this chapter hopes to provide a useful starting point for further explorations into the integration of urban policy and policy design. Indeed, the incorporation of policy design into urban policy processes can provide policymakers with a powerful set of tools for assessing existing urban policy efforts and planning future urban policy interventions in a more integrated manner, considering and addressing existing policy legacies that may otherwise adversely impact new policy interventions.

Future research directions may therefore focus on further conceptual explications of the linkages between policy design and urban policy. These efforts may also involve the application of any potential new theoretical insights to other smart cities. The continued proliferation of smart cities across the world – and the potential impacts that smart city initiatives can have on their inhabitants – suggest an urgent need for closer attention to and research on the policy processes involved in the design, formation, and governance of a smart city.

Note

1 The ruling People's Action Party (PAP) has consistently won a comfortable majority in all general elections since independence.

References

Albino, Vito, Umberto Berardi, and Rosa M. Dangelico (2015). "Smart Cities: Definitions, Dimensions, Performance, and Initiatives." *Journal of Urban Technology* 22 (1): 3–21.

Angelidou, Margarita (2014). "Smart City Policies: A Spatial Approach." *Cities* 41 (Supplement 1): S3–S11.

Bakıcı, Tuba, Esteve Almirall, and Johnathan Wareham (2012). "A Smart City Initiative: The Case of Barcelona." *Journal of the Knowledge Economy* 4 (2): 135–148.

Balakrishnan, Vivian (2016). "Opening Speech by Dr Vivian Balakrishnan, Minister-in-Charge of the Smart Nation Initiative." at Smart Nation Innovations/Innovfest UnBound. Marina Bay Sands Expo and Convention Centre, Singapore. www2.imda.gov.sg/news-and-events/Media-Room/archived/ida/Speeches/2016/opening-speech-by-dr-vivian-balakrishnan-minister-for-foreign-affairs-and-minister-in-charge-of-the-smart-nation-initiative-at-smart-nation-innovations-innovfest-unbound.

Baldwin, Robert, Colin Scott, and Christopher Hood (Eds.) (1998). *A Reader on Regulation.* Oxford: Oxford University Press.

Batty, Michael (2013). "Big Data, Smart Cities and City Planning." *Dialogues in Human Geography* 3 (3): 274–279.

Béland, Daniel (2007). "Ideas and Institutional Change in Social Security: Conversion, Layering, and Policy Drift." *Social Science Quarterly* 88 (1): 20–38.

Bemelmans-Videc, Marie-Louise, Ray C. Rist, and Evert Vedung (Eds.) (1998). *Carrots, Sticks, and Sermons: Policy Instruments and Their Evaluation.* Piscataway, NJ: Transaction Publishers.

Bhandari, Mamik (2017). "Is Data Singapore's Next Big Bet?" *The Straits Times,* 6 February.

Bressers, Hans, and Pieter-Jan Klok (1988). "Fundamentals for a Theory of Policy Instruments." *International Journal of Social Economics* 15 (3/4): 22–41.

Calder, Kent E. (2016). *Singapore: Smart City, Smart State*. Washington, DC: Brookings Institution Press.

Chan, Meng Lai, Ying Lau, and Shan Ling Pan (2008). "E-government Implementation: A Macro Analysis of Singapore's E-government Initiatives." *Government Information Quarterly* 25 (2): 239–255.

Chang, Ha-Joon, and Ilene Grabel (2004). *Reclaiming Development: An Alternative Economic Policy Manual*. London: Zed Books Ltd.

Chng, Grace (2016). "Smart Nation Report Card: Let's Get Digital." *The Straits Times*, 22 May.

Crivello, Silvia (2015). "Urban Policy Mobilities: The Case of Turin as a Smart City." *European Planning Studies* 23 (5): 909–921.

Dameri, Renata P. (2017). "Urban Smart Dashboard. Measuring Smart City Performance." In *Smart City Implementation*, 67–84. New York: Springer International Publishing.

Doelen, Frans C.J. van der (1998). "The 'Give-and-Take' Packaging of Policy Instruments: Optimizing Legitimacy and Effectiveness." In *Carrots, Sticks and Sermons: Policy Instruments and Their Evaluation*, edited by Marie-Louise Bemelmans-Videc, Ray C. Rist, and Evert Vedung, 129–146. Piscataway, NJ: Transaction Publishers.

Economic Policy Board (2016). "Industries" [online]. Singapore Economic Development Board – Investing Business in Singapore. /content/edb/en/industries.html (accessed 15 February 2017).

Elmore, Richard F. (1987). "Instruments and Strategy in Public Policy." *Review of Policy Research* 7 (1): 174–186.

Filipponi, Luca, Andrea Vitaletti, Giada Landi, Vincenzo Memeo, Giorgio Laura, and Paulo Pucci (2010). "Smart City: An Event Driven Architecture for Monitoring Public Spaces with Heterogeneous Sensors." In *2010 Fourth International Conference on Sensor Technologies and Applications (SENSORCOMM)*, 281–286. IEEE, Venice/Mestre, Italy. doi:10.1109/SENSORCOMM.2010.50.

Gil-Garcia, J. Ramon (2012). "Towards a Smart State? Inter-agency Collaboration, Information Integration, and Beyond." *Information Polity* 17 (3/4): 269–280.

Gil-Garcia, J. Ramon, Theresa A. Pardo, and Taewoo Nam (2016). "A Comprehensive View of the 21st Century City: Smartness as Technologies and Innovation in Urban Contexts." In *Smarter as the New Urban Agenda: A Comprehensive View of the 21st Century City*, edited by J.R. Gil-Garcia, T.A. Pardo, and N. Taewoo, 1–19. New York: Springer International Publishing.

Goldsmith, Stephen, and Susan Crawford (2014). *The Responsive City: Engaging Communities Through Data-Smart Governance*. San Francisco, CA: Jossey-Bass.

Goodspeed, Robert (2015). "Smart Cities: Moving Beyond Urban Cybernetics to Tackle Wicked Problems." *Cambridge Journal of Regions, Economy and Society* 8 (1): 79–92.

Grabosky, Peter N. (1995). "Regulation by Reward: On the Use of Incentives as Regulatory Instruments." *Law & Policy* 17 (3): 257–282.

Greco, Ilaria, and Massimiliano Bencardino (2014). "The Paradigm of the Modern City: SMART and SENSEable Cities for Smart, Inclusive and Sustainable Growth." In *Computational Science and Its Applications – ICCSA 2014*, edited by B. Murgante et al., 579–597. New York: Springer International Publishing.

Gubbi, Jayavardhana, Rajkumar Buyya, Slaven Marusic, and Marimuthu Palaniswami (2013). "Internet of Things (IoT): A Vision, Architectural Elements, and Future Directions." *Future Generation Computer Systems* 29 (7): 1645–1660.

Gunningham, Neil, Peter Grabosky, and Darren Sinclair (1998). *Smart Regulation: Designing Environmental Policy.* New York: Oxford University Press.

Hacker, Jacob S. (2004). "Privatizing Risk Without Privatizing the Welfare State: The Hidden Politics of Social Policy Retrenchment in the United States." *The American Political Science Review* 98 (2): 243–260.

Hollands, Robert G. (2008). "Will the Real Smart City Please Stand Up?" *City* 12 (3): 303–320.

Hood, Christopher (1986). *The Tools of Government.* London: Chatham House Publishers.

Howlett, Michael (2000). "Managing the 'Hollow State': Procedural Policy Instruments and Modern Governance." *Canadian Public Administration* 43 (4): 412–431.

Howlett, Michael (2004). "Beyond Good and Evil in Policy Implementation: Instrument Mixes, Implementation Styles, and Second Generation Theories of Policy Instrument Choice." *Policy and Society* 23 (2): 1–17.

Howlett, Michael (2011). *Designing Public Policies: Principles and Instruments.* London: Routledge.

Howlett, Michael, and Jeremy Rayner (2007). "Design Principles for Policy Mixes: Cohesion and Coherence in 'New Governance Arrangements'." *Policy and Society* 26 (4): 1–18.

Howlett, Michael, and Jeremy Rayner (2013a). "Patching vs Packaging in Policy Formulation: Assessing Policy Portfolio Design." *Politics and Governance* 1 (2): 170–182.

Howlett, Michael, and Jeremy Rayner (2013b). "Patching vs Packaging in Policy Formulation: Complementary Effects, Goodness of Fit, Degrees of Freedom and Feasibility in Policy Portfolio Design." *Annual Review of Policy Design* 1 (1): 1–19.

Huff, William G. (1995). "The Developmental State, Government, and Singapore's Economic Development Since 1960." *World Development* 23 (8): 1421–1438.

Infocomm Development Authority of Singapore (2014). "Singapore Lays Groundwork to be World's First Smart Nation." News Release. Singapore: Infocomm Development Authority of Singapore.

Juniper Research (2016). *Worldwide Smart Cities: Energy, Transport & Lighting 2016–2021.* Basingstoke: Juniper Research.

Kitchin, Rob (2014). "The Real-time City? Big Data and Smart Urbanism." *GeoJournal* 79 (1): 1–14.

Kitchin, Rob, and Gavin McArdle (2016). "Urban Data and City Dashboards: Six Key Issues." Working Paper No. 21. Maynooth: Maynooth University.

Lasswell, Harold D. (1951). "The Policy Orientation." In *The Policy Sciences: Recent Developments in Scope and Method,* edited by D. Lerner and H.D. Lasswell, 3–15. Stanford, CA: Stanford University Press.

Lasswell, Harold D. (1971). *A Pre-view of Policy Sciences.* New York: American Elsevier Pub. Co.

Lee, Hsien Loong. (2014). "Smart Nation: Better Living, More Opportunities, Stronger Communities." Speech at Smart Nation Launch. Smart Nation and Digital Government Office, Government of Singapore. www.smartnation.sg/whats-new/speeches/smart-nation-launch.

Lee, Jung Hoon, Robert Phaal, and Sang-Ho Lee (2013). "An Integrated Service – Device – Technology Roadmap for Smart City Development." *Technological Forecasting and Social Change* 80 (2): 286–306.

Lim, Yan Liang (2016). "Trust Between Citizens, Government Key for Smart Nation: PM Lee Hsien Loong." *The Straits Times*, 12 July.

Long, Simon (2015). "The Singapore Exception." *The Economist*, 18 July.

Low, Linda (2001). "The Singapore Developmental State in the New Economy and Polity." *The Pacific Review* 14 (3): 411–441.

Low, Linda (2006). *The Political Economy of a City-State Revised*. Singapore: Marshall Cavendish.

Mahizhnan, Arun (1999). "Smart Cities: The Singapore Case." *Cities* 16 (1): 13–18.

MasterCard (2016). "MasterCard and Singapore Economic Development Board to Cooperate on Urban Mobility, Tourism and Trade" [online]. MasterCard Social Newsroom. http://newsroom.mastercard.com/press-releases/mastercard-and-singapore-economic-development-board-to-cooperate-on-urban-mobility-tourism-and-trade/ (accessed 15 February 2017).

Meijer, Albert, and Manuel P.R. Bolívar (2016). "Governing the Smart City: A Review of the Literature on Smart Urban Governance." *International Review of Administrative Sciences* 82 (2): 392–408.

Ministry of National Development (2015). "OneService Mobile App – Making It Easier for You to Report Municipal Issues" [online]. Municipal Services Office. www.mnd.gov.sg/mso/press-oneservice.htm (accessed 23 February 2015).

Misuraca, Gianluca, Francesco Mureddu, and David Osimo (2014). "Policy-Making 2.0: Unleashing the Power of Big Data for Public Governance." In *Open Government: Opportunities and Challenges for Public Governance*, edited by Mila Gasco-Hernandez, 171–181. New York: Springer.

Murinde, Victor, and Kupukile Mlambo (2011). "Development-Oriented Financial Regulation." Birmingham: Birmingham Business School. www.new-rules.org/storage/documents/g20-fsb-imf/murinde-kups.pdf.

Neirotti, Paolo, Alberto De Marco, Anna C. Cagliano, Giulio Mangano, and Franchesco Scorrano (2014). "Current Trends in Smart City Initiatives: Some Stylised Facts." *Cities* 38: 25–36.

Norris, Donald F., and Christopher G. Reddick (2013). "Local E-Government in the United States: Transformation or Incremental Change?" *Public Administration Review* 73 (1): 165–175.

Noveck, Beth S. (2015). *Smart Citizens, Smarter State: The Technologies of Expertise and the Future of Governing*. Cambridge, MA: Harvard University Press.

Perera, Charith, Arkady Zaslavsky, Peter Christen, and Dimitrios Georgakopoulos (2014). "Sensing as a Service Model for Smart Cities Supported by Internet of Things." *Transactions on Emerging Telecommunications Technologies* 25 (1): 81–93.

Perry, Martin (1997). *Singapore: A Developmental City State*. Chichester: Wiley.

Rayner, Jeremy, and Michael Howlett (2009). "Introduction: Understanding Integrated Policy Strategies and Their Evolution." *Policy and Society* 28 (2): 99–109.

Resch, Bernd, Rex Britter, and Carlo Ratti (2012). "Live Urbanism – Towards SENSEable Cities and Beyond." In *Sustainable Environmental Design in Architecture*, edited by Stamatina T. Rassia and Panos M. Pardalos, 175–184. New York: Springer.

Shelton, Taylor, Matthew Zook, and Alan Wiig (2015). "The 'Actually Existing Smart City'." *Cambridge Journal of Regions, Economy and Society* 8 (1): 13–25.

SNPO (2016). "About Smart Nation" [online]. Singapore: Smart Nation Programme Office. www.smartnation.sg/about-smart-nation (accessed 22 October 2016).

SNPO (2017a). "Smart Nation Initiatives" [online]. Singapore: Smart Nation Programme Office. www.smartnation.sg/initiatives/ (accessed 15 February 2017).

SNPO (2017b). "Smart Homes" [online]. Singapore: Smart Nation Programme Office. www.smartnation.sg/initiatives/Living/smart-homes (accessed 14 February 2017).

Sriramesh, Krishnamurthy, and Milagros Rivera-Sánchez (2006). "E-government in a Corporatist, Communitarian Society: The Case of Singapore." *New Media & Society* 8 (5): 707–730.

Stiglitz, Joseph E., Jamie Jaramillo-Vallejo, and Yung Chal Park (1993). *The Role of the State in Financial Markets*. Washington, DC: World Bank.

Stimmel, Carol L. (2015). *Building Smart Cities: Analytics, ICT, and Design Thinking*. Boca Raton, FL: Auerbach Publications.

Tan, Kenneth P. (2012). "The Ideology of Pragmatism: Neo-liberal Globalisation and Political Authoritarianism in Singapore." *Journal of Contemporary Asia* 42 (1): 67–92.

Thelen, Kathleen (2004). *How Institutions Evolve: The Political Economy of Skills in Germany, Britain, the United States, and Japan*. Cambridge and New York: Cambridge University Press.

Townsend, Anthony M. (2014). *Smart Cities: Big Data, Civic Hackers, and the Quest for a New Utopia*. New York: W.W. Norton & Company.

Watts, Jake M., and Newley Purnell (2016). "Singapore Is Taking the 'Smart City' to a Whole New Level." *Wall Street Journal*, 25 April.

Willke, Helmut (2007). *Smart Governance: Governing the Global Knowledge Society*. Frankfurt: Campus Verlag.

Woo, Jun Jie (2015). "Beyond the Neoliberal Orthodoxy: Alternative Financial Policy Regimes in Asia's Financial Centres." *Critical Policy Studies* 9 (3): 297–316.

Woo, Jun Jie (2016a). *Singapore as an International Financial Centre: History, Policy and Politics*. London: Palgrave Macmillan.

Woo, Jun Jie (2016b). *Business and Politics in Asia's Key Financial Centres: Hong Kong, Singapore and Shanghai*. Singapore: Springer.

Woodhouse, Alice (2016). "Hong Kong Faces Challenge From Singapore in 'Smart City' Planning." *South China Morning Post*, 22 June.

Woodside, Kenneth (1986). "Policy Instruments and the Study of Public Policy." *Canadian Journal of Political Science* 19 (4): 775–794.

Zanella, Andrea, Nichola Bui, Angela Castellani, Lorenzo Vangelista, and Michele Zorzi (2014). "Internet of Things for Smart Cities." *IEEE Internet of Things Journal* 1 (1): 22–32.

Zygiaris, Sotiris (2013). "Smart City Reference Model: Assisting Planners to Conceptualize the Building of Smart City Innovation Ecosystems." *Journal of the Knowledge Economy* 4 (2): 217–231.

3 The politics of advancing governance reform and curbing corruption in the metropolitan city

The case of Jakarta, 2012–2017

Vishnu Juwono and Elva Sagita Cindra

When the mayor of the small Indonesian town of Solo, Joko Widodo (known as "Jokowi") won the election to become Governor of Jakarta in 2012, there were high hopes that he and his Deputy Governor Basuki Tjahya Purnama (known as "Ahok") would bring more accountable, free, and transparent governance to the city. Jakartans elected the two men due to their credible track records in leading much smaller towns or regions. As they did not come from the usual political elites based in Jakarta, Jokowi and Ahok promised a new approach to governance – from a leadership style that was humbler and more responsive to the voice of the poor, to confronting the established patronage networks built by the political elites that bred corruption in Jakarta.

During his short stint as governor (2012–2014), Jokowi was able to project a different style, with the help of the mass media. He was seen as more receptive to the needs of the poor, with his frequent surprise visits around the city, making sure that his programs were on track. His healthcare and education programs, which also targeted the poor, contributed to his soaring popularity among Jakartans but also made him a national figure. With this high approval rating, Jokowi entered – and won – the presidential race in 2014.

This resulted in Ahok, Jokowi's deputy, becoming Governor of Jakarta. In contrast to Jokowi, Ahok's leadership style was characterized by his no-nonsense approach, directly confronting lazy and often corrupt bureaucrats. He was also known for his responsive governance style. For instance, he set up a rapid-response team that would quickly respond to people's various demands, like fixing the hole in the street. However, Ahok's period in office was not without controversy. His close links with powerful property developers alarmed the anti-corruption activists, while his robust approach to bureaucrats led to the Jakarta government struggling to disburse its budget. Ahok was eventually forced to step down in 2017, when he was convicted in a blasphemy case; he was replaced by his Deputy, Djarot, until his term ended in November 2017.

This chapter assesses whether Jokowi and Ahok were able to deliver their promises to provide more accountable, transparent, and responsive governance as well as to curb corruption. It aims to contribute to the existing literature by focusing on governance and anti-corruption reform by local government, especially the government of DKI Jakarta under Jokowi and Ahok. It applies political pluralism combined with Burns' political leadership theory as a theoretical framework with the aim of identifying the proponents and opponents of governance reform and anti-corruption initiatives in Jakarta during 2012–2017. The chapter thus aims to provide a comprehensive review of the progress and regress of governance reform in the Province of Jakarta under the leadership of Jokowi and Ahok.

Literature review

A number of studies about Jokowi focus primarily on his term as Mayor of Solo, with his populist public service policy (Bunnell et al., 2018; A. Hamid, 2014; S. Hamid, 2012). Abdul Hamid (2014) argues that Jokowi's victory in the 2012 gubernatorial election was seen as a triumph of populism, based on his positive image as a leader, primarily when he was serving as Mayor of Solo. Several factors contributed to the emergence of Jokowi as an alternative leader for Jakarta, including the low level of trust toward government and lack of confidence toward political parties, rampant corruption in Jakarta, the critical stance of Jakartan youth, and strong demands for a more responsive political leader.

Similarly, Sandra Hamid (2012) claims that the results of the Jakarta gubernatorial election conveyed a message of discontent with the status quo and desire for change. Despite facing an incumbent who was supported by the major political parties in the local parliament, Jokowi secured a victory through two rounds of voting, demonstrating that political party coalitions do not necessarily determine election outcomes, especially when there is a charismatic figure in the race. Bunnell et al. (2018) argue that Solo acted as a political launch pad for Jokowi as he sought to translate some of his mayoral accomplishments in Solo to his governorship of Jakarta.

Other studies have focused on Jokowi's time as president (Hatherell, 2014; Kurniawan and Utami, 2017; Mietzner, 2014). Mietzner (2014) argues that Jokowi's victory in the presidential election meant that Indonesia's democracy could be preserved. The 2014 presidential election featured a formidable populist challenge from Prabowo Subianto, Suharto's former son-in-law, who promised more robust leadership and a return to the indirect electoral mechanisms with which Suharto had ruled Indonesia for 32 years. In comparison, Jokowi's populism was pragmatic, moderate, and inclusive. Jokowi looked and sounded like an average lower-middle-class Indonesian, which made him seem like the antithesis of typical Indonesian elite politicians (Mietzner, 2014: 114).

Kurniawan and Utami (2017) focus on the Jakarta Post's open endorsement of Jokowi in the presidential election. The Jakarta Post used its power to influence the point of view of many in society by presenting the purportedly "right side" of Jokowi during the campaign. Hatherell (2014), however, argues that Jokowi's success was not solely due to his being the darling of the media: instead, his success thus far is based on his ability to make representative claims that are judged, by a large proportion of those he formally represents, as desirable.

Meanwhile, although some of the literature on Ahok addresses his anti-corruption efforts, the majority focuses on his leadership style, especially at the time of the blasphemy case (Hatherell and Welsh, 2017; Manurung, 2016; Setijadi, 2017). Hatherell and Welsh (2017) outline Ahok's careful construction of his decisive leadership style, as he successfully set up a dichotomy between his own clean, anti-corruption image and the image of his corrupt and ineffective rivals. Manurung (2016) highlights Ahok's blunt remarks, especially toward corrupt public officials. While sometimes controversial, Ahok offered a refreshing alternative to Jakartans, who were fed up with corrupt and hypocritical leaders. However, Setijadi (2017) points out that some voters did not like Ahok's personality and brash attitude. This was evident in pre-election polls, which showed that, while voters were supportive of Ahok's policies and his strong work ethic, they did not find him to be a likable figure.

There has been relatively little literature to date about Jokowi's anti-corruption reform efforts during his governorship. One recent study on anti-corruption efforts (Juwono, 2019) focuses on Jokowi's presidency rather than his time as Governor of Jakarta. For his term as governor, most studies focus on his populist policies such as the one-door integrated services system or the Jakarta Smart Card (*Kartu Jakarta Pintar*) and Jakarta Health Card (*Kartu Jakarta Sehat*). This chapter aims to help fill this gap in the existing literature by examining governance and anti-corruption reform at the level of local government, especially the government of DKI Jakarta under the leadership of Jokowi and Ahok.

Methodology

This research on which the chapter is based employed a qualitative approach to the analysis of a complex problem faced by Jokowi and Ahok during their period in office in Jakarta. The research is descriptive; that is, it searches out facts and credible interpretations to make a factual and accurate description of the effects and nature of – and relationships among – the phenomena studied (Cresswell, 2013: 263). The data employed are mainly from secondary sources, including academic journal articles, book chapters, and articles in national newspapers and weekly magazines. The chapter also provides a document review of various rules and regulations that were issued by the government of Jakarta. All these data were then processed according to the theoretical framework described in the following section.

Theoretical framework

In this chapter, we apply two theoretical frameworks to help analyze the progress and regress of governance reform in the Province of Jakarta under the leadership of Jokowi and Ahok. The first of these analytical frameworks is political pluralism, which is well-suited for identifying political rivalry in situations involving governance reform. The political pluralism approach advocates the need for high-quality democracy, whether at the local or national level. This internationally recognized approach is associated with the work of American political scientist Robert Dahl, from his early writings in the 1950s to his seminal book of 1998 entitled *On Democracy*.

Dahl's political pluralism is complemented by the political actors approach, which is used to identify how resources are mobilized and distributed democratically through state institutions to reduce inequality (Dahl, 1998: 169). As many studies show, at least in the context of Indonesia, the resources under the control of political reformers are usually limited, while other political actors, such as oligarchs, possess a substantial amount of resources. Dahl also shows that wealth is not the only valuable resource when it comes to achieving political goals.

Pepinsky (2014) has developed the political pluralism approach further by outlining the importance of policy as an object of political contestation between political actors. He argues that "political actors engage in politics to produce policies that they favor" (ibid.: 83). Although the oligarchy has enormous economic resources at its disposal, it does not always win political battles and is not always able to impose its will. The political pluralism framework is useful because it describes the continuous political struggle between progressive groups and the oligarchy.

However, the political pluralism framework alone will not be sufficient for our purposes. As suggested previously, political pluralism can be seen as the dependent variable that is affected by political actors, who can be seen as the independent variables. To complement the framework of political pluralism, we also use the political leadership framework. This framework analyzes the interactions between leaders and their followers; it was first introduced by Burns, who identified two types of political leadership – transactional leadership and transformational leadership (Burns, 2010: 4).

According to Burns, transactional leaders' relationship with their followers is based on merely exchanging one thing for another – jobs for votes, subsidies for campaign contributions – as in political campaigns for parliament or for the executive, both at the local and national level. On the other hand, transformational leaders are more compelling and genuine, because they emerge from the fundamental needs, aspirations, and values of their followers. As a result, transformational leaders are expected to produce social change that will meet their followers' needs (ibid.). We would argue that an additional category should be added: semi-transformational leadership. This type of leadership is expected to bring about changes but changes that are less far-reaching than under transformational leadership and also vulnerable, as the changes could be reversed. Unlike transactional leaders, semi-transformational leaders do not enact changes based solely on the exchange motive but out of personal idealism or, in the case of groups, collective virtue. By applying Burns' framework, this chapter aims to evaluate the leadership of political actors who were able to execute a policy that brought about significant progress in the context of governance reform and anti-corruption measures.

Table 3.1 Types of political leadership, based on Burns

Type of leadership	Outcome
Transformational leaders	Emerge from the fundamental wants, needs, aspirations, and values of their followers
Transactional leaders	Interaction with their followers is based on exchange, e.g., jobs for votes or subsidies for campaign contributions
Semi-transformational leaders	Expected to bring about changes, but less far-reaching than under transformational leadership

Source: Burns (2010)

Findings and discussions

The track record of Jokowi and Ahok

Jokowi was Mayor of Solo (Surakarta) from 2005 to 2012. Many believe that his excellent track record as mayor helped him to win the Jakarta gubernatorial election in 2012 (Suaedy, 2014). During his time as mayor, Jokowi often traveled around the city to meet residents and businesses, a practice known as *blusukan*. He continued this habit after being elected as Governor of Jakarta. This open approach not only got a positive response from people but also increased his media exposure. Part of Jokowi's success has been his ability to engage with people from different backgrounds.

In 2005, Jokowi campaigned for Solo as a beautiful city without corruption (Baker, 2013). His objective was to revitalize Solo as a clean, safe place to live and work. One of his successes, highlighted by the media, was the 2006 relocation of street vendors without conflict or violence. Street vendors were moved from Banjarsari Gardens to a new market place opened in Kithilan Semanggi. This relocation created a model for further street vendor relocations and was an early indication of Jokowi's consensual approach to solving problems in Solo.

Jokowi has won numerous noteworthy awards (Tempo, 2008). In 2008, he won Leadership Awards from the Ministry of Administrative and Bureaucratic Reform of the Republic of Indonesia in cooperation with Leadership Park magazine. In the same year, he was chosen by Tempo magazine as one of just ten regents or mayors from 472 districts and cities across the country. The selection was based on three criteria: public service, transparency, and friendliness in the business world. Two years later, in 2010, he won the Bung Hatta Anti-Corruption Award. According to one of the judges, Betti Alisjahbana, Jokowi was a leader who sympathized with the life of the poor people in Solo (Fadillah, 2013). Under his leadership, the city of Solo experienced rapid change. With the motto of "Solo: The Spirit of Java", Jokowi was able to provide excellent service. "As a result, local revenue (PAD) from the market, originally Rp 7 billion, rose to Rp 12 billion in 2008" (quoted in Fadillah, 2013). In 2013, Jokowi won the same award again, this time as Governor of Jakarta. In 2011, he was named by Gatra magazine as

Best Mayor, and in 2012 he was nominated in the Best Mayor in the World competition held by the World Mayor Foundation, winning third place.

Jokowi received extensive national media exposure as a potential leader through his support for Esemka, a national car project conducted by vocational high school (*Sekolah Menengah Kejuruan*, SMK) students in Surakarta (Hamid, 2014: 90). In January 2012, Jokowi campaigned for Esemka and used the car as his official car, even though it had not yet passed the feasibility tests. His actions won him widespread support and coverage from the national media. His fame grew further when he rejected a plan by the Governor of Central Java to build a shopping mall over the ex-Saripetojo Ice Factory – a cultural heritage site.

Jokowi's deputy, Ahok, had served as Regent of East Belitung from 2005 to 2010. In 2006, Tempo magazine chose him as one of ten figures who had changed Indonesia (Tempo, 2006). Ahok tackled two main problems: education and health. Under his leadership, the East Belitung government abolished tuition fees from primary school to high school, and dozens of academically accomplished students were given scholarships to Trisakti University, Jakart and Bangka-Belitung University. He also scrapped fees for doctors, medicine, hospitals, and ambulances, making them free for his citizens.

Ahok was known for his combative leadership style, especially with corrupt officials, which later brought him both praise and controversy (Tempo, 2006). During his time as Regent of East Belitung, bureaucrats who were caught neglecting their work during office hours were directly sanctioned, and any promotion was delayed. Ahok argued that his confrontational style was part of his effort to uphold integrity (Hatherell and Welsh, 2017: 179). The issue of corruption is always part of public discourse in Indonesia. Corrupt officials, including local leaders, being detained by the Corruption Eradication Commission (KPK), became almost daily news, creating an urgent need to clean up the leadership of the country. Ahok succeeded in projecting himself as an honest and different leader, contrasting himself with those who were corrupt. He won numerous prestigious awards, such as Anti-Corruption Figure (2007), Bung Hatta Anti-Corruption Award (2013), and Anti-Gratification (2015).

The clean track record of both Jokowi and Ahok was one of the factors that brought them success in the Jakarta gubernatorial election. In September 2012, Jokowi was able to defeat incumbent governor Fauzi Bowo, who was supported by most of the major political parties (Bunnell et al., 2018: 1070). Only two main political parties supported Jokowi and Ahok: Megawati's PDI-P and Prabowo's Greater Indonesia Movement (Gerindra) party. In the words of Bunnell et al. (ibid.):

> Political commentators have highlighted several aspects of Jokowi's electability, including the popularity of his down-to-earth, "polite populist" style . . . the professionalism of his campaign team, their use of social media in reaching out to younger voters . . . and the fact that, unlike his incumbent rival, Jokowi had no direct connection with (authoritarian) New Order politics.

Programs of the Jokowi–Ahok era

The signature programs under the Jokowi and Ahok administration focused on social welfare, bureaucratic reform, infrastructure, and developing a transportation system. During the campaign, Jokowi had introduced what he called *Kartu Jakarta Pintar* (KJP – Jakarta Smart Card) and *Kartu Jakarta Sehat* (KJS – Jakarta Health Card) (Aziza, 2016). KJP is a program to provide educational access for the poorest citizens of DKI Jakarta; it includes education support up to Rp 240,000, which is distributed monthly. With this, the least well-off students can afford to get an education up to high school or vocational school with full financial help from the budget of the provincial government of DKI Jakarta. Jokowi first launched 3,013 KJP cards on 1 December 2012. In the previous month, DKI Jakarta launched KJS, distributing a total of 3,000 cards in six DKI Jakarta areas, for the trial phase (Desyani, 2012). KJS recipients can enjoy free health services at all public hospitals in DKI Jakarta and basic treatment at 88 hospitals in partnership with DKI Jakarta.

A few months later, Jokowi started to reform the bureaucracy and introduced the so-called Jobs Auction (*Lelang Jabatan*) (Akuntono, 2013). Jobs Auction is a merit-based test as well as an open selection process for appointing high-level officials and heads of sub-districts in Jakarta. The test includes identifying the candidates' vision and mission and assessing their track record and performance. Ahok thought that many officials of the DKI Jakarta provincial government were not in the right jobs; Jobs Auction was seen as a way to minimize the potential for corruption, collusion, and nepotism (known collectively by the acronym KKN). Ahok wanted to ensure that the selection process that was conducted by the Regional Personnel Board (BKD) was open and accountable. The selection process was to provide opportunities for all civil servants to participate in healthy and merit-based competition. One appointment resulting from the Jobs Auction initiative that created controversy was the appointment of a Christian ward chief in the majority Muslim area of Lenteng Agung. This led to protests from a conservative Islamic group (McRae, 2013: 301). Both Jokowi and Ahok fully backed the ward chief, arguing that officials should be judged only on their competencies. This defense of their appointment for the Lenteng Agung ward chief set an excellent precedent (ibid.), which proved useful for Jokowi's future presidential campaign.

However, the bureaucratic reforms also attracted some criticism. Nirwono Joga, an urban planning expert, was quoted as saying that the bureaucratic reform did not improve the local budget disbursement rate, which had ranged between 45% and 65% over the previous five years. Instead, the budget was being spent more on the operational costs of and capital injections for regionally owned enterprises (BUMD): "It means that the SKPD [local work unit], despite the bureaucratic reform, is not able to perform their duty. Because so many projects are still pending, the bidding in the procurement process could be considered failed because the budget is not adequately disbursed" (quoted in Sari, 2017).

On 2 September 2013, less than a year after his election as governor, Jokowi launched the project Tanah Abang Market Block G to relocate street vendors

(Bunnell et al., 2018: 1070). The relocation of street vendors in the vicinity of Tanah Abang to a more suitable building, named Block G, replicated the policy Jokowi had carried out in Solo. Once again, he adopted the so-called *blusukan* style involving impromptu site visits, fostering direct relations with street vendors. Approximately 1,000 street vendors were relocated into Block G, with the benefit of free rent for the first year.

The launch of the new building created momentum to clean up the chaotic Tanah Abang area. Block G was strategically located right next to Tanah Abang station, and at first the stalls in Block G were crowded with visitors, as Jokowi had expected. However, after some time, visitor numbers dropped, and the block began to seem deserted – just as the traders had predicted. When Jokowi left his post as governor of Jakarta and became president of Indonesia, the vendors returned to the streets around Tanah Abang. During his tenure as governor, Ahok carried on the struggle to control the Tanah Abang street vendors. However, he prioritized law enforcement to drive out street vendors, asserting that he would continue to discipline those who insisted on selling their wares on sidewalks and roadsides (Akbar, 2017).

One of Jokowi's successes as governor was the revitalization of Pluit Reservoir Park (Waduk Pluit) and Rio Ria Reservoir (Waduk Ria Rio) in North Jakarta (Taylor, 2015). Residents who were living in informal housing there were relocated to flats built by his predecessor, Governor Fauzi Bowo. This relocation was reminiscent of Jokowi's resettlement of riverbank dwellers from Pucang Sawit in Solo, which had similar aims. In both cases, Jokowi built relations with the affected community members through lunch invitations and informal discussions. Another success was building a mass transportation system for Jakarta, including the ground-breaking mass rapid transit (MRT) underground train. Jokowi was able to execute an integrated mass transportation plan that had been prepared by a former governor, Sutiyoso.

Jokowi and Ahok's other famous program was the one-door integrated public services policy (Rudi, 2015). This program sought to integrate all licensing and non-licensing services within the same area, to improve productivity and efficiency in terms of procedures, time, and cost. The integrated public services covered the areas of housing, public works, spatial planning, transportation, environment, education, health, and land, and were available in all sub-districts throughout Jakarta to bring public services directly to the community.

A study conducted by the International Finance Corporation and World Bank in 2012 showed that acquiring a business license in Jakarta took 45 days; this was longer than any of the other 20 cities in the study (Arifianto, 2015). Jokowi's response to this was to establish the one-door integrated service to replace the previous licensing system, which was scattered across several agencies. This new system was started in mid-2013 and was ratified through Regulation No. 12 of 2013 on One-Door Integrated Licensing (PTSP). However, it was only in January 2014 that a particular agency serving PTSP was formed under the name of One-Door Integrated Services Agency (BPTSP). The results of a poll conducted by Kompas Research and Development Institute showed that the one-door integrated public service unit was well-received by the citizens of Jakarta (ibid). Of respondents who had processed documents through this new system, 80% stated that the integrated system was better than the previous service.

According to the assessment of the Ombudsman, the one-door integrated services program places DKI Jakarta in the "green zone" of public services (Taylor, 2017), under a three-zone classification related to the public service performance of local government. The green zone represents an excellent performance, the yellow zone a moderate performance, and the red zone a poor performance. The assessment was the result of a review conducted in May–July 2017, when Ahok and his deputy Djarot Saiful Hidayat still led the city government. The one-door integrated services system was also awarded the label of "excellent" public service provider by the Ministry of Administrative Reform and Bureaucracy Reform (Hilmi, 2018). There are six assessment factors included in the award: policy (which accounts for 30%), professionalism of human resources (18%), public service information system (15%), consultation and management complaints (15%), facilities and infrastructure (15%), and public service innovation (7%). The one-door integrated services system achieved the highest score across 34 provinces in Indonesia.

Programs of the Ahok–Djarot era

In November 2014, Ahok officially became Governor of DKI Jakarta, replacing Jokowi. One of his first acts was to launch an electronic budgeting (e-budgeting) system for preparing the local revenue and expenditure budget (APBD). There was a number of factors behind this move, including the low disbursement of Jakarta's expenditure in the budget in 2013 and the fact that during Ahok's time as Deputy Governor some of the budget items that had been scrapped began to reappear (Evan, 2015). The new e-budgeting system would minimize potential corruption and make the budget more transparent to the public. Agus Rahardjo, Chairman of the Corruption Eradication Commission (KPK), praised Ahok for this new e-budgeting mechanism (Adzkia, 2016). According to Agus, e-budgeting encourages the public to participate and oversee the government's budget performance.

The legal basis for e-budgeting was established by Law No. 23 of 2014 on Regional Government (Tamaela, 2015). According to Law No. 23, Article 391, paragraphs (1) and (2), the government shall provide information related to regional development and regional finance. The article also states that government information should be managed by a local government system. E-budgeting is also supported by Article 387 on innovation, in the same law. In 2015, however, a serious conflict arose between Ahok and the regional parliament of Jakarta (DPRD) over a local budget:

> At this time, the DPRD put forward a budget that was significantly larger than that which had been proposed by Ahok. Ahok refused to accept the

DPRD's version and instead submitted his version to the home ministry. This resulted in public conflict between members of the DPRD and Ahok.

(Hatherell and Welsh, 2017: 179)

Immediately after this dispute, a survey was conducted by Lingkaran Survei Indonesia on the public's response to Ahok's conflict with the DPRD (Table 3.2). Of the 1,200 respondents, the survey found that "an overwhelming majority (72.85 percent) . . . believed the argument made by Ahok that public officials were likely to be involved in stealing state assets" (ibid.: 182).

Another policy of Ahok's that had the support of the community was the closure of some rogue entertainment venues and nightclubs (Ros, 2014), including, among others, Stadium Discotheque and Mille's. The nightclubs were closed for violating the rules of Regional Regulation (Perda) No. 6 of 2015 on Tourism, which deals with the sale and use of drugs or addictive substances in a location. The venues lost their business registration certificates. In the case of Stadium, Ahok claimed that the action was necessary because Stadium had already committed too many violations; various warnings had been issued, but nothing had changed.

In terms of infrastructure, one measure that Ahok undertook to overcome congestion was the building of the Semanggi interchange (Carina, 2017). The work was carried out by contractor PT Wijaya Karya and completed within one and a half years. The community widely praised it as an innovative project. The development was paid for not from the local budget (APBD) but using compensation for additional floor area (KLB) claimed from PT Mitra Panca Persada, with a value of about Rp 360 billion. Jakarta Gubernatorial Decree No. 210/2016 allows the owners of properties located in KLB bonus areas to construct additional floors in exchange for building public facilities (Indonesia Institute of Deliverology, 2017). KLB enables property owners to build taller buildings with a higher utility rate and value. In return, the city gets new or renovated public facilities, equal to the property value increase.

However, while the regulation seems to offer a fair deal, it exploits KLB as a source of funding without considering the land-use implications (ibid.). According to the institute, the city had not carried out sufficient preliminary studies to support the claim that the Semanggi interchange would reduce traffic congestion. It also discounted the concerns of communities who are directly affected

Table 3.2 Survey of public response to Ahok's conflict with the DPRD

	All participants	*Jakarta participants*	*Muslim participants*	*Non-Muslim participants*
Supported Ahok	60.77%	70%	57.2%	83.31%
Supported DPRD	22.65%	20%	25.48%	4.18%
Unsure	16.58%	10%	17.20%	12.51%

Source: Lingkaran Survei Indonesia, 2015, in Hatherell and Welsh (2017: 182)

by the granting of additional KLB. For example, according to the Constitution, permitting taller buildings means taking away part of the air space that belongs to the public (Sarwanto, 2016). The city was desperately in need of more public space, but it was opening another window to corruption by avoiding scrutiny. Bambang Widjojanto, a former Commissioner of the Corruption Eradication Commission (KPK), expressed his concern that the KLB policy of DKI Jakarta provincial government represented a new form of corruption (ibid.). This policy, according to Bambang, caused low budget disbursement; in the first half of 2015 budget absorption in DKI Jakarta was under 25% and a year later had not reached 50%.

Jakarta suffers from recurrent flooding; Ahok decided to tackle this problem with a major flood mitigation project (van Voorst and Padawangi, 2015), which entails a restructuring of the river and the relocation of communities near the area. Relocations have also been conducted for several other purposes, including reservoir normalization, coastal embankment construction, and the revitalization of green open spaces. According to Indonesian law, it is forbidden to inhabit riverbanks, which are supposed to serve as water catchment areas. Nevertheless, around 3.5 million slum dwellers have settled along the city's riverbanks, unable to afford housing in other areas of Jakarta.

For some people, the prospect of eviction is even more threatening than floods. Starting in 2015, the flood mitigation plan involves widening and deepening the city's rivers, meaning the evacuation and enforced resettlement of 34,000 river-bank dwellers. Most of them are likely to be evicted without adequate compensation, as residents do not possess formal land rights according to the current land registration system. According to a 2015 report published by the Jakarta Legal Aid Institute (LBH Jakarta), some 3,200 people were forcibly displaced between 2007 and 2012 (Zulfikar, 2016). By 2015, some 8,145 families and 6,283 business units had been forced to leave the land they had occupied for decades.

In 2015, many families and businesses were victims of forced eviction, such as the evictions in Kampung Pulo in August 2015. The number of cases increased from 113 in 2015 to 193 in 2016 (Parikesit, 2017), with forced evictions occurring in five areas of Jakarta. There were 35 forced eviction sites in North Jakarta, 23 in East Jakarta, 55 in Central Jakarta, 41 in West Jakarta, and 39 in South Jakarta (ibid.). Forced evictions are nothing new in Jakarta: during the previous administrations of Presidents Sukarno and Suharto, the government carried out mass expulsions to fulfill the dreams of city planners and to serve the personal interests of a few privileged developers.

Moreover, Indonesia's transition to democracy has not led to the cessation of forced evictions (Sheppard, 2006). From the governorship of Sutiyoso to that of Ahok, thousands of poor people in Jakarta have witnessed security forces destroying their homes. This destruction of property occurs with little notice, due legal process, or proper compensation. Many residents complain that they were given little warning or received confusing information. All they know is that their homes were flattened, and they were given only a short time to collect their belongings and leave. Furthermore, they received either no compensation at all or minimal levels of compensation that did not adequately cover the losses they suffered. It is not surprising that thousands of poor people in Jakarta live in fear that, one day, security forces and bulldozers will come to their community.

The Jakarta government justifies many of the evictions by claiming that it is safeguarding public order, expelling people who violate private or state property, or clearing land for infrastructure projects. However, the government has used excessive force to evict and has failed to provide alternative housing or other assistance. Interviews with LBH Jakarta on evictions in Kampung Aquarium, North Jakarta, refer to violence, short notice, and lack of a clear explanation for evictions.

> The use of violence has undoubtedly violated human rights. Evictions conducted by DKI Jakarta involving the police, security officers, and Indonesian national armed forces have caused thousands of people and businesses to lose their houses. Until now, it remains unclear what standard procedure the government is using. There should be sufficient notice from the head of the local area: proper warning is necessary. However, notifications are too sudden and do not give enough time for the people to prepare their leave.[1]

Another of Ahok's controversial policies is reclamation (Johan, 2017), which is undertaken by the government to increase the amount of useable land and for conservation within the coastal area. Jakarta Bay is a reclamation project on the North Coast (Pantura) of Jakarta. The reclaimed area is vast, totaling 5,152 hectares or 51.5 million square meters. Jakarta Bay reclamation covers 17 islands (Islands A through Q), stretching from the west to the east side of North Beach Jakarta. Of the 17 islands, 13 (Islands A to M), with a total area of 3,560 ha (35.6 million m²), are located in the elite areas of Pantai Indah Kapuk (PIK), Pluit, and Ancol. Opinions about the reclamation project are divided, as indicated in Table 3.3.

Table 3.3 Opinions about Jakarta Bay reclamation

	For	Against
1	Increases open space for the development of Jakarta	Disrupts the life of coral reefs, Bentos, mangrove forests
2	Brings profits to build Jakarta	Potentially disrupts submarine cables
3	Develops the area of North Jakarta	Causes flooding due to reclamation extending the river mouth
4	Strengthens the flow into the sea	Disturbs the work of fishermen
5	Reduces the risk of abrasion	May increase sedimentation at the river mouth
6	Provides a source of clean water for North Jakarta	May become a new dumping ground for waste and cause smell pollution
7	Acts as a dam to withstand sea-level rise	May cause the island to sink

Source: Litbang Kompas, in Rosalina (2016)

According to Ahok, reclamation is necessary for economic growth (Belarminus, 2017). It is expected to generate approximately a million jobs. If all planned reclamation is implemented, the economic gain is estimated to reach Rp 158 trillion. However, Ahok was also criticized for giving preference to the interests of certain conglomerates in the case of the Jakarta Bay reclamation project (Widiyoko, 2017). According to Ian Wilson (2017), Ahok had close links with big property development companies such as the Agung Podomoro Group, Agung Sedayu Group, and Sinarmas Group. However, Widiyoko (2017) argues that the biggest beneficiaries of Ahok's term as governor were state-owned enterprises (SOEs). These SOEs are either owned by the national government (*Badan Usaha Milik Negara* or BUMN) or by the regional government (*Badan Usaha Milik Daerah*, or BUMD). In the fiscal years 2013–2015, Widiyoko claims, capital injections into these companies from the provincial budget amounted to more than Rp 12.72 trillion, while the Jakarta government's total equity in all its BUMD stood at around Rp 20 trillion. He found the most significant projects in Jakarta Bay were awarded to Jaya Konstruksi Manggala Pratama Tbk (JKON), a subsidiary of the Jaya Group. Another primary beneficiary of big contracts was Wijaya Karya Tbk (WIKA), a national SOE. Other national SOEs dominate major projects in Jakarta, such as Waskita Karya, Pembangunan Perumahan, Adhi Karya, and others (ibid.).

In 2016, Ahok became entangled in a blasphemy case (Hatherell and Welsh, 2017: 175–176). It began when Ahok gave a speech during a working visit at Pramuka Island, Kepulauan Seribu, on 27 September. In his defense, Ahok argued that he was making a point about the use of the Quran by his political opponent and not about the Quranic verse itself. But the comment provoked a wave of public anger from Muslim communities that led to mass protests and calls for Ahok to be arrested for blasphemy. He was named as a suspect while campaigning for re-election, which contributed to his defeat in the 2017 Jakarta gubernatorial elections.

Jokowi and Ahok as semi-transformational leaders

As noted earlier in this chapter, the political leadership framework identifies two types of leaders, with the nature of the political regime and the structure of society helping to determine whether a transactional or a transformational leader emerges (Burns, 2010). Transformational leaders are more likely in developing countries like Indonesia, where there are profound social crises that demand change (Hermann, 1979: 121). Although, as also noted earlier, the political pluralism approach advocates the need for a high-quality democracy, whether at the local or national level, the expansion of electoral politics in Indonesia since 1998 has not led to substantial democratic reforms (Fukuoka, 2012: 53). The exercise of predatory power through money, politics, and political thuggery still constitutes a significant part of political contestation.

The dynamics of present-day Indonesian politics cannot be understood without reference to oligarchs, particularly business elites who have established economic assets independent of the state. Many of the "old faces" continue to dominate politics and business in Indonesia, while new ones are drawn into the same predatory practices that have defined politics in Indonesia for decades (Hadiz and Robison, 2013: 35). Looking at the case of Jakarta in the period 2012–2017, Jokowi and Ahok represented fresh faces that gave new hope to Indonesia's democracy with their credible track records. Burns (2010) relies on the notions of motives and values and their impact on purpose and behavior. Jokowi and Ahok were seen as leaders who would be able to bring a significant change for Jakarta. The population, especially its youth, expected them to be capable of establishing a more accountable, free, and transparent governance in a city that was known to be riddled with systemic corruption.

Jokowi and Ahok's track records were evident in the numerous awards that they had won, such as the Bung Hatta Anti-Corruption Award. They were seen as a refreshing contrast to corrupt and incompetent elites. During their time as the governor and deputy governor of DKI Jakarta, their primary programs were aimed at meeting fundamental needs and producing a social change for the poor. Their priorities were social welfare, bureaucracy reform, infrastructure, and developing a mass transportation system. The public service programs that were best known by the people, including the Jakarta Smart Card in the field of education and the Jakarta Health Card in the health sector, helped poor people to access services necessary to meet minimum living needs.

Jokowi carried out bureaucratic reform, such as the introduction of the Jobs Auction, in an attempt to minimize the potential for corruption, collusion, and nepotism. With this reform, the ward and sub-district heads were to be chosen through an open selection process and appointed according to their capabilities. Ahok's best-known program as Governor of DKI Jakarta was the application of the e-budgeting system. E-budgeting was expected to minimize the potential for corruption and to make the budget more transparent to people. As described earlier, Ahok experienced conflicts with the provincial parliament of Jakarta (DPRD) when he refused to accept the DPRD version of a budget that differed significantly from his own. Ahok was known for his "aggressive" attitude in running his programs; this proved to be a double-edged sword that made him both liked and disliked at the same time.

Based on these findings, the leadership of Jokowi and Ahok can be categorized according to Burn's political leadership theory. We would argue that both Jokowi and Ahok can be seen as semi-transformational leaders. According to Burns (2010: 4), transformational leaders emerge from the fundamental wants, needs, aspirations, and values of their followers. Thus, transformational leaders are expected to produce social change and satisfy their followers' needs. Jokowi and Ahok were not able to fully meet these characteristics due to their respective circumstances. Jokowi's time as governor was too short to institute a systematic change in the bureaucracy, as he was elected President of Indonesia in 2014 after being a governor for only two years. For Ahok, after a promising start, his combative communication style gradually undermined his effectiveness in governing. Ahok's political opponents managed to capitalize on his reckless language through the blasphemy case, which resulted in Ahok losing decisively in the 2017 election, securing just 42% of the votes compared to the 58% of his opponent, Anies Baswedan.

Conclusion

The chapter has attempted to evaluate the track records of Jokowi and Ahok in terms of the progress and regress of governance reform within the Province of Jakarta, using political pluralism and political leadership as an analytical framework. Political pluralism helps to explain the political dynamic of the rivalry between progressive and conservative groups in the context of strengthening democracy in Indonesia. Political pluralism is the dependent variable that was affected by the political actors as the independent variables. To complement political pluralism, we applied the framework of political leadership first introduced by Burns (2010). Burns identified two types of political leadership – transactional leadership and transformational leadership – but, as explained earlier, we recognize a further category, the semi-transformational leadership type.

Jokowi and Ahok did not come from the usual powerful close-knit political elite that is mostly based in Jakarta. This led to high hopes that they would bring a new approach to governance with their previous credible track records as local government leaders. Unfortunately, they were not able to meet all the criteria ascribed to transformational leaders by Burns, because the two men faced political complexities of their own, which hampered their legacies in pushing further governance reform and anti-corruption efforts in Jakarta Province. Our analysis, therefore, concludes that Jokowi and Ahok fell into the category of semi-transformational leaders while they served as governor and deputy governor of Jakarta in the period 2012–2017. This shows that being a reform-minded leader is not, on its own, sufficient to bring about significant governance reform. A conducive political environment is also essential, in the form of both critical mass support as well as political support from the top elites. As clearly shown, Jokowi and Ahok were not able to secure consistent levels of such support in their governance reform and anti-corruption efforts.

Note

1 Interview with Jakarta Legal Aid Institute (LBH Jakarta), 2017.

References

Adzkia, Aghnia (2016). "KPK Puji Program e-Budgeting Ahok (KPK Praise Ahok's E-budgeting Program)." *CNN Indonesia*, 13 January. www.cnnindonesia.com/nasional/20160113093418-20-103912/kpk-puji-program-e-budgeting-ahok (accessed 9 July 2018).

Akbar, Jihad (2017). "Membandingkan Cara Jokowi, Ahok, dan Anies Atasi Semrawut Tanah Abang (Comparing Jokowi, Ahok and Anies in Dealing with Mismanagement in Tanah Abang)." *Kumparan*, 23 December. https://kumparan.com/

@kumparannews/membandingkan-cara-jokowi-ahok-dan-anies-atasi-semrawut-tanah-abang (accessed 6 July 2018).

Akuntono, Indra (2013). "Jokowi: Kita Bertindak Ada Konsep (Jokowi: We Act Based on Concept)." *Kompas*, 14 March. https://nasional.kompas.com/read/2013/03/14/1504468/jokowi.kita.bertindak.ada.konsep (accessed 9 July 2018).

Arifianto, Budiawan Sidik (2015). "Acungan Jempol untuk Pelayanan Satu Pintu (Thumbs up for One-stop Service)." *Kompas*, 19 February. https://megapolitan.kompas.com/read/2015/02/19/07180071/Acungan.Jempol.untuk.Pelayanan.Satu.Pintu (accessed 6 July 2018).

Aziza, Kurnia Sari (2016). "Memahami KJP dan KIP (Understanding KJP and KIP)." *Kompas*, 31 October. https://megapolitan.kompas.com/read/2016/10/31/10102701/memahami.kjp.dan.kip?page=all (accessed 7 July 2018).

Baker, Brian (2013). "Mayor of the Month for February 2013 Joko Widodo (Jokowi) Governor of Jakarta." www.citymayors.com/mayors/jakarta-widodo.html (accessed 9 July 2018).

Belarminus, Robertus (2017). "Saat Ahok Ditanya Reklamasi Untuk Siapa (When Ahok Was Asked Who Will Benefit From the Reclamation)." *Kompas*, 3 April. https://megapolitan.kompas.com/read/2017/04/03/08505951/saat.ahok.ditanya.reklamasi.untuk.siapa (accessed 8 July 2018).

Bunnell, Tim, Rita Padawangi, and Eric C. Thompson (2018). "The Politics of Learning From a Small City: Solo as Translocal Model and Political Launchpad." *Regional Studies* 52 (8): 1065–1074.

Burns, James M. (2010). *Leadership*. New York: Harper Perennial Modern Classic.

Carina, Jessi (2017). "Simpang Susun Semanggi yang Dimulai Ahok, Diselesaikan Djarot, dan Akan Diresmikan Jokowi (The New Development of Semanggi Bridge Started in Ahok Era, Finalized in Djaror, Launched by Jokowi)." *Kompas*, 31 March. https://megapolitan.kompas.com/read/2017/07/31/08040941/simpang-susun-semanggi-yang-dimulai-ahok-diselesaikan-djarot-dan-akan?page=all (accessed 8 July 2018).

Cresswell, John (2013). *Research Design: Pendekatan Kualitatif, Kuantitatif, dan Mixed (Qualitative, Quantitative, and Mixed Approaches)*. Yogyakarta: Pustaka Pelajar.

Dahl, Robert A. (1998). *On Democracy*. New Haven, CT: Yale University Press.

Desyani, Anggrita (2012). "Kartu Jakarta Sehat Diluncurkan (Health Service Card Jakarta Is Launched)." *Tempo*, 10 November. https://metro.tempo.co/read/440925/kartu-jakarta-sehat-diluncurkan (accessed 6 July 2018).

Evan (2015). "Begini Sistem Kerja E-Budgeting Versi Ahok (This Is How the E-budgeting System Works Under Ahok)." *Tempo*, 3 March. https://metro.tempo.co/read/646591/begini-sistem-kerja-e-budgeting-versi-ahok (accessed 9 July 2018).

Fadillah, Ramadhian (2013). "Jokowi dan Ahok akan hadiri Bung Hatta Anti Corruption Award (Jokowi and Ahok Will Attend Bung Hatta Anti-corruption Award Ceremony)." *Merdeka*, 31 October. www.merdeka.com/jakarta/jokowi-dan-ahok-akan-hadiri-bung-hatta-anti-corruption-award.html (accessed 5 July 2018).

Fukuoka, Yuki (2012). "Oligarchy and Democracy in Post-Suharto Indonesia." *Political Studies Review* 11 (1): 52–64.

Hadiz, Vedi R., and Richard Robison (2013). "The Political Economy of Oligarchy and the Reorganization of Power in Indonesia." *Indonesia* 96: 35–57.

Hamid, Abdul (2014). "Jokowi's Populism in the 2012 Jakarta Gubernatorial Election." *Journal of Current Southeast Asian Affairs* 33 (1): 85–109.

Hamid, Sandra (2012). "Indonesian Politics in 2012: Coalitions, Accountability, and the Future of Democracy." *Bulletin of Indonesian Economic Studies* 48 (3): 325–345.

Hatherell, Michael (2014). "Repertoires of Representation and an Application to Indonesia's Jokowi." *Representation* 50 (4): 439–451.

Hatherell, Michael, and Alistair Welsh (2017). "Rebel With a Cause: Ahok and Charismatic Leadership in Indonesia." *Asian Studies Review* 41 (2): 174–190.

Hermann, Margaret (1979). "Review: Burns on Political Leadership." *Political Psychology* 1 (1): 121–123.

Hilmi, Alfan (2018). "Pelayanan Terpadu Satu Pintu Jakarta Raih Predikat Sangat Baik (One-stop Service in Jakarta Achieves the Best Performance)." *Tempo*, 25 January. https://metro.tempo.co/read/1053942/pelayanan-terpadu-satu-pintu-jakarta-raih-predikat-sangat-baik (accessed 6 July 2018).

Indonesia Institute of Deliverology (2017). "What Is Wrong with Semanggi Interchange?" http://deliverology.org/en/2017/09/whats-wrong-semanggi-interchange (accessed 13 July 2018).

Johan, Daniel (2017). "Harta di Balik Reklamasi Teluk Jakarta (The Treasure Behind the Jakarta Bay Reclamation)." *Detik News*, 27 July. https://news.detik.com/kolom/d-3432904/harta-di-balik-reklamasi-teluk-jakarta (accessed 13 July 2018).

Juwono, Vishnu (2019). "Kepemimpinan Politik dalam Mendorong Inisiatif Anti Korupsi (Political Leadership in Pushing for Anti-corruption Initiatives)." *Prisma* 38 (2): 63–71.

Kurniawan, Eri, and Amalia Dwi Utami (2017). "The Representation of Joko Widodo's Figure in the Jakarta Post." *Indonesian Journal of Applied Linguistics* 6 (2): 341–350.

Manurung, Hendra (2016). "The Effect of Basuki 'Ahok' Tjahaya Purnama Leadership Style on Indonesia Democracy (2012–2016)." Lembaga Ilmu Pengetahuan Indonesia (LIPI) International Conference on Social Sciences and Humanities 2016: 803–812.

McRae, Dave (2013). "Indonesian Politics in 2013: The Emergence of New Leadership?" *Bulletin of Indonesian Economic Studies* 49 (3): 289–304.

Mietzner, Marcus (2014). "How Jokowi Won, and Democracy Survived Indonesia's 2014 Elections." *Journal of Democracy* 25 (4): 111–125.

Parikesit, Gangsar (2017). "Data LBH, Jumlah Penggusuran di Jakarta Meningkat (Based on Data by LBH, the Number of Evictions in Jakarta is Increasing)." *Tempo*, 13 April. https://metro.tempo.co/read/865754/data-lbh-jumlah-penggusuran-di-jakarta-meningkat (accessed 9 July 2018).

Pepinsky, Thomas B. (2014). *Beyond Oligarchy: Wealth, Power, and Contemporary Indonesian Politics.* Ithaca, NY: Cornell University Press.

Ros (2014). "Satu Jam Bersama Ahok: Ahok Cerita Beking di Balik Penutupan Diskotek Stadium (One Hour with Ahok: Ahok Backing Story behind the Stadium Disco Closing)." *Detik News*, 7 November. https://news.detik.com/berita/2742065/ahok-cerita-beking-di-balik-penutupan-diskotek-stadium (accessed 5 July 2018).

Rosalina, Puteri (2016). "Jalan Panjang Reklamasi di Teluk Jakarta, dari era Soeharto sampai Ahok (Long Road of Reclamation in Jakarta From Soeharto to Ahok Era)." *Kompas*, 4 April. https://megapolitan.kompas.com/read/2016/04/04/10050401/Jalan.Panjang.Reklamasi.di.Teluk.Jakarta.dari.era.Soeharto.sampai.Ahok (accessed 9 July 2018).

Rudi, Alsadad (2015). "Ahok Luncurkan 'One Day Service' Perizinan di PTSP (Ahok Launched 'One Day Service' in Integrated Public Service)." *Kompas*, 13 August.

https://megapolitan.kompas.com/read/2015/08/13/06540321/18.Agustus.
Ahok.Luncurkan.One.Day.Service.Perizinan.di.PTSP (accessed 6 July 2018).

Sari, Nursita (2017). "Catatan Prestasi Pembangunan Jakarta 5 Tahun Terakhir (A
Note on Jakarta's Development Achievements in the Past Five Years)." *Kompas*,
13 October. https://megapolitan.kompas.com/read/2017/10/13/09375261/
catatan-prestasi-pembangunan-jakarta-5-tahun-terakhir (accessed 5 July 2018).

Sarwanto, Abi (2016). "Denda koefisien lantai bangunan disebut gaya korup-
tif baru (Fine for the Additional Floor in Developing New Building is a New
Type of Corruption)." *CNN Indonesia*, 9 December. www.cnnindonesia.com/
nasional/20161209234543-12-178639/denda-koefisien-lantai-bangunan-dise
but-gaya-koruptif-baru (accessed 12 July 2018).

Setijadi, Charlotte (2017). "The Jakarta Election Continues: What Next for Embat-
tled Governor Ahok?" *ISEAS Perspective* 18: 1–8.

Sheppard, Bede (2006). "Human Rights Watch Report: Condemned Communities Forced Evictions in Jakarta." *Human Rights Watch*, 5 September. www.hrw.
org/report/2006/09/05/condemned-communities/forced-evictions-jakarta
(accessed 12 October 2019).

Suaedy, Ahmad (2014). "The Role of Volunteers and Political Participation in the
2012 Jakarta Gubernatorial Election." *Journal of Current Southeast Asian Affairs*
33 (1): 111–138.

Tamaela, Tara Marchelin (2015). "Sistem E-budgeting yang Digunakan Ahok Dini-
lai Punya Dasar Hukum (E-budgeting System Used by Ahok Is Considered to
Have a Legal Basis)." *Kompas*, 3 March. https://megapolitan.kompas.com/
read/2015/03/03/19570601/Sistem.Ebudgeting.yang.Digunakan.Ahok.Dinilai.
Punya.Dasar.Hukum (accessed 12 October 2019).

Taylor, Gloria Safira (2017). "Pelayanan Publik Pemprov DKI Era Ahok Masuk Predikat Baik (Public Service in Ahok Era Is in the Category of Good)." *CNN Indonesia*,
5 December. www.cnnindonesia.com/nasional/20171205142148-20-260251/
pelayanan-publik-pemprov-dki-era-ahok-masuk-predikat-baik (accessed 6 July 2018).

Taylor, John (2015). "A Tale of Two Cities: Comparing Alternative Approaches to
Reducing the Vulnerability of Riverbank Communities in Two Indonesian Cities."
Environment and Urbanization 27 (2): 621–636.

Tempo (2006). "10 tokoh yang mengubah Indonesia (10 Figures that Changed
Indonesia)." *Tempo Magazine* 30 (2), 25 December: 5–6.

Tempo (2008). "Sedikit Orang Baik di Republik yang Luas (The Few Good People in
this Vast Republic)." *Tempo Magazine* 20 (3), 22 December: 11–12.

van Voorst, Roanne, and Rita Padawangi (2015). "Floods and Forced Evictions in
Jakarta." *New Mandala*, 21 August. www.newmandala.org/floods-and-forced-
evictions-in-jakarta/ (accessed 15 July 2018).

Widiyoko, Danang (2017). "Ahok and the Rise (and Fall?) of the State Capital." *New
Mandala*, 7 June. www.newmandala.org/ahok-rise-fall-state-capital/ (accessed 10
July 2018).

Wilson, Ian (2017). "Jakarta: Inequality and the Poverty of Elite Pluralism." *New
Mandala*, 19 April. www.newmandala.org/jakarta-inequality-poverty-elite-pluralism/
(accessed 12 October 2019).

Zulfikar, Muhammad (2016). "Forced Evictions in Jakarta: More than Losing Homes."
Huffpost blog 25 April. www.huffingtonpost.co.uk/muhammad-zulfikar-rakhmat/
forced-evictions-jakarta_b_9758944.html (accessed 9 July 2018).

4 Ideology of pragmatism

Singapore's domestic policy

Charles Chao Rong Phua

> We were in no position to be fussy about high-minded principles. We had to make a living.
>
> Lee Kuan Yew

In 2015, Singapore celebrated its first 50 years as an independent state (Kwa Chong Guan et al., 2009). Singapore's success has been credited variously to luck, meritocracy, and pragmatism, among other factors (Parameswaran, 2015). Several academics and practitioners have described Singapore as pragmatic, but many have omitted to explain in any detail what pragmatism in Singapore means, despite the fact that the multiplicity of interpretations implies a certain degree of conflict over the precise meaning of the term. In his book *Singapore: Identity, Brand, Power*, Kenneth Paul Tan summarizes the most frequently implied conceptualizations of the term as: "acting in a non-dogmatic but instrumental way", having "little patience for philosophy, theory, or finely nuanced and elaborate arguments", being "willing to learn . . . from best practices available anywhere in the world", taking "a realist perspective on human nature", having "little patience for intangible, even qualitative, values in its materialist world", and being "managerial in . . . orientation to leadership" (Tan, 2018: 17–19).

As Tan notes, pragmatism tends to have specific connotations when used in a policy context, effectively functioning as a synonym for "realist" most of the time. However, this is just one possible perspective; other interpretations of Singaporean pragmatism within the policy domain can be identified and examined. This chapter seeks to do just that. First, it will explain Singapore's own definition of pragmatism via interviews with Singapore leaders in a literature review. Second, it will illustrate how pragmatism works in practice, focusing on Singapore's domestic issues. Third, it will discuss the "ideology of pragmatism" and its promoters. In the course of the chapter, I intend to argue that while the Singapore government's fixation on pragmatic policymaking was originally a logical response to the difficult circumstances that prevailed immediately following independence, it later became an article of faith and a way to counter and pre-empt criticism, with developmental authoritarian attitudes toward politics prevailing long after development had been achieved.

Literature review: pragmatism and realism in Singapore's foreign policy

The focus on pragmatism in analyzing Singapore's political decision-making can be traced back to the beliefs of founding fathers Lee Kuan Yew and Goh Keng Swee. As Lee Kuan Yew said in a 1994 speech to parliament, "If a thing works, let's work it, and that eventually evolved into the kind of economy that we have today [sic]. Our test was: Does it work?"[1] Similarly, in 1977, Goh Keng Swee had emphasized the importance of practical benefits over signaling:

> It might have been politically tempting to rid ourselves of institutions and practices that bore, or seemed to bear, the taint of colonial associations. Had we done so we would have thrown away a priceless advantage for the sake of empty rhetoric.[2]

Over time the pragmatic tendencies of the founding fathers became ingrained within the culture of both the People's Action Party (PAP) and the civil service, as described by Jon Quah (2010) and Neo Boon Siong and Geraldine Chen (2007). As Neo and Chen put it:

> The founding generation of leaders – Lee Kuan Yew, Goh Keng Swee, and, to a certain extent, Hon Sui Sen – in their own ways, shaped the ethos and values of the Singapore public service, and the way it defined and approached its key functions.
>
> (Neo and Chen, 2007: 147–148)

The most detailed examination of pragmatism in Singapore's governance can be found in Kenneth Paul Tan's article, "The Ideology of Pragmatism" (2012). In this piece, Tan examines the Singapore government's use of pragmatism to justify political authoritarianism in an era of neoliberal globalization. He argues that pragmatism is regarded as an ideology justifying strong political control on a performance legitimacy basis. While ideology may, on the face of it, appear antithetical to pragmatism, Singapore has nevertheless elevated pragmatism to a similar status to that enjoyed by ideologies in more ideological states (see also Tan, 2017). This chapter will explore this idea of a Singaporean "ideology of pragmatism" in more detail.

In addition to Tan's in-depth exploration of the concept, Michael Hill and Lian Kwen Fee (1995) and Chua Beng Huat (1997) also mention the "ideology of pragmatism" in their books: Hill and Lian describe the politics of nation-building, while Chua's reference occurs in the context of a discussion of communitarian ideology in Singaporean democracy. Their remarks on the ideology of pragmatism can be contrasted with the position of Chan Heng Chee, who preferred to take Singapore's pragmatism at face value, describing the country as an administrative state (1975) and devoid of ideology (1976). Indeed, the historical electoral dominance of the PAP confounds the issue to a degree, since there is little competition to compel the PAP to distinguish itself in ideological terms.

In terms of foreign relations, Singapore's foreign policy is frequently described as "realist". Michael Leifer (2000) is generally seen as the defining work on Singapore's realist foreign policy, although the topic has also been tackled by Kawin Wilairat (1975), Chan Heng Chee (1988), Bilveer Singh (1999), and Alan Chong (2006). Leifer himself was a realist in his outlook; his thesis was essentially that Singapore is small and had to cope with vulnerability and was therefore obliged to take a realist position. While Leifer's general thesis of vulnerability due to geography is a persuasive one, his position nevertheless cannot adequately explain the occasional liberal tendencies of Singapore's foreign policy as described in Narayanan Ganesan's *Realism and Interdependence in Singapore's Foreign Policy* (2005) or the "economic interdependence and regional institution-building" posited by constructivist Amitav Acharya's *Singapore's Foreign Policy: The Search for Regional Order* (2008).

This apparent contradiction was earlier highlighted by Acharya (1998), who described Tommy Koh as a pragmatic idealist. However, this term was thinly defined and referred only to Koh's perspective on diplomacy, not to Singaporean policy in general. Koh himself, in a eulogy for Lee Kuan Yew in March 2015, described the first principle of Singapore's foreign policy as pragmatism:

> First, our foreign policy is based on pragmatism and not on any doctrine or ideology. The scholars who have written that Singapore's foreign policy is based on realism are mistaken. If it were based on realism, we would not have attached so much importance to international law or to the United Nations. Our constant lodestar is to promote the security and prosperity of Singapore.
>
> (Koh, 2015)

Koh thus refutes the idea of Singapore as a purely realist state. He alludes to the importance of international law but grounds his emphasis on a constructivist point of view – seeing law as a way to frame mindsets. This can be contrasted with Ganesan's (2005) focus on the liberal order as created via economic interdependence and Acharya's (2008) focus on regional institution-building. Similarly, Prime Minister Lee Hsien Loong recently summarized the key fundamentals behind Singapore's foreign relations, concluding that: "Singapore can continue to be the master of its own destiny on the global stage by adopting a 'balance between realism and idealism' to defend and advance its interests abroad" (Chong Zi Liang, 2015).

Chong's (2006) article on "abridged realism" offers what is probably the most detailed examination of pragmatism in Singapore's foreign policy. Chong articulates the underlying nuances of the pragmatic and liberal qualifiers (pragmatic realism, liberal realism, and pragmatic idealism) affixed to the positions of Sinnathamby Rajaratnam, Lee Kuan Yew, Tommy Koh, and Kishore Mahbubani. Despite portraying a highly nuanced landscape of foreign policy thinking, however, Chong's process-tracing approach to analyzing the positions of foreign policy leaders is based on an attempt to deduce their foreign policy beliefs from their speeches; it does not offer a comprehensive framework for describing pragmatism in Singapore's policymaking more generally.

While pragmatism in foreign policy has attracted the most scholarly attention, some authors have also addressed pragmatism in other specific domains. Schein (1996), for example, provides a detailed and comprehensive analysis of pragmatism as practiced by the Economic Development Board (EDB), while Neo and Chen (2007) look in detail at the ways in which pragmatic philosophy has become ingrained within the public administration, producing a self-replicating internal system. This chapter seeks to unpack the whys and hows of pragmatism in Singapore's policy framework.

Singapore: an ideology of pragmatism

While many analyses of Singaporean policymaking (particularly those produced by leaders or former leaders) have taken official declarations of adherence to purely pragmatic strategies at face value, others have taken the position that, perversely, the Singapore government's focus on pragmatic policymaking has, over time, worked to create a state "ideology of pragmatism". As Tan (2019: 17–19) argues: "By doggedly describing itself as pragmatic, the Singapore state is actually disguising its ideological work and political nature through an assertion of the absence of ideology and politics". In other words, pragmatism has effectively taken on the same function that ideology occupies in ideological states. The Singapore narrative is: Singapore is only a city-state, with no hinterland, we must work to be "at the table, not on the menu" (Jayakumar, 2015); we must be pragmatic to survive.[3] In this respect, pragmatism has been institutionalized in the mindset of the administration and the leadership; the selection of candidates for future leadership in the bureaucracy and politics, using a suite of measures that includes perceived pragmatism, further deepens the institutionalization of the ideology of pragmatism at high levels. In practice, this translates into a standard operating procedure used within both politics and administration. This begins with a focus on facts-based strategic analysis of the situation, scenario planning with regard to the various possibilities, checklist-based decision-making, and flexibility at all levels. We will elaborate further using a policy process approach.

During the agenda-setting and policy-formulation phases of the policy process, Singapore leaders use a fact-based or inductive analysis of the situation. This is seen as the fundamental "added value" contributed by the governmental elites.[4] The same procedure applies when revising existing policies that have proved unsuccessful or unpopular. One obvious example would be the case of the hugely unpopular Graduate Mothers Scheme (an openly eugenics-based policy that provided incentives for women with university degrees to have more children), which will be discussed in more detail later in this chapter. While Lee Kuan Yew's authoritarian treatment of internal opponents who resisted co-optation into the PAP system is well-known, he nevertheless remained open to argument on the part of those whose loyalty was not under question as a means to both elucidate facts and develop better strategies. As Bilahari Kausikan put it:

> Mr. Lee suffered no fools. He often tried to intimidate you into agreement. But this is not the same thing as being intolerant. . . . Even when he did not agree, he listened. He never thought that he had all the answers. He never hesitated to change his mind if the situation warranted it.[5]

Cabinet meetings were not used to simply rubber-stamp Lee's decisions.[6] It was recorded, for instance, that Lee and Goh Keng Swee often quarreled over policy positions, and Lee would relent if Goh's logic was sufficiently persuasive. At the same time, Goh shared Lee's preference for immediate, fact-based analysis and personal verification of facts.[7] As defense minister, Goh was famous for carrying out spot-checks: he would fly in by helicopter or arrive by car, unannounced, to observe the "unrehearsed" conduct of military life. After retiring as prime minister (serving first as senior minister and later minister mentor), Lee continued to devote himself to surveying and analyzing changes in the international situation and recommended policy changes via the Cabinet accordingly. It can be seen as an endorsement of his fact-based adaptability that Senior Minister Lee's views continued to be sought (and were thus apparently considered sufficiently uncontroversial) by the international community as an elder world statesman, by capitalist and socialist states, and by democratic and authoritarian governments (Allison et al., 2013: xiii–xxiii).

However, pragmatism as per the Singaporean vision of the concept does not mean a complete reliance upon short-term expediency. In fact, during policy formulation, Singapore prides itself on long-term scenario planning and futures thinking. Once again, this is a reflection of Lee Kuan Yew's own vision of the role of a leader: "My job is to be a long-range radar, to look ahead and then share with the government and give them my advice".[8] Scenario planning was imported from Shell Petroleum and actively practiced in various ministries (I have myself been actively involved in the practice and teaching of the method). Diverse scenario-planning methodologies (such as "future forward" and "future backward"), which are now widely available in open source literature, were also used. Former head of the Civil Service, Peter Ho was a firm believer in these methods and established the Centre for Strategic Futures in 2009 reporting directly to the Prime Minister's Office. Various ministries now have dedicated staff responsible for "futures" work. Where futures methodologies attempt to anticipate new complexity and unexpected events, scenario planning takes a linear, goal-oriented approach.[9] A practical example of this long-term planning can be found in Singapore's urban planning system. Urban planners work with three types of plans: concept plans, which cover 30–40-year time spans, master plans which seek to operationalize and adjust concept plans in shorter time periods of 5–10 years, and development guide plans. Singapore is divided into 55 planning areas, and plans for future developments are prepared by the Urban Redevelopment Authority in the form of development guide plans to systematically and transparently communicate to the private sector (Centre for Liveable Cities, 2016: 16, 81–82, 86–87). For example, the 1971 Concept Plan sets out the development needs of a projected population of four million by 1992. Similarly, the 1991 Concept Plan incorporated 55 Development Guide Plans, which in turn fed into the 1998 Master Plan.

During policy formulation, Singapore's pragmatic approach has often led it to favor policy hybrids and thus innovation. The solution selected for a particular problem is often not based on one or another theoretical or ideological system but a hybrid. For example, while the PAP was initially influenced by pro-collective/ egalitarian aims of Fabian socialism, it realized that full-scale welfare provision would bankrupt the state. Hence a hybrid system was chosen: a capitalist economy with welfare measures in housing, education, and healthcare. While the PAP's exact positioning on the left–right continuum has fluctuated over time, its fondness for the idea of a hybrid model has remained constant since 1965 (Neo and Chen, 2007: 166–177).

Lee Hsien Loong's successful resolution of the KTM railway dispute with then Prime Minister Najib Razak in 2010 can be seen as a typical policy hybrid. This disagreement centered on 217 hectares of land owned by the Malaysian Government, via the Federated Malay States Railways company (later Keretapi Tanah Melayu or KTM). As a result of the shared history of the two countries, KTM had possession of a corridor of land and several buildings deep within Singapore territory, presenting both a potential threat to national security and an obstacle to urban planning. In the end, rather than assigning sovereignty over the land in question to one party or another, it was decided to co-develop the land under the state-owned enterprises Temasek Holdings of Singapore and Khazanah Nasional of Malaysia. At the time this was widely seen as an innovative solution, though it has since been suggested as a way to resolve various other territorial disputes. Another example of pragmatism-as-adaptability in Singapore–Malaysia relations can be seen in the matter of water trading. Singapore signed three water agreements with Malaysia in 1961, 1962, and 1990, under which the Malaysian authorities would sell water to water-scarce Singapore at mutually agreed prices. The 1961 water agreement was due to expire in 2011, and, during the renewal negotiations, the Malaysian side announced its intention to raise the raw water price.[10] Under pressure to achieve water independence from Malaysia, Singapore chose to put some of its energy into technological innovation rather than focusing purely on negotiation strategies. As well as enhancing water catchment areas and developing water desalination programs, scientists in Singapore invented a reverse osmosis process to reclaim water from latrines.[11] This technological solution to the problem also allowed Singapore to negotiate with Malaysia from a much stronger position.

Singapore has also made concerted efforts to institutionalize pragmatic decision-making. As mentioned earlier, the debate process in pre-cabinet and cabinet meetings aims to ensure that blind spots and feasibility of proposed policies are actively addressed by ministers who have held similar ministerial portfolios before (Yahya, 2018). The logic and common sense of a policy will always be analyzed to ensure soundness and coherence. Resource availability is a key criterion, given that Singapore is a small state with limited resources; policies that require too many resources and for which the costs outweigh the benefits will not be approved. This resource availability check ensures that policy designs can be implemented within Singapore's means and capabilities. Lastly, there is a check on systemic effects to ensure policies do not bring short-term benefits at the expense of long-term costs.[12]

During the policy-implementation phase, Singapore's small state and tightly-knit government becomes an advantage. The close relationship between politicians and civil servants means that during implementation the feedback loop from implementers to decision-makers is short, allowing for tactical adjustments, operational changes, and even policy reversals to be made.

Examples of pragmatic policymaking in Singapore

This section provides several short studies of pragmatism in Singaporean policymaking. These are examples of the Singapore government making a clear and conscious decision to put sentiment to one side and focus on what it perceived to be the national interest at the time. The examples include population control, a field that has seen many of the most widely publicized policy reversals; the policy U-turn involving the Graduate Mothers Scheme; and pragmatism in economic development and racial and religious matters.

Population control policies

While the majority of feedback loops and decisions on policy reversals tend to be internal to government and little-publicized, the many twists and turns of the government's population control policies have been well-documented and widely commented upon (Straughan et al., 2009).

Like many other nations, Singapore experienced a post-war baby boom between 1945 and 1965. However, while in most countries this was a reflection of rapid GDP growth and increased prosperity, in Singapore population growth outstripped economic growth. In land-scarce Singapore, over-population was a perennial threat, and high occupancy rates in the pre-independence slums created conditions for disease to thrive. Moreover, the withdrawal of British troops and the split from Malaysia had led to mass unemployment. While various attempts had been made by government and private organizations to control population growth, it was only following independence in 1965 that the government was able to take a strong line. Abortion and sterilization were legalized in 1970, and a raft of disincentives to large families was gradually introduced, grouped together under the heading of the "Stop at Two" policy. Maternity leave was rescinded beyond the second child, and large families were given lower priority when it came to public housing and education. However, these policies coincided with the beginning of Singapore's developmental explosion, which led to massive economic growth and a corresponding increase in living standards. The result was an over-correction. In 1975, the total fertility rate dropped below the 2.1 births per woman required to maintain a stable replacement rate. By 1986, the government recognized that the falling birth rate had become enough of a problem to create a future demographic time bomb, and brought in a selection of pro-natalist policies, grouped under the heading "Have-Three-or-More" (if you can afford it).

Despite the government's best efforts, however, the natural trend toward lower birth rates in more developed societies was never successfully counteracted, and the number of children born per woman continued to drop. Today it stands at around 1.2. While the government has maintained its pro-natalist policies, it has also made the pragmatic choice to search for other solutions to its population woes. The result has been a highly adaptable and economy-driven immigration policy, under which foreign workers are accepted or repatriated at rates that precisely track economic indicators. Under this policy, large-scale immigration is used to drive continued growth, being justified to the public as the only practical way to maintain living standards if locals refuse to have larger families (Yang et al., 2017).

Lee Kuan Yew acknowledged that the Stop at Two policy had been too successful, leading to a collapse in birth rates and a growing demographic challenge.

> Referring to criticism that it had been wrong, Mr Lee wrote: "Yes and no." Without lower population growth, unemployment and schooling problems would not have been solved, he argued. "But we should have foreseen that the better-educated would have two or fewer children, and the less-educated four or more." In hindsight, "we would have refined and targeted our campaign differently" right from the 1960s, he said. . . . "I cannot solve the problem and I have given up," he said, leaving the task to the new generation of leaders.
>
> (*Today Online*, 2015)

The Graduate Mothers Scheme

One of the first policies adopted under the pro-natalist banner was the specifically targeted Graduate Mothers Scheme. This policy was explicitly eugenicist in nature, reflecting the perspectives of Lee Kuan Yew and many of his colleagues, who were concerned that the drop in birth rates experienced during the 1970s, following the introduction of the Stop at Two policies and increased economic growth rates, had predominantly affected well-educated Singaporeans, who had benefitted most from economic development (Yap, 2003). Lee argued that if the less academically gifted maintained a higher birth rate than their better-endowed colleagues, the result would be a net decline in general intelligence. Moreover, the apparent preference of educated men for less educated wives was liable to create an imbalance in supply and demand at the top end of the scale, as highly educated women refused to "marry down" (Lyons-Lee, 1998).

In 1984 a raft of policies was introduced with the intention of incentivizing childbearing among women with university degrees. As well as tax rebates and preferential access to public housing, they would also have priority when it came to making school choices. While the unpopularity of these policies could reasonably have been anticipated, the extent of the backlash was not. Citizens were particularly outraged by the priority school choice policy, given that it appeared to compound advantages enjoyed by a social and genetic elite, while consigning others to perpetual under-class status. The policy was as unpopular among its beneficiaries as it was among those who would have lost out as a result and contributed to a shock election result in the same year, with a 12.8% swing against the ruling PAP (Quah, 1985). Although the majority of the government supported the policy, they nevertheless accepted that the electoral price to be paid for its introduction was a sign that they had underestimated the strength of public sentiment on the issue. In 1985, the most controversial aspects of the policy were scrapped (Palen, 1986).

As Goh Chok Tong put it:

> It was not sustainable. By then even those of us who were in favour of it knew the political costs. It may cost us to lose the election. That was the time when we began to modify. We were all pragmatists on what was doable and what was not.
>
> (quoted in Peh, 2019: 157)

The economic development board

Goh Keng Swee's "fact-based" pragmatism can be seen in his decision to experiment with export-oriented growth when the rest of the developing world favored import substitution. Goh surveyed the economic development models of the world and was not convinced that the import-substitution model would work for Singapore as "our domestic market was too small and we lack natural resources".[13] Hence, the geography of Singapore (its size, demographics, lack of natural resources) compelled policymakers to think of alternatives to the widely accepted panacea that was import substitution at the time.[14] Singapore therefore experimented with an alternative model, which soon proved itself appropriate to the city-state's situation; nevertheless, aware of the dangers of being lulled into complacency by this short-term success, the Economic Development Board (EDB) continued to tweak and update policy as Singapore's economic situation evolved. The EDB's willingness to drop previously successful strategies when circumstances indicated that an alternative approach was likely to yield even better results is well-documented by Schein (1996: 99–101).

Despite the EDB's resounding success in helping the country's economic development, the government took pains to avoid complacency and the accretion of red tape, subjecting the organization to continual upgrades, including a root-and-branch reform in the 1980s. Even personnel who had played crucial roles in creating the economic prosperity enjoyed in Singapore at that point were moved to other departments if it was felt that their skills were no longer suited to dealing with an economy that was now increasingly focused on higher value-added goods and services. Chairman Philip Yeo described the change thus: "Because economic development is dynamic, we have to continually maintain and improve Singapore's competitive advantage" (ibid.). The idea that to stay in place is to fall behind is one that has become increasingly commonplace in Singapore as it has developed. Where pragmatic policies were originally justified by an urgent need to catch up with the rest of the developed world, they are now justified by the equally urgent need to stay ahead of the rapidly industrializing nations of East Asia. As PM Lee Hsien Loong put it:

> It is really a tidal wave, a tsunami coming in our direction and the only way to get out of the trouble is to rise above the tsunami by training ourselves, developing expertise and doing things which they cannot do yet in China but which we can do now in Singapore so that we can make a living for ourselves in order to improve our lives.
>
> (Lee Hsien Loong, 2011)

Learning from Japan

While many countries favor evidence-based economic policy, in the Singapore case this often had to be pursued in the face of sentiment. Just as with the maintenance of colonial institutions despite anti-colonial feelings, economic policy had to be conducted despite misgivings. Thus, the PAP's original leaning toward Fabian socialist principles, when faced with the need to raise revenue and boost activity, quickly transformed into a pro-business, low-tax policy.

A similar trend can be seen in Singapore's willingness to openly acknowledge the inspiration it took from Japanese development policy, despite the brutal nature of Japan's wartime occupation of Singapore. The post-independence leadership made a conscious decision to avoid reliance upon anti-Japanese sentiment as a prop to their own legitimacy – in contrast with many of their counterparts in China and Korea, for example (Cho Il Hyun and Park Seo-Hyun, 2011). When Japan grew into an economic giant, the Singapore leadership set aside any nationalist or personal resentment (despite many of them having experienced the occupation) and analyzed the strengths of the Japanese Ministry of Trade and Industry (MITI), the role of state-led capitalism in rejuvenating the Japanese economy, and the cultural strengths of the Japanese economic program. Regardless of its wartime record, the focus was entirely upon the lessons that could be learned from Japan's present growth. South Korea, Taiwan, Hong Kong, and Singapore followed and adapted the Japanese model of state-led capitalism in a Japanese "flying geese formation", although with a greater or lesser willingness to admit the source of their inspiration. This story has been widely recounted in business management and area studies (e.g., Wong, 2009). Singapore took a conscious decision to adopt a functional approach toward learning without becoming emotionally fixated on Japan's past.

In recent years a similar trend has driven engagement with China. Despite severe misgivings regarding China's foreign ambitions, Singapore has been among the leaders when it comes to economic cooperation with the PRC, while nevertheless doing its best to maintain a neutral political position.

Religious knowledge in schools

Race and religion are particularly sensitive areas in Singapore, with the government tending to take a hard line when it comes to issues that may have adverse consequences for racial and religious harmony. Threats to either can be heavily sanctioned under sedition laws, and intensive social engineering policies have been implemented to prevent the creation of mono-ethnic or single-religion areas. Similarly, immigration and birth rates are carefully monitored to ensure that the ratios between the various races in Singapore remain broadly similar to those that prevailed at independence.

Despite the high degree of governmental intervention in this area, however, policies on the matter are not doctrinaire. Not being driven by reasons of principle but rather being angled toward a particular outcome, policies can be modified in response to events. In 1984 a new subject, Religious Knowledge, was introduced in Singapore's secondary schools. The goal, as described by Goh Keng Swee, was to provide an "intellectual basis which will bind the various moral qualities we deem desirable into a consistent system of thought" (as cited in Ong and Moral Education Committee, 1979: iii) – itself a thoroughly pragmatic aim. This, in turn, was aimed at reinforcing a sentiment of local attachment in the face of the growing prevalence of "Western values" among the younger generation. As Lee Hsien Loong later put it, "Religion is a strong force in Singapore society. . . . It's a positive force in our society but which we have to manage because we have so many religions" (quoted in Tan Hui Yee, 2009). Pupils could choose to take classes on the Bible (in English), Islam (in English or Malay), Buddhism (in English or Chinese), Confucian ethics (in English or Chinese), Hinduism (in English) or Sikhism (in English). The curriculum was implemented in a particularly pragmatic way, focusing on using each religion to help inculcate values that were deemed beneficial to Singaporean society as a whole (such as the importance of doing good works), rather than advocating any particular belief system. Similarly, the textbooks used were carefully curated to provide objective information, rather than to attempt to instill devotion (Tan, 2008).

While the program may seem relatively inoffensive, it had been scrapped by 1989 and replaced with a general Civic and Moral Education course. In practice, the fact that the course options had only been available in specific languages (and thus to particular ethnic groups) was perceived to have accentuated ethnic differences. It was also felt that the choice of certain religions upon which to focus had the effect of compromising the state's neutrality. This, combined with more aggressive proselytizing by certain religious movements, led to a gradual redefinition of the government's position with regard to religion, with the state repositioning itself as a neutral regulator rather than an interventionist actor (Musa, 2017).

The "ideology of pragmatism" in the context of Singapore's geography

While Singapore's ideology of pragmatism has spread throughout all spheres of policymaking, it was originally institutionalized in the name of national survival, predicated upon a perceived sense of vulnerability when faced with much larger neighbors and a lack of domestic resources.

Geography has generally been the most important factor influencing Singapore's perception of its own lack of power and hence its sense of vulnerability (Leifer, 2000). Its small size originally made it a "price-taker nation", with a relative lack of negotiating power. While this has been remedied to a large degree through the country's rapid growth and its possession of a currency, an army, and a sovereign wealth fund, all of which punch well above their weight, the siege mentality has remained, as described earlier (Mahbubani, 2017). At independence, Singapore's lack of natural resources rendered its continued survival dependent upon the goodwill of other countries, in the sense that it lacked the option of self-sufficiency that is available to larger states that have an agricultural hinterland and hydrocarbon and mineral resources. This translated into a particular conception of its place in the world: Singapore's existence was not a given, and the nation-state had to constantly strive to ensure its relevance to the rest of the world and to certain great powers such as the USA and China, whilst maintaining its sovereign status (Singh, 1999: 15–17).

Singapore's position as a land-scarce and largely encircled state also influenced its relatively strong line on national sovereignty, demonstrated, for example, by Singapore's pro-active diplomacy behind ASEAN and the UN's condemnation of Vietnam's invasion of Cambodia (Ang, 2013). The fact that Singapore is a Chinese majority state sandwiched between larger states with Muslim majorities (Indonesia and Malaysia) has tended to compound the siege mentality and Singapore's cautious navigation of the Malay world (Rahim, 2009: 58), as well as influencing Singapore's decision to be the last Southeast Asian state to officially recognize China.

While history and socio-cultural factors have played a role in fostering pragmatism, these in turn are strongly influenced by geography, meaning that the latter can be said to be the root cause of Singapore's pragmatism (Singh, 1999: 15–17). In its early years in power, the senior PAP leadership openly asserted the predominance of geography in determining its strategic orientations, and while Singapore's political system is pluralistic (with various weak actors), the Prime Minister is the dominant leader, the strongest agent, and plays a disproportionate role in setting the agenda for other actors. Civil society and media often make a conscious choice to avoid commenting on issues known to be sensitive – mainly those relating to religion, race, and foreign policy – although precisely what constitutes a sensitive issue varies over time (Lee, 2002). Traditional media focus almost entirely on factual reporting, with commentators who express inconvenient opinions risking their careers (Yip Wai Yee, 2017). Even the Opposition generally agrees with the incumbent government on the coverage and approach taken toward such sensitive issues. In 2017, for example, Low Thia Kiang, then secretary-general of the Workers' Party, gave a speech about the implications of a rising China for Singapore's place in the world:

> Low identified Singapore's foreign policy position as well as strategic part-
> ners, and then questioned if "our foreign policy principles need to be updated
> in view of the changing world order". The speech drew praises from both
> the Foreign Minister and Prime Minister Lee Hsien Loong on their Face-
> book accounts. PM Lee wrote: "Some opposition MPs made good speeches
> too. Mr Low Thia Kiang set out succinctly how the strategic landscape is
> changing, and how this challenges our foreign policy. He asked: how can we
> protect and advance the national interest of our multi-racial country?" For-
> eign minister Vivian Balakrishnan also noted that Low posed a "thoughtful
> question" reflecting the level of "bipartisan support for our foreign policy
> efforts".
>
> (Ong, 2018)

In Singapore, in other words, "politics stops at the water's edge" with politicians, regardless of party affiliation, being united on foreign policy aims and broad strategies. This, in itself, works to reinforce the PAP's dominance over national narratives and conceptual frameworks, with the ideal of a strong leader required to preserve a vulnerable state eventually becoming self-perpetuating.

Singapore's small size and lack of natural resources has always been cited in the national narrative to justify why Singapore must be thankful that it is still in existence, why Singaporeans must work hard and not take survival and prosperity for granted, and why the government must be strong, relatively unchallenged, constantly think and plan ahead, and execute with caution. Elite homophily is likely to have been one of the dominant factors behind the institutionalization of the ideology of pragmatism. It is not surprising that a government that sees pragmatism as the principle driving its own and the nation's survival will be likely to attract, select, and promote new members who embody the same values. The criteria used in assessing civil servants have traditionally been summarized under the acronym HAIR (Helicopter, Analysis, Imagination, Reality), all of which are strongly linked to the government's self-perceptions: "helicopter" refers to the ability to see the big picture, to take a bird's eye view of any given issue; "analy-sis" means the application of economic cost-benefit analysis approaches to aid decision-making; "imagination" and "reality" (or realism) refer to the ability to come up with solutions that are both creative and practical (Neo and Chen, 2007: 351–353). The use of these highly pragmatic values to select candidates for high office have contributed to the institutionalization of the Singaporean ideology of pragmatism.

In a similar vein, once accepted into the party or bureaucratic system, recruits find themselves encouraged to pursue training in fields that are perceived to be of solid practical use to the party and/or the nation. During the developmental phase of Singapore's existence, the early cohorts of scholars within the Public

Service Commission were only permitted to study engineering.[15] This included functionaries in apparently unrelated fields, such as foreign affairs; thus career diplomats such as Kishore Mahbubani ended up with at least some experience of studying more "practical" fields. In later years, while more freedom was given to civil servants and other leaders wishing to pursue their education, the focus tended to be on economics, reflecting both the economic training of that generation of leaders and the perceived need for economic skills in government, as state management of the national economy became more data-driven and the financial sector grew to make up a much bigger part of the national GDP.[16]

Conclusion

Singapore's pragmatic policymaking was originally the fruit of its geographical constraints, insofar as the adaptive, unsentimental approach to politics taken by Lee Kuan Yew and his early lieutenants can be seen as a strategically reasonable response to difficult circumstances. Over time, however, pragmatism transformed from a spontaneous response to a specific set of geographical constraints into a fully-fledged state narrative. The "ideology of pragmatism" has become more entrenched through the selection of talent that reflects the personal and political qualities that earlier generations of leaders valued in themselves.

Pragmatism in foreign policy has generally been less controversial than in domestic policy. In foreign policy, the continued presence of outside threats can be used to justify pragmatic decision-making. In domestic policy, this "external risk" justification has grown less persuasive in recent years, with the decline of the communist threat. The result has been increasing calls for a more principle-driven approach to politics. Such calls have often focused on national identity as a starting point, demanding reduced immigration and greater pressure upon new immigrants to integrate. Interestingly, however, these demands are often couched in terms that are themselves redolent of the old pragmatic PAP-style politics, with commenters arguing their point based upon the need for national cohesion in order to ensure long-term survival, rather than upon nationalistic sentiments alone. If even those arguing against pragmatism do so using essentially pragmatic arguments, this seems to suggest that the phenomenon is well and truly ingrained within Singapore's political life.

Notes

1 Lee Kuan Yew, Speech in Parliament on the White Paper on Ministerial Salaries, 1 November 1994 (cited in Han Fook Kwang et al., 1998: 109).
2 Goh Keng Swee, as cited in Austin (2004), quoted in Neo Boon Siong and Geraldine Chen (2007: 166–167).
3 Lim Siong Guan, personal interview, 3 April 2017.
4 See the contribution of Ng Kok Song in *Up Close with Lee Kuan Yew: Insights from Colleagues and Friends* (Various authors, 2015: 153).
5 See the contribution of Bilahari Kausikan in *Up Close with Lee Kuan Yew: Insights from Colleagues and Friends* (Various authors, 2015: 160).

6 Suppiah Dhanabalan, personal interview, 17 January 2018.
7 Wang Gungwu, personal interview, 12 August 2016.
8 Ng Kok Song in *Up Close with Lee Kuan Yew: Insights from Colleagues and Friends* (Various authors, 2015: 153).
9 Lecture by Peter Ho, 'Scenario Planning and Horizon Scanning, 5 September 2013, for module 'Evolving Practices of Governance in Singapore' taught at Lee Kuan Yew School of Public Policy.
10 See: http://eresources.nlb.gov.sg/infopedia/articles/SIP_1533_2009-06-23.html (accessed 31 March 2019).
11 Reverse osmosis has been pioneered by Hyflux, a Singapore-based company once linked with Temasek.
12 Suppiah Dhanabalan, personal interview, 17 January 2018.
13 Suppiah Dhanabalan, personal interview, 17 January 2018.
14 Ibid.
15 Lim Siong Guan, personal interview, 3 April 2017.
16 Ibid.

References

Acharya, Amitav (1998). *The Quest for World Order: Perspectives of a Pragmatic Idealist*. Singapore: Institute of Policy Studies and Times Academic Press.
Acharya, Amitav (2008). *Singapore's Foreign Policy: The Search for Regional Order*. Singapore: World Scientific.
Allison, Graham, Robert D. Blackwill, and Ali Wyne (2013). *Lee Kuan Yew: The Grand Master's Insights on China, the United States, and the World*. Cambridge, MA: MIT Press.
Ang Chen Guan (2013). *Singapore, ASEAN and the Cambodian Conflict 1978–1991*. Singapore: NUS Press.
Austin, Ian Patrick (2004). *Goh Keng Swee and Southeast Asian Governance*. Singapore: Marshall Cavendish Academic.
Centre for Liveable Cities (2016). *Urban Development: From Urban Squalor to Global City*. Singapore: Centre for Liveable Cities.
Chan Heng Chee (1975). "Politics in an Administrative State: Where Has the Politics Gone?" Occasional Papers Issue 11. Singapore: Department of Political Science, University of Singapore.
Chan Heng Chee (1976). *Dynamics of One Party Dominance*. Singapore: Singapore University Press.
Chan Heng Chee (1988). "Singapore: Domestic Structure and Foreign Policy. Final Draft." In *Asia and the Major Powers: Domestic Politics and Foreign Policy*, edited by Robert A. Scalapino et al., 280–305. Berkeley: Institute of East Asian Studies, University of California.
Cho, Il Hyun, and Park Seo-Hyun (2011). "Anti-Chinese and Anti-Japanese Sentiments in East Asia: The Politics of Opinion, Distrust, and Prejudice." *The Chinese Journal of International Politics* 4 (3): 265–290.
Chong, Alan (2006). "Singapore's Foreign Policy Beliefs as 'Abridged Realism': Pragmatic and Liberal Prefixes in the Foreign Policy Thought of Rajaratnam, Lee, Koh and Mahbubani." *International Relations of the Asia Pacific* 6 (2): 269–306.
Chong, Zi Liang (2015). "Singapore Diplomacy 50 Years On." *Straits Times*, 6 December. www.straitstimes.com/politics/singapore-diplomacy-50-years-on (accessed 31 March 2019).

Chua Beng Huat (1997). *Communitarian Ideology and Democracy in Singapore.* Abingdon: Routledge.

Ganesan, Narayanan (2005). *Realism and Interdependence in Singapore's Foreign Policy.* Abingdon: Routledge.

Han, Fook Kwang, Warren Fernandez, and Sumiko Tan (1998). *Lee Kuan Yew: The Man and His Ideas.* Singapore: Straits Times Press.

Hill, Michael, and Lian Kwen Fee (1995). *The Politics of Nation Building and Citizenship in Singapore.* London: Routledge.

Jayakumar, Shunmugam (2015). *Be at the Table or Be on the Menu: A Singapore Memoir.* Singapore: Straits Times Press.

Koh, Tommy (2015). "Remembering Lee Kuan Yew: Our Chief Diplomat to the World." *Straits Times,* 25 March. www.straitstimes.com/singapore/remembering-lee-kuan-yew-our-chief-diplomat-to-the-world (accessed 31 March 2019).

Kwa, Chong Guan, Derek Thiam Soon Heng, and Tai Yong Tan (2009). *Singapore, a 700-year History: From Early Emporium to World City.* Singapore: National Archives of Singapore.

Lee Hsien Loong (2011). "National Day Rally Speech." PMO, 14 August. www.pmo.gov.sg/Newsroom/prime-minister-lee-hsien-loongs-national-day-rally-2011-speech-english (accessed 4 May 2019).

Lee, Terence (2002). "The Politics of Civil Society in Singapore." *Asian Studies Review* 26 (1): 97–117.

Leifer, Michael (2000). *Singapore's Foreign Policy: Coping With Vulnerability.* Abingdon: Routledge.

Lyons-Lee, Lenore (1998). "The 'Graduate Woman' Phenomenon: Changing Constructions of the Family in Singapore." *Sojourn: Journal of Social Issues in Southeast Asia* 13 (2): 309–327.

Mahbubani, Kishore (2017). "Treat China and Trump with Respect in 2017." *Straits Times,* 11 February.

Musa, Mohammad Alami (2017). "Engaging Religion with Pragmatism: The Singapore State's Management of Social Issues and Religious Tensions in the 1980s." RSIS Working Paper Series No. 305. Singapore: S. Rajaratnam School of International Studies.

Neo, Boon Siong, and Geraldine Chen (2007). *Dynamic Governance: Embedding Culture, Capabilities and Change in Singapore.* Singapore: World Scientific.

Ong, Tanya (2018). "Number of Times PAP Praise Opposition Few and Far Between But It Has Happened Before." *Mothership,* 16 May. https://mothership.sg/2018/05/pap-praising-opposition-history/ (accessed 31 March 2019).

Ong, Teng Cheong and the Moral Education Committee (1979). "Report on Moral Education." Singapore National Printers.

Palen, J. John (1986). "Fertility and Eugenics: Singapore's Population Policies." *Population Research and Policy Review* 5 (1): 3–14.

Parameswaran, Prashanth (2015). "10 Lessons from Lee Kun Yew's Singapore." *The Diplomat,* 24 March. https://thediplomat.com/2015/03/10-lessons-from-singapores-success/ (accessed 1 January 2019).

Peh, Shing Huei (2019). *Tall Order: The Goh Chok Tong Story.* Singapore: World Scientific Publishing Company Pte. Limited.

Quah, Jon S.T. (1985). "Singapore in 1984: Leadership Transition in an Election Year." *Asian Survey* 25 (2): 220–231.

Quah, Jon S.T. (2010). *Public Administration Singapore Style.* Singapore: Talisman.

Rahim, Lily Zubaidah (2009). *Singapore in the Malay World: Building and Breaching Regional Bridges.* Abingdon: Routledge.

Schein, Edgar (1996). *Strategic Pragmatism: The Culture of Singapore's Economic Development Board.* Cambridge, MA: MIT Press.

Singh, Bilveer (1999). *The Vulnerability of Small States Revisited: A Study of Singapore's Post-Cold War Foreign Policy.* Yogyakarta: Gadjah Mada University Press.

Straughan, Paulin Tay, Angelique Chan, and Gavin Jones (2009). "From Population Control to Fertility Promotion: A Case Study of Family Policies and Fertility Trends in Singapore." In *Ultra-Low Fertility in Pacific Asia,* edited by Gavin Jones, Paulin Tay Straughan, and Angelique Chan, 199–221. Abingdon: Routledge.

Tan, Charlene (2008). "The Teaching of Religious Knowledge in a Plural Society: The Case for Singapore." *International Review of Education* 54 (2): 175–191.

Tan, Hui Yee (2009). "Best Not to Bring Back Religious Classes in Schools." *Straits Times*, 18 September.

Tan, Kenneth Paul (2012). "The Ideology of Pragmatism: Neo-Liberal Globalisation and Political Authoritarianism in Singapore." *Journal of Contemporary Asia* 42 (1): 67–92.

Tan, Kenneth Paul (2017). *Governing Global-city Singapore: Legacies and Futures After Lee Kuan Yew.* Abingdon: Routledge.

Tan, Kenneth Paul (2018). *Singapore: Identity, Brand, Power.* Cambridge: Cambridge University Press.

Today Online (2015). "Policies for the Bedroom and Beyond." 23 March. www.todayonline.com/rememberinglky/policies-bedroom-and-beyond (accessed 31 March 2019).

Various authors (2015). *Up Close with Lee Kuan Yew: Insights From Colleagues and Friends.* Singapore: Marshall Cavendish.

Wilairat, Kawin (1975). *Singapore's Foreign Policy.* Singapore: ISEAS Press.

Wong, John (2009). "East Asian Experiences of Economic Development." *East Asian Policy* 1 (4): 48–54.

Yahya, Yasmine (2018). "Lim Hng Kiang: Longest-serving MTI Minister Who Prefers Talking Trade to Getting Personal." *Straits Times*, 27 April.

Yang, Hui, Peidong Yang, and Shaohua Zhan (2017). "Immigration, Population, and Foreign Workforce in Singapore: An Overview of Trends, Policies, and Issues." *HSSE Online* 6 (1): 10–21.

Yap, Mui Teng (2003). "Fertility and Population Policy: The Singapore Experience." *Journal of Population and Social Security (Population)* 1 (Suppl.): 643–658.

Yip, Wai Yee (2017). "Mediacorp Apologises for Remarks on Najib in TV Show." *Straits Times*, 6 April.

5 Planning a new capital in Central Asia

The case of Nur-Sultan (Astana), Kazakhstan

Michael Waschak[1]

Introduction

Shortly after declaring its independence from the Soviet Union in 1990, the government of Kazakhstan decided to break with its Soviet past and relocate its capital from the city of Almaty on the country's southern border to a more central location. Accompanying this geographic change were the aspirations of a new beginning for the nation and its people in a place that could be designed and planned as a new Kazakh capital city. The decision to move the capital was made on 6 July 1994, and on 10 December 1997 the city of Akmola, a more northern town closer to the geographic center of the country, replaced Almaty to become the independent nation's capital. Originally designated Astana (Kazakh for "capital"), the city was renamed Nur-Sultan in 2019 in honor of Nursultan Nazarbayev, the first president of the Republic who had led Kazakhstan for 30 years and who had resigned in March that year. Given the recent celebration of the 20th anniversary of Astana as the capital and the ongoing political changes, this is an ideal time to reflect on the origins of the city and to explore how strong, centrally controlled planning has affected urban development in a resource-rich, non-democratic state.

This city, like all capital cities, serves many purposes. It provides physical spaces with unique security, transportation, and logistical challenges for the operations of government; it serves as a center of national culture and education, it provides spectacular landmarks that reflect the goals, aspirations, and history of a people; and it provides a community for the diverse populations that typically accumulate in and around a capital city. The development of Nur-Sultan encompasses all of these elements, offering an instructive case to observe the formation and advancement of national identity even as physical infrastructure continues to be built. Many of the difficulties in planning Nur-Sultan's built environment parallel the challenges in other regional states since the breakup of the Soviet Union.

This chapter will briefly explore the development of urban planning and the history of the Central Asian region and will then develop a case study of the city of Nur-Sultan through the three lenses identified earlier: first as a set of physical spaces that provide the structures necessary to meet the physical, security, transportation, and logistical burdens of a capital city; second as a center of culture and a monument to the people of Kazakhstan; and third as a livable community for a diverse capital city population where people live, work, learn, and play. It will then explore the lessons that can be learned from both the old and new neighborhoods of the city in the context of Nur-Sultan's current process of centralized urban planning – lessons of particular relevance for those interested in studying the intersection of state power and urban planning in the developing and developed worlds. Finally, I will argue that the powerful forces shaping the city would benefit from greater public participation in the planning process – a more community-based approach to planning future development.

Urban planning and the history of Nur-Sultan (Astana)

Cities have been *planned* in various ways since people first began living together in higher densities. Urban planning is used as a tool to deliberately organize humanity's domination over the environment in ways that provide humans with living and working spaces that are functional and attractive. Moreover, leaders and rulers want their cities, especially capital cities, to be attractive and secure as these characteristics represent the virtues and power of the leader. Populations participate in the development of their leadership's spectacular vision and architecture to distinguish themselves from residents of less impressive and thus less powerful states. Further, "developmental discourses frequently fashion the people's happiness as an element of their own prestige" (Koch, 2018: 149). Thus, providing attractive monuments, security, and a healthy environment for the people is in the best long-term interest of the leaders.

Built into the use of monumental architecture is a kind of paternalistic assumption that the benevolent leader is right to use the state's riches to provide a positive environment for the populace (Geertz, 1983). Various non-compatible uses need to be separated, such as keeping noxious waste facilities away from living spaces (space planning), and systems to move people efficiently from living spaces to working spaces need to be designed (transportation planning). Over time, as resource use becomes more intense and humans start to recognize the limits to their consumption, planning for resource conservation and the future becomes critical (sustainable development). These various aspects of planning communities have evolved into two broad themes: planning for physical spaces and planning for positive societal development.

Traditional urban planning theory has focused on a linear progression from a centrally controlled process of needs recognition through project design and implementation (Le Breton and Henning, 1961; Brooks, 2002), coupled with various approaches to crafting physical spaces that shape society and humanity into better and higher versions of themselves (e.g., Howard, 1898; LeCorbusier, 1929). Over recent decades, however, planning theories have evolved and expanded to take on more collaborative, interactive, community-based, and sustainability-focused characteristics (e.g., Agger and Sorensen, 2018; Jacobs, 1962: Grabow and Heskin, 1973; Habermas, 1962; Healy, 1997; Innes, 1995;

Norton, 2005). In affluent democratic societies, urban planning is now typically considered to be a part of the dialogue among planning professionals, the people, and their elected representatives.

The notion that a planned community has the potential to add some greater social value to humanity has been a core theme in urban design since at least 1516 when Sir Thomas Moore penned his book *Utopia*. Planners have sought to develop urban environments to improve the lives of residents and visitors based upon their vision of what raises humans to their highest level (societal/advocacy planning). These paternalistic utopian visions transfer or reinforce the values of the powerful down to the population as a whole.

Key figures and concepts in modern planning of the 19th and 20th centuries include socially motivated planners like Ebenezer Howard (Garden Cities), Frank Lloyd Wright (Broadacre City) and Le Corbusier, Charles-Édouard Jeanneret (the Radiant City), as well as men like Frederick Law Olmsted Jr. who participated in the City Beautiful movement (Cohen, 1992; Fishman, 1977). Each of these men sought to design communities that would serve and shape society according to their particular vision. Driving the more collaborative approaches to planning cities is the American notion that the best way for people to live together and structure their physical spaces is to be determined by the individual people involved (Goodspeed, 2016). Unfortunately, early utopian visions and much modern urban development, lack the participation and consent of the residents whose lives would be theoretically shaped by building and living in these planned communities.[2]

A similar critique can be applied to the development of Nur-Sultan. The creation of visual spectacles through strong central planning in the resource-rich Republic of Kazakhstan has been focused on providing a new sense of national identity and a clear separation from the Soviet past (Koch, 2018). The first president and his administration promulgated Kazakh values and a particular identity even while underscoring the importance of diversity and respect for all persons. The structure of Nur-Sultan as a showpiece representing the highest ideals of the Kazakh culture encourages citizens to see themselves as something different from and better than their neighbors who lack such a spectacular capital city. Furthermore, it provides a poignant visual, suggesting Kazakh power, status, and wealth that "others" can see from the outside (Koch, 2018: 3).[3]

To emphasize the crucial role of the city, Nur-Sultan is metaphorically as well as physically located in the geographic center of the territory of Kazakhstan. Moving the capital to this new location was both a symbolic and practical decision. It implied that the government was for all of Kazakhstan and that its territorial integrity would be preserved following the country's independence from the former Soviet Union. Additionally, this new location provided an opportunity to restructure the relationships of city and regional governance with the new capital. And finally, the new location would provide a physical venue for creating the iconic symbols of the new, independent Republic of Kazakhstan.

Kazakhstan and its new capital provide an important example of rapid, large-scale urban development and decision-making in a non-democratic state in a territory with a long and interesting history. There is evidence that humans have lived in the region since the Paleolithic (Stone Age) period and that there has been trade among the nomadic horse cultures in the region since at least the Bronze Age (Outram et al., 2010, 2012). The region was the site of frequent conflicts as there are no physical barriers to ward off invaders on the flat, open steppe. This led to interest and invasions from a variety of neighbors: regular incursions by Russian, Chinese, Mongol, and Turkic invaders brought changes in leadership and economic conditions as the steppe peoples were driven from nomadic to more settled lifestyles and back again to nomadic ways.

However, one relationship is historically especially important. As their ethnic identity coalesced, the Kazakh nomads began to develop a closer relationship with the Russians, beginning in the 18th and 19th centuries. Seeking aid against southern invaders, the three main Kazakh Zhuzes (clans) turned to the Russians for help against raiders from the Xinjaing region of China. The Russians saw the potential benefits of controlling the region and over time exerted greater and greater influence, culminating in Kazakhstan becoming a Soviet Republic when the Soviet Union was formed in the early 20th century. Close contact with Russians led to significant changes in the region's ethnic mix and the lifestyles of the people, which continue to have important effects. Since independence, Kazakhstan has sought to diminish or at least balance the power of their northern neighbor over the country.

The majority of the country's population is ethnic Kazakh (63%) with ethnic Russians accounting for 24% and other minorities including Uzbeks, Ukrainians, Uygurs, Tatars, Germans, Chinese, Koreans, and others making up about 13%.[4] The new capital, Nur-Sultan, has rapidly grown to be a diverse and vibrant city and is currently the second largest city in Kazakhstan (after the former capital of Almaty).

Kazakhstan's sizeable territory makes it the ninth-largest country on earth. It is completely land locked, but it bridges the Asian and European continents. Thus it has provided important trade routes throughout history and formed part of the ancient Silk Road connecting Asia to Europe. In addition to its historical geographical value, the country is still important in the Central Asian region today. It has the largest and most powerful economy in the region among former Soviet States, and it continues to be a center of trade among the region's powers. This role is increasing in importance as China begins its new Belt and Road Initiative, announced in 2013. This plan envisages the building of land routes to European markets through Central Asia/Kazakhstan and sea routes to markets in South Asia and the Middle East.

Nur-Sultan (Astana) as a physical space

Nur-Sultan is very much a tale of two cities. The Ishim River is the dividing line through the city with the right bank of the river representing the older and established parts of the city, built in the Soviet era, and the left bank, full of new high-rise buildings, parks, and monuments, representing the vibrant and newly established sections constructed since the capital moved to the city. The city is an interesting case to consider when it comes to architecture, with the two parts of the city clearly representing different eras. The space of the city is divided between old and new, both metaphorically and physically.

The right bank, for the most part, is a classic Soviet town with homogeneous apartment buildings painted in pastel colors, narrow streets often with sidewalks lined by mature trees and cozy communal playgrounds and yards. Some people say that it looks more organic and natural than the more "artificial" left bank. Other people say it has a "spirit of the city" that the new part has not yet acquired. I would argue that these perceptions are the result of greater communication among the residents and the various actors making development plans over long periods of time. The right bank is far more connected to the residents and is what Nur-Sultan was before it became one of the most important national brands, a new capital.

Khrushchyovka Nur-Sultan

The left bank neighborhoods and buildings, designed at different times by a variety of famous architects, foreign and local, represents the new city – a place that is striving to become a modern metropolis, an attraction for people and money from all over the world. Apartments and government buildings on the left bank are of modern design, built in large blocks and often covered by ubiquitous alucobond (mirrored aluminum composite materials). There is no one style in which buildings are constructed, but rather a mix of styles – a bit of oriental, a bit of Western, a bit of futuristic, and sometimes decidedly strange. Not everyone considers this beautiful, but it seems that most of the people still like the boldness and speed with which the new capital has been developing.

The old city and right bank of the Ishim River

The majority of buildings on the right bank of the river were constructed during Soviet times when the city was called Tselinograd (Russian: Целиноград). The familiar three- to five-story apartment buildings[5] that are commonly found in former Soviet cites are called *Khrushchyovkas* (built during the term of the general secretary of the Communist Party Nikita Khrushchyov and named after him). They are quite large and constructed of bricks or large concrete blocks, following a standard low-cost design as a symbol of the equality that socialism was promoting. There are usually three or four apartments on each floor. The individual apartments are typically quite small (30–60 square meters on average).

There are three primary types or sizes of residential apartments found in Khrushchyov architecture: one-room (e.g., a single room with a combined sleeping and living space and an attached kitchen and bathroom), two-room (e.g., a separate sleeping room with a combined use sleeping/living room, kitchen and a bathroom) and three-room. In recent years many owners in Nur-Sultan have changed the original designs and made apartments more comfortable for themselves. The changes may include creating more space by eliminating walls between two rooms, creating more modern open floor plans.

The right bank has evolved organically to serve the needs of residents. The development of neighborhoods has resulted in a community with many open markets, like the one located on Beibitshilik Street. The salespeople at these small, popular, green stalls are referred to as grannies (women in their 60s and 70s). The products they sell are natural, often local produce, which is one of the reasons why these open markets are still so popular among the citizens in the city. However, as the economy has strengthened following independence and the move of the capital, people's wants have been changing, and some of the bigger open markets have been transformed into huge modern supermarkets like Alem or Shanghai that offer residents more choices and better prices on imported goods.

A classic example of Soviet-era educational architecture is the building that belongs to the polytechnic vocational college on Beibitshilik Street.[6] The buildings of educational institutions like this one usually have high ceilings and long corridors along the entire length of the building. Today the basement of the building is rented out to a pharmacy, and a branch of the local bank is situated in the next building. Most of the first floors of the residential houses were privatized for business in the time of the transition of Nur-Sultan to becoming the capital. Walking near these buildings you might see small shops, beauty salons, dental clinics, and notaries' offices on the lower floor. Most of the business activity on this side of the city is based in these first-floor former apartments of the older buildings.[7]

These first-floor offices sometimes extend into public spaces and parking areas, limiting pedestrian sidewalk space. However, the Akimat of Nur-Sultan (the city municipality), tries to make open spaces more comfortable for citizens and guests of the city. In many places there are tree-lined avenues between building and roads, and along the Duken uly street, the municipality has placed benches to form a gathering space that blocks out a parking zone.

The citizens of the right bank of the river are mostly people who have been living in Nur-Sultan since Soviet times or moved here in the 1990s. It is common to see older people walking or sitting on benches. Typically, they have known each other for years and know most of the neighbors. The culture and atmosphere of the right bank certainly differs from what people experience when they cross the bridge over Ishim River. The right bank maintains the spirit of Tselinograd and Akmola, in its history and architecture style. However, the appearance of the city changes, the closer it gets to the Ishim River. Older buildings have been replaced by new ones. The river is the conventional border where the old city ends and the new city starts. Looking at the left bank from the opposite side of the river, there is no "gray" and "boring" Soviet style architecture to be seen. There is only a mesmerizing view of the new capital that was designed and is being constructed as a showpiece of Kazakhstan's new position among the nations of the world.

The new city and the left bank of the Ishim River

The development of the new elements of Nur-Sultan, mostly on the left bank of the Ishim River and to the south and west, did not occur organically or by accident. The late Kisho Kurokawa, a well-known Japanese architect, drew up the original plans for the center of the new capital in 1998 as part of a design competition. Following his design, the city center has developed along a wide promenade running east to west across the center of the city and intersected at the President's Palace by the Ishim River. The design is in a style reminiscent of the City Beautiful movement in the United States, with large parks, promenades, and avenues surrounded by grand buildings (described in more detail later); the city has developed spectacular visual characteristics similar to other great capitals around the globe.[8]

One illustrative example of how life and residences differ between the old and the new parts of the city is found in the popular Highvill Astana, also known as the "Manhattan of Astana city". Located along the city's main promenade, Highvill is situated on the border of old and new. This residential and mixed-use estate is comprised of eight blocks located across the street from the Palace of Peace and Reconciliation and the Khazret Sultan Mosque. In contrast to the Soviet era five-story buildings without elevators, Highvill buildings vary from 18 to 34 floors. The infrastructure of this complex is highly advanced and designed in a way that keeps residents separate from the older elements of the city and allows them to enjoy the facilities without leaving the complex area. It has stores, supermarkets, kindergartens and childcare centers, healthcare facilities, cafes and restaurants offering various national cuisines, sport centers and gyms, dance studios, learning centers, beauty salons, and more. The security and convenience of immediate access to all these amenities permits the high quality of life demanded by the busy people who live in the capital. Some residents describe Highvill as a peculiar kind of "separate state" that has been formed by the elite community of the residents. This separateness is reinforced by the level of security required by dignitaries and other residents and rigorously maintained in the complex. Strangers do not have access to the courtyards, and the entrances are strictly managed by personnel of the Highvill residential complex.

Built in 2010, the administrative–residential complex on Water-Green Boulevard further east along the promenade has many similar features. The futuristic buildings of this complex consist of the business offices and apartments of the national ruling party and other elites. All necessary amenities like parking or cleaning are available in the building. Just across the city's main promenade lies the Keruen shopping mall, and just a short walk further up the park is the Baiterek monument.

Continuing along the promenade there are the residential complexes Nursaya Elite (on the left) and Nursaya Bonita (on the right). The names of these apartment buildings are translated from Kazakh: "Nur" means light and "Saya" means shadow. "Elite" and "Bonita" were taken from two construction companies, Elite Stroy and Bonita Engineering. Both complexes are situated along the Nurzhol Boulevard in the center of the left bank, not far from the government's House of Ministries, Presidential Palace, and the Baiterek monument. Part of Nursaya Elite is home to state officials such as the deputies of the parliament, who live there during their terms in office. There is a closed parking zone with security all around.

The apartments in the new part of the city are bigger than those on the right bank. In Nursaya, for example, apartments range in size from one-room apartments covering 48–52 square meters to four-room luxury apartments of more than 130 square meters. There are popular shops, cafes, and restaurants located on the first floors of these buildings that were specifically designed for commercial purposes, and the nation's monuments are clearly visible to everyone living in the left bank complexes.

Nur-Sultan (Astana) as a monument to Kazakhstan

Since the breakup of the Soviet Union, the leadership of Kazakhstan has had to navigate the country through the contentious geography of its position between the world powers of Russia to the north and China to the south. In order to promote national unity and to build an image of power and prosperity, the capital city has developed a number of examples of monumental architecture. Among these, the Baiterek Tower dominates the center and the long open-air promenade that traverses the city, east to west. Close by, the Khan Shatyr Entertainment Center – a tent-like structure representing the traditional housing of Kazakh nomads – anchors one end of the promenade, and to the east the pyramid of the Palace of Peace and Justice anchors the right bank of the river. The blue-domed Ak Orda Presidential Palace, with a similar design to the White House in Washington DC, sits on the left bank of the Ishim River. A little further to the west lies Nur-Sultan's new Nurly Zhol Railway Station, and to the south are the Nazarbayev University and the site of the 2017 World Energy Expo.

The desire to position the country as a model and world-leader for promoting peace and global security goes back to the region's historical epics and folk tales. One such story is described in President Nazarbayev's 2008 book, *The Kazakhstan Way*, in which the notion of peace and its importance to the nation is illustrated through the legend of the sacred Samruk bird. According to legend, the Samruk builds its nest on top of the Baiterek (the tree of life) and lays its golden egg (the sun). However, every year the dragon said to live at the base of the tree comes to eat the bird's golden egg. This story represents the eternal battle between evil and good, summer and winter, and the light and darkness in the world. In another folk tale a man named Yer Tostik comes along and kills the dragon, thereby saving the golden egg. For his heroic action, the Samruk rewards him by helping him to escape from the underground world. In this legend, kindness, mutual assistance, and cooperation help to defeat the enemy. Thus, the legend of the Samruk and Baiterek is a representation of independent Kazakhstan's aspiration to live in peace while working with its neighbors.

Baiterek Tower

Today people in Nur-Sultan recall these stories when they view the 97-meter tall Baiterek Tower that rises from a raised plaza in the center of town. It is made up of a narrow cylindrical shaft (containing elevators), surrounded by white branch-like girders flaring out at the top in a representation of a tree. There is a 22-meter diameter sphere representing the sun at the top of the tower. An emblem of Baiterek Tower is included in the logo of the city, on postcards, and even on the national currency. This use of historically important Kazakh imagery is designed to connect the Kazakh people to their new capital and to the nation.

Similarly drawing on historical local imagery, the Khan Shatyr Entertainment Center is a multi-level shopping and entertainment facility in the form of a giant tent. The Kazakh people were largely nomadic prior to Soviet times. The imagery of this historical living space pushes back against the time when the Soviets forced the Kazakhs to give up their traditional nomadic culture, become sedentary, and plant crops so that they might be more easily controlled.

Khan Shatyr Entertainment Center

In another example, the visual symbolism of the pyramid of the Palace of Peace and Justice connects Kazakhstan to the ancient pyramids of the world. It was built to commemorate the first Congress of Leaders of World and Traditional Religions held in 2003 connecting the diverse people of Kazakhstan to the many differing religious traditions of others from around the globe. Inspired by the success of the first event, the first president, Nursultan Nazarbayev, proposed the construction of the Palace of Peace to symbolize the spirit of Kazakhstan, where cultures, traditions, and representatives of various nationalities co-exist in peace and harmony.

Norman Foster, the main architect of the Palace, designed the building to represent all the world's religions in one place. The building forms a pyramid with a square base of 62 × 62 meters and a height of 62 meters, which is almost half the height of the Great Pyramid of Cheops (139 meters). Pale granite was used for the lower section of the pyramid, while stained glass was used for the upper section. The peak of the pyramid is covered by a colored light design by Brian

Clarke, featuring 130 doves symbolizing 130 nationalities living in Kazakhstan. Natural light pours in from the top of the pyramid to the auditorium at the very bottom through a glass lens that reflects the light. The design engineers used a steel and concrete skeleton that is able to resist the expansions and contractions caused by the extreme weather conditions in Nur-Sultan, where the temperature can vary from –40 to +40 degrees Celsius.

The US White House is seen the world over as a symbol of America's democracy and leadership in the world. In Nur-Sultan the gleaming white Ak Orda Presidential Palace, situated in a bend of the Ishim River, provides a visual connection to the imagery and power of the United States. This political symbolism helps to show outsiders that Kazakhstan is not a puppet of Russia, nor is it intimidated by its powerful southern neighbor China, but it is instead an international power in its own right.

Ak Orda Presidential Palace

This use of this powerful imagery and its meaning is consistent with the actual relationship with the United States. Since independence, Kazakhstan has maintained friendly relations with the USA; this connection to the world's greatest superpower gives outsiders a view of Kazakhstan as a peer of such a powerful nation. Maintaining this relationship has included accepting American assistance to remove enriched uranium from the territory when Kazakhstan took the remarkable step of giving up its nuclear weapons arsenal in 1995.[9] The Kazakhstan leadership therefore relies on imagery such as that represented in the Ak Orda Presidential Palace to demonstrate its prestige and power in the region and in the world.

In addition to leadership on the local and international stage, Nur-Sultan represents the connectivity of all Kazakh people. Aiding this connectivity is the modern Nurly Zhol Railway Station, on what will be the western edge of the main promenade through the city, once it is completed. The enormous station was designed to use 70% green technologies (e.g., solar and geothermal power and rainwater collection for cleaning and irrigation). The routes from the station are intended to connect all regions of Kazakhstan with the new capital.

Looking to the future, the city became the home of the Nazarbayev University in 2010. Designed with the mission of educating the young and giving them the advantages of an international, English-language education without leaving the country, the university complex has been rapidly built on the same grand scale as the best of the city's monuments. It sits across the highway from the Mega Silkway shopping mall and the site of the Expo 2017 Astana, dedicated to future energy. The Nazarbayev University, the National Defense University and the Expo 2017 complex – which is to be turned into a business development center – mark the southern boundaries of the new city.

Nazarbayev University

In addition to these great monuments and grand buildings, the city is criss-crossed with numerous smaller parks and promenades, the Triumphal Arch

Mangilik El, monuments to historical figures, grand mosques, a botanical garden, wonderful museums, an Opera House styled after Russia's Bolshoi, and the Triumph of Astana office complex styled after one of Stalin's Seven Sisters. The vistas dazzle from the air and from a distance. In the spring and summer, people throng to walk along the riverfront among the imposing buildings, but when winter comes the lifestyle of the Kazakh people changes.

Nur-Sultan (Astana) as a livable community

Nur-Sultan is a community of contrasts. The city has been centrally planned based upon the wishes of the country's leaders and the designs of the planner, Kurokawa. The new part of the city, located primarily on the left bank of the Ishim River, represents the city as a modern capital with wide thoroughfares and grandiose buildings. A great deal of attention has been paid to how it looks and, as mentioned earlier, what it represents. However, as a living space at a human scale, it has some significant drawbacks that derive from the city's approach to urban planning.

The differences on the two sides of the river illustrate the evolution of the city from a small town called Akmola to the modern Central Asian capital, Astana/Nur-Sultan. The older part of the city represents the city in its pre-capital days as a former Soviet regional center. It was designed according to Soviet styles and standards and has developed organically over time. This organic development has tied the local residents closely to their neighborhoods and their neighbors. Further, as time has passed, the needs of the local residents have been taken up by the community so that they are met, often in creative ways. This community-level planning is missing from the new city.

While some families have lived on the right bank for generations, people living on the left bank are rarely even second-generation residents. Most are families that arrived in Nur-Sultan after it became the capital. In addition, there are a lot of expatriates who work in international companies and organizations, diplomats based in the embassies, and immigrants from neighboring countries who mostly work in construction. During its 20 years as the capital, Nur-Sultan has attracted many new residents with new job and life opportunities: thousands of people have relocated to the city since 1998. Today the population exceeds one million permanent registered citizens and many more who stay on a temporary basis. Thus, the demand for housing is very high among citizens and can be compared only to Kazakhstan's largest city, the former capital of Almaty in the south. The new left bank of Ishim River has been actively under construction since 2000, becoming the center of political life once the majority of government ministries and other international and local state actors moved to the left bank.

The interaction between residents and the physical spaces of the city can be felt through the unofficial nicknames given to houses or other buildings by citizens. For example, one building officially called the business center Astanalyk (Metropolitan) is more commonly known as "the syringe" due to its shape. Parts of the city are often known locally by the names of nearby residential complexes rather than by the names of streets or addresses of houses. This works well for the locals, but it can be frustrating for visitors.

Conclusions

For most visitors coming to the capital of Kazakhstan, their first impression coming from the airport is likely to be of the monuments, the imposing buildings, grand parkways, and public spaces that have been and will continue to be scaled for visual impact.[10] From the street or from the air above the city, Nur-Sultan is in many ways becoming what great leaders of the past would have aspired to build. From a distance it looks impressive and serves as a shining example of what the Kazakhs hoped to achieve. However, in order to meet the goals of the social planners of the past, current planners need to spend more time thinking through how people do – and will – live among the monuments.

Nur-Sultan is a city that for many Kazakhs lacks the soul of the more established city of Almaty, which previously served as the nation's capital. More attention needs to be paid to how people actually live in the city and to the likely needs of future generations of residents and visitors. The scale of the monumental architecture is visually appealing in the tradition of the City Beautiful movement. In winter, however, temperatures can drop as low as –50 C, and steppe winds blow snow into near whiteouts, making much of the city far less usable to residents for a large part of the year.[11] Moreover, the city was intentionally designed in a modular fashion in which different parts of the city serve specific purposes. However, far less attention was paid to providing a means for people to get from one part of the city to another: walking distances between building complexes that are no problem in the warmer months become impossible as winter closes in. Nur-Sultan is currently very much an automobile town but without the road and parking infrastructure to support the large number of cars. Some local planners argue that this is intentional, to promote the use and development of demand for public transit – but no comprehensive transit plan exists. For example, most bus lines are private, without specific timetables, and the light rail system that was to operate between the international airport and the new railroad terminal has been placed on indefinite hold. For now, residents will have to go on struggling with traffic jams and very limited parking at many of the worksites around the city.

Strong centralized planning has driven Nur-Sultan's spectacular growth according to the desires of the first president, Nazarbayev. This rapid growth was facilitated by the wealth generated by the extractive use of Kazakhstan's enormous natural resources. However, since the drop in oil prices following the collapse of 2014, these revenues have dried up, and development has stalled. With the ongoing changes in Kazakhstan's political regime, this seems a good time to consider a different, more collaborative style of city planning that gives greater consideration to the needs of the residents living in the city space than to the image of the city as perceived by others living farther away.

The experiences of Asian cities like Nur-Sultan need to be taken seriously by planners and policy scholars alike. Dismissing the development of Asian capitals in resource-rich autocracies as nothing more than grand experiments in creating flashy images for powerful men is lazy scholarship. Nowhere else are the contrasts of local and other, rich and poor, and powerful and not powerful so starkly illustrated. Planners have a role in facilitating communication so that the needs and interests of the residents are incorporated into development plans for the future.

Notes

1 An early version of this chapter was drafted in collaboration with eight students from the Nazarbayev University Graduate School of Public Policy: Almas Akhmediya, Nargiza Chorieva, Kuanysh Kalachev, Alexandra Kogay, Aigerim Makenova, Ulpan Shegenova, Adilbek Sultanov, and Medet Yessimkhanov.
2 The notion that living in a particular physical space would have an impact on the psyche of the residents has been popular among planning theorists. However, well-meaning elites often do not understand the communities and societies they want to change well enough to make a positive impact (see for example, Jacobs, 1962).
3 This is a one-way communication to the people and others and lacks the beneficial elements encompassed in the latest versions of collaborative planning theory.
4 See: http://worldpopulationreview.com/countries/kazakhstan-population/
5 Five floors was the maximum that the Soviets would allow without elevators, so most such buildings in former Soviet states have five floors.
6 For the history of the college, see the website "The Polytechnic College of Astana,1994–2017. The history of the college" at: http://polytech.kz/istoriya/ (accessed 16 April 2018). Available in Kazakh or Russian.
7 Renting the first floor to businesses is a widespread modern design practice and is used on the left bank as well. Providing mixed uses and services in residential buildings reduces the need for transportation from home to work and for accessing basic needs.
8 There are a number of useful internet resources available. Строительная компания HighVill: http://highvill.kz/A (accessed 27 April 2018); Bazis-A, "On the Water-Green Boulevard Administrative-housing estate": http://en.bazis.kz/ our_objects/ready/item/na_vodnozelenom_bulvare/; (accessed 24 April 2018); Elitestroy, "The Nursaya Residential Cluster": www.elitstroy.kz/en/projects/ nursaya/ (accessed 24 April 2018); Bonita Engineering, "Residential complex Nursaya South quarter in Astana": http://bonita.kz/en/residential-complex-nursaia-south-quarter-in-astana/ (accessed 24 April 2018).
9 As one of the largest of the Soviet Republics, Kazakhstan had 1,410 USSR nuclear warheads stationed in its territory – one of the largest nuclear arsenals on earth at that time.
10 The impact of these vistas is somewhat less appreciated during the winter months when fewer people come to visit.
11 First snows come as early as September, and spring creeps in only in April. Typically temperatures are below freezing (as low as -50) for about six to seven months of the year.

References

Agger, Annika, and Eva Sorensen (2018). "Managing Collaborative Innovation in Public Bureaucracies." *Planning Theory* 17 (1): 53–73.
Brooks, Michael P. (2002). *Planning Theory for Practitioners.* London: Routledge.

Cohen, Jean-Louis (1992). *Le Corbusier and the Mystique of the USSR: Theories and Projects for Moscow*. Princeton, NJ: Princeton University Press.

Fishman, Robert (1977). *Urban Utopias in the Twentieth Century*. New York: Basic Books.

Geertz, Clifford (1983). *Centers, Kings and Charisma: Reflections on the Symbolics of Power*. New York: Basic Books.

Goodspeed, Robert (2016). "The Death and Life of Collaborative Planning Theory." *Urban Planning* 1 (4). http://doi.org/10.17645/up.v1i4.715.

Grabow, Stephen, and Allan Heskin (1973). "Foundations for a Radical Concept of Planning." *Journal of the American Institute of Planners* 39 (2): 106–114. https://doi.org/10.1080/01944367308977664.

Habermas, Jurgen (1962 trans 1989). *The Structural Transformation of the Public Sphere: An Inquiry Into a Category of Bourgeois Society*. Cambridge: Polity.

Healy, Patsy (1997). *Collaborative Planning: Shaping Places in Fragmented Societies*. Vancouver: University of British Columbia Press.

Howard, Ebenezer (1898). *To-morrow: A Peaceful Path to Real Reform* (Republished 1902 as *Garden Cities of To-morrow*). London: Swan Sonnenschein & Co., Ltd.

Innes, Judith E. (1995). "Planning Theory's Emerging Paradigm: Communicative Action and Interactive Practice." *Journal of Planning Education and Research* 14 (3): 183–189.

Jacobs, Jane (1962). *The Death and Life of Great American Cities*. New York: Random House.

Koch, Natalie (2018). *The Geopolitics of Spectacle: Space, Synecdoche, and the New Capitals of Asia*. Ithaca, NY: Cornell University Press.

Le Breton, Preston P., and Dale A. Henning (1961). *Planning Theory*. Upper Saddle River, NJ: Prentice Hall.

LeCorbusier (Charles-Edouard Jeanneret) (1929). *The City of To-morrow and Its Planning*. London: John Rodher Press.

Nazarbayev, Nursultan (2008). *The Kazakhstan Way*. Astana: Stacey International.

Norton, Bryan G. (2005). *Sustainability: A Philosophy of Adaptive Ecosystem Management*. Chicago, IL: University of Chicago Press.

Outram, Alan K., Alexei. Kasparov, Natalie A. Stear, Victor Varfolomeev, Emma Usmanova, and Richard P. Evershed (2012). "Patterns of Pastoralism in Later Bronze Age Kazakhstan: New Evidence From Faunal and Lipid Residue Analyses." *Journal of Archeological Science* 39 (7): 2424–2435.

Outram, Alan K., Natalie A. Stear, Alexei Kasparov, Emma Usmanova, Victor Varfolomeev, and Richard P. Evershed (2010). "Horses for the Dead: Funerary Foodways in Bronze Age Kazakhstan." *Antiquity* 85 (327): 116–128.

6 New Asian Statism

Toward an understanding of Asia's 21st-century urban transformation

Kris Hartley

Asia's late-20th-century economic surge has generated scholarly reflection about state-led growth amidst rapid globalization and domestic economic and political liberalization. Within this frame, a more focused literature has examined Asian cities as platforms of interaction between two contradictory forces: central planning and global capital (Carroll, 2017; Carroll et al., 2019; Shatkin, 2019; Taşan-Kok and Baeten, 2011). This bi-polarity informs studies that view cities as a product of negotiations and collaborations between states and markets. However, this approach may be too narrow to describe the complex dynamics currently shaping Asia's urban growth. Amidst halting democratization and devolutionary reforms, citizens are playing an increasingly influential role in policymaking about issues like environmental management, urban revitalization, and the protection of vernacular architectural heritage. Indeed, these movements have taken a critical view of elite political and economic cronyism that arguably characterizes Asia's 20th-century model of national developmentalism – with government intervention in the economy deemed "undemocratic" (Park et al., 2012: 17). This trend is poised to gather momentum as Asia's developmental states (the four Asian Tigers: Hong Kong, Singapore, South Korea, and Taiwan), now decades into economic restructuring, not only experience the democratizing pressures that accompany long-term income growth and socio-economic mobility but also must react to changing market dynamics regarding innovation and knowledge economies (Hartley et al., 2018). The purpose of this chapter is to introduce and discuss a framework that serves as an original descriptive tool for more deeply probing the conceptual and practical implications of these dynamics. Using the "RICE" framework, based on the concepts of resilience, innovation, and civic enterprise, the chapter endeavors to bring clarity to Asia's disruptive collision involving market liberalization, developmentalism, and an emergent popular self-determinism. In so doing, the chapter and framework also articulate research frontiers related to the study of Asian cities in the 21st century.

Conceptualizing developmental models in the literature

To understand trends impacting Asia's urban growth, it is necessary first to understand the emerging forces shaping national development. This chapter introduces the notion of "New Asian Statism" to conceptualize the political-economic context in which 21st-century Asian urbanism materializes. Specifically, it describes a governance regime in which three sectors (state, market, and society) are being opportunistically seen by policymakers as mutually supportive facilitators of urban development. Within this context, the more applied role of the RICE framework is to operationalize the interdependent roles of these three actors, providing a descriptive template for understanding how New Asian Statism is institutionalized. The actors each play a unique role. The state facilitates the functioning of institutions and infrastructure, the efficient and effective coordination of government activities, and the provision for general social welfare. The first two of these tasks accord with the prevailing mandates of the new public management paradigm (see Cheung and Scott, 2003 for an overview of such paradigms in Asia), while the third varies in degree across nations based on political appetite for government intervention. The private sector – as the central player in markets – channels capital toward productive ends to serve consumers, generate value, and accumulate economic gains. Manifestations of this state–market dichotomy in the context of Asia's developmental and socio-cultural legacies reveal tensions between hierarchical models of public-organizational governance and efficiency-based managerialism (Jingjit and Fotaki, 2010). To economic growth models long dominated by the state–market dialectic, New Asian Statism adds non-corporate civil society (hereafter "civil society"), a third-wave phenomenon copiously addressed in literature about Asia's political economy (Alagappa, 2004; Brook and Frolic, 1997; Douglass and Friedmann, 1998; Haynes, 2013; Keane, 2013; Rodan, 2013; Roniger and Güneş-Ayata, 1994). As neoliberalism continues to merge with developmentalism, state power devolves and public–private partnerships emerge (Hackworth, 2007; Park et al., 2012). New Asian Statism describes a regime of quasi-neoliberalism in which non-corporate civil society plays a greater role in governance, policymaking, and public service delivery.

The role of the state and markets in economic development is well-studied and summarized, needing no further acknowledgment in this chapter. However, a growing literature about the emerging role of civil society deserves mention for its relevance to the chapter's assumption about increased balance and collaboration among all sectors. The role of civil society in urban growth has been variously explored in the literature. Woolcock (1998) introduces a social capital framework that examines the interplay between top-down and bottom-up approaches to development. His dimensions of analysis include state–society relations ("synergy") and corporate coherence and capacity ("organizational integrity"). While this approach is valuable both for its classification of states (collapsed, weak, rogue, and developmental) and for its effort to capture a broad sweep of regime types, the implied state–society duality succumbs to a conceptual bi-polarity that largely overlooks the contributions of non-corporate and non-market actors. While the structures and processes of urban governments are relevant to the institutional elements of the RICE framework, the behaviors that occur within those structures – at both the organizational and individual levels – call for the integration of scholarship about urban development with that of entrepreneurial governance.

Laden with meaning in both the Western academic literature and popular media, entrepreneurship is a variously applied concept that typically refers to the resourceful and opportunistic activities of individuals in a commercial setting. However, entrepreneurship can be seen as both a public sector and a civil society behavior. From the perspective of public policy, entrepreneurship has received recent but incomplete scholarly attention, typically in service only to studies about individual political or managerial agency within the context of policy change. For example, the multiple streams framework (Kingdon and Thurber, 1984), punctuated equilibrium theory (Baumgartner and Jones, 1993), and advocacy coalition framework (Sabatier, 1999) describe in various ways the enterprising efforts of individuals as policy entrepreneurs and issue-driven groups as advocates of policy agendas. Among studies focusing on individuals are Seifert's (2014) study of policy entrepreneurs in the parliaments of Europe and Asia and Capano's (2009) study of leadership in policy change. According to Audretsch and Link (2012), there has been little conceptual convergence of frameworks that explain the role of entrepreneurship in a broader developmental sense. Examining the treatment of entrepreneurship and innovation within three economic paradigms (neoclassical, Keynesian, and Schumpeterian), Audretsch and Link insist that related policy is ambiguous and scholarship lacking in consensus.

Finally, in examining entrepreneurship it is necessary to acknowledge the dominance of Western conceptualizations of the term and to consider the possibility of its uniquely Asian embodiment. One common lens for examining differences in perceptions about entrepreneurship between Western and Asian settings is the idea of willingness to accept risk (higher in the former) and the stigmatization of business failure (higher in the latter) (Begley and Tan, 2001). In a study comparing the motivation behind entrepreneurial behavior in Hong Kong and Singapore, Ang and Hong (2000) find risk-taking, persistence, and self-determinism to be explanatory factors. More recently, Smith and Kaminishi (2019) argue that differences in entrepreneurial behaviors between Western and Asian contexts may not only be overstated but also biased by Western-based analytical frames and simplistic cultural dichotomies. Given the geographical convergence of ideas and models about business and entrepreneurship at a general level, this chapter's arguments are built largely on understandings about entrepreneurship as developed in the academic literature; it acknowledges that this literature has a Western perceptual bias.

The framework introduced in this chapter invokes the concept of civic enterprise (Hartley, 2018), extending firm-based entrepreneurship models (e.g., that proposed by Miles et al., 2005) in a way that stimulates discussions about entrepreneurship as a collaborative multi-sectoral behavior. This reading of entrepreneurship blends public and private agency in the context of planning and implementing development strategies. Multi-sectoral collaboration has already been explored as a phenomenon in which interests are dominated by a particular sector. For example, Swyngedouw (2005) explores the notion of governance-beyond-the-state, arguing that the evolution from government to governance has cloaked market interests in "socially innovative figures of horizontally organized stakeholder arrangements" (ibid.: 2003). Likewise, Gerometta et al. (2005) build on studies of civil society in urban governance to argue that the erosion of the welfare state elevates the importance of entrepreneurial community organizing and the so-called third sector (the sector comprising organizations that are neither public nor for-profit and that operate in the social enterprise, civic, and charity realms). Reading the struggles of civil society through concepts of inequality and exclusion, the authors argue that social innovation is possible only when marginalized groups are mobilized and included in a pluralistic governance process. Studies of public sector entrepreneurship have also explored the behavior of agents within policy systems; these include initiative and innovation among local officials and the role of entrepreneurship in governance efficiency (Oakerson and Parks, 1988), government–firm relations and entrepreneurship as enablers of innovation (Klein et al., 2010), ecological entrepreneurship networks to address sustainable agricultural practices (Marsden and Smith, 2005), and public entrepreneurs as teams that transform systems from within (Bernier and Hafsi, 2007). Discussions about entrepreneurship in the Asian context, particularly among the Asian Tigers, must account for the strong hierarchical culture of the state as a whole and its subsidiary agencies.

Many studies take an unduly narrow view of the scope and power of public entrepreneurship, confining it to internal (e.g., process and systemic) reforms and ignoring its potential role in external initiatives like economic development. The concept of collaborative governance can be the vehicle through which private sector-focused discussions about entrepreneurship engage the policy sciences literature. The concept has a mature and somewhat stagnant literature in public administration, with studies addressing the role of citizens as governance participants (Vigoda, 2002) and the emerging necessity of new skill-sets for public managers (Huxham and Vangen, 2013; Weber and Khademian, 2008). Innes and Booher (2003) argue that collaborative governance is a useful mechanism to leverage public and private sector capacity where agencies lack power and jurisdiction. This chapter recognizes the role of civic enterprise in collaborative urban and regional development, not only in practical application but also as an emerging theoretical paradigm. Indeed, the influence of neoliberalism on cities and dynamics inherent to the developmental state itself are broadening the role of non-government sectors and may transform the "developmental city" into an "entrepreneurial city" (Park et al., 2012). At the same time, insights from literature about civil society in the Western context should be treated with caution, as the role of civil society and its evolution by Western standards is considerably divergent from Asian contexts. Only recently has a robust civil society – as defined by these Western standards – begun to emerge in Asia to the degree that its potential to counterbalance statism and corporatism (and their collaborative models) can be seriously discussed.

This chapter's line of argument about the RICE framework makes its primary contribution at the intersection of literatures about urban and regional governance (with reference to institutional structure), policy development (process), and entrepreneurship (behavior). As such, the framework and ideas behind it extend the literature in several ways. First, it contributes to understandings about how multi-sector and intergovernmental models for the delivery of public goods and infrastructure can support growth and resilience at the urban and regional scale. Second, it establishes the basis for empirical studies about the under-explored topic of creative and innovative policymaking in rapidly developing cities and regions. Finally, it illustrates how the agency of governance units, insofar as they are granted autonomy, combines with that of civil society in localized development initiatives, embodying the concept of civic enterprise.

Use of frameworks in the literature

In systematizing inquiry and facilitating cross-case comparison of institutional and related factors, scholars have used frameworks and their derivatives to identify variables, relationships, and testable hypotheses. Ostrom (2011) argues that the interchangeable use of the terms "framework", "theory", and "model" adds confusion to scholarly analysis. In what she describes as a nested structure, frameworks provide a general set of variables and a meta-theoretical language, theories make testable assumptions about the relevance of specific framework elements and their variables, and models identify relationships among particular variables. Healey (2006) examines urban governance frameworks and the many dimensions that define them, including actors, networks, structures, and processes. Her study of the relationship between structures and individual agency is pertinent to the applications of resilience (structure) and entrepreneurship (behavior) as described in the previous section. The literature boasts abundant coverage of the individual roles of resilience, innovation, and citizen entrepreneurship (conceptualized in this chapter as civic enterprise) in economic development. Aside from the popular multiple streams, advocacy coalition, and punctuated equilibrium frameworks, others receiving attention in policy process and change research are Ostrom's (1985) Institutional Analysis and Development (IAD) framework and her Socio-ecological Systems (SES) framework (Anderies et al., 2004) and Schmid's (2008) Situation, Structure, Performance (SSP) framework.

Extending the literature's long-time focus on institutions as a determinant of governance quality and developmental outcomes, Hall and Taylor (1996) propose three "new institutionalisms" (rational choice, sociological, and historical) to address a broad range of change dynamics relevant to the policy process and governance structures. Pierre (1999) likewise examines institutional dynamics between nation-states and localities, proposing a four-type model of governance: managerial, corporatist, pro-growth, and welfare. His study considers national-level conditions ("external dimensions") in analyses of urban governance, and his use of participants, objectives, instruments, and outcomes provides an ordered analytical framework. However, the role of national context as distinct from the urban environment is incidental and under-conceptualized, with both contexts pooled into his four governance types. This complicates application of his model to cross-national analysis where one analytical context is distinct from another (e.g., national versus urban). Although some elements relevant to national-level analysis are appropriate to urban and regional levels, the peculiarities of problems faced by cities – practical challenges as well as governance constraints – deserve a uniquely tailored framework. One example is Hartley's (2017) transboundary governance framework for water management in China's Pearl River Delta Region, accounting for regional governance conditions while considering the individual interests of sub-regional jurisdictions and Hong Kong's unique context as a separate governance "system".

When examining the role of actors in urban governance, particularly as classified across sector types, the literature on policy sub-systems (Howlett et al., 1995) is helpful. Frameworks incorporating policy sub-systems have been utilized by studies of network–outcome dialectics (Marsh and Smith, 2000), the relationship between citizen advocacy groups and legislators (Berry, 1999), interactions in special policy arenas (Freeman, 1965), policy networks as social relationships among actors (Klijn, 1996), and policy monopolies through structures supported by "powerful ideas" (Baumgartner and Jones, 1993). In spite of the many efforts to conceptualize sub-systems, McCool (1998) critiques related frameworks for having limited validity in describing real-world situations, difficulty in establishing causality, and the misfortune of being poorly applied by scholars. Despite the fact that the sub-systems perspective still has relevance in the current generation of governance literature, the literature exploring and refining the concept as a methodological tool appears to be approaching maturity within current understandings of the topic, giving way to more recent curiosities in the field of policy studies such as capacity (Wu et al., 2015), regimes (Howlett, 2009), and tools and instruments (Howlett et al., 2015). Furthermore, the context in which policies are made has also come into increasing analytical focus, including a recent revival of the concept of wicked problems and the struggle of public policies to address them, as evidenced by special issues about the topic in the journals *Policy and Society* (Termeer et al., 2019) and *Policy Design and Practice* (Hartley et al., 2019). Despite the broad sweep of policy and governance studies introducing analytical and conceptual frameworks, no studies or frameworks appear to have combined resilience, innovation, and civic enterprise (elements of New Asian Statism) into an internally consistent framework relevant at the sub-national level.

The RICE framework

The RICE framework operationalizes New Asian Statism by examining three abstractions (structure, process, and behavior) that define urban and regional governance within the context of social, economic, and political liberalization. The definition of each application is specific to this framework. Resilience is the structural capacity of governance institutions to adapt to exogenous change, particularly concerning institutional characteristics such as hierarchy, jurisdiction, and autonomy. The efficacy of structural design can be exhibited in a variety of ways, such as the speed of administrative reforms, the ability to capture economic opportunities, and the responsiveness of governments to situational threats. Given that resilience is the capacity to adapt or evolve, high levels of resilience would seem to correlate in successful situations with high levels of innovation. With resilience a characteristic of any system having high adaptive potential, it can thus be seen as an "emergent" or flexible property operating at the edges or outside of what can be controlled by policy. According to Kuecker and Hall (2011: 25), "When systems reach the bifurcation point [point of divergence at which a system either renews itself or tips into collapse], the innovations necessary for emergence into an adaptive, self-reproducing system are often discovered or implemented".

Innovation refers to creative processes within government and is distinguished from private sector innovation, which has been examined by many studies of knowledge economies, economic development, agglomeration and clustering, and other topics related to urban growth. Public sector innovation can include creative approaches to policy development and inventive reforms to administrative procedures. Civic enterprise is entrepreneurial behavior arising from multi-sectoral collaboration engaging government, private sector, and non-market civil society (e.g., advocacy groups, non-profit organizations, and individuals). This behavior can be applied to a variety of initiatives including social enterprise and entrepreneurship and more generally in policy domains like urban development and environmental management.

While there is, in general, a theoretical consensus regarding the definition and function of government as opposed to that of the private sector, civil society has been more variously conceptualized. For example, Swyngedouw (2005: 1996) offers a struggle-laden conceptualization of civil society as: "the pivotal terrain from which social transformative and innovative action emerges and where social power relations are contested and struggled over". Similar conceptualizations of civil society, for example that by Kuecker (2004) in a study of political movements in Latin America, focus on its emergence as a collective action phenomenon in response to a state emptied of its apparatus and capabilities by neoliberalism. The approach to civil society in the RICE framework differs from that of Swyngedouw, Kuecker, and others in two ways. First, it recognizes the collaborative realm as the arena in which innovation takes place. The term "civic enterprise" encompasses the intentionally complementary efforts of the state, market, and civil society within the urban context. Second, it does not focus on power struggles of the Marxian or neo-Gramscian type. This chapter's examination of civil society as a collaborative agent does not deny the validity of power struggles or the value of understanding them (particularly in the context of civil society as a front of resistance against neoliberalism or statist authoritarianism), but the concept of civic enterprise is conceptually limited in order to focus the analysis on operational and administrative mandates of urban growth. As such, the concept, for this framework's purpose, is not necessarily rooted in grievance but may help to problematize understandings about the role of neoliberalism in the developmental state.

The RICE framework's three applications focus on the interactions of interventionist governance and entrepreneurial activity in urban growth (whether by policy design or by assertion of market interests); the applications are therefore particularly relevant to Asia in capturing the economic and social contexts of liberalizing developmental states (examples of which can be found in Park et al., 2012). While it may be applicable beyond Asia, the intention of the framework is to focus on the rapidly developing countries of Southeast Asia and the mature economies of East Asia. The latter are restructuring toward knowledge and service industries and the former from agriculture and resource extraction to manufacturing or from low value-added to higher value-added manufacturing. In both case types, the legacy of economic central planning is being tested by external structural forces, with the circumstantial mandate of globalization and its policy bedfellow neoliberalism requiring modest to significant reforms in governance amidst a shrinking state; this ultimately leads to what this chapter has already described as New Asian Statism.

The RICE box (Figure 6.1) is a representation of how the three applications (as parameters) of the framework combine to yield a taxonomy of governance paradigms. For expediency, each application is measured on a low–high scale; nevertheless, the model acknowledges that there is more subtlety in the degree to which each application is realized. The purpose of the RICE box is to specify how New Asian Statism, the Asian embodiment of liberalizing developmentalism, is situated within a larger panoply of governance paradigms. The term "liberalizing" in this context refers to movement toward more open and competitive systems within a nation's economy, politics, and society – whether through policy intentionality (a legacy of "statism") or through the more organic (and "new") forces driving markets and civic enterprise. The RICE box also enhances the external

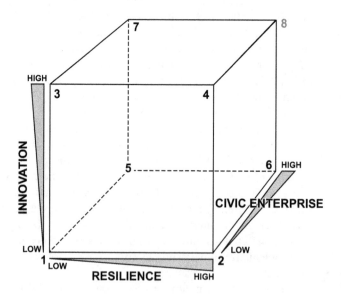

Figure 6.1 The RICE box

Table 6.1 Proposed taxonomy of national governance types emerging from the RICE box

Point in box	Paradigm Label	Resilience (Structure)	Innovation (Process)	Civic Enterprise (Behavior)
1	Failed dictatorships	Low	Low	Low
2	Entrenched dictatorships	Medium	Low	Low
3	Post-Communist transition states	Low	High	Low but growing
4	Developmental authoritarian states	Mostly high	High	Low
5	Failed anarchic states	Low	Low	High
6	Western welfare states	High	Medium	High
7	Western capitalist states	Mostly low	High	High
8	Liberalizing developmental states (New Asian Statism)	High	Mostly high	Medium and growing

validity of New Asian Statism as a conceptual tool by enabling the identification of alternative governance paradigms beyond New Asian Statism, as understood through differing parameter settings. In addition to establishing the conceptual basis and theoretical justification of the RICE framework, the RICE box is more broadly applicable and has descriptive power in a variety of governance contexts. Its relevance therefore extends beyond the confines of this chapter.

Table 6.1 extends the RICE box to an analytical plateau, building on Woolcock's four classifications of states cited previously in this chapter's literature review. Despite its use of a low–high continuum, the box's description of each application of the RICE framework is not normative or necessarily value-laden. For example, high resilience may not necessarily be a desirable characteristic if it extends from the effects of regime entrenchment; systemic adaptability can enable the perpetuation of malevolent government practices and elite policy capture by maintaining or improving performance on rudimentary sources of political legitimacy like economic growth. Nevertheless, the framework implies that resilience – regardless of the ends it serves – is necessary for flexible urban economic governance amidst systemic turbulence and uncertainty. Governance paradigms with high levels of innovation employ outward-looking processes that support growth-oriented policies; normative judgments vary depending on perspectives about the distributional and ethical implications of globalization.

Toward a 21st-century research agenda for Asian cities

The concluding section of this chapter briefly describes the applicability of the RICE framework to the study of the local–national policy dialectic and closes with a call for more attention to complex policy problems confronting urban governments. The chapter's analytical purpose in situating urban governance within a national context is twofold: to methodically account for exogenous factors influencing urban governance and to enhance the RICE framework's external validity. First, the scope, function, and efficacy of sub-national governments are in part a product of national-level governance conditions. While there is a variety of approaches to and degrees of decentralization and devolution across Asia, in most cases national governments retain a degree of control that can be described as anywhere from moderate to dominant. The high levels of federalization seen in some Western states (e.g., Switzerland) have thus far failed to gain credibility in Asia, despite recent democratizing pressures. Furthermore, national governments have fiscal and borrowing authority for many of the types of infrastructure investments that determine urban competitiveness (in contexts, unlike Singapore, where national and urban government jurisdictions are not coterminous). The second purpose for considering national conditions in studying cities and regions is to generate control variables that account for national contexts; this allows urban governments to be benchmarked against regional and global peers while holding common explanatory factors constant.

The broader research program proposed in this chapter intends to contribute to the dialogue among scholars, practitioners, and students about the design of policy systems, methods for analyzing them, and innovative approaches to reforming them. This call for additional research concludes with the connection between the RICE framework and existing work about flexible governance for economic growth. The concept of flexible economic opportunism is introduced by Hartley (2014) as:

> a governance model for theory and practice that emphasizes adaptability and pragmatism over ideology and patronage. It advocates timely accommodation of global economic trends, enabled by a structural orientation towards economic competitiveness and policy pragmatism. The model's fundamental proposition is that supportive institutional and administrative conditions can nurture an environment where evidence guides policy and innovation drives governance. As such, flexible economic opportunism is not a belief system or a normative philosophy, but a systemic architecture that most efficiently accommodates the will of the state – as expressed through any number of different political systems – while maximizing competitive potential.
>
> (Hartley, 2014: 1)

The RICE framework adds a methodological element to urban and regional applications of flexible economic opportunism, in particular the institutional and administrative conditions that enable evidence-based policy. While flexible economic opportunism primarily concerns economic growth and global competitiveness at the national level, its principal tenets (pragmatism and alignment of institutional and administrative characteristics) can inform studies about urban and regional governance using the RICE framework's analytical approach. Further, the framework and flexible economic opportunism share a broad ambition to be applicable across governance regime types. Resilience, innovation, and civic enterprise can be pursued or simply enabled by urban and regional governments within a broad array of political systems, including "light" authoritarian and one-party-dominant states (e.g., Singapore or China), liberalizing developmental states (South Korea), and liberal "Western-style" democracies (Sweden). On a cautionary note, however, the difficulty of realizing the combination of elements in the RICE framework through policy practice should not be underestimated; thornier questions about equity, sustainability, and socio-economic marginalization are politically negotiated, and this process varies in effectiveness and democratic representativeness across regime types. Future research should therefore consider the extent to which elements of the framework come together by intention or serendipity and which types of political systems facilitate or enable that convergence.

The shift in capital and production to Asia and to rapidly developing countries, along with Asia's continued emergence as a center not only for production but also for the generation and funding of new ideas, is a significant moment in global history. Nevertheless, at this time there also appears to be a mismatch between theory and practice across three nascent tensions that will arguably define Asia's 21st-century growth: an enterprising and footloose global private sector, a creative civil society yearning for quality of life and a voice in governance, and governments trapped between the comfortable legacy of central planning on the one hand and the unpredictable realm of economic opportunity and existential threats on the other. In addressing this emerging New Asian Statism, the RICE framework represents a systematic and internally coherent analytical approach to understand how urban governments can operate under evolving and often turbulent circumstances. Both the RICE framework and flexible economic opportunism are an effort to gain theoretical purchase on the evolution of governance models (structures, processes, and behaviors) in an age of global instability and disruption precipitated by interconnected, synchronous, and intractable crises (Hartley et al., 2019). The speed of adaptability in governance design and function typically lags behind rapidly morphing global trends, generating urgency for flexible governance models that are at once actionable, grounded in theoretical rigor, and calibrated both to what is known and what cannot be easily predicted.

In closing, it is helpful to situate the argument of this chapter within the broader sweep of neoliberalism and its ability or otherwise to address the aforementioned systemic crises. New Asian Statism as an emerging phenomenon stands at the tense front between government and private sector pre-eminence. As the term "developmental" implies intentional movement toward development, the term "liberalizing" implies movement toward free markets, if not also toward political openness and contestability. However, the logical destination is not necessarily a full apotheosis of the private sector in shaping human affairs, nor does the term "statism" imply that all neoliberal transformation occurs at the blessing or planning of the state. Rather, the replication of neoliberal ideologies and institutions both defines and is defined by New Asian Statism in an endogenous and dialectical process. Indeed, neoliberalism creates favorable conditions for elements of the RICE framework (resilience, innovation, and civic enterprise). For example, Joseph (2013: 38) argues that resilience "is best understood as a neoliberal form of governmentality that places emphasis on individual adaptability". The notion of resilience – and indeed innovation and civic enterprise as well – is not incompatible with Hayekian-inspired neoliberal constructs. Elements of the RICE framework (especially civic enterprise) describe collective action and community mobilization within a public commons; it is the latter that neoliberalism seeks to replace with market-based systems. Future work should thus examine the extent to which urban issues (and, beyond that, global crises and wicked problems) can be effectively managed by statism or neoliberalism as rusty tools – or by New Asian Statism as either an emergent hybrid of the two or a unique third way.

References

Alagappa, Muthiah (Ed.) (2004). *Civil Society and Political Change in Asia: Expanding and Contracting Democratic Space.* Stanford, CA: Stanford University Press.

Anderies, John M., Marco A. Janssen, and Elinor Ostrom (2004). "A Framework to Analyze the Robustness of Social-Ecological Systems From an Institutional Perspective." *Ecology and Society* 9 (1): 18. www.ecologyandsociety.org/vol9/iss1/art18/.

Ang, Swee Hoon, and Don G.P. Hong (2000). "Entrepreneurial Spirit Among East Asian Chinese." *Thunderbird International Business Review* 42 (3): 285–309.

Audretsch, David B., and Albert N. Link (2012). "Entrepreneurship and Innovation: Public Policy Frameworks." *The Journal of Technology Transfer* 37 (1): 1–17.

Baumgartner, Frank R., and Bryan D. Jones (1993). *Agendas and Instability in American Politics.* Chicago, IL: University of Chicago Press.

Begley, T.M., and W.L. Tan (2001). "The Socio-cultural Environment for Entrepreneurship: A Comparison Between East Asian and Anglo-Saxon Countries." *Journal of International Business Studies* 32 (3): 537–553.

Bernier, Luc, and Taïeb Hafsi (2007). "The Changing Nature of Public Entrepreneurship." *Public Administration Review* 67 (3): 488–503.

Berry, Jeffrey M. (1999). *The New Liberalism: The Rising Power of Citizen Groups.* Washington, DC: Brookings Institution Press.

Brook, Timothy, and B. Michael Frolic (Eds.) (1997). *Civil Society in China.* Armonk, NY: M.E. Sharpe.

Capano, Giliberto (2009). "Political Change and Policy Change: Some Notes on the Role of Leadership as a Theoretical and Empirical Problem." Paper presented at the XXI IPSA World Congress of Political Science, 12–16 September.

Carroll, Toby (2017). "Capitalism, Contradiction and the Onward March of Variegated Neoliberalism in Southeast Asia." In *The Political Economy of Emerging Markets*, edited by Richard Westra, 135–158. London and New York: Routledge.

Carroll, Toby, Judith Clifton, and Darryl S.L. Jarvis (2019). "Power, Leverage and Marketization: The Diffusion of Neoliberalism From North to South and Back Again." *Globalizations* 16 (6): 771–777.

Cheung, Anthony B.L., and Ian Scott (2003). "Governance and Public Sector Reforms in Asia: Paradigms, Paradoxes and Dilemmas." In *Governance and Public Sector Reform in Asia: Paradigm Shifts or Business as Usual?*, edited by Anthony B.L. Cheung and Ian Scott, 1–24. London and New York: Routledge.

Douglass, Mike, and John Friedmann (Eds.) (1998). *Cities for Citizens: Planning and the Rise of Civil Society in a Global Age.* Hoboken, NJ: John Wiley & Sons.

Freeman, John Leiper (1965). *The Political Process: Executive Bureau – Legislative Committee Relations.* New York: Random House.

Gerometta, Julia, Hartmut Haussermann, and Giulia Longo (2005). "Social Innovation and Civil Society in Urban Governance: Strategies for an Inclusive City." *Urban Studies* 42 (11): 2007–2021.

Hackworth, Jason (2007). *The Neoliberal City: Governance, Ideology, and Development in American Urbanism.* Ithaca, NY: Cornell University Press.

Hall, Peter A., and Rosemary C.R. Taylor (1996). "Political Science and the Three New Institutionalisms." *Political Studies* 44 (5): 936–957.

Hartley, Kris (2014). *Can Government Think? Flexible Economic Opportunism and the Pursuit of Global Competitiveness.* New York: Routledge.

Hartley, Kris (2017). "Environmental Resilience and Intergovernmental Collaboration in the Pearl River Delta." *International Journal of Water Resources Development* 34 (4): 525–546.

Hartley, Kris (2018). "Cultural Policy and Collaboration in Seoul's Mullae Art District." *Geoforum* 97: 177–188.

Hartley, Kris, Glen Kuecker, and Jun Jie Woo (2019). "Practicing Public Policy in an Age of Disruption." *Policy Design and Practice* 2 (2): 163–181.

Hartley, Kris, Jun Jie Woo, and Sun Kyo Chung (2018). "Urban Innovation Policy in the Post-developmental Era: Lessons From Singapore and Seoul." *Asia & the Pacific Policy Studies* 5 (3): 599–614.

Haynes, Jeffrey (2013). *Democracy and Civil Society in the Third World: Politics and New Political Movements.* Hoboken, NJ: John Wiley & Sons.

Healey, Patricia (2006). *Urban Complexity and Spatial Strategies: Towards a Relational Planning for Our Times.* London and New York: Routledge.

Howlett, Michael (2009). "Governance Modes, Policy Regimes and Operational Plans: A Multi-level Nested Model of Policy Instrument Choice and Policy Design." *Policy Sciences* 42 (1): 73–89.

Howlett, Michael, I. Mukherjee, and J.J. Woo (2015). "From Tools to Toolkits in Policy Design Studies: The New Design Orientation Towards Policy Formulation Research." *Policy & Politics* 43 (2): 291–311.

Howlett, Michael, Michael Ramesh, and Anthony Perl (1995). *Studying Public Policy: Policy Cycles and Policy Subsystems.* Cambridge: Cambridge University Press.

Huxham, Chris, and Siv Vangen (2013). *Managing to Collaborate: The Theory and Practice of Collaborative Advantage.* London and New York: Routledge.

Innes, Judith E., and David E. Booher (2003). "The Impact of Collaborative Planning on Governance Capacity." Berkeley, CA: Institute of Urban and Regional Development, University of California.

Jingjit, Rutaichanok, and Marianna Fotaki (2010). "Confucian Ethics and the Limited Impact of the New Public Management Reform in Thailand." *Journal of Business Ethics* 97 (1): 61–73.

Joseph, Jonathan (2013). "Resilience as Embedded Neoliberalism: A Governmentality Approach." *Resilience* 1 (1): 38–52.

Keane, John (2013). *Civil Society: Old Images, New Visions.* Hoboken, NJ: John Wiley & Sons.

Kingdon, John W., and James A. Thurber (1984). *Agendas, Alternatives, and Public Policies.* Boston, MA: Little, Brown and Company.

Klein, Peter G., Joseph T. Mahoney, Anita M. McGahan, and Christos N. Pitelis (2010). "Toward a Theory of Public Entrepreneurship." *European Management Review* 7 (1): 1–15.

Klijn, Erik-Hans (1996). "Analyzing and Managing Policy Processes in Complex Networks: A Theoretical Examination of the Concept Policy Network and Its Problems." *Administration & Society* 28 (1): 90–119.

Kuecker, Glen D. (2004). "Latin American Resistance Movements in the Time of the Posts." *History Compass* 2 (1). https://doi.org/10.1111/j.1478-0542.2004.00126.x.

Kuecker, Glen D., and T.D. Hall (2011). "Resilience and Community in the Age of World-system Collapse." *Nature and Culture* 6 (1): 18–40.

Marsden, Terry, and Everard Smith (2005). "Ecological Entrepreneurship: Sustainable Development in Local Communities Through Quality Food Production and Local Branding." *Geoforum* 36 (4): 440–451.

Marsh, David, and Martin Smith (2000). "Understanding Policy Networks: Towards a Dialectical Approach." *Political Studies* 48 (1): 4–21.

McCool, Daniel (1998). "The Subsystem Family of Concepts: A Critique and a Proposal." *Political Research Quarterly* 51 (2): 551–570.

Miles, Raymond E., Grant Miles, and Charles Curtis Snow (2005). *Collaborative Entrepreneurship: How Communities of Networked Firms Use Continuous Innovation to Create Economic Wealth*. Stanford, CA: Stanford University Press.

Oakerson, Ronald J., and Roger B. Parks (1988). "Citizen Voice and Public Entrepreneurship: The Organizational Dynamic of a Complex Metropolitan County." *Publius: The Journal of Federalism* 18 (4): 91–112.

Ostrom, Elinor (1985). "Formulating the Elements of Institutional Analysis." Paper presented at Workshop in Political Theory and Policy Analysis, Indiana University, Bloomington.

Ostrom, Elinor (2011). "Background on the Institutional Analysis and Development Framework." *Policy Studies Journal* 39 (1): 7–27.

Park, B., R.C. Hill, and A. Saito (Eds.) (2012). *Locating Neoliberalism in East Asia*. Chichester: Wiley-Blackwell.

Pierre, Jon (1999). "Models of Urban Governance: The Institutional Dimension of Urban Politics." *Urban Affairs Review* 34 (3): 372–396.

Rodan, Garry (Ed.) (2013). *Political Oppositions in Industrialising Asia*. London and New York: Routledge.

Roniger, Luis, and Ayşe Güneş-Ayata (Eds.) (1994). *Democracy, Clientelism, and Civil Society*. Boulder, CO: Lynne Rienner Publishers.

Sabatier, Paul A. (1999). *Theories of the Policy Process*. Boulder, CO: Westview Press.

Schmid, A. Allan (2008). *Conflict and Cooperation: Institutional and Behavioral Economics*. Hoboken, NJ: John Wiley & Sons.

Seifert, Jan (2014). *Policy Change and Legislative Policy Entrepreneurship*. Singapore: Lee Kuan Yew School of Public Policy.

Shatkin, Gavin (2019). "The Planning of Asia's Mega-conurbations: Contradiction and Contestation in Extended Urbanization." *International Planning Studies* 24 (1): 68–80.

Smith, Andrew, and Miriam Kaminishi (2020). "Confucian Entrepreneurship: Towards a Genealogy of a Conceptual Tool." *Journal of Management Studies* 57 (1) 25–56. https://doi.org/10.1111/joms.12439.

Swyngedouw, Erik (2005). "Governance Innovation and the Citizen: The Janus Face of Governance-beyond-the-State." *Urban Studies* 42 (11): 1991–2006.

Taşan-Kok, Tuna, and Guy Baeten (Eds.) (2011). *Contradictions of Neoliberal Planning: Cities, Policies, and Politics*. Dordrecht: Springer Science & Business Media.

Termeer, Catrien J.A.M., Art Dewulf, and Robbert Biesbroek (2019). "A Critical Assessment of the Wicked Problem Concept: Relevance and Usefulness for Policy Science and Practice." *Policy and Society* 38 (2): 167–179.

Vigoda, Eran (2002). "From Responsiveness to Collaboration: Governance, Citizens, and the Next Generation of Public Administration." *Public Administration Review* 62 (5): 527–540.

Weber, Edward, and Anne M. Khademian (2008). "Managing Collaborative Processes: Common Practices, Uncommon Circumstances." *Administration & Society* 40 (5): 431–464.

Woolcock, Michael (1998). "Social Capital and Economic Development: Toward a Theoretical Synthesis and Policy Framework." *Theory and Society* 27 (2): 151–208.

Wu, Xun, M. Ramesh, and Michael P. Howlett (2015). "Policy Capacity: A Conceptual Framework for Understanding Policy Competences and Capabilities." *Policy and Society* 34 (3–4): 165–171.

Part 2
Delivering public value

7 Realization of universal health coverage through social health insurance expansion

An appraisal of policy capacity in China and Indonesia

Si Ying Tan and Wei Yang

Introduction

Universal health coverage (UHC) is one of the most prioritized policy goals for many developing countries aiming to fast-track their social development (Hsiao and Shaw, 2007). Within the context of the expansion of smart cities across the world, UHC has been touted as one of the key strategies in the smart cities action plan (Centre for Liveable Cities, 2018). In India, for instance, there has been a call to improve and transform the health system so that it can become more responsive and more efficient not just in serving the health needs of the entire population but also in realizing its socio-economic potential to boost the medical tourism industry in the country (Reddy, 2015). One of the biggest financing instruments leveraged to achieve UHC is the aggressive expansion of social health insurance (SHI). SHI expansion is seen as instrumental as it enables governments to achieve basic health policy objectives of widening health coverage but also to strengthen their political support (Greer and Méndez, 2015). Based on the principle of population risk-pooling and either contributory or subsidized financing mechanisms, SHI can be either mandatory or voluntary (Hsiao and Shaw, 2007). For formal sector employees, SHI financing involves employers and employees each paying a certain percentage of contributions. In developing countries with a larger proportion of informal sector workers, government subsidies often complement voluntary contributions for the risk-pooling mechanism to work effectively (ibid.).

This chapter aims to examine the policy capacity of two of the largest and most populous developing countries in the world – Indonesia and China – and to analyze the degree to which different domains of policy capacity are critical in achieving UHC through the expansion of SHI programs in the two countries. Early this century, both Indonesia and China joined the bandwagon of setting UHC as a health policy target by introducing two of the largest state-controlled SHI schemes in the world. Governments from both countries were ambitious in expanding the coverage of their SHI programs to the entire population in their respective pledges to achieve UHC by 2020. When SHI schemes were first rolled out in the two countries in the late 20th century, less than a quarter of the population had health insurance coverage (Barber and Yao, 2010; Rokx, 2009). Two decades later, the UHC targets seem to have diverged in terms of SHI coverage: while China's sweeping reforms had successfully paved the way to achieving UHC by 2011 (Yu, 2015), Indonesia's progress on UHC has been more incremental. As of July 2018, a total of 75% of the Indonesian population was covered by SHI (BPJS-Health, 2018).

Given that the two countries shared fairly similar policy trajectories at the initial stage of reform, experienced a similar developmental stage from the 1940s to the late 1970s, and faced similar constraints embedded within their large and decentralized health systems, it is of both policy and theoretical interest to decipher why China has achieved its target much faster than Indonesia. It is also important to understand and differentiate the policy trajectories undertaken by both countries in achieving their respective goals. Hence, this chapter poses the following research questions: what policy trajectories have been followed by China and Indonesia in achieving UHC and how do they diverge? To what extent does policy capacity matter in accelerating reforms?

This analysis and appraisal of SHI systems in Indonesia and China will argue that the difference in the ways policy capacity is harnessed and developed by the government is the main explanatory factor in the divergence of SHI expansion in Indonesia and China. In particular, this chapter applies the definitions and operationalization of a proposed framework that comprises six domains of system-level policy capacity in order to appraise the speed, breadth, and depth of health reforms by tracing the development of SHI expansion in both countries. Policy capacity is broadly conceptualized as the skills and resources needed to achieve a policy goal (Painter and Pierre, 2005; Wu et al., 2015). Notably, this chapter finds that the ability of the Chinese Communist Party to maintain nimble and tactical relationships with its sub-national counterparts, its enormous capacity in rolling out a plethora of policy pilots and experiments alongside SHI reform, and its commitment to systematically increase the supply-side capacity of the Chinese health system are some of the most instrumental factors in explaining what amounts to a stellar SHI performance for a large developing economy.

The chapter is organized as follows: the next section lays out and explains policy capacity as the conceptual framework of this analysis. This is followed by a description of the respective histories of SHI expansions in Indonesia and China, after which the policy capacity of the respective health systems in the context of SHI expansions will be analyzed. This analysis is then followed by a cross-jurisdictional comparative analysis of SHI expansion in Indonesia and China. In the concluding section, the remaining challenges faced by SHI systems in both countries – and the policy implications of those challenges – are discussed.

Conceptual framework: policy capacity in policy reform

Academic interest in studying policy capacity as an important ingredient in public policy and public administration surfaced in the 1980s. Conceived under the framework of capacity building in an era that saw an increasing demand from international donor agencies to boost the sustainability of development in developing countries, policy capacity emphasizes skills-building and staff training as means of increasing public organizational performances and impacts (Honadle, 1981; LaFond et al., 2002; Potter and Brough, 2004). In recent years, this concept has been used to explain and analyze a wide range of government activities beyond the field of public administration. In health policy, the policy capacity of various actors in the government has proved to be one of the most critical ingredients in ensuring good coordination when instituting system-wide reforms in the health sector (Gleeson et al., 2009; Tan, 2018).

Defined by Painter and Pierre (2005: 2) as "the ability to marshal the necessary resources to make intelligent collective choices about and set strategic directions for the allocation of scarce resources to public ends", policy capacity interacts with administrative capacity and state capacity to form core components of governing capacity. There are two different aspects to policy capacity: one focuses on the hardware of government, which requires having optimal financial resources and the right technical expertise in public policymaking; the other builds on the software of government and emphasizes the creation of accountability and trust from the citizens toward the state, to maintain the currency of their political support (Painter and Pierre, 2005). This chimes with Woo et al.'s (2015) call to build citizens' trust as the basis for constructing legitimation capacity within the government.

Since then, several major publications have contributed to the conceptual development of policy capacity (Peters, 2015; Wu et al., 2015). In Wu et al.'s framework, policy capacity encompasses three major competencies/skills (operational, analytical, and political), as well as capabilities/resources at three different levels (individual, organizational, and systemic). Operational capacity includes the ability to implement policies as intended by policymakers among street-level bureaucrats (Gleeson et al., 2009; O'Toole and Meier, 2010; Peters, 2015). Analytical capacity means having both technical and analytical expertise to manage tasks that involve different degrees of difficulty (Peters, 2015), including making evidence-informed decisions (Newman et al., 2017) and formulating technocrat-driven policies (Howlett, 2009). Political capacity is broadly conceptualized as the ability to mobilize diverse societal interests and navigate a complex political environment in order to achieve political goals (Dunlop, 2015; Pal and Clark, 2015).

Building on Wu et al.'s (2015) framework, Saguin et al. (2018) have attempted to broaden the conceptualization of policy capacity at three levels of government – macro, mezzo, and micro – to create a more granular framework in the analysis of policy capacity. Specifically, at the macro or system level, policy capacity, which often involves reforms implemented by major actors such as international pacts, national governments, and sub-national governments, comprises six different domains: institutional capacity, administrative capacity, regulatory capacity, fiscal capacity, financial capacity, and political capacity (see Table 7.1). Each of these domains is postulated as important in understanding policy capacity at the highest level of policy reforms.

Table 7.1 Policy capacity at the macro (system) level

Level of capacity	Key actors	Capacity domains	Definitions/Operationalizations
Macro (System level)	International pacts/ alliances Regional pacts/ alliances National government Sub-national government	Institutional capacity	• Capacity to adopt policy ideas and make intelligent choices in the design of policy • Capacity to make strategic policy decisions and steer systemic adoption of those decisions
		Administrative capacity	• Capacity to identify, formulate and implement policy decisions and ensure the uniformity of implementations
		Regulatory capacity	• Capacity to monitor and enforce established rules and procedures via a distinct regulatory structure
		Fiscal capacity	• Capacity to control government spending through the monitoring of financial operations, making sound long-term budget decisions, improving budget process and transparency, and achieving structural balance • Capacity to raise and collect revenues from taxes in accordance with the tax policy for public consumption
		Financial capacity	• Capacity to generate additional revenues • Capacity to control and regulate economic activities
		Political capacity	• Capacity to mobilize societal support and consent in the pursuit of different policy goals • Capacity to coordinate and control diverging interests to compromise in the policy process

Source: adapted from Saguin et al., forthcoming (2018)

Methods

The six different domains of the policy capacity framework mentioned earlier provide a systematic conceptual frame for analyzing the performance of the respective areas of UHC implementation, highlighting the two countries' achievements and shortfalls. To compare the policy trajectories in UHC attainment for Indonesia and China, we used a comparative case study approach (George and Bennett, 2005). We combined different types of secondary data sources, which included journal articles, book chapters and grey literature such as policy documents, reports from multilateral organizations, and news articles. Combining different data sources enabled the triangulation of data as well as the construction of richer case narratives for each country. In analyzing these data, we performed both within-case and cross-case analyses. We first conducted within-case analysis by mapping out the development of health policy reforms that led to SHI expansion in both countries by using process tracing for each case. Process tracing, which is an established technique in case study method, aims at "inductively identifying complex interaction effects from causal variables that are not independent of each other" (ibid.: 212) in order to "identify single path or different paths to an outcome" (ibid.: 215). The appraisals of policy capacity for both cases were then conducted as cross-case analyses by first analyzing the overall policy capacity in SHI expansion within each case, before comparing them across the six different system-level capacity domains. As the capacity domains do not represent measurable indicators, we apply only the definitions and operationalizations of the domains in our appraisal.

The history of SHI expansion in Indonesia

Early reform: the promise of economic growth in the post-independence era (1945–1992)

The health system in Indonesia was first established by the Dutch colonial government in the early 20th century. *Askes* (Health Insurance for Civil Servants), one of the earliest SHI schemes, was started in 1945, after Indonesia attained national independence. It carried the colonial legacy of providing mandatory health insurance for civil servants with a comprehensive package of free health services, mandating 2% monthly salary contribution from the members (Rokx, 2009). Subsequently, *Askes Persero* (Health Insurance for the Police and Militaries) was established in 1968. This SHI scheme was targeted at both active and retired military personnel and their dependents (Rokx, 2009; Thabrany et al., 2003).

The New Order government in Indonesia led by President Suharto from 1967 to 1996 ushered in unprecedented economic growth, with massive investment in the public sector and public infrastructure in the early years of his leadership. These initial economic achievements were bolstered by two oil booms in the 1970s (Suryahadi et al., 2014). The annual average growth rate of real GDP in Indonesia from 1970 to 1995 was reported at 6.7% – outwardly satisfactory for a middle-income country. However, critics opined that this seemingly impressive growth concealed structural weaknesses inherent within the Indonesian economy, such as the constant capital outflow due to financial liberalization and average annual inflation of 10% in the same period (Francis, 2012).

Following *Askes* and *Askes Persero*, *Jamsostek* (Worker's Social Security) was introduced in 1992 to provide health insurance and other social security measures – such as work-accident insurance, death benefits, and old-age savings – to formal sector workers (Suryahadi et al., 2014). The mandatory contributions for *Jamsostek* came entirely from the employers and amounted to 3% of salary for single employees and 6% for married employees.

Rollback of reform: Asian financial crisis and economic downturn (1997–1999)

The contagion of the Asian financial crisis that first hit Thailand in 1977 affected many other Asian countries including Indonesia, resulting in the worst economic performance in the country's history. Indonesia experienced a GDP growth of -13.1% in 1998, and its national budget turned from surplus in the early 1990s to deficit post-crisis (Francis, 2012). This situation was compounded by other unexpected negative impacts, including the devaluation of the Indonesian currency six times in less than a year, a sharp rise in the unemployment rate, and soaring inflation. The downturn in the Indonesian economy during this period had a serious impact on the economic conditions of average households and reduced most low-income households to a state of extreme poverty virtually overnight (Suryahadi et al., 2014; Waters et al., 2003). The incidence of absolute poverty ballooned from 11.3% of the total population in 1996 to 23.3% in 1999 (Francis, 2012).

In the immediate aftermath of the crisis, an empirical analysis of the impacts of the Asian financial crisis on healthcare in Indonesia showed that household expenditure on health had decreased markedly both in absolute terms and in terms of percentage of overall spending, largely due to the increased costs of imported drugs and treatment costs in governmental health centers. The public health system had also been seriously hit by reductions in public healthcare expenditure as government budgets for healthcare shrank (Waters et al., 2003).

A groundswell of discontent caused by the pervasive negative impacts of the currency devaluation gradually manifested in increasing opposition to the dictatorship of the New Order regime, creating waves of political unrest and civilian demonstrations that eventually paved the way for the downfall of President Suharto in 1998 (Suryahadi et al., 2014).

Extension of reforms: democratic transition and social health insurance expansion (1998–2013)

The downfall of Suharto ushered in a democratic transition in Indonesia as new actors who had campaigned heavily for reform emerged in the policy arena. In the battle to woo voters and secure political support, politicians resorted to electoral populism, with promises of social welfare expansion, better social services provision, free healthcare, and free education becoming dominant narratives in most of the electoral campaigns at that time (Aspinall and Warburton, 2013).

The first major wave of reforms took place in 2004 when the newly elected President Susilo Bambang Yudhoyono's government introduced a free and basic healthcare program, known as *Askeskin* (Health Insurance for the Poor), to be rolled out at the national level. It was intended to expand health insurance coverage to low-income citizens who were largely reliant on the informal sector (Aspinall, 2014). The financing of *Askeskin* was substantially different from the earlier SHI schemes as the premiums were entirely financed from public revenues (Suryahadi et al., 2014). The fiscal commitment to such an enormous welfare expansion arguably held the key to Yudhoyono's rise during his campaign, from electoral underdog to popular leader (Aspinall, 2014). In 2008, *Askeskin* was converted into a new SHI scheme known as *Jamkesmas* (Suryahadi et al., 2014).

In addition to *Jamkesmas*, which was administered by the central government, the inception of decentralization in 2001 that endowed local governments in Indonesia with higher fiscal and administrative autonomy also resulted in the flourishing of local health insurance schemes known as *Jamkesda*; these were intended to cover parts of the populations that were not covered under *Jamkesmas* (Trisnantoro et al., 2014). The concurrent existence of *Jamkesmas* and *Jamkesda* enabled more poor households to be included in SHI schemes.

Consolidation of reform: the roll-out of JKN (national health insurance scheme)

The political ambition to expand SHI throughout the country was crystallized when President Yudhoyono announced in 2013 the plan to roll out a new National Health Insurance program, *Jaminan Kesehatan Nasional* – known as *JKN* – from January 2014 onwards. *JKN* aims to consolidate all existing SHI schemes in the country (*Askes, Askes Persero, Jamsostek, Jamkesmas* and *Jamkesda*) into a single-payer national health insurance system (Trisnantoro et al., 2014). With the announcement of a high-profile policy reform to unify the previously fragmented SHI schemes that offer different benefits packages, the Indonesian government signaled its political commitment to be the guardian of healthcare for its citizens. Reporting directly to the President of Indonesia, BPJS-Health – a third party payer that contracts with both public and private health providers – became the agency tasked with the implementation of *JKN* (Tan, 2018). The key features of Indonesia's SHI schemes are brought together in Table 7.2.

This major political move to consolidate all SHI schemes into a single-payer system required more financial resources from the Indonesian central government as it had to absorb the SHI premiums of 86.4 million members new to *JKN*, who were previously covered by local SHI schemes such as *Jamkesda* (The Economist, 2014). At the same time, the Indonesian government promised to include more medical benefits for *JKN* enrollees, ranging from minor illnesses such as influenza to expensive treatment such as open heart surgery, dialysis, and cancer therapies (ibid.). In 2014, *JKN* was reported to cover 121.6 million people, close to half of Indonesia's population of 252 million (ibid.), making it one of the biggest SHI programs in the world. The transition from President Yudhoyono to the new president, Joko Widodo, in October 2014, was accompanied by further promises to remove fuel subsidies so as to free up resources from

Table 7.2 Key features of various social health insurance schemes in Indonesia

	ASKES (Health Insurance for Civil Servants)	JAMSOSTEK (Workforce Social Security)	JAMKESMAS (Health Insurance for the Poor)	JKN (National Health Insurance)
Started	1968	1992	2008 (evolved from ASKESKIN, which was started in 2004)	2014
Target population	Civil servants, retired civil servants, retired military personnel, and veterans	Private employees in corporations with >10 employees or that pay a salary >Rp 1 million (USD 76.30) a month	Poor and near-poor	Entire Indonesian population
Enrollment	Mandatory	Voluntary	Voluntary	Voluntary
Coverage	16.6 million[a]	5.0 million[a]	76.4 million[a]	180 million[b]
Risk-pooling	Yes	Yes (conditional on participation as members can opt out)	No	Yes (national level)
Cost-sharing	Yes (if members want to upgrade class or branded drugs out of formulary)	No	No	No
Financing mechanism	Contributory regime: 2% of basic + 1% government; no ceilings	Contributory regime: 3% of salary for single employees, 6% of salary for married employees; ceiling Rp 1 million (USD 76.30) per month (since 1993)	Subsidized regime: Rp 6,500 (USD 0.50) per capita per month	Contributory regime: 3% of salary from employer and 2% of salary from employee in public sector; 4% of salary from employer and 1% of salary from employee in private sector; USD 36–72 per annum for non-salaried and non-poor informal-sector workers.

Financing source	Ministry of Finance	Employers (100%)	National budget (APBN) allocated in the Ministry of Health's budget (block grant) by Ministry of Finance.	Multiple sources. Financing sources for contributory regime enrollees (formal-sector employees, civil servants and self-employed personnel) comprising a combination of personal and employers' contributions. Financing sources for subsidized regime enrollees are from the district and central government budget
Designated health providers	Mostly contracted public health centers and public hospitals	Mixed; Public and private providers	All community health centers and public hospitals and selected empaneled private hospitals	All public providers (community health centers and public hospitals) and selected private providers that contract with BPJS-Health
Services covered	Comprehensive, no specific exclusion; Drugs are covered if prescribed within formulary; Cost-sharing available when services fall outside basic benefit package	Comprehensive; Cancer treatment, cardiac surgery, hemodialysis, and congenital diseases are excluded; Drugs are covered if prescribed within formulary; No cost-sharing	Comprehensive; Drugs are covered if prescribed within formulary	Medical (all services that are assessed to be medically necessary at the primary, secondary, and tertiary levels) and non-medical (accommodation and emergency transportation to health facilities)

Source: adapted and modified from Tan (2018a)

[a]coverage as of 2013; [b]coverage as of September 2017

the government budget for more investment in social services and healthcare as part of the government's drive to achieve UHC by 2019 (Sambijantoro, 2014).

The history of social health insurance expansion in China

Early reform: collectivist welfare regime (1951–1978)

China was a rising star in public health system performance among the developing countries prior to 1978. The communist party regime led by Mao Zedong transformed the public health landscape in China by taking complete ownership in the operations and financing of healthcare, ranging from large specialized health facilities in the urban areas to small township clinics in the rural areas, a phenomenon that was typical of communist societies during that period. The so-called barefoot doctors formed the bulk of human resources in the health sector at the time, delivering both affordable and effective healthcare in China. They were perceived to be the core actors in expediting the improvement of health outcomes in China between 1952 and 1982 – an improvement marked by a dramatic reduction in infant mortality from 200 to 34 per 1,000 live births and an almost miraculous increase in life expectancy from 35 to 68 years (Blumenthal and Hsiao, 2005). The health system in China during this period included three social insurance schemes that covered almost the entire population of China: the Government Insurance Scheme (GIS) for employees of state-owned companies, Labour Insurance Scheme (LIS) for the urban population, and Cooperative Medical System (CMS) for the rural population (Ramesh et al., 2013).

Rollback of reform: economic liberalization and minimalist welfare regime (1978–1998)

The liberalization of the Chinese economy from a centrally planned economy to a market economy, a bold decision taken by then-premier Deng Xiaoping in 1978, spurred phenomenal economic growth in China over the ensuing three decades. However, it also resulted in the demise of the government's role in the public health system. Deng spearheaded an ideological shift in China's welfare philosophy turning an egalitarian state into a highly individualistic and market-oriented system, advocating for a "family responsibility system" in the rural sector and emphasizing family as the first line of social protection (Liu, 2002). From 1978 to the 1990s, the Chinese government placed economic growth as the top priority in China's developmental agenda; the price it paid was a widening of health disparities and deterioration of health outcomes for large numbers in the rural population (Huang, 2014).

The minimalist welfare approach adopted by the Chinese government shook the fundamental structure of the public health system, which had been heavily state-dependent prior to the economic transformation. As the government reduced its fiscal responsibility in public health provision, public hospitals became privatized, resulting in the transfer of ownership and operations to private providers (Gu and

Zhang, 2006). The CMS collapsed as a result of the privatization of agricultural collectives in rural areas, leaving the barefoot doctors unemployed and 900 million rural citizens uninsured (Blumenthal and Hsiao, 2005). The changes in public healthcare provision saw the share of national health spending as a percentage of total government spending reduced from 32% in 1978 to 15% in 1999 (ibid.), while out-of-pocket spending as a share of total spending increased from 23.2% to 57.8% (Liu and Rao, 2006).

The devolution of financial autonomy from the state to private entities also created health disparities between the rural and urban populations and between rich and poor, as privatization of the public health system resulted in cost escalation, impeding access to healthcare by the poor (Liu, 2002). Health inequality in China became a serious phenomenon, characterized by widening discrepancies in the infant mortality rate (IMR) and maternal mortality rate (MMR) between urban and rural China. In 1999, the IMR was reported to be 37 in rural areas as opposed to 11 in urban areas, while the MMR was reported to be 39 in rural area and 14 in urban areas (Blumenthal and Hsiao, 2005).

Extension of reforms: signaling of legitimacy and SHI expansion (1998–2009)

The widening health disparity between urban and rural areas was a worrisome situation for political leaders, as levels of public grievance increased. The negative repercussions on the impoverished rural population, which made up 70% of the total population in China, were seen as a threat to the authoritarian Communist Party regime with its firm belief that political order and stability were prerequisites to sustainable economic growth (Blumenthal and Hsiao, 2005; Liu and Rao, 2006). In a sign of the government's desire to secure political legitimacy, the Health Ministry, led by Dr Zhang Wenkang in the late 1990s, took the initiative to push for healthcare to be given priority on the political agenda (Liu and Rao, 2006). Academic research also played a role in bringing healthcare to the attention of top policymakers in China from the late 1990s onward. The publication of the World Health Report in 2000 rang a political alarm bell for Communist Party leaders as the report highlighted the relatively lower level of health financing in China as compared to many other upper-middle-income countries (ibid.).

A preliminary wave of SHI reform in China occurred with the introduction of Urban Employees Basic Medical Insurance (UEI) in 1998 – a government health insurance scheme that was mandatory for urban formal sector workers. The subsequent wave of reforms from 2003 – including the New Rural Cooperative Medical Insurance Scheme (NRCMS), which initially enrolled 8 million of the rural population – marked the beginning of the full government response to address the urban–rural health disparity. It was also a strong signal of the Communist Party's political commitment to the grand ambition of universal health coverage by 2020. In 2007, the Urban Residents Basic Medical Insurance (URI) was launched, targeting urban migrant workers as well as the non-employed (children, students, elderly, and disabled). By 2008, 87% of the total Chinese population was covered by one or other of the major state-controlled health insurance schemes (Meng and Tang, 2010).[1]

Escalation of reforms: three-phase public health reforms and the expansion of policy pilots

In 2009, a three-phase health development blueprint was unveiled by the Chinese government as a major development plan to strengthen supply-side readiness by 2020. In the first phase, spanning 2009–2012, a total of USD 125 billion was injected into the health sector to finance development and programs in five key areas: expanding SHI, strengthening primary care, establishing an essential medicines program, ramping up public healthcare services, and implementing pilot reforms in public hospitals (Li and Fu, 2017). Policy experimentation and pilots became central and were prioritized by the government as instruments to inform policies (Husain, 2017). For instance, 17 cities were selected as pilot cities for public hospitals in the first phase (Li and Fu, 2017).

In the second phase (2012–2015), the Chinese government reaffirmed its promise and commitment to the same health developmental focus as the first phase but increased its attention on public hospital reforms. Another 83 cities across China were added as pilot cities in order to step up efforts to strengthen the supply-side of healthcare (ibid.). In the third phase, which started in 2015, an integrated health system with improved interface between primary care and higher-level care through ongoing reforms was envisioned (ibid.). Moreover, in further attempts to improve the efficiency and equity of the existing SHI system, the Chinese government announced a merger between URI and NRCMS to form the new Urban and Rural Residence Medical Insurance (URRMI) scheme in 2016 (Shan, 2016). Table 7.3 provides an overview of the various SHI schemes in China.

Capacity for SHI reform and expansion in Indonesia

While the earlier Indonesian SHI schemes were comprehensive and targeted, their coverage remained limited, benefiting only a small segment of the population. Prior to the introduction of *Askeskin*, extending health coverage for a vast majority of Indonesian population remained an unreachable goal.

The performance and uptake of *Jamsostek* in the early years of its roll-out were not impressive. Due to its non-mandatory design, which gave certain employers who had already enrolled their employees in some other private health insurance schemes the option of non-enrollment, its membership had expanded very slowly. In addition, its low wage ceiling, high administrative costs, low service quality, and the poor management of its healthcare providers did not promote its uptake (Thabrany et al., 2003). *Jamsostek* was further criticized for failing to cover a substantial proportion of informal sector workers (Aspinall, 2014).

Askes and *Askes Persero* had also suffered from similar capacity issues. These two schemes were bogged down with fundamental design problems such as poor

Table 7.3 Key features of various social health insurance schemes in China

	NCMS	UEI	URI	URRMI
Date started	2003 (Pilot scheme was initiated in four provinces)	1998 (pilot scheme was initiated in 1994)	Pilot since 2007	Rolled out in phases since January 2016
Target population	Rural residents	Urban employee	Urban residents without formal employment	Urban residents without formal employment and rural residents
Enrollment	Participation is usually voluntary at household level but could be enforced once the county joins the NCMS	Participation is mandatory for all urban residents with formal employment	Voluntary (household level)	Voluntary
Coverage	805 million rural population	271 million urban employees	264 million urban residents	Those who are not covered under the UEI scheme
Risk pooling	County level	City level	City level	County level
Reimbursement rate, ceiling and deductibles	Deductibles, reimbursement rates, and ceilings are set by the county governments. The rates depend largely on the types of health providers	Deductibles, reimbursement rates, and ceilings are set by the city government. The rates depend largely on the types of health providers	Deductibles, reimbursement rates, and ceilings are set by the city government. However, deductibles, reimbursement rates, and ceilings are different for children, elderly, and other urban residents. These rates also depend on the types of health providers	Deductibles, reimbursement rates, and ceilings are set by the county governments. The rates depend largely on the types of health providers

(*Continued*)

Table 7.3 (Continued)

	NCMS	UEI	URI	URRMI
Financing mechanism	In western and central China, the central government assisted the local government in providing finance for the scheme. In the more affluent eastern and coastal regions, financing the premium was mainly through local governments. Government subsidies increased from RMB 42.1 in 2005 to RMB 308.5 in 2012	A total of 8% of employees' monthly payroll needs to be contributed to the scheme, with the employee paying 2% and the employer paying the remaining 6%	In general, an annual premium provided by the government should be no less than RMB 40 per year per person. In addition, the government provides extra subsidies to disabled children, children from poor families, poor disabled elderly above 60. Insured urban residents who live in affluent provinces are likely to receive better benefit packages compared with those who live in less affluent provinces	In the preliminary phase, financing mechanism differs in each county. Generally, premiums are financed via a combination of self-contribution and government subsidies
Designated health facilities	All levels of public health facilities	All levels of public health facilities	All levels of public health facilities	All levels of public health facilities
Covered services	In-patient services, catastrophic out-patient services, some prevention care services	In-patient services, catastrophic out-patient services, some prevention care services	Mainly cover in-patient services and catastrophic out-patient services.	In-patient services (up to 75%) and out-patient services.

Source: adapted from Tan et al. (2018)

quality, limited coverage, and adverse selection, which resulted in a significant upsurge of healthcare expenditures that were not proportionate to the increased premiums paid by the members. This caused service providers to back off and become unwilling to serve *Askes* members (Thabrany et al., 2003).

Despite the increased political commitment to the expansion of SHI embodied in the roll-out of *JKN* in 2014, serious questions about the fiscal sustainability of this ambitious program remain. One recent report suggests that *JKN* is fast becoming insolvent (Heriyanto, 2018). The deficits reported by BPJS-Health have been skyrocketing over the years, hitting Rp nine trillion (USD 69.3 million) in 2017 (ibid.). The weakness of Indonesia's public finances over recent years – demonstrated by its continuous struggle with fiscal deficits since the Asian financial crisis in 1997 – has also hindered its ability to progressively expand SHI to a wider population (Francis, 2012). A mere 2.2% of the total government budget is allocated to healthcare, which is seen as inadequate to protect the poor from financial risks, given the high costs associated with treating major catastrophic illnesses (Suryahadi et al., 2014). The country's total health expenditure (THE) as a percentage of GDP remained relatively low throughout the period 1995–2012, when compared to China and other Southeast Asian counterparts in the same period (WHO, 2014).

The limited fiscal space for health was compounded by systemic issues in operations and service delivery that have so far proved insurmountable. Ongoing under-investment in service delivery within the public health system led to severe shortages both in hospital beds and human resources for health (Meliala et al., 2013; Suryahadi et al., 2014). Based on official World Health Organization estimates, the number of hospital beds was 0.9 per 1,000 population in 2012, and the density of physicians that year was 0.204 per 1,000 population, while in 2015 the density of nurses or midwives was 13 per 10,000 population (WHO, 2016). The fact that these service ratios were lower than other countries with similar income levels (Rokx, 2009) highlights a serious and fundamental supply-side issue in public health delivery in Indonesia. Current regulations allow for dual practice: public healthcare professionals can apply for a license to work in two private settings, provided that their minimum number of service hours in the public setting is fulfilled. However, an observational study identified that many of them did not adhere to this provision and practiced fewer hours within the public setting than required by the regulations (Meliala et al., 2013). The regulations were often not enforced, and no penalties were imposed by the regulatory agencies on those who flouted them (ibid.).

Capacity for SHI reform and expansion in China

Once NRCMS, one of the largest SHI schemes in China, was announced, strong administrative and financial support from the state ensued. In order to scale up NRCMS in rural areas, extra-budgetary support from the government increased ten-fold between 2003 and 2012, raising the level of funds pooling in each county and boosting the financing capacities of the NRCMS county offices (Meng and Xu, 2014). In a high-profile workshop aiming to address public concerns and

expectations in 2006, President Hu Jintao announced that the Chinese government would increase its commitment in healthcare with an additional injection of
RMB 850 million (approximately US$ 124 billion) of government funding into
a three-year health development plan to run from 2009 to 2012 (Yu, 2015). This
financial investment in health would focus on five major areas of health financing, three of which were: to expand insurance coverage, to increase government
spending on public services, and to strengthen primary care facilities in China
(Yip and Hsiao, 2009). The three-phase health development plan announced by
the central government, alongside the 12th and 13th five-year plans in health
development, represent major financial and political commitments to strengthen
the supply-side of the health system at a time when SHI enrollment in China was
fast expanding (Li and Fu, 2017).

China's economic growth over the past three decades has been phenomenal
in global terms and has outperformed most developing countries. With the
exception of 1989 and 1990, China achieved 5–15% of real annual GDP growth
between 1980 and 2017 (IMF, 2018). This stellar economic growth has enabled
China to finance healthcare in a consistent fashion. For instance, China's annual
total health expenditure (THE) was on average 4–5% of its GDP from 1995 to
2015, while its SHI spending as a percentage of THE also increased by leaps
and bounds from 2000 to 2015 (WHO, 2018). Out-of-pocket expenditure as a
percentage of THE declined consistently during the same period. The Chinese
government's ability to boost its health spending while containing out-of-pocket
expenditure shares for the past two decades, while highly laudable, is not an
entirely unique phenomenon. A cross-country econometric analysis established
that high overall government spending on health and low out-of-pocket shares
are signs of a health financing transition, away from a low spending system with
high out-of-pocket expenditures to a high spending system with better risk-
pooling mechanisms (Fan and Savedoff, 2014). These patterns also indicate the
high fiscal capacity of the state. To date, China's public health spending is much
higher than many low- and middle-income countries and is on par with developed
countries like the USA and South Korea (Eggleston, 2012).

In the meantime, a plethora of policy pilots and experiments have been undertaken in the bid to reform rural SHI programs, payment systems, and public
hospital management in various counties and cities over the past two decades
(Husain, 2017; Li and Fu, 2017). The decision to endow local governments
with the autonomy to tinker with the policy design and policy implementation of
various central policy directives is both pragmatic and unorthodox for an authoritarian regime. These policy experiments and pilots are pragmatic in that they
allow effective diffusion of learning and multiplication of best practices across
sub-national jurisdictions, either through codification of best policy models into
the national institutional framework or through the organic spread of policy ideas
in the form of inter-governmental information exchanges facilitated by site visits,
training, and exchange of documentation (Husain, 2017). On the other hand,
rolling out policy experiments is seen as an unorthodox move in that central
government continues to receive fresh policy ideas from the bottom up and to

witness transformative innovations at the local level without loosening its grips in controlling the overarching agenda (Heilmann, 2008).

Cross-jurisdiction appraisal of policy capacity for UHC realization and SHI expansion

Institutional capacity

The ability of China to engage in ongoing policy experimentations and pilots as tools to facilitate policy learning symbolizes high institutional capacity and effective command-and-control at the central level. Whether these pilots and experiments are conducted through simple geographic expansion of existing programs or through academic evaluation of different SHI schemes, public hospital reforms, and provider payment reforms (Husain, 2017), they reflect the nimbleness of the central government in treading a fine line between giving local governments the autonomy to modify the design and implementation of policies and retaining its hierarchical control over those same local governments (Yuan et al., 2017). By contrast, Indonesia – although sharing the same overall policy ambition – lacks systematic, government-led efforts to roll out policy experiments in different localities in order to identify policy solutions that are time-sensitive and context-specific.

Administrative capacity

With regard to administrative capacity to deliver health services effectively on the supply-side, both China and Indonesia face constraints in terms of their endowment of human resources for health and health infrastructures. For instance, in 2015, the number of nursing and midwifery staff in China was 24 for every 10,000 head of population. Although slightly higher than the 13 for every 10,000 in Indonesia (WHO, 2016), this falls short of the world standard of 29 for every 10,000 (The Statistics Portal, 2018). Similarly, in 2017 China had only 0.03 public health centers for every 1,000 head of population, while the figure for Indonesia was around 0.04 (CEIC, 2018a, 2018b). The "General Practitioner System" announced by the Chinese government in 2011, providing financial incentives for health workers to be posted to remote areas and standardizing the certification and licensure for physicians, was seen as a progressive move in boosting the capacity of primary healthcare in China (Eggleston, 2012). Indonesia, on the other hand, is held back by enormous gaps in health service delivery and continual yearly deficits as a result of a surge in health demand from its population after the roll-out of *JKN*.

Regulatory capacity

Coordinated policy implementation between the central and local governments, especially in ensuring effective roll-out of the SHI schemes, hinges on the supervisory and regulatory roles assumed by the central government. While this issue has always been a major challenge in large and decentralized countries, in China the central government has taken concrete steps to facilitate the expansion of SHI since the beginning of the reform period, by implementing many government-led regulations and effective incentive structures. One of the keys to the successful expansion of the NRCMS scheme, for instance, is the presence of a strong and clear regulatory role for the central government, coupled with its use of implementation metrics – such as speed of expansion as performance incentives for local governments – to expand health coverage for the population (Yuan et al., 2017). Indonesia has not yet been able to set up a central taskforce that could effectively monitor policy implementation in its 500 sub-national jurisdictions. The failure of regulatory authorities to issue warnings or take action against health professionals who do not fulfil their minimum required duties in the public health sector – for fear of losing them altogether to the private sector – highlights Indonesia's enforcement issues (Meliala et al., 2013).

Fiscal capacity

Statistics on the total health expenditure (THE) and general-government health expenditure (G-GHE) of the two countries show a stark difference between Indonesia and China (see Figures 7.1–7.5). China has consistently increased its expenditure in health, while Indonesia had not been able to do so. Figure 7.1 indicates that, between 2000 and 2016, China spent 4–5% of its gross domestic product (GDP) on health, while Indonesia spent only about 2–3% of its GDP on health in the same period.

Figure 7.2 shows G-GHE as a percentage of THE in both Indonesia and China. At the beginning of the century, the G-GHE percentage for Indonesia, at

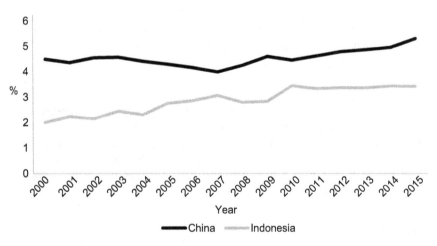

Figure 7.1 Total Health Expenditure (THE) as % Gross Domestic Product (GDP)
Source: WHO (2018)

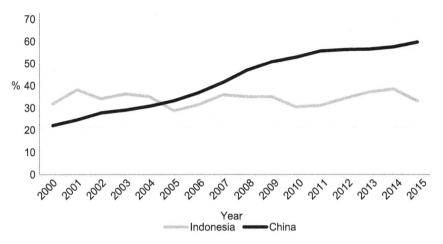

Figure 7.2 G-GHE as % of Total Health Expenditure (THE)
Source: WHO (2018)

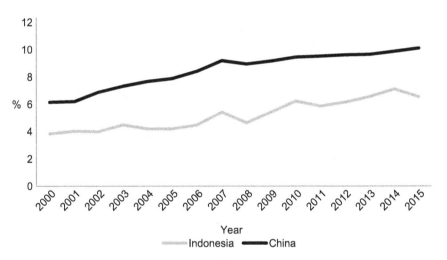

Figure 7.3 G-GHE as % of General Government Expenditure (G-GE)
Source: WHO (2018)

about 32%, was higher than that for China. However, in Indonesia this percentage remained stable for the next 15 years, whereas China has gradually increased the government share in health spending, with G-GHE as a percentage of THE rising steadily from 22% in 2000 to 60% in 2015 (WHO, 2018).

Figure 7.3 reports G-GHE as a percentage of general-government expenditure (G-GE). The graph shows clearly that the Chinese government has consistently

allocated more expenditure to health compared to Indonesia. Moreover, the percentage increased steadily in China, from 6.2% in 2000 to 10.1% in 2015, whilst
Indonesia recorded a much lower increase, from 3.8% in 2000 to 6.5% in 2015
(ibid.).

Figure 7.4 shows SHI spending as a percentage of THE. Again, China has
ramped up its SHI spending with a sevenfold increase from 2000 to 2015. For
Indonesia the pattern is much less regular and shows a relatively consistent
upward climb only after 2014, the year *JKN* was rolled out (ibid.).

Another indicator that reflects a government's fiscal capacity in health is the
out-of-pocket share as a percentage of THE. In Figure 7.5, China exhibits a clear
downward trend from 60% in 2000 to 32% in 2015. Indonesia, on the contrary,
shows a winding and gradual but generally upward trend over the same period,
rising from 45% in 2000 to 50% in 2015 (ibid.).

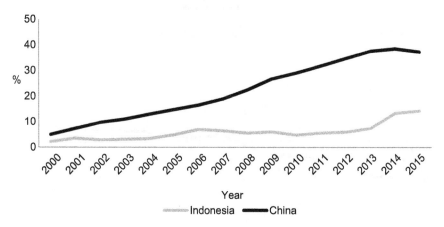

Figure 7.4 SHI as % of Total Health Expenditure (THE)
Source: WHO (2018)

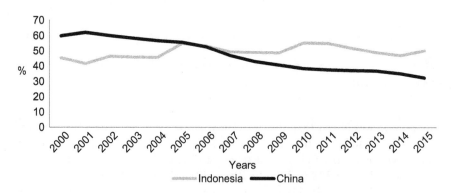

Figure 7.5 OOP as % of Total Health Expenditure (THE)
Source: WHO (2018)

Financial capacity

Figure 7.6 shows that China's economic growth has outperformed emerging and developing economies since the 1980s, with an impressive annual real GDP growth rate of more than 5% in most years over the last four decades, reaching double-digit growth in four different periods (1984–1985, 1987–1988, 1992–1995, 2003–2007) (IMF, 2018). While Indonesia generally maintained an economic growth rate of between 2% and 9% in the same period, it dipped into negative growth (–13.1%) in 1998, during the Asian Financial Crisis (ibid.). The relatively higher and sustained growth in China has generated additional revenues, which allowed China to leverage larger investments in healthcare. Indonesia's economic plunge in the late 1990s, on the other hand, compounded its inability to free up more financial resources for healthcare, resulting in its weaker capacity to resolve supply-side issues in the health system.

Political capacity

Both Indonesia and China have demonstrated high political capacity in UHC implementation and SHI expansion. In China, the recognition that healthcare for all was inherent in the socialist-based social structure of the country enabled the top leaders to reverse course in the late 1990s, away from a neoliberal minimalist welfare philosophy that had allowed the free market to drive up health costs in the 1980s and 1990s (Yu, 2015). In Indonesia, high political capacity for UHC was demonstrated by the proliferation of local SHI schemes (*Jamkesda*) over the last two decades, even though central government was rolling out the nationwide *Jamkesmas* scheme at the same time. The election promise of UHC helped district heads to get elected after decentralization measures had given citizens the right to directly vote for their city mayors and/or district governors

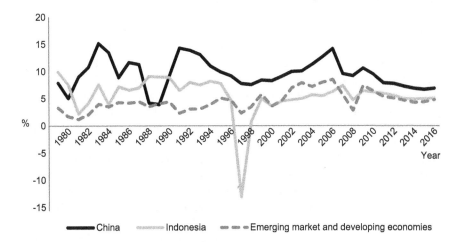

Figure 7.6 Real GDP growth (annual % change)
Source: IMF (2018)

(Aspinall, 2014). The popular *Jamkesmas* and *Jamkesda* schemes created a path dependency, which eventually culminated in the roll-out of a national health insurance program by the central government in 2014 (Pisani et al., 2017).

Conclusion: implementation challenges and policy implications

This chapter has shown the strong explanatory power of policy capacity in differentiating between the policy trajectories of Indonesia and China in their quests to achieve UHC. While both countries demonstrated low administrative capacity and high political capacity in UHC implementation, China has exhibited a higher policy capacity overall and has achieved its UHC target ahead of its timeline. Nevertheless, fundamental health system challenges remain, preventing both countries from advancing other health policy goals associated with the realization of UHC. In particular, out-of-pocket expenditures as a percentage of THE remained relatively high in both Indonesia and China in 2015 as compared to the WHO recommended standard of 15–20% (Shan et al., 2017). The uneven distribution of healthcare resources to urban and rural areas, including human resources for health, creates urban–rural inequities and inter-jurisdictional disparities in both countries that hinder UHC progress (Huang, 2014; Meliala et al., 2013). In Indonesia, most specialist doctors remain concentrated in urbanized areas and on the more populous and wealthier island of Java (Meliala et al., 2013).

There are also ongoing issues and concerns pertaining to the design of the SHI schemes. In China, a cross-sectional survey examining the perceived performance of the health insurance system among public health managers and administrators in four provinces revealed that a large proportion of respondents were pessimistic about the achievements of the Chinese health system (Shan et al., 2017). Despite widening health coverage, perceived limited financial protection, inequity of various SHI schemes, lack of portability of funds for floating populations, and ineffective supervision were found to be some of the main concerns among the respondents. In Indonesia, policymakers face the challenge of identifying ways and means to effectively increase the coverage of SHI among informal sector workers, dubbed as the "missing middle" in SHI enrollment. Here, a cross-sectional survey has debunked the myth that it was high SHI premiums that prevented informal sector workers from enrolling in SHI programs: instead, the study found that lack of health services within the vicinity and lack of insurance literacy were two major factors that contributed to the low rates of enrollment (Dartanto et al., 2016). Indeed, lack of SHI coverage among informal sector workers, lack of supply-side readiness, and the mismatch between policy design and fiscal sustainability of SHI systems were found to be the three main challenges in implementing UHC in developing countries more generally (Bredenkamp et al., 2015).

The previous findings have important policy implications for both Indonesia and China and for many other developing countries that are currently expanding their SHI programs. Strengthening the supply-side capacity of the public health system is the foremost challenge for most developing countries, and this agenda has to be tackled in parallel with the quest to achieve the UHC target. To realize this goal, governments should step up measures to strengthen financial investment in healthcare facilities and human resources for health. They also need to engage in evidence-informed policy by improving health technology assessments and health reform evaluations at both national and sub-national levels (Bredenkamp et al., 2015).

The wide adoption of policy experimentation and pilots by the Chinese government as major initiatives of health system strengthening is commendable and is worth emulating. Besides this, improving regulatory capacity by establishing a robust supervisory structure within the health system in order to minimize administrative lapses should be prioritized as a key aspect of the health reform agenda. Reforming SHI systems also necessitates constant experimentation and flexibility with the incentive structures of the health financing system, such as provider payment and performance incentives, to identify optimal solutions that can control health costs without compromising the quality of healthcare (Tan and Melendez-Torres, 2018). Last but not least, levelling the playing field for all SHI enrollees should be another priority. Deliberate measures should be deployed to improve access to and utilization of healthcare provision for all segments of the population, especially informal sector workers, those on low incomes, and those living in geographically depressed areas. Only when healthcare access and uptake are substantially enhanced can UHC live up to its original promise of improving health for all. Any country that realizes this mission will significantly improve its livability and enhance equity among its citizens.

Note

1 This figure breaks down as follows: NRCMS: 68%; UEI: 15%; URI: 4%.

References

Aspinall, Edward (2014). "Health Care and Democratization in Indonesia." *Democratization* 21 (5): 803–823. https://doi.org/10.1080/13510347.2013.873791.

Aspinall, Edward, and Eve Warburton (2013). "A Healthcare Revolution in the Regions." *Inside Indonesia* 111. www.insideindonesia.org/a-healthcare-revolution-in-the-regions-2.

Barber, S.L., and L. Yao (2010). "Health Insurance Systems in China: A Briefing Note." World Health Report 2010 Background Paper 37. Geneva: WHO. www.who.int/healthsystems/topics/financing/healthreport/37ChinaB_YFINAL.pdf.

Blumenthal, David, and William Hsiao (2005). "Privatization and Its Discontents – The Evolving Chinese Health Care System." *New England Journal of Medicine* 353 (11): 1165–1170. https://doi.org/10.1056/NEJMhpr051133.

BPJS-Health (2018). "BPJS-Health: Enrollment of JKN Participants." https://bpjs-kesehatan.go.id/bpjs/.

Bredenkamp, Caryn, Timothy Evans, Leizel Lagrada, John Langenbrunner, Stefan Nachuk, and Toomas Palu (2015). "Emerging Challenges in Implementing Universal Health Coverage in Asia." *Social Science & Medicine* 145: 243–248. https://doi.org/10.1016/j.socscimed.2015.07.025.

CEIC (2018a). "China Premium Database." www.ceicdata.com/en/products/china-economic-database.

CEIC (2018b). "Indonesia Premium Database." www.ceicdata.com/en/products/indonesia-economic-database.

Centre for Liveable Cities (2018). "ASEAN Smart Cities Network." Singapore: Centre for Liveable Cities. www.clc.gov.sg/docs/default-source/books/book-asean-smart-cities-network.pdf.

Dartanto, Teguh, Jahen Fachrul Rezki, Wahyu Pramono, Chairina Hanum Siregar, Usman Bintara, and Hamdan Bintara (2016). "Participation of Informal Sector Workers in Indonesia's National Health Insurance System." *Journal of Southeast Asian Economies* 33 (3): 317–342. http://10.0.5.75/ae33-3c.

Dunlop, Claire A. (2015). "Organizational Political Capacity as Learning." *Policy and Society* 34 (3–4): 259–270.

The Economist (2014). "Indonesia Launches Universal Healthcare." *The Economist Intelligence Unit*, 13 January. www.eiu.com/industry/article/1071418091/indonesia-launches-universal-healthcare/2014-01-13.

Eggleston, K. (2012). "Health Care for 1.3 Billion: An Overview of China's Health System." Asia Health Policy Program Working Paper 28. Stanford, CA: Stanford University.

Fan, Victoria Y., and William D. Savedoff (2014). "The Health Financing Transition: A Conceptual Framework and Empirical Evidence." *Social Science & Medicine* 105: 112–121. https://doi.org/10.1016/j.socscimed.2014.01.014.

Francis, S. (2012). "Fiscal Policy Evolution and Distributional Implications: The Indonesian Experience." IDEAs Working Paper Series 01/2012. www.mappingfinance.org/uploads/wp_2012_01.pdf.

George, A.L., and A. Bennett (2005). *Case Studies and Theory Development in the Social Sciences.* Cambridge, MA and London: MIT Press.

Gleeson, Deborah H., David G. Legge, and Deirdre O'Neill (2009). "Evaluating Health Policy Capacity: Learning From International and Australian Experience." *Australia and New Zealand Health Policy* 6 (1): 3. https://doi.org/10.1186/1743-8462-6-3.

Greer, Scott L., and Claudio A. Méndez (2015). "Universal Health Coverage: A Political Struggle and Governance Challenge." *American Journal of Public Health* 105 (S5): S637–639. https://doi.org/10.2105/AJPH.2015.302733.

Gu, E., and J. Zhang (2006). "Health Care Regime Change in Urban China: Unmanaged Marketization and Reluctant Privatization." *Pacific Affairs* 79 (1): 49–71.

Heilmann, Sebastian (2008). "Policy Experimentation in China's Economic Rise." *Studies in Comparative International Development* 43 (1): 1–26.

Heriyanto, Devina (2018). "Q&A: BPJS Kesehatan, Health for All Indonesians." *The Jakarta Post*, 7 April. www.thejakartapost.com/academia/2018/04/06/qa-bpjs-kesehatan-health-for-all-indonesians.html.

Honadle, Beth Walter (1981). "A Capacity-building Framework: A Search for Concept and Purpose." *Public Administration Review* 41 (5): 575–580. https://doi.org/10.2307/976270.

Howlett, Michael (2009). "Policy Analytical Capacity and Evidence-based Policymaking: Lessons From Canada." *Canadian Public Administration* 52 (2): 153–175.

Hsiao, W., and R. Shaw (2007). *Social Health Insurance for Developing Nations.* Washington, DC: The International Bank for Reconstruction and Development/World Bank.

Huang, Xian (2014). "Expansion of Chinese Social Health Insurance: Who Gets What, When and How?" *Journal of Contemporary China* 23 (89): 923–951. https://doi.org/10.1080/10670564.2014.882617.

Husain, Lewis (2017). "Policy Experimentation and Innovation as a Response to Complexity in China's Management of Health Reforms." *Globalization and Health* 13 (1): 54. https://doi.org/10.1186/s12992-017-0277-x.

IMF (2018). "IMF Data Mapper: Real GDP Growth (Annual Percent Change)." International Monetary Fund. www.imf.org/external/datamapper/NGDP_RPCH@WEO/OEMDC/ADVEC/WEOWORLD.

LaFond, Anne K., Lisanne Brown, and Kate Macintyre (2002). "Mapping Capacity in the Health Sector: A Conceptual Framework." *The International Journal of Health Planning and Management* 17 (1): 3–22. https://doi.org/10.1002/hpm.649.

Li, Ling, and Hongqiao Fu (2017). "China's Health Care System Reform: Progress and Prospects." *International Journal of Health Planning and Management* 32 (3): 240–253. https://doi.org/10.1002/hpm.2424.

Liu, Yuanli (2002). "Reforming China's Urban Health Insurance System." *Health Policy* 60 (2): 133–150.

Liu, Yuanli, and Keqin Rao (2006). "Providing Health Insurance in Rural China: From Research to Policy." *Journal of Health Politics, Policy and Law* 31 (1): 71–92. https://doi.org/10.1215/03616878-31-1-71.

Meliala, Andreasta, Krishna Hort, and Laksono Trisnantoro (2013). "Addressing the Unequal Geographic Distribution of Specialist Doctors in Indonesia: The Role of the Private Sector and Effectiveness of Current Regulations." *Social Science & Medicine* 82: 30–34. https://doi.org/10.1016/j.socscimed.2013.01.029.

Meng, Q., and S. Tang (2010). "Universal Coverage of Health Care in China: Challenges and Opportunities." World Health Report 2010 Background Paper 7. Geneva: WHO. www.who.int/healthsystems/topics/financing/healthreport/7ChinaM_T.pdf.

Meng, Q., and K. Xu (2014). "Progress and Challenges of the Rural Cooperative Medical Scheme in China." *Bulletin of the World Health Organization* 92 (6): 447–451.

Newman, Joshua, Adrian Cherney, and Brian W. Head (2017). "Policy Capacity and Evidence-based Policy in the Public Service." *Public Management Review* 19 (2): 157–174.

O'Toole, Laurence J., and Kenneth J. Meier (2010). "In Defense of Bureaucracy." *Public Management Review* 12 (3): 341–361.

Painter, M., and J. Pierre (2005). "Unpacking Policy Capacity: Issues and Themes." In *Challenges to State Policy Capacity: Global Trends and Comparative Perspectives*, edited by Martin Painter and Jon Pierre, 1–18. Basingstoke: Palgrave Macmillan.

Pal, Leslie A., and Ian D. Clark (2015). "Making Reform Stick: Political Acumen as an Element of Political Capacity for Policy Change and Innovation." *Policy and Society* 34 (3–4): 247–257.

Peters, B. Guy (2015). "Policy Capacity in Public Administration." *Policy and Society* 34 (3–4): 219–228. https://doi.org/10.1016/j.polsoc.2015.09.005.

Pisani, Elizabeth, Maarten Olivier Kok, and Kharisma Nugroho (2017). "Indonesia's Road to Universal Health Coverage: A Political Journey." *Health Policy and Planning* 32 (2): 267–276. https://doi.org/10.1093/heapol/czw120.

Potter, Christopher, and Richard Brough (2004). "Systemic Capacity Building: A Hierarchy of Needs." *Health Policy and Planning* 19 (5): 336–345. http://doi.org/10.1093/heapol/czh038.

Ramesh, M., Xun Wu, and Alex Jingwei He (2013). "Health Governance and Health-care Reforms in China." *Health Policy and Planning* 29 (6): 663–672.

Reddy, K. Srinath (2015). "India's Aspirations for Universal Health Coverage." *The New England Journal of Medicine* 373 (1): 1–5.

Rokx, C. (2009). *Health Financing in Indonesia: A Reform Road Map.* Washington, DC: World Bank Publications.

Saguin, Kidjie, Si Ying Tan, and Nihit Goyal (2018). "Mapping Scientific Research on Policy Capacity: A Bibliometric Analysis and Qualitative Framework Synthesis." Paper presented at International Workshop on Public Policy, Pittsburgh.

Sambijantoro, S. (2014). "Jokowi Backs Plans to End Fuel Subsidies." *The Jakarta Post*, 2 May. www.thejakartapost.com/news/2014/05/02/jokowi-backs-plan-end-fuel-subsidies.html.

Shan, Juan (2016). "Health Insurance Policies for Rural, Urban Residents Merged." *China Daily*, 12 January. www.chinadaily.com.cn/china/2016-01/12/content_23049243.htm.

Shan, Linghan, Qunhong Wu, Chaojie Liu, Ye Li, Yu Cui, Zi Liang, Yanhua Hao, et al. (2017). "Perceived Challenges to Achieving Universal Health Coverage: A Cross-sectional Survey of Social Health Insurance Managers/administrators in China." *BMJ Open* 7 (5). http://bmjopen.bmj.com/content/7/5/e014425.abstract.

The Statistics Portal (2018). "Density of Nursing and Midwifery Personnel as of 2013, by Region (per 10,000 population)." www.statista.com/statistics/280159/density-of-nursing-and-midwifery-personnel-by-region/.

Suryahadi, Asep Yadi, Vita Febriany, and Athia Yumna (2014). "Expanding Social Security in Indonesia: The Processes and Challenges." Working Paper 2014–14. Geneva: UNRISD. www.unrisd.org/80256B3C005BCCF9/(httpAuxPages)/B31ACAA3F1FF4206C1257D9C0052B44F/$file/Suryahadi et al.pdf.

Tan, Si Ying (2018). "Bureaucratic Autonomy and Policy Capacity in the Implementation of Capitation Payment Systems in Primary Healthcare: Comparative Case Studies of Three Districts in Central Java, Indonesia." *Journal of Asian Public Policy* 12 (3): 330–350. https://doi.org/10.1080/17516234.2018.1459150.

Tan, Si Ying, and G.J. Melendez-Torres (2018). "Do Prospective Payment Systems (PPSs) Lead to Desirable Providers' Incentives and Patients' Outcomes? A Systematic Review of Evidence From Developing Countries." *Health Policy and Planning* 33 (1): 137–153. http://doi.org/10.1093/heapol/czx151.

Thabrany, H., A. Gani, M.L. Pujianto, and B.B. Mahlil (2003). "Social Health Insurance in Indonesia: Current Status and the Plan for National Health Insurance." Paper presented at Social Health Insurance Workshop WHO SEARO, New Delhi, 13–15 March.

Trisnantoro, L., T. Marthias, and D. Harbianto (2014). "Universal Health Coverage Assessment: Indonesia." Global Network for Health Equity. http://gnhe.funsalud.org.mx/Documentos/UHCDay/GNHEUHCassessment_Indonesia.pdf.

Waters, Hugh, Fadia Saadah, and Menno Pradhan (2003). "The Impact of the 1997–98 East Asian Economic Crisis on Health and Health Care in Indonesia." *Health Policy and Planning* 18 (2): 172–181. https://doi.org/10.1093/heapol/czg022.

WHO (2014). "World Health Statistics 2014: Part III Global Health Indicators." Geneva: World Health Organization. www.who.int/gho/publications/world_health_statistics/EN_WHS2014_Part3.pdf.

WHO (2016). "Global Health Workforce Statistics." Geneva: World Health Organization. http://apps.who.int/gho/data/node.main?showonly=HWF.

WHO (2018). "Global Health Expenditure Database." Geneva: World Health Organization. http://apps.who.int/nha/database.

Woo, Jun Jie, M. Ramesh, and Michael Howlett (2015). "Legitimation Capacity: System-level Resources and Political Skills in Public Policy." *Policy and Society* 34 (3–4): 271–283.

Wu, Xun, M. Ramesh, and Michael Howlett (2015). "Policy Capacity: A Conceptual Framework for Understanding Policy Competences and Capabilities." *Policy and Society* 34 (3–4): 165–171. http://doi.org/10.1016/j.polsoc.2015.09.001.

Yip, Winnie, and William C. Hsiao (2009). "Non-evidence-based Policy: How Effective Is China's New Cooperative Medical Scheme in Reducing Medical Impoverishment?" *Social Science & Medicine* 68 (2): 201–209. http://doi.org/10.1016/j.socscimed.2008.09.066.

Yu, Hao (2015). "Universal Health Insurance Coverage for 1.3 Billion People: What Accounts for China's Success?" *Health Policy* 119 (9): 1145–1152. https://doi.org/10.1016/j.healthpol.2015.07.008.

Yuan, Beibei, Weiyan Jian, Li He, Bingyu Wang, and Dina Balabanova (2017). "The Role of Health System Governance in Strengthening the Rural Health Insurance System in China." *International Journal of Equity in Health* 16: 44. https://doi.org/10.1186/s12939-017-0542-x.

8 Building the city from abroad
Viet Kieu and the rights to Saigon

Hung Vo and Donna Doan Anderson

Introduction

In recent decades, political and economic reforms through Vietnam's Doi Moi ("Renovation Era") have led to dramatic transformations in Saigon.[1] Since opening its doors to market reform and global capital penetration, Saigon's urban landscape has seen intense development, including the rapid construction of new urban centers on former agricultural land. Even as Vietnam continues to privatize state-owned enterprises and allow for the inheritance, transfer, exchange, leasing, and mortgaging of land-use rights, the state maintains full ownership of the land. With business and government often in collusion, urban space becomes a site of political, economic, and social contestation (Wendel and Aidoo, 2015).

This chapter examines the broad implications for the people, planning, and politics of the city by discussing the economic role played by overseas Vietnamese, also known as Viet Kieu, in Saigon's development. Using historical and contemporary analyses as well as ethnographic fieldwork, it explores the emerging impacts of temporary and permanent Viet Kieu returnees on the built environment in Saigon. To understand contemporary transformations in Saigon, we trace the history of international actors in the city and how integration into global economies has continued to challenge the development of the city. Facilitated by enabling state policies, the diaspora's remittances have become co-opted to accelerate exclusionary, large-scale urban development projects. The chapter begins by delineating the historical trajectory of urban development in Saigon, before analyzing the emerging impacts of Viet Kieu returnees on the built environment. We argue that, rather than advancing development, remittances promote dependency through exclusionary urban development.

Saigon's development history

With established commercial, monetary, and taxation systems, Saigon has remained the financial and economic capital of Vietnam since the Nguyen Dynasty of 1802–1945 (Nguyen et al., 2016: 17). Under colonialism, the French introduced modern urban planning to Cochinchina (the most southern region of Indochina) in the mid-19th century (ibid.). Naming Saigon the administrative and commercial hub for south Cochinchina created the need for the first master plans that would guarantee the city's development to meet French imperial needs (Wright, 1991). As laboratories or experimental terrains (*champs d'experience*), colonial cities became the ontological locations for aspiring young architects and administrators to exercise their radical ideas on what were considered "unadulterated primitive lands" in the *outre mer* (ibid.). A plan for the city was crafted in 1861 by one such radical French military engineer, Colonel Coffyn, who envisioned a "future metropolis of 2,500 hectares and half a million people that would allow for state, collective and private land ownership under colonial supervision" (Wright, 1991: 168. This was a truly aspirational vision, given that there were roughly 600 European residents and 50,000 Vietnamese and Chinese occupants within the city at the time.

Coffyn's population projection for Saigon was unrealized for over a century, and the number of inhabitants did not begin to proliferate until the latter half of the 20th century. Following colonial liberation at the end of World War II, the country was divided into the Democratic Republic of Vietnam in the North and the Republic of Vietnam in the South. Under the influence of the United States and its neoliberal ideology, domestic planners tried to make designs based on Western planning theories, but failed to facilitate Saigon's growth (Huynh, 2015). However, mass migration from the North to the South during the Vietnam War (1955–1975) swelled Saigon's population, leading to severe housing shortages (Nguyen et al., 2016). The South Vietnamese government responded with three plans – the Hoang Hung plan (1958), Ngo Viet Thu (1960), and Doxiadis (1962) – although they all had limited success due to lack of resources as a result of the ongoing Vietnam War (ibid.).

With the end of the war in 1975, Saigon lost both its status as South Vietnam's capital and its name. The new communist government adopted a centralized socialist system that abandoned private ownership and established collectivization of agricultural land (Coit, 1998; Nguyen et al., 2016: 17). This central planning period (1975–1985) did little for Saigon's development, which led to economic restructuring in 1986. The Doi Moi, meaning renovation or renewal, shifted Vietnam's focus from isolated, centralized policies to a more market-driven economy, open to foreign investment. This restructuring permitted the granting of land-use rights to organizations and individual land users under the administration of the state. In the years following the enactment of the Doi Moi, Vietnam continued to loosen its land-use laws to allow private capital (1991), the right to use land for joint ventures of domestic and foreign investors (1998), and large-scale projects and commercialization (2003) (Nguyen et al., 2016: 18).

The market liberalization of the 1990s enabled Vietnam to pursue much-needed infrastructure projects and to embark on a series of urban redevelopment projects. Situated within global frameworks of pressures toward a "new metropolitan mainstream", Saigon began to prioritize brash developments in an effort to increase competition and promote economic growth, at the cost of vernacular urban form and architecture. "[A]rticulated as a norm that defines what is to be regarded as urban or metropolitan while also presenting certain standards and processes for urban planning and design" (Schmid, 2012: 54), these developments raised concerns over the power and influence of capital on the everyday life of urban dwellers.

The new metropolitan mainstream

Beginning in the late 2000s, Vietnam began to strictly enforce street clearance policies to reduce "congestion", promote public order, and increase food safety (Kim, 2015). Not alone in its efforts, Vietnam joined other countries from Singapore to Mexico in waging battles against the informal sector. Masked by the rhetoric of beautification and revitalization are more insidious aspirations of exclusion by decision-makers keen on shaping the city to their liking. The complexities of this contestation and how it has been localized are explored in detail by Annette Kim in *Sidewalk City: Remapping Public Space in Ho Chi Minh City* (2015). Contrary to popular concerns over public health and pedestrian flow, Kim argues that such narratives are ill-informed and do not reflect the reality of what happens on the ground. While housing tenure and its accompanying rights have experienced protection under the law in Vietnam, this is a privilege only afforded to those who own property, despite the lack of a formal property rights regime in the country.

In 2017, the *New York Times* published a telling article on the policies encroaching on Saigon, titled "Efforts to Ease Congestion Threaten Food Culture in Southeast Asia" (Ives, 2017). While street food is affected, the underlying current reveals a more insidious effort to curb the informal sector in favor of a sanitized urban form characteristic of many Western cities. In making sense of this trend in Saigon, anthropologist Erik Harms contends that beauty has become a form of control in the "new Saigon" (Harms, 2012). Specifically, Harms argues that "discourses of beauty can and often do support the agendas of dominant elites" (ibid.: 737). The redevelopment of Saigon's Thu Thiem district, masterminded by Massachusetts-based firm Sasaki, was undertaken by the city administration using the rhetoric of "blight" or "urban wastelands" (Harms, 2014: 313). This type of legitimizing narrative is reminiscent of much US city-planning undertaken in the name of urban renewal. This is most evident in Jane Jacobs' (1992) work but also in Herbert Gans' 1962 landmark ethnographic study of the working-class residents in the West End neighborhood of Boston (Gans, 1982 [1962]). The difference in the case of Saigon, half a century later, is that, unlike the US, Vietnam's pursuit of the strategy reflects its desire to attract foreign capital.

Vietnam's increasing integration into the global economy has obvious ramifications for the population, primarily invoking concerns of displacement with the influx of foreign capital flows and investment. Municipal intervention in public space is not a one-off intervention in what authorities could consider a matter of regulatory enforcement; rather, it fits within the country's broader goals and strategies around attracting foreign direct investment (FDI). Many of the country's street-clearance policies emerged in the early 2000s, when the intake of FDI was beginning to increase. Harms, in exploring the consequences of two redevelopment projects in Saigon – Phu My Hung and Thu Thiem – frames this tension directly: such new development projects, he claims, represent one part "urban experiment" and another part "moral project" (Harms, 2016: 9). These new urban zones, as they are called, aim to "build a new 'urban civilization' and urban 'civility'" (ibid.) that stand in contrast to the perceived chaos and anarchy associated with the use of public space. Because the street vendors do not fit the image of Vietnam's new moral awakening, they are disenfranchised through the legal system, their security or precarity dependent on the negotiations they conduct or the empathy they invoke in the authorities (Kim, 2015).

If public space could ever be considered a site of democratic engagement, it is becoming increasingly scrutinized for purposes of political surveillance and moral policing (Low, 2006; Sevilla-Buitrago, 2014). This Western conceptualization of space is complicated within a developing world context such as Vietnam, where the communist party has complete control of land and people. While the government can easily be blamed for enacting regressive policies, a closer look reveals that emerging exclusionary policies are not entirely disconnected from transnational capital flows.

Diaspora dollars and the role of remittances

While existing research focuses on foreign capital as an important engine of urban development, few researchers have interrogated the different forms of capital. Attracting FDI is critical for developing countries starved of capital. Since joining the World Trade Organization in 2007, Vietnam's average pool of annual FDI has leapt from USD 2.5 billion in 2000–2005 to USD 8.4 billion in 2008–2014 (OBG, 2017). While these investments account for up to 21% of Vietnam's annual GDP and are the focus of broader contemporary debates on globalization, another form of global capital, remittances, remains overlooked. The International Monetary Fund divides remittances into three broad categories: 1) personal money transfers; 2) compensations, wages, or salaries; and 3) capital transfers. In Vietnam, remittances often reach levels that are as high as FDI – or even higher, as between 2010 and 2014. In fact, there is a noticeable positive relationship between remittances and growth in FDI, as illustrated in Figure 8.1. This study presents a first attempt to connect diaspora remittances to processes of urban development and exclusion in Saigon.

In 2015, Saigon received nearly USD 4.4 billion in remittances, 22% of which went into real estate and 72% into starting businesses. In 2017, Saigon received the highest share of remittances in the country, with an inflow of USD 5.2 billion, representing an increase of 18% (Das, 2018). According to the Vietnam Investment Review (2018),

> The last quarter [of 2018] marks the moment when Vietnam will receive the largest amount of remittance for the year in comparison with other channels such as securities, gold and foreign currencies. The real estate sector is considered a potential channel to attract this investment.

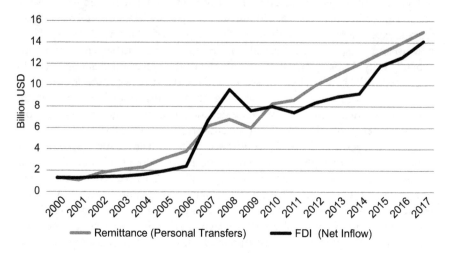

Figure 8.1 Remittances and FDI in Vietnam 2000–2017

Source: Author recreation based on World Bank data under CC BY-4.0.

Source: https://data.worldbank.org/indicator/BX.KLT.DINV.CD.WD?locations=VN and https://data.worldbank.org/indicator/BX.TRF.PWKR.CD.DT?locations=VN

While historically remittances were intended to support family members left behind, in 2017 only an estimated 6% of remittances were for kinship support (Das, 2018).

The economic influence of first-generation Vietnamese migrants, also known as Viet Kieu, has enabled Vietnam to emerge as one of the fastest-growing economies of Asia, growing at an annual rate of 7.3% a year between 1990 and 2010 (Donor Working Group, 2012: 10). Many members of this diaspora, from a variety of socio-economic classes, engage in a transnational citizenship bridging the USA and Vietnam. Viet Kieu "navigate the apparent disconnect between ideal cultural models of the space they live in and the everyday realities of their actual lives" (Harms, 2011: 3) by shifting their identities, roles, and capital dependent on the space they occupy. Thus, the types of remittances they make – economic and social, formal and informal – reflect the complicated roles that their influence and their dollars play in Saigon's development.

As a result of the Vietnam War, huge numbers migrated from South Vietnam to countries including the United States, Australia, and Canada.[2] Years of closed authoritarian policies stunted economic growth and prevented many migrants from returning until diplomatic ties were re-established between the USA and Vietnam in 1995. Meanwhile, with the Doi Moi economic restructuring that opened Vietnam's economy in 1986, Viet Kieu began pouring billions into the development of Saigon. Formal remittances, such as direct money transfers, account for upwards of 10% of Vietnam's GDP, with an estimated USD 11.9 billion being sent in 2016 (Tyabaev et al., 2016). As is characteristic of developing countries with large diaspora populations overseas, remittances play a significant role in the development of the city, often reaching levels equivalent to foreign aid and FDI combined (Thai, 2014). Although migrant money has been a significant contributor to Vietnam's growth, its role is complicated and has created an ambivalence, an "in-between-ness" as to who has the right to the city. This is similar to Erik Harms' description of the residents of Hoc Mon as "neither wholly inside nor outside, but uncomfortably both" (Harms, 2011: 3).

For many migrants, their engagement with the homeland is dependent on the state and international legal frameworks. Since macroeconomic restructuring began in the late 1980s, the Vietnamese government has continued to loosen its authoritarian grip in order to entice Viet Kieu and their dollars to return home. When it removed the 5% tax on remittances in 1997, the flow of remittances through formal channels significantly increased, largely taking the form of individual contributions such as supplemental income toward a family's living expenses (Thai, 2014). However, the government's range of economic incentives has not been able to stop informal money transfers, such as so-called pocket exchanges, gift giving, or spending money upon returning to the homeland. These informal remittances are estimated to supplement recorded remittances by at least 50% (Thai, 2014: 21; World Bank, 2005).

The Vietnamese government estimated that more than half a million migrants returned to Vietnam to visit in 2008 – a significant increase from the 8,000 just 20 years earlier (Chan and Tran, 2011). Although informal remittances are not included in reported figures, it is clear to see how a stable flow of financial remittances would make a remarkable impact on the economy of a city like Saigon.[3] The increased role of these remittances has spawned two dominant models within the literature: the *dependency model*, which argues that remittances increase inequality, generate a culture of migration, and encourage unnecessary consumption and the *development model*, which argues that remittances help poor countries to achieve economic growth by raising household income levels.[4]

In the specific case of Vietnam, Thai (2014) highlights the transnational nature of the Viet Kieu. Focusing on the largely altruistic motives and the complex social dynamics related to money circulation in Saigon, Thai introduces the concept of the "transnational expenditure cascade" (ibid.: 25). This "cascade" exists through "the impacts that giving and spending money among migrant members of transnational families have had on the spending habits of other migrants, their non-migrant relatives, and Vietnamese society in general" (ibid.: 26). Thai's research identifies many Viet Kieu living as low-wage workers in the US who regularly send money to families in Vietnam or take drastic measures to save money to spend upon returning. In so doing, they confound their status and social class by converting their low incomes in the US to high incomes in Vietnam. The transnational expenditure cascade thus allows Viet Kieu to move beyond binary categorizations of Weberian and Marxist theoretical traditions, which examine class divisions within the same national economy and society or within macro/micro and "first and third world" approaches (ibid.: 29; see also Frank, 1967; Radhakrishnan, 2011: 17; Wallerstein,

1974). This allows a greater examination of the tensions surrounding the "in-between" nature of the Viet Kieu's financial remittances as currencies of care and of status, fulfilling both economic and social needs.

Returning migrants, whether temporary or permanent, carry with them not only money to spend and share with their family and friends back home but their diverse experiences, perspectives, and opinions from abroad. As a result, their financial and social remittances can also carry positive outcomes for capital-seeking developers but negative implications for those operating in the informal sector. In this sense, the Vietnamese diaspora is just one of many examples of a transnational community whose members have multiple identities and involvements that are not cemented either to their homelands or to their host countries.

Examining remittances solely through an economic lens limits our understanding of the "in-between" status of the Viet Kieu. More attention needs to be given to social remittances including ideas, values, norms, and concepts that migrants transfer to their homelands (Levitt, 1998). Social remittances recognize that diaspora migration patterns are not linear but transnational and cyclical in nature. Just as migrants bring values and ideas to their host countries, this process then "affects what they [migrants] send back to non-migrants who either disregard or adopt these ideas and behaviors, transforming them in the process, and eventually re-remitting them back to migrants who adopt and transform them once again" (Levitt and Lamba-Nieves, 2011: 3). As a form of non-financial capital, social remittances may involve change in community practices, improving infrastructure, engaging in political behavior, gender and familial roles, and generating new business and trade targeting the diaspora's new transnational class (Isaakyan and Triandafyllidou, 2017: 2789).

The transnational class

Diaspora networks and urban exclusion

The global financial crisis in the mid- to late-2000s undermined much of the economic progress Vietnam had made since the Doi Moi restructuring, prompting the government to prioritize the economic and social capital of the Viet Kieu (Sassen, 2000). Recognizing the potential impact of a transnational citizenry, the Vietnamese government responded with a series of legal changes beginning with Resolution 36, passed in 2004, which was the "first clear articulation of the fact that [the Vietnamese government] considered Vietnamese people both at home and abroad as equally important to national unity" (Koh, 2015: 185). The Investment Law of 2005 provided Viet Kieu with preferential land rents and reductions in corporation tax, personal income tax, and tariffs on machinery imports for those making business investments. In addition, Decree 71 (issued on 8 August 2010) allowed those who hold "Vietnamese nationality" and those of "Vietnamese origin" to own any number of houses, as long as their work was relevant to state agencies and contributing to national development (ibid.: 186).

Thai (2014: 101) suggests that merchants capitalize on low-wage migrant networks by opening businesses that are specifically priced for migrants with foreign capital and by maintaining feelings of "old" Saigon in their businesses in order to target migrants wishing to re-engage with their pre-migration years. However, "it is not difficult encountering social divisions within the new Saigon, which reflect how class and gender are encoded in different axes of the city" (ibid.: 99; see also Caldeira, 1996). The efforts made on behalf of some Viet Kieu to engage in an "authentic" Vietnamese lifestyle further exacerbate their "in-between-ness". At the same time, returnees also begin to establish businesses that cater to other overseas Vietnamese. We spoke to one Vietnamese American businessman who had returned permanently to Vietnam, who designed and sold homes exclusively to other returnees.[5]

Although reliable data on permanent returnees are scarce, Harris (2015) cites figures from a Communist party website claiming that roughly 3,000 Viet Kieu returned to Saigon between June 2004 and June 2013, with an additional 9,000 holding long-term residential permits for work or investment. A search for new opportunities, cultural pressures, gendered expectations, and the lack of adventure and fulfillment in their careers motivate high-skilled migrants to re-engage with Vietnam. These "returnees [are] distinct from other high skilled expatriates as they make cultural efforts to blend in with locals while also asserting their simultaneous foreignness" (Nguyen-Akbar, 2017: 1117). In her ethnographic study of the "1.5 generation", Mytoan Nguyen-Akbar notes that these members of the diaspora occupy a third, "in-between space" that separates them from working- and middle-class locals in Vietnam (ibid.). This is exemplified in the residential areas that returnees live in: "hems", or densely populated residential alleyways off major streets, offer a more authentic Saigonese experience than the exclusive home rentals in secluded neighborhoods or high-rises in the center of the city, which are created to attract foreigners.

Elite enclaves, restricted mobility

In the same ways that the local economy responds to the diaspora's actual or projected interests, returnees exert preferences that are materialized in the built environment. This primarily manifests in their indirect appropriation of public space through their housing preferences. Increasingly, new housing projects in Saigon are becoming gated. In areas where there are no gates, guards are deployed to monitor who comes in and out of the site. In one visit to a popular housing enclave for overseas Vietnamese built by the Vinhome conglomerate, a guard stopped Hung's motorbike and demanded identification from him and his driver. While the road was public and not marked as private, pseudo enforcement personnel patrolled the perimeters and kept out unwanted guests.

Retired Viet Kieu represent one of the largest capital-wielding investment groups, according to interviews with developers and government officials.[6] Retirees returning to Saigon seek the conveniences they were accustomed to back in the United States. A form of social remittances, these retirees bring Westernized preferences for order, sanitation, and urban form, which become physically constitutive. According to Savills, a major developer in Vietnam, many opt to purchase luxury properties: "Their favourite option is apartments in the medium and high-end segments with one or two bedrooms. . . . Viet Kieu want to buy houses in Vietnam for asset accumulation or to lease out" (quoted in Ngoc, 2018). This has arguably fueled property development and speculation, such as the 252-unit Viet Kieu Village on the periphery of Saigon.[7] The Viet Kieu Village represents one of the most regulated examples of the built environment. The development began directly after the Vietnamese government had relaxed regulations on foreign property ownership for Viet Kieu who could prove their Vietnamese origins;[8] only those who could prove their connection to the diaspora were allowed to purchase properties and reside in the community. Over the course of two decades, the law was changed three times to make it increasingly easy for overseas Vietnamese to purchase property.

The diaspora's preferences and investment patterns in Saigon coincide with Gavin Shatkin's "real estate turn" in urban politics in Southeast Asia, in which governance regimes align their strategies to propel real estate development (Shatkin, 2016). Members of the diaspora and their remittances do not introduce new forms of exclusion to the city; rather, they intensify existing forms of exclusion by enabling large-scale capitalist urban development projects. One of Vietnam's largest real estate developers and brokers sought to sell as much as 20% of its housing stock to overseas Vietnamese, according to an interview with one of its sales agents.[9] The ability of Viet Kieu returnees to impact the real estate market is further extended by their unique relationship with the Vietnamese government, which courts their investment and their return. As a result, rather than creating the assumed positive outcomes, remittances perpetuate the dependency model through increasing inequality. This is accomplished through the separation of foreign elites from the domestic populace.

The rights and privileges that both low-wage and high-skilled returnees enjoy in Saigon become a lens through which to analyze the insecurity of informal workers in the city. The returnees belong to a growing group of actors staking claims on and trying to shape the city. Within the context of state strategies for national development, which include exploiting the capital and talents of the diaspora, they become privileged actors in this process. In creating the social and public infrastructure necessary to encourage their return and long-term stay, the state has engaged in targeted, large-scale development projects. Informal workers – among those most affected by exclusionary public space – become victims of these changes, cast aside as a nuisance. During a drive around a new development site in Phu My Hung, the district in which Viet Kieu Village is located, my motorbike driver was prevented from entering a commercial waterfront area. The policeman who stopped our vehicle offered no explanation. Frustrated, my driver exclaimed, "Phu My Hung does not belong to you!"

Although the entry of the diaspora network (and their capital) is heralded by the international community as a new actor on the development stage, their capital poses considerable development challenges. The tightening of control over public space is seen through new developments and speculative real estate projects. Erik Harms (2016: 60) documents the public regulations that accompanied the newly constructed Phu My Hung district, such as signs in the parks requiring visitors to "behave a cultural and civilized lifestyle at public spaces [sic]". Diaspora return and engagement in the urban life in Saigon can be argued to have accelerated this "new mainstream cosmopolitanism" in the city.

Debates on globalization have focused on firms and corporations as the parties responsible for urban change through speculation. Our research suggests that the influence from diaspora networks, especially in a country with a large, capital-heavy diaspora, can make similar claims on urban space. These claims coalesce with state desires to transform Saigon into a new global city. New actors with new claims have helped to perpetuate existing inequalities in the city, especially among the most vulnerable population, operating in the informal sector. Public space becomes one of the battlegrounds where this tension is most apparent.

Conclusion

Centralized bureaucratic interventions, such as the creation of the State Committee for Overseas Vietnamese Affairs, further incentivize business by overseas Vietnamese. Housed under the Ministry of Foreign Affairs, the State Committee for Overseas Vietnamese Affairs manages programs including conferences on economic development, summer camps for Viet Kieu children, and the expansion of Vietnamese education abroad (VOV, 2016). However, it is the annual "Homeland Spring" (Xuan Que Huong) program directed toward Viet Kieu returning for the lunar New Year holiday (VOV, 2018) that most clearly demonstrates the bureaucratic intention to create a transnational Vietnamese citizenry.

While completing fieldwork in January 2019, Hung was invited, through connections in the State Committee, to attend the Homeland Spring 2019 celebration. The Ho Chi Minh City Hall welcomed nearly 1,000 Viet Kieu for what appeared to be a celebration dedicated completely to the overseas Vietnamese community. On the bright stage, next to a large bust of Ho Chi Minh, was an image of the city's skyline – a metaphor of the city's ambition as well as foreshadowing what would unfold throughout the evening. Represented in the list of speakers were city leaders as well as notable Viet Kieu who have contributed to the city, all of whom urged the attendees to support the city's long-term development and aspiration to become a "smart city," emphasizing the aspect of "homeland". The message was clear: given their tremendous capital potential, the Viet Kieu are an indispensable part of the city's future development.

By problematizing diasporic capital and positioning it in a broader set of questions about governance, this chapter has explored issues of citizenship and urban change by treating "return migrants as an analytical entity" (Chan and Tran, 2011). As globalization continues to intensify across major and secondary cities around the world, it sets the conditions for "new economic possibilities, social spaces and political constellations" (Ong, 2000: 55–56). Some scholars see economic globalization as market liberalization in the form of capital deregulation and expansion in FDI (Brenner, 1999); others explore the socio-cultural dimensions of globalization, noting the new ways in which collective identities are created from an intermixing and exchange of people, commodities, and information (Appadurai, 1996). Within these shifting definitions, the Viet Kieu represent a force for globalization, given Viet Nam's path of global economic integration. While immigrants are often considered the "other", fixing them within the context of "processes whereby global elements are *localized*, international labor markets are constituted and cultures from all over the world are de- and re-territorialized" allows them to become central figures in globalization (Sassen, 2000: 83, italics in original).

Increasing capital flows and integration appear to go hand-in-hand with greater regulation and erosion of public life. In order to achieve its development aspirations, the state aligns itself with the interests of foreign firms and their capital, the consequences of which are well known: people and their livelihoods are displaced for the sake of capitalist growth. Between 2008 and 2011, over 1.5 million people in Vietnam registered complaints with the government related to displacement, submitting over 600,000 petitions. In 2010, the government announced that Saigon needed to implement 500 projects that would require the clearance of 83,000 households (Phúc Huy, 2010). These projects could not have been accomplished by the state alone but required the active involvement of foreign investments. As this chapter has demonstrated, while FDI is a critical element in the Vietnamese economy, so are remittances from the diaspora. The ebb and flow of overseas Vietnamese capital has played a key role in the urban development of Saigon.

If the current trend continues, the inflow of remittances will continue to rise and be absorbed by a specialized sector of the real estate market. There is the potential for this capital to be directed toward sustainable growth if the necessary regulatory framework is created and enforced: however, given the state's metropolitan vision for Saigon and its deliberate strategy of soliciting overseas support, any effort to modulate remittances appears unlikely. While remittances have often been hailed as a tool for development, our analysis shows that remittances can accelerate and intensify existing exclusionary practices in the city and therefore promote dependence. This chapter thus raises some important policy questions: how can the government make best use of diasporic capital to support Saigon's developmental needs? What measures can be taken to curb exclusionary urban growth?

Old actors have acquired new roles in contemporary Saigon. Behind the bustle of the city is a new group of elites who spend limited amounts of time in the city but who hold significant capital power. As the state continues to align itself with foreign capital, it is orienting the city toward becoming an attractive destination for overseas Vietnamese. Vietnam's integration into the global economy since the turn of the millennium has been due, in large part, to diaspora dollars. While legislation and various government programs have made it easier for Viet Kieu to return and work in Vietnam, "substantial ambiguities and bureaucratic inefficiency have undercut these measures", forcing Viet Kieu to adopt a "cautious, wait-and-see approach toward the country" (Koh, 2015: 174). The Viet Kieu have introduced new opportunities and economic potential to the development of Saigon, but at the same time these pose a threat to locals' right to the city. Increased awareness around the challenges of governing of a global city like Saigon requires a broader, more holistic approach that incorporates both local residents and more transitory populations.

Notes

1 In this chapter, we have chosen to refer to Ho Chi Minh City as Saigon throughout, as the majority of the diaspora in the United States as well as the city's residents use this name. We have also chosen not to employ diacritic marks in Vietnamese words and names, for the sake of smoother reading.
2 Estimates put the numbers at 1.3 million in the USA (in 2014), 227,000 in Australia (mid-2015) and 183,000 in Canada (also mid-2015); see Zong and Batalova (2016).
3 For general information on remittances as important supplements to developing countries' economies, see Ratha (2013); Ratha and Mohapatra (2007); Solimano (2003).
4 For more on the dependency model see Kpodar and Le Goff (2011); for the development model see OECD (2006).
5 Interview with a local business owner who has asked to remain anonymous, January 2019.
6 Interviews with officials from the State Committee for Overseas Vietnamese Affairs in Saigon, January 2019.
7 The Viet Kieu Village was conceived as a development project in 2002, and construction completed in 2008. INTRESCO, formerly a state-owned development company, built the project with widespread support from government officials keen on building a strong relationship with the diaspora. To the government, providing easy access to local housing for overseas Vietnamese was the key to securing their long-term engagement with the country.
8 Interview with a former public relations manager of INTRESCO, January 2019.
9 Interview with a sales agent in a large real estate brokerage firm, January 2019.

References

Appadurai, Arjun (1996). *Modernity at Large: Cultural Dimensions of Globalization.* Minneapolis, MN: University of Minnesota Press.

Brenner, Neil (1999). "Globalisation as Reterritorialisation: The Re-scaling of Urban Governance in the European Union." *Urban Studies* 36 (3): 431–451.

Caldeira, Teresa P.R. (1996). "Fortified Enclaves: The New Urban Segregation." *Public Culture* 8 (2): 303–328. https://doi.org/10.1215/08992363-8-2-303.

Chan, Yuk Wah, and Thi Le Thu Tran (2011). "Recycling Migration and Changing Nationalisms: The Vietnamese Return Diaspora and Reconstruction of Vietnamese Nationhood." *Journal of Ethnic and Migration Studies* 37 (7): 1101–1117.

Coit, K. (1998). "Housing Policy and Slum Upgrading in Ho-Chi-Minh City." *Habitat International* 22 (3): 273–280. http://doi.org/10.1016/s0197-3975(98)00011-3.

Das, Koushan (2018). "Remittances to Vietnam on the Rise." *Vietnam Briefing News*, 7 May. www.vietnam-briefing.com/news/remittances-vietnam-rise.html/ (accessed 20 April 2019).

Donor Working Group (2012). *Vietnam Development Report 2012: Market Economy for a Middle-Income Vietnam*. Hanoi: Vietnam Development Information Center.

Frank, Andre Gunder (1967). *Capitalism and Underdevelopment in Latin America*. New York City: NYU Press.

Gans, Herbert J. (1982 [1962]). *The Urban Villagers: Group and Class in the Life of Italian-Americans*. New York: Simon and Schuster.

Harms, Erik (2011). *Saigon's Edge: On the Margins of Ho Chi Minh City*. Minneapolis, MN: University of Minnesota Press.

Harms, Erik (2012). "Beauty as Control in the New Saigon: Eviction, New Urban Zones, and Atomized Dissent in a Southeast Asian City." *American Ethnologist* 39 (4): 735–750.

Harms, Erik (2014). "Knowing Into Oblivion: Clearing Wastelands and Imagining Emptiness in Vietnamese New Urban Zones." *Singapore Journal of Tropical Geography* 35 (3): 312–327.

Harms, Erik (2016). *Luxury and Rubble: Civility and Dispossession in the New Saigon*. Oakland, CA: University of California Press.

Harris, Scott (2015). "Returning to the Homeland, Vietnamese Americans Make their Mark." *Los Angeles Times*, 30 April.

Huynh, Du (2015). "The Misuse of Urban Planning in Ho Chi Minh City." *Habitat International* 48: 11–19.

Isaakyan, Irina, and Anna Triandafyllidou (2017). "'Sending So Much More Than Money': Exploring Social Remittances and Transnational Mobility." *Journal of Ethnic and Racial Studies* 40 (15): 2787–2805.

Ives, Mike (2017). "Efforts to Ease Congestion Threaten Street Food Culture in Southeast Asia." *New York Times*, 29 April. www.nytimes.com/2017/04/29/world/asia/sidewalk-food-vendors-hanoi-bangkok-jakarta.html (accessed 20 April 2019).

Jacobs, Jane (1992). *The Death and Life of Great American Cities*. New York: Vintage Books. Print.

Kim, Annette Miae (2015). *Sidewalk City: Remapping Public Space in Ho Chi Minh City*. Chicago, IL: University of Chicago Press.

Koh, Priscilla (2015). "You Can Come Home Again: Narratives of Home and Belonging Among Second-Generation Việt Kiều in Vietnam." *Journal of Social Issues in Southeast Asia* 30 (1): 173–214.

Kpodar, Kangni, and Maelan Le Goff (2011). "Do Remittances Reduce Aid Dependency?" IMF Working Paper 11/246. Washington, DC: International Monetary Fund.

Levitt, Peggy (1998). "Social Remittances: Migration Driven Local-Level Forms of Cultural Diffusion." *The International Migration Review* 32 (4): 926–948.

Levitt, Peggy, and Deepak Lamba-Nieves (2011). "Social Remittances Revisited." *Journal of Ethnic and Migration Studies* 37 (1): 1–22.

Low, S.M. (2006). "The Erosion of Public Space and the Public Realm: Paranoia, Surveillance and Privatization in New York City." *City & Society* 18 (1): 43–49.

Ngoc, Bich (2018). "Property Market Fueled by Viet Kieu." *Vietnam Investment Review*, 11 March. www.vir.com.vn/property-market-fuelled-by-viet-kieu-57049.html.

Nguyen, Thanh Bao, D. Ary A. Samsura, Erwin van der Krabben, and Anh-Duc Le (2016). "Saigon – Ho Chi Minh City." *Cities: The International Journal of Urban Policy and Planning* 50: 16–27.

Nguyen-Akbar, Mytoan (2017). "The Formation of Spatial and Symbolic Boundaries Among Vietnamese Diasporic Skilled Return Migrants in Ho Chi Minh City, Vietnam." *Sociological Perspectives* 60 (6): 1115–1135.

OBG (2017). "Foreign Direct Investment and Trade in Vietnam Continue to Climb." *Oxford Business Group*, 10 December. https://oxfordbusinessgroup.com/overview/bucking-trend-foreign-direct-investment-and-trade-continue-climb (accessed 20 April 2019).

OECD (2006). "International Migrant Remittances and their Role in Development." In *International Migration Outlook 2006*, edited by OECD, 140–159. Paris: OECD.

Ong, Aihwa (2000). "Graduated Sovereignty in South-east Asia." *Theory, Culture & Society* 17 (4): 55–75.

Phuc Huy (2010). "TP.HCM: noi thieu noi thua nha tai dinh" [HCMC Short of Space and Homes for Resettlement]. *Tuoi Tre*, 11 January.

Radhakrishnan, Smitha (2011). *Appropriately Indian: Gender and Culture in a New Transnational Class*. Durham, NC: Duke University Press.

Ratha, Dilip (2013). "The Impact of Remittances on Economic Growth and Poverty Reduction." MPI Policy Briefs, September. Washington, DC: Migration Policy Institute.

Ratha, Dilip, and Sanket Mohapatra (2007). "Increasing the Macroeconomic Impact of Remittances on Development." Development Prospects Group. Washington, DC: World Bank.

Sassen, Saskia (2000). "The Global City: Strategic Site/New Frontier." *American Studies* 41 (2/3): 79–95.

Schmid, Christian (2012). "Henri Lefebvre, the Right to the City, and the New Metropolitan Mainstream." In *Cities for People, not for Profit: Critical Urban Theory and the Right to the City*, edited by Neil Brenner, Peter Marcuse, and Margit Mayer, 42–62. London and New York: Routledge.

Sevilla-Buitrago, Alvaro (2014). "Central Park Against the Streets: The Enclosure of Public Space Cultures in Mid-nineteenth Century New York." *Social & Cultural Geography* 15 (2): 151–171.

Shatkin, Gavin (2016). "The Real Estate Turn in Policy and Planning: Land Monetization and the Political Economy of Peri-urbanization in Asia." *Cities* 53: 141–149.

Solimano, Andres (2003). "Remittances by Emigrants: Issues and Evidence." Working Paper 2003/98. Helsinki: World Institute for Development Economic Research (UNU-WIDER).

Thai, Hung Cam (2014). *Insufficient Funds: The Culture of Money in Low-Wage Transnational Families*. Stanford, CA: Stanford University Press.

Tyabaev, Andrey E., Svetlana F. Sedelnikova, Nguyen Th Hong Bach Lien, and Yaroslav N. Lopukhin (2016). "Capital Investment of Overseas Vietnamese to the Economy of the Socialist Republic of Vietnam." SHS Web of Conferences, 28. https://doi.org/10.1051/shsconf/20162801105.

Vietnam Investment Review (2018). "Real Estate Transactions to Increase in Q4." *Vietnam Investment Review*, 13 October. www.vir.com.vn/real-estate-transactions-to-increase-in-q4-63073.html?fbclid=IwAR19lY_6upqh-CY7zoQRke8nnSmzCGm6VhGCRlEekt-wge4_kKPI72RlwrLw.

VOV (2016). "Summer Camp Opens for Young Expats." *The Voice of Vietnam*, 13 July. http://vovworld.vn/en-US/news/summer-camp-for-young-vietnamese-expats-opens-452742.vov (accessed 19 February 2019).

VOV (2018). "Overseas Vietnamese Treated to Homeland Spring Program." *The Voice of Vietnam*, 8 February. http://vovworld.vn/en-US/current-affairs/overseas-vietnamese-treated-to-homeland-spring-program-618089.vov (accessed 12 May 2019).

Wallerstein, Immanuel (1974). "The Rise and Future Demise of the World Capitalist System: Concepts for Comparative Analysis." *Comparative Studies in Society and History* 16 (4): 387–415.

Wendel, Delia Duong Ba, and Fallon Samuels Aidoo (Eds.) (2015). *Spatializing Politics: Essays on Power and Place*. Cambridge, MA: Harvard University Graduate School of Design.

World Bank (2005). "Global Economic Prospects 2006: Economic Implications of Remittances and Migration." Global Economic Prospects and the Developing Countries (GEP) Report 34320. Washington, DC: World Bank. http://documents.worldbank.org/curated/en/507301468142196936/Global-economic-prospects-2006-economic-implications-of-remittances-and-migration.

Wright, Gwendolyn (1991). *The Politics of Design in French Colonial Urbanism*. Chicago, IL: University of Chicago Press.

Zong, Jie, and Jeanne Batalova (2016). "Vietnamese Immigrants in the United States." *Migration Policy Institute*, 8 June. www.migrationpolicy.org/article/vietnamese-immigrants-united-states-3.

9 Negotiating block size in Shanghai

Historical superblock or New Urbanist small block?

Daixin Dai and George Frantz

Introduction

Over the past decade there has been a debate over the merits of the traditional configuration of cities in China. The focus of discussions has been on the size of city blocks and the advantages, perceived or otherwise, of the American urban design template of small city blocks, vigorously promoted by the New Urbanist movement (Calthorpe, 2013; Lee and Ahn, 2003), versus the large city blocks that have been the organizing structures of Chinese cities for some three millennia. These large city blocks, which are the norm in China, are referred to in the USA as "superblocks".

The superblock is substantially larger than a traditional city block in many American cities. The 104 superblocks analyzed for this study ranged in size from 2.3 hectares (hereafter "ha") to 97 ha in area. Of these superblocks, 57 – or 55% of the sample – are eight ha (approximately 20 acres) or larger. A superblock is often bounded by arterial streets designed to move high volumes of traffic efficiently; however, many superblocks in older sections of cities, including New York City and Shanghai, are bounded by two-lane streets. Within the superblock a network of lanes, characterized by low volumes of traffic, limited vehicular passage, and restricted visibility at intersections and turns, carry local traffic and provide access to residences and businesses. Moreover, in contrast to the streets surrounding the superblock, these lanes have multiple functions, serving as vehicle, pedestrian, and bicycle routes.

Historical and cultural contexts are key to how urban form and space are defined. Urban centers in China date back to 5000 BCE, and urban planning as a discrete practice emerged there over 3,000 years ago. The superblock is an old urban form, the earliest known plan incorporating the concept being the plan for the new city of Chengzhou (near present day Luoyang, Henan province), drafted in 1036 BCE by the Chinese official Zhou Li. Zhou Li laid out his new city in accordance with specific principles that he recorded and later codified in the *Kao-Gongji* or the *Ancient Chinese Encyclopedia of Technology* (Jun, 2013). His plan for Chengzhou became a template for city planning in China, to be replicated over and over again in the new capital cities of multiple dynasties, up to and including Beijing.

The large city block as an organizing form in Chinese cities was thus well established when William Penn's plan for Philadelphia (1682) and James Oglethorpe's plan for Savannah (1733) established the small city block grid as the organizing framework for American cities. Many cities in the USA – Philadelphia and Savannah being but early examples – were originally laid out as speculative real estate ventures. This practice has its roots in the system established by the English crown at the beginning of European colonization: control of land was granted to individuals or corporations, with the expectation that there were profits to be made from the land in the "New World". Frontage on a public street was maximized as a means of maximizing lot prices. The city as real estate venture was especially influential in the layout of cities in the Western USA in the latter part of the 19th century, as railroads used the sale of land granted by the US government as a means of financing their construction.

The bias toward the automobile and the West's history of automobile-oriented urban planning, in the USA especially, is very evident in many of the arguments against the use of the superblock. Smooth, efficient vehicular traffic circulation is a paramount urban planning objective in US cities, and, historically in the USA, this has been achieved through the use of dense urban street grids. The new guidance on city block size in China, issued by the State Council of the Peoples Republic in February 2016, turns away from China's urban planning tradition by promoting smaller city blocks; this reflects a modern-day bias in favor of the automobile, as a key objective of breaking up the superblocks is to improve traffic circulation and relieve congestion.

For the purposes of this case study, the characteristics of city blocks in Shanghai (China), Kyoto (Japan), Taipei (Taiwan), and New York City (USA) were examined for a number of attributes such as size, extent, and character of automobile and pedestrian infrastructure and "walkability".[1] Shanghai was chosen because it is the largest city in China and has a history of urban planning dating to the late 1800s that reflects indigenous urban planning as well as substantial foreign interventions and influences, including in the question of city block size. Kyoto and Taipei were chosen as examples of the long-standing presence of the superblock elsewhere in Asia: in Kyoto since before 800 CE, in Taipei since the 1880s. New York City was chosen because it is the largest and one of the most densely populated Americans cities, and its city grid, based on the small city block, is considered an American planning icon. It was also selected because, since the early 20th century, a number of superblocks have appeared within the urban fabric of the city. Of the 23 New York superblocks identified from satellite imagery, 14 (61%) were carved out of the existing urban fabric through demolition and consolidation; the remaining nine (39%) were developed on greenfield sites. Eleven of the superblocks were developed as public housing by the New York City Housing Authority.

The superblock in the United States has come under criticism from planners in recent years for a variety of alleged issues, from disrupting automobile traffic patterns and shifting the burden of traffic onto surrounding streets, to reducing the walkability of cities, to creating exclusive "gated communities". In the suburban context in the USA, the preponderance of ultra-low-density cul-de-sac streets resulting in super-sized blocks has been decried for creating a near total dependence on the automobile, a hostile pedestrian environment, and social isolation. True though this may be, these suburban "superblocks" bear no relationship to or lineage with the superblocks of Shanghai, Kyoto, Taipei, or New York City, nor are they comparable, given their location within the suburban context, their predominantly single-family detached housing, and their density.

More darkly, although contradicted by the history and functionality of superblocks in New York City and the millennia of experience in China and elsewhere in Asia, superblocks have been labeled sociological disasters, havens of poverty and crime (Calthorpe, 2013). This line of argument is derived from the high-profile failure of a number of public low-income housing projects in US cities, most notably the notorious Priutt-Igoe in St. Louis, MO and the Cabrini Green low-income housing projects in Chicago. Despite the numerous other documented faults of such public housing projects, such as incompetent management, racial discrimination, corruption, gross failures in maintenance and upkeep, and lack of basic amenities for residents, planners and the popular press have pointed to block size as a major factor (Kan et al., 2017; Texeira, 2019). Yet elsewhere superblock-based public housing projects such as those developed and maintained by the New York City Housing Authority have succeeded in providing low-income housing in a livable urban environment, as has market-rate housing such as the seminal Stuyvesant Town and Peter Cooper Village in Manhattan, and Parkchester in the Bronx. These superblock-based, high-density urban communities built in the 1940s continue to provide good-quality living environments for their residents today.

Shanghai and the Chinese superblock

This "superblocks are bad urban design" message has been transmitted to and accepted by urban planners in China in recent decades and is now reflected in Central Government guidance. In February 2016, China's State Council released a new set of urban development guidelines designed to improve urban planning practice in the country, fostering more sustainable, pedestrian-based urban areas with improved access to commercial areas, public parks, and other public services (Shepard and Huang, 2016).

City planners in Shanghai did contemplate moving to the small city block concept earlier in the 20th century. The Shanghai General Plan, begun in 1927 and completed in 1931, was a series of planning documents created by the Shanghai City Committee under the Guomingtang. It included both general regional plans for the city and its hinterland and detailed urban plans for specific sections of the city under Republic of China control. One of its most ambitious proposals was to develop a new center for City of Shanghai administrative functions and a major commercial center in Wujiaochang, north of the International Concession. Very much influenced by Western planning thought, the master plan proposed a New Administration District with a cruciform street layout incorporating several squares, a city administrative building, library, museum, and other public build-ings. A series of new streets radiating from a point southwest-west of the New Administration District would connect this new Chinese administered area to the rest of the city to the south. But the most radical feature of the new plan was the use of small city blocks in a grid pattern. These smaller city blocks ranged in size from approximately 75 meters by 145 meters (1.25 ha.) to 90 meters by 170 meters (1.5 ha.) (Gao, 2012). Implementation commenced with the mapping and construction of some of the streets and public buildings. In June 1934, the Mayor's Building was completed and opened (ibid.). The 1937 Japanese invasion stopped further implementation of the Shanghai General Plan, however, and sat-ellite imagery for the Wujiaochang area reveals that while some of the proposed radial streets were constructed utilizing small city blocks, the smaller city block pat-tern was mostly abandoned. Today just over 105 city blocks occupy an area where in 1931 over 860 were envisioned.

The 1949 Greater Shanghai Plan, 3rd Draft, completed in May 1949, was produced by a team of architects and planners that included German expatriate architect Richard Paulick and urban planners Jin Jingchang, Zhong Yaohua, and Cheng Shifu. They blended Howard's Garden City concepts with Eliel Saarin-en's Organic Decentralization theory. They proposed 11 new satellite districts on the edges of central Shanghai, each home to between 500,000 and one million residents. More importantly, the 1949 draft plan embraced continued use of the superblock, primarily as a means to reduce street intersections and intersection conflicts for pedestrians but also to ensure efficient and fluid movement of traf-fic along urban arterials. The plan advocated block sizes of 400 meters by 800 meters for commercial development and 600 meters by 1,000 meters for residen-tial areas. To further control impacts of heavy urban traffic, the plan also recom-mended a hierarchy of streets. While broad arterials would move traffic efficiently through the metropolitan area, streets within the proposed neighborhood units would be no wider than two traffic lanes (Shanghai Urban Planning Commit-tee, 1949: 95). The plan was not adopted, but many of its concepts, including the large city block, survived and continued to influence plans completed since liberation.

In the newly adopted Shanghai Master Plan 2017–2035, the city is upending the planning doctrine established in the 1949 Greater Shanghai Plan, 3rd Draft. The 2035 Master Plan calls for developing a "small, human-oriented urban spa-tial fabric" and for increased control over the size and scale of the city block in order to "control street block sizes within appropriate walking distances by increasing the road network density" (Shanghai, 2018: 62). Advocates of the smaller American-style city block generally posit that smaller blocks equal a more developed street network that gives drivers more options as they move through the community, provides more street frontage for shops and services, and increases the walkability of the city and neighborhood. In contrasting block sizes in cities in China and the USA, Calthorpe has argued that superblocks in China, divided by wide arterial streets, contribute to traffic congestion, whereas a denser network of narrower streets can both better optimize the flow of traffic and improve safety for pedestrians (Calthorpe Associates). In this auto-centric viewpoint, more streets provide drivers with more options, thus improving traffic flow. This ignores that fact that, while in the USA urban transportation is dominated by the movement of automobiles, in China it is still very much dominated by pedestrian and bicycle movement.

In its report *Urban China: Toward Efficient, Inclusive and Sustainable Urbanization*, the World Bank repeats the argument for smaller city blocks, calling for a "finer grain" street system such as that found in Paris and other European cities (World Bank et al., 2014: 145). It attributes to such finer grain street systems more optimized traffic flows because they create more direct routes for traffic. Pedestrian mobility is also purported to be enhanced. Whether small blocks and many streets actually improve pedestrian safety and enhance pedestrian mobility, in large cities in particular they do expose the pedestrian to greater volumes of traffic and higher traffic speeds and to higher levels of traffic noise and air pollution than do the lanes within a superblock.[2] The lower speed limits (30 kph or less), constricted street widths, blind corners and curves, and the competing pedestrian and bicycle traffic make lanes and alleys very unattractive to cut-through traffic.

At the same time, this finer grain street network alluded to in the World Bank's prescription for curing the alleged ills of the superblock –

[a] high density of narrow streets with close intersections creates a vibrant, safe, and walkable urban landscape. Destinations tend to be within walking distance, and the system of close intersections enables the pedestrian to change direction easily. The connectivity of streets of different sizes ensures the continuity of public space that is an essential feature for walkability.

(ibid.)

– actually describes the character of the contemporary residential superblock in Shanghai and other Chinese cities, as well as the historic superblocks in cities such as Kyoto and Taipei.

Other arguments favoring smaller city blocks over superblocks in China are that more street-facing shops generate more pedestrian traffic (Shepard and Huang, 2016) and that more streets means more sidewalks and thus increased walkability (Hamidi and Ewing, 2014). This may be so, but as illustrated across so many sprawling, low-density suburbs throughout the USA, more street-facing shops attract more pedestrian traffic only if there are pedestrians living within a walkable distance and there are sidewalks to accommodate them. These arguments also ignore the reality in China, where arterial-fronting superblock perimeters often provide the types of dynamic, pedestrian-dominated commercial areas that American urban planners pine for. In the post-1990 Minhang District of Shanghai, in the vicinity of the Dongchuan Road Metro station, approximately 24% of the total street frontage is commercial space; in Putuo District, approximately 32% of the street frontage within the Caoyang neighborhood is occupied by commercial space. These arguments for small city blocks are unfortunate in that they ignore some three millennia of urban planning practice as well as the 20th-century thinking embodied in both the Garden City movement in Shanghai and the seminal 1949 Greater Shanghai Plan, 3rd Draft.

The role of population size and density

Population size and density are critical factors that distinguish cities in China and the rest of Asia from the USA. For this case study, city blocks in Shanghai, Kyoto, and Taipei were compared to city blocks in the 10 most densely populated cities in the USA. The mean population density of the four Asian city blocks studied – 14,764 persons/km^2 – outstrips the mean population density of the 10 most densely populated cities in the USA by a factor of almost 2.5 times.[3] This higher density in the Asian cities permits much greater reliance by residents on walking and cycling and provides a critical mass of passengers necessary to support investment in the kind of dense mass transit network that makes the automobile superfluous. In fact, all four of the Asian city areas studied are served by one or more metro/ subway station. Their population densities also provide the critical mass to eco- nomically sustain neighborhood-oriented retail development within easy walking distances of homes. All four study areas are characterized by numerous small shops meeting the daily needs of residents, as well as restaurants and the offices of doctors and other professional service providers.

Suggesting the adoption of American-style small blocks in the name of effi- ciency in the movement of traffic thus ignores a number of factors that distinguish the Chinese city from the American city. First and foremost, as already hinted, are population size and population density: only nine US cities have populations that exceed 1,000,000 persons, and only 33 have populations that exceed 500,000 persons. The majority of major US cities have population densities of less than 2,000 persons/km^2 (5,130 persons/mi^2). Of the 200 largest US cities, only 44 have population densities in excess of 2,000 persons/km^2, well below that of the typical city in China; only five US cities have population densities in excess of 5,000 persons/km^2 (12,820/mi^2).

This low density in US cities has resulted in much greater dependence on the automobile, but it also translates into much lower traffic volumes in typical American residential neighborhoods, due to fewer residents and dwellings and less local traffic. Within the urban cores, however, the small block grid has gener- ated significant volumes of traffic through residential neighborhoods, especially those on the periphery of city centers, introducing high levels of noise, exhaust emissions, and dust, dramatically affecting air quality and substantially lowering the quality of life. This is most evident in older neighborhoods close to the down- town centers of cities in the USA, where former boulevards have evolved into major arterial streets. With the increasing levels of traffic generated by suburban sprawl, the quality of life in what were often upper-class neighborhoods in the 19th century deteriorated in the 20th century to the point at which the higher- income residents abandoned these areas for the suburbs, and they devolved into strips of offices, retail, and low-rent apartments. The lower density of typical

American cities also precludes the critical mass of population necessary to economically sustain small-scale neighborhood retail development or the dense network of primary schools that would enable children to walk to school. Walkability of a neighborhood is only relevant when there are destinations to walk to.

The advocacy for smaller city blocks that favors the movement of the automobile ignores many of the benefits of the superblock concept for residents of the high-density metropolis. Vehicular traffic is dramatically reduced, and, where permitted, it is more often than not sharing the roadway with a much larger number of pedestrians and bicycles. In this environment, vehicular speed and movement are subordinated to the safety of the pedestrian and cyclist. Land dedicated to wider streets and the separate sidewalk infrastructure for pedestrians within the typical small block grid can be dedicated to personal and community green space within a superblock. In New York City, planners have often been permitted to ban the automobile from the core of the superblock, turning those areas over entirely to the residents for their use and enjoyment. In many cities in China, locating schools within the superblock has reduced the exposure of children to high volumes of traffic at multiple street intersections on their walks to and from school.

The configuration of the city block

Returning to Zhou Li's city plan for the new city of Chengzhou in 1036 BCE, the superblock was conceived as the basic building block of the new city. In his plan the typical city block (superblock) measured about 334 meters per side and covered approximately 10.9 ha (Jun, 2013). The original city as a whole covered approximately 180 ha (0.67 mi^2). A key aspect of Zhou's principles of urban design was conceptualizing the city as a series of modules. Initially, the new city of Chengzhou was of a specific size, but his modular design permitted an orderly expansion of the city. His imprint can be found in many cities in China today and continues to shape the urban form in the 21st century.

Modern superblocks come in a variety of shapes from irregular and curvilinear forms such as those found at Radburn, New Jersey; Greenbelt, Maryland; and the older sections of Shanghai, to the late-20th and early 21st-century rectilinear blocks which have been the catalyst for the current policy debates in China and the USA. Physically, superblocks in the USA and China are characterized by a lack of lanes that pass straight through the blocks and directly connect streets on either side. In Kyoto and Taipei, the majority of lanes do pass directly through the superblocks. Inside the superblock, not all pedestrian pathways are dedicated to pedestrian use only. In the cases of Kyoto, Shanghai, and Taipei, pathways within the superblock may be shared with the bicycle, motorbike, and automobile. Cars and other vehicles may be permitted, but they are the subordinate to the pedestrian and the bicycle as a transportation form. Vehicular speeds are reduced to 30 kph/20 mph or less. This is accomplished through a combination of: 1) setting maximum legal speed limits; 2) physical design elements such as narrow lanes (no more than five meters in width), with tight curves, restricted visibility, and control devices such as speed bumps and "stop" intersections; and 3) the often-larger volumes of pedestrian and bicycle traffic sharing the same path.

The pedestrian pathway, whether along a busy arterial road or within the super-block, must be attractive and enticing to city residents. Along arterial roads, the sidewalks must be adequately sized to safely accommodate the anticipated pedestrian traffic without excessive congestion and must provide designated pedestrian crossings, a well-established tree canopy (a critical element in semi-tropical and tropical climates), and clear signposting. The appeal of pedestrian pathways, whether inside or outside the superblock, is enhanced by dynamic commercial enterprises, an attractive built environment including pleasing architecture, as well as seating and other amenities that encourage residents to linger and promote the myriad social interactions triggered when people congregate.

A survey of superblocks in New York City, Shanghai, Taipei, and Kyoto was conducted as part of our investigation. In the case of Shanghai, we looked at superblock development from five sections of the city: the Old City (pre-European era), Luwan/French Concession (late 19th/early 20th centuries), Putuo District (1950s/1960s), Xinzhuang (1980s/1990s), and southern Minhang District (late 20th/early 21st centuries) to trace their evolution. In New York City, superblocks were developed as both public and private housing communities. Numerous superblocks were created throughout the city beginning in the 1930s in order to provide sites for public housing projects. In Manhattan they were often part of pre-World War II slum clearance and urban renewal projects. To make way for Metropolitan Life's Stuyvesant Town and Peter Cooper Village projects in 1944, some 24 blocks were cleared. (NYT Archive, 1943). In Brooklyn, Queens, and the Bronx, they were often greenfield developments, such as the Parkchester development on 121 acres in the Bronx.

Some 1,800 years after the construction of Chengzhou, the Japanese Emperor Kanmu adopted the superblock concept when he established his new capital city of Kyoto in 794 CE, using the T'ang capital of Chang'an as his model (Ebrey et al., 2006). Taipei, like Shanghai, is a relatively new city, dating to the mid-1800s and the Qing Dynasty of China. The design for the city was drawn up under Emperor Guangxu and development began in 1882. Following the long-standing Chinese urban planning practice, it was laid out in a rectilinear form, with superblocks, in what is now the northern portion of Zhongzheng District where the Presidential Office Building and other Taiwanese government buildings are located. After World War II, Taipei continued to expand eastward away from the Tamsui River, but urban planners maintained the superblock form as the basic urban organizing unit.

Today superblocks can vary significantly in size. Our study of 104 superblocks in the four cities uncovered a wide variation in block sizes, both within and between the cities (Table 9.1). The median size of superblocks sampled in the four cities ranges from five ha in Taipei to 21 ha in Kyoto. The median sizes in New York City and Shanghai are relatively close: 9.3 and 9.6 ha respectively. The mean size of the superblocks of Kyoto is by far the greatest, at 31.7 ha, followed by New York City at 14 ha, Shanghai at 12 ha, and Taipei at just 6.7 ha. The

Table 9.1 Sampling of superblock sizes, New York City, Kyoto, Shanghai, and Taipei

City	Sample Size	Median Block Size (ha)	Smallest Block Size (ha)	Largest Block Size (ha)	Median Dimension (North-South) (meters)	Median Dimension (East-West) (meters)
Kyoto, Japan	15	21	5.7	96.9	468	573
New York City, USA	22	9.3	6	73	289	311
NYC Housing Authority	11	7	6	19	295	274
Private Rentals, Co-ops, Condominiums	11	12	7	73	283	440
Shanghai, China	51	9.6	2.7	46.3	325	390
Old City	6	15	2.7	46.3	268	523
Luwan/French Concession	12	7	5.2	20.2	325	155
Putuo/Caoyang Xincun	12	6	2.8	13.3	280	185
Xinzhuang	9	8	3.9	22.4	195	460
Minhang District	12	18	15.8	24.8	428	425
Taipei, Taiwan	16	5	1.2	23.8	295	178

sampling of 15 superblocks to the west and south of the Imperial Palace in Kyoto also shows that Kyoto has the largest variation in terms of block sizes, ranging between 5.7 ha and 96.9 ha, followed by New York City, where the variance is between six ha and the 73 ha Co-Op City superblock in the Bronx. The largest superblock identified in Shanghai, 46.3 ha, is located not in the modern Minhang suburb but in the old city.

The outside dimensions of the sample blocks were calculated from satellite imagery. Given that the common city block is not uniformly rectilinear but most often trapezoidal or another irregular polygon shape, average north to south and east to west dimensions were calculated. The blocks in Kyoto and Minhang District, Shanghai, exhibited the largest outside dimensions – in fact, substantially larger block sizes – than the other study samples. In Kyoto the median dimension north to south is 468 meters, and the median dimension east to west is 573 meters. In Minhang the median dimension north to south is 428 meters and east to west 425 meters. At the smaller end, Putuo District and Taipei are closely aligned in terms of outside block dimensions: median north to south and east to west block dimensions in Putuo are 280 and 185 meters respectively; in Taipei they are 195 meters and 178 meters respectively. Median block size in Putuo is slightly larger: six ha versus five ha in Taipei.

The smaller size superblocks in New York City, specifically those occupied by NYC Housing Authority public housing, can be attributed to early 20th-century urban renewal in the city. The majority of these blocks appear to have resulted from the consolidation of three or four former city blocks into new development sites. The larger, privately developed superblocks, on the other hand, were mostly built on greenfield sites in peripheral areas of Brooklyn, Queens, and the Bronx, where larger land parcels still existed. The 46 ha Parkchester site in the

Bronx, developed between 1939 and 1942, was a former Catholic home and farm for boys. The 73 ha Co-op City was developed on former wetlands along the Hutchinson River at the eastern edge of the Bronx between 1966 and 1973.

In New York and Shanghai, the streets and alleys within the superblock are most often cul-de-sacs that bar through traffic, in effect limiting vehicle traffic to that of residents. In the case of the New York City blocks in Table 9.1, perimeter parking lots dominate, leaving the interior portions of the superblocks as strictly pedestrian spaces. In the case of Shanghai, the alleys and lanes form extensive cul-de-sac systems, which rarely extend through a block to another street. Even on the few through connections, the route is so tortuous – with twists and turns and blind intersections – that it is exceedingly undesirable to a driver.

Kyoto and Taipei differ from New York and Shanghai in the layout of their superblocks. In these two cities the internal lanes and alleys of the superblocks generally pass through from one side of the blocks to the other, but they are usually five meters or less in width and often only permit one-way automobile and truck traffic. The travel lane is also shared with pedestrians, motorbikes, and bicycles, creating obstacles and slowing traffic. Narrow lanes and the proximity of buildings create blind intersections and sharp turns, again resulting in a route that most drivers would choose to avoid if possible.

The large city blocks that dominate in Shanghai, Kyoto, and Taipei create urban enclaves nested within the matrix of arterial streets, which form islands of livability in the metropolis, buffering residents from heavy traffic, incompatible land uses, and other undesirable features of the urban landscape and providing a higher-quality living environment within the city. Although the American blocks accommodate similar functions, the term "superblock" merely describes physical form, whereas "enclave" encompasses social and environmental attributes of that form.

In the typical Shanghai superblock, mixed-use buildings facing onto the streets contain retail shops and services catering to residents, while shielding the interior of the block from arterial traffic and noise. High masonry walls, grilled fences, and landscaped areas set back from the streets and sidewalks also provide effective delineation between interiors of blocks and city streets. Within many blocks, small shops catering to residents' needs, community centers, schools, childcare and senior centers, and parks and playgrounds can be found. Interior streets and alleys function as a shared transportation resource, with the automobile subordinated to pedestrian and bicycle traffic, as described previously. Access to the block is restricted to a few points along the perimeter of the block, and in many cases the entry points are for pedestrians only.

Immediately apparent in city block configurations in two areas of Shanghai, in Kyoto, in Taipei, and two areas of New York City is the dominance of lanes in the urban fabric of the Asian examples and the dominance of through streets and arterials in New York City. The superblock and lane network in the Caoyang Xincun area of Putuo District (#1), the first units of which were constructed in 1952 (SUCRDI, 2018), is notable in that it was a prototype *xincun* (workers' village) designed in accordance with the Garden City and the block/street network design principles laid out in the 1949 Greater Shanghai Plan, 3rd Draft. Caoyang Xincun and its superblock and lane configuration would become a template for new residential development in Shanghai right through to the development of the Minhang District, begun in the 1990s (#2). Key features include one or more central spines that terminate deep within the block, either as a cul-de-sac or a T-junction with another lane, with secondary lanes branching off from the spine. Intersections are generally constricted, forcing drivers to turn sharply and reduce their speed even further. On-street parking, sometimes in unauthorized, informal spaces, intrudes into traffic lanes. Buildings, shrubs, and other landscaping can reduce sight ranges to four to five meters or less. Finally, the lanes serve not only for motor vehicles but also for bicycles and pedestrians, requiring care and attention on the part of drivers. The size of the superblocks in Shanghai and elsewhere has grown considerably since the construction of Caoyang Xincun: those in the Minhang sample area range between 15.8 ha and 24.8 ha, with a median size of 18 ha, while those in the Putuo sample area range between 2.8 ha and 13.3 ha, with a median size of six ha.

The superblock configurations in Kyoto and Taipei differ significantly from those of the Shanghai examples in that the lane networks in those cities typically extend all the way through the superblocks to the bordering arterial streets, directly connecting one side to the other. Nonetheless, the constricted width of the lanes, coupled with on-road parking; multiple low-visibility intersections; and competing use by pedestrians, bicycles, and motorbikes, are a strong deterrent to through traffic. This is in stark contrast to the grids of Manhattan and Queens, which, while providing drivers with multiple options for traveling through the city, do so at a significant cost to the livability of urban neighborhoods and the quality of life for the residents living along those streets.

In the two examples of superblocks in Manhattan and Queens shown on the maps, the Stuyvesant Town and Peter Cooper Village complexes (1944) in Manhattan stand out, as do the New York City Housing Authority superblocks in Queens. The lanes in Stuyvesant Town do not penetrate into the core of that community, instead looping through tenant parking areas and back onto the street. One lane extends east to west through Peter Cooper Village, but it was designed with several sharp turns to slow traffic and make it unattractive as a through street. The blocks in Queens are entirely pedestrian with the exception of some parking lots on the periphery.

The six sample areas are relatively close in terms of the total amounts of streets and lanes, with a mean combined length of 47,334 meters and median combined length of 42,991 meters. Manhattan in New York City has the lowest combined length, 37,369 meters of streets and lanes, while Taipei has the highest amount, 62,920 meters.

In terms of the World Bank's "fine grain street" network, Queens, with some 38,882 meters of street length, would qualify as the finest-grained network of streets, followed by Manhattan. The street network in Kyoto is by far the least fine-grained of the six sample networks, with only 8,505 meters of street network. In terms of total streets plus lanes network, Taipei has the finest-grained street

Table 9.2 Comparison of aggregate lengths of lanes and streets in the sample city block systems in Kyoto, New York, Shanghai, and Taipei

	Streets (meters)	Lanes (meters)	Total Streets + Lanes (meters)	Proportion of Lanes to Streets
Kyoto	8,505	32,157	40,662	3.78095238
New York – Manhattan	32,983	4,386	37,369	0.13297759
New York – Queens	38,882	2,174	41,056	0.05591276
Shanghai – Putuo/Caoyang	17,409	39,663	57,072	2.27830433
Shanghai – Minhang	10,846	34,080	44,926	3.14217223
Taipei	21,685	41,235	62,920	1.90154485

network, with some 62,920 meters of street and lane network, followed by the networks in Putuo and Minhang districts in Shanghai. Manhattan and Queens lag well behind Taipei, with only 37,3689 meters and 41,056 meters respectively.

In terms of the proportional differences between total length of lanes to length of streets, the contrast between the small block fabric of New York and the super-block fabric of the Asian cities is dramatic. The street networks in the Queens and Manhattan sample areas dominate the transportation network, whereas in the other four sample areas in Kyoto, Shanghai, and Taipei, lane lengths dominate street lengths by factors of 3.78, 3.14, 2.28, and 1.90 times respectively. Because the street networks in Kyoto, Shanghai, and Taipei are dominated by lanes, they do not serve vehicular traffic nearly as well as the street networks in New York City. They do, however, serve the resident populations of the superblocks in those cities by providing a dense network of pedestrian and bicycle paths within the superblock through the shared use of the lanes.

Porosity and walkability

Porosity is a measure of the ease with which the residents of a superblock and others can pass in and out of the neighborhood. In the case of the superblock, porosity is an important factor influencing the walkability (or lack thereof) for superblocks. Lower porosity can be an indicator of a lower level of walkability, since with fewer entry/exit points, residents must often walk extra distances to the designated points. As noted later, porosity varies widely among sample areas.

Historically, walking distance has been a key measure in determining what is walkable. Clarence Perry in the 1920s based his neighborhood concept on the five minute/0.25-mile walking distance radius (Perry, 1998 [1929]). Perry's neighborhood concept has spread throughout the world (Mehaffy et al., 2014; Miao, 2003). However, recent evidence indicates that walkable distances in the USA are much higher than Perry's 0.25-mile radius. According to Agrawal and Schimek, in 2001 the mean walking-trip length for the US was estimated to be 0.62 miles (Agrawal and Schimek, 2007), while Pucher et al. (2011), using data from the US National Household Travel Surveys, derived an estimate of 0.61 miles. In their analysis of data from the 2009 National Household Travel

Surveys, Yang and Diez-Roux (2012) calculated that over 65% of trips on foot were in excess of 0.25 mile, while 18% were in excess of one mile in length.

A major premise of this chapter is that walkability – and consequently the accessibility of the city to its residents – is a critical ingredient in the livability and the social and ecological sustainability of the city. Walkability enhances the rights of city residents to their city (Wang, et al. 2017). Pedestrian-based transportation and pedestrian-orient public spaces – sidewalks but also parks and other green space – also provide enhanced opportunity for direct public contact between city residents, as they move through their neighborhoods and districts (ibid.). This holds true also for the semi-private space of the superblock interior. Per Wang, "planning and policies aiming to improve city welfare and citizens wellbeing should work to forge and to revitalize public space and consider that streets, roads, paths, passes are the nexus of much of the multi-functionality in cities" and that "mobility is also balanced with placemaking and local commerce with active living people" (ibid.). As Jane Jacobs points out in *The Death and Life of Great American Cities* (1961), a bustling sidewalk that incorporates the clear demarcation between public and private space, actively utilized buildings along it, and many "eyes upon the street" are critical in attracting a robust flow of both residents and strangers walking along it. Busy superblock lanes create the same environment, without the large volumes of vehicular through traffic that characterize most urban arterial streets.

Key arguments against the superblock in Chinese cities have been the issues of walkability and distance to destinations beyond the superblock. The focus of the argument is the porosity of superblocks, the robustness of connections between the superblock and the public street network, particularly in comparison to the American small city block. The number of entry and exit points into and out of the superblocks in the six sample areas was determined utilizing a combination of maps, satellite imagery, and on-site documentation. The perimeters of superblocks were then calculated using street center-lines derived from maps and satellite imagery and aggregated for each sample area. The number of entry and exit points per 100 meters was then calculated for each superblock to arrive at an estimate of porosity and aggregated for each sample area. The results are shown in Figure 9.1.

It is immediately obvious that the superblocks in the two Shanghai sample areas are far less porous that those in Kyoto, New York City, or Taipei. Superblocks in those three cities have between 2.1 and 4.4 times as many exit and entry points per 100 meters as superblocks in the Minhang sample area and between 1.5 and 2.1 times as many entry and exit points per 100 meters as superblocks in the Putuo sample area. In the case of Kyoto and Taipei, the typical lane emerges directly onto one of the surrounding streets or arterials, giving those superblocks a high level of porosity. In the case of Queens, the single cluster of six superblocks is comprised of relatively small superblocks with proportionally more street frontage and dense networks of walkways within the blocks.

The lack of porosity in the sample superblocks in Shanghai is due to the historical use of walls in Chinese cities to delineate neighborhoods and to provide

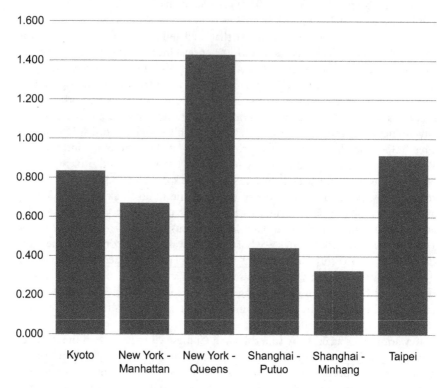

Figure 9.1 Number of entry and exit points per 100 meters

residents with a sense of security. Walled residential compounds and walled neighborhoods date back centuries in China, and this is reflected in contemporary Shanghai. In the Minhang sample area there are on average 3.4 entry and exit points per block; in the Putuo sample area, there are on average 4.6 entry and exit points per block. This lack of porosity restricts the ability of residents to enter or exit the superblock to only a few locations. But while superblocks in Minhang and Putuo exhibit the least amount of porosity, this does not translate into less walkability for residents, nor is porosity a difficult issue to address.

In the case of Minhang, 20 of the 37 entry points meet the public street within or immediately adjacent to a commercial area, and the entire sample area is within a 0.25-mile radius of any one of these 20 entry points. The commercial areas are each comprised of a diverse mix of retail goods and services, including food, clothing, hardware and household goods, auto repair shops, banks, restaurants, medical offices, and government services offices. The Zhiye Plaza shopping mall at the corner of Dongchuan and Shiping roads is a three-level mall with approximately 45,000 m^2 of floor area, including a large supermarket. Measured along streets and sidewalks – public bicycle and pedestrian infrastructure – approximately 43% of the Minhang sample area is within Agrawal and Schimek's 0.62-mile walking range.

In the Putuo sample area, only 28 of the 123 entry points meet the public street within or immediately adjacent to a commercial area. Because the commercial nodes in Putuo are smaller and more scattered through the area, however, only a 17-ha portion, representing about 7% of the sample area, is located more than a 0.25-mile radius of a commercial area. At the core of the sample area is the three-story, 49,000 m² Caoyang Shopping Mall, which is within a 0.62-mile walking distance of over 80% of the sample area.

Thus the low levels of porosity of the superblocks in the Minhang and Putuo sample areas do not detrimentally impact walkability. In terms of pedestrian infrastructure such as sidewalks, the distances to services are eminently walkable, regardless of block size. It can be argued that these neighborhoods and the neighborhoods of the Kyoto and Taipei sample areas are more walkable than the neighborhoods of Manhattan and Queens, particularly from the standpoint of pedestrian safety and comfort. Within the superblocks, pedestrians and cyclists are not subjected to the levels of traffic, with their associated speed, noise, and air pollution, that are encountered on public thoroughfares in New York City. Rather, they are walking in an environment where a substantial portion of their walk is along a narrow lane where there are fewer automobiles and other motor vehicles, where vehicle speeds are dramatically curtailed, and where the automobile is subordinated to pedestrians and cyclists.

Conclusion

It remains to be seen whether and in what form the State Council's February 2016 urban development guidelines will be implemented in the coming decades and what effect they will have. The superblock has served the cities of China and their residents well for some 3,000 years. The timing of the new policy, in an era of climate change concerns and continued investments in bicycle and pedestrian facilities and in public transportation, is not auspicious.

Arguments setting forth the benefits of smaller blocks and a finer-grained urban street grid, while valid in the context of the sprawling, low-density, low-population, automobile-dominated cities in the USA and other high-income countries, tend to fall apart in the context of the high-density and still very much bicycle- and pedestrian-oriented cities of China. They ignore basic facts on the ground, such as the already dynamic street environment in the typical Chinese city and the concentrations of neighborhood commercial development adjacent to superblocks, both made possible by population density, proximity, and walkability. They ignore the comfort and safety afforded pedestrians in the low-traffic, low-speed lanes within the superblock, instead advocating an environment where vehicular traffic dominates the life of the neighborhood. They ignore the implications of placing schools, community centers, and other neighborhood services adjacent to busy streets, as opposed to nesting them within superblocks.

This is not to argue that the superblock doesn't warrant any scrutiny or that there is no need for change. The porosity of superblocks in Chinese cities can and should be addressed as the country continues to grow and expand its cities. It may not be necessary to increase porosity in superblock design, but it is important to ask the question of "porosity for whom?" The emphasis in the debate to date has been porosity for all, to the benefit of the automobile user. More consideration should be given to the impacts of a fine-grained urban street pattern on pedestrians and cyclists and on residents of the apartments and condominiums who would be coping with the street traffic situated just beyond their front door.

Any improvements in porosity should also address the matter of the entry points for cyclists and pedestrians in the superblocks. Even if there is no major issue with regard to walkability in terms of distance and infrastructure in places like Minhang and Putuo in Shanghai and in other cities throughout China, selected improvements in pedestrian infrastructure, in the form of a greater number of conveniently located entry and exit points, would enhance the attractiveness of non-automobile transportation to city residents. As with the historical layout of the interior superblock lane, the improved pedestrian and bicycle infrastructure should be designed in a manner that protects the high-quality living environment that residents within the superblock currently enjoy.

The superblock as an urban form has served the residents of Chinese cities well through the unprecedented shift in population from rural to urban since 1949 and through the meteoric rise of the automobile in China over the past 40 years. It has been – and continues to be – a useful urban planning tool in keeping the automobile at bay and creating high-quality residential environments within some of the most densely populated cities in the world. If not implemented very carefully, the new small-block oriented urban design guidelines adopted by the Central Government, based on Western planning models biased toward the personal automobile, threaten to upend a successful approach to providing attractive, good-quality, human-scale, and sustainable residential environments for inhabitants of its cities.

Notes

1 We utilize Ann Forsyth's definition of walkability in our discussion, namely "the very basic physical infrastructure to get from one place to another . . . a continuous path with some reasonable surface and no major hazards", and "that destinations are close enough to get to in a reasonable time on foot" (Forsyth, 2015: 10).
2 As noted earlier, for the purpose of this study, a lane is a street with a width of five meters or less, characterized by low volumes of traffic, limited vehicular passage, and restricted visibility at intersections and turns, which is designed to carry local traffic and provide access to residences and businesses.
3 The relatively low population density of Minhang District in Shanghai is due largely to the estimated 35% of the district dedicated to industrial development or agricultural uses.

References

Agrawal, Asha Weinstein, and Paul Schimek (2007). "Extent and Correlates of Walking in the USA." *Transportation Research Part D* 12: 548–563.

Calthorpe, Peter (2013). "Point of View: Q & A." *Metropolis Newsletter*, 23 July. www.metropolismag.com/Point-of-View/July-2013/Q-A-Peter-Calthorpe/ (accessed 23 March 2015).

Calthorpe Associates (undated). "Low Carbon Cities: Practices for China's Next Generation of Growth." Pamphlet.

Ebrey, Patricia, Anne Walthall, and James B. Palais (2006). *Pre-modern East Asia: To 1800*. Boston, MA: Houghton Mifflin.

Forsyth, Ann (2015). "What Is a Walkable Place? The Walkability Debate in Urban Design." *Urban Design International* 20 (4): 274–292.

Gao, Sangni (2012). "Shanghai Urban Planning History Review." TS.

Hamidi, Shima, and Reid Ewing (2014). "A Longitudinal Study of Changes in Urban Sprawl Between 2000 and 2010 in the United States." *Landscape and Urban Planning* 128: 72–82.

NYT Archive (1943). "Housing Plan Seen as a 'Walled City': Civic Groups Oppose Post-War Metropolitan Life Project, Citing Lack of Schools." *New York Times*, 20 May.

Jacobs, Jane (1961). *The Death and Life of Great American Cities*. New York: Random House.

Jun, Wenren (2013). *Ancient Chinese Encyclopedia of Technology: Translation and Annotation of Kaogong Ji* (The Artificers' Record). London and New York: Routledge.

Kan, Har Ye, Ann Forsyth, and Peter Rowe (2017). "Redesigning China's Superblock Neighbourhoods: Policies, Opportunities and Challenges." *Journal of Urban Design* 22 (6): 757–777. https://doi.org/10.1080/13574809.2017.1337493.

Lee, Chang-Moo, and Kun-Hyuck Ahn (2003). "Is Kentlands Better Than Radburn? The American Garden City and New Urbanist Paradigms." *Journal of the American Planning Association* 69 (1): 50–71.

Mehaffy, Michael, Sergio Porta, and Ombretta Romice (2014). "The 'Neighborhood Unit' on Trial: A Case Study in the Impacts of Urban Morphology." *Journal of Urbanism: International Research on Placemaking and Urban Sustainability* 8 (2): 199–217. https://doi.org/10.1080/17549175.2014.908786.

Perry, Clarence (1998 [1929]). *The Neighbourhood Unit*. London and New York: Routledge/Thoemmes Press.

Pu, Miao (2003). "Deserted Streets in a Jammed Town: The Gated Community in Chinese Cities and Its Solution." *Journal of Urban Design* 8 (1): 45–66.

Pucher, John, Ralph Buehler, Dafna Merom, and Adrian Bauman (2011). "Walking and Cycling in the United States, 2001–2009: Evidence From the National Household Travel Surveys." *American Journal of Public Health* 101 (Supplement 1): S310–S317.

Shanghai (2018). *Shanghai Master Plan 2017–2035*. Shanghai: Shanghai Urban Planning and Land Resource Administration Bureau.

Shanghai Urban Planning Committee (1949). *Greater Shanghai Plan, 3rd Draft* (大上海都市计), edited by Shanghai Urban Design Research Institute. Shanghai: Tongji University Press.

Shepard, Wade, and C.C. Huang (2016). "China's Urban Policy Unit Just Met for the First Time in 38 Years. Here's What It Recommended." *City Metric*, 9 March. www.citymetric.com/fabric/china-s-urban-policy-unit-just-met-first-time-38-years-here-s-what-it-recommended-1904 (accessed 12 July 2016).

Texeira, Lauren (2019). "Building China: Rise of the Superblock." *RADII*. https://radiichina.com/building-china-rise-of-the-superblock/.

Wang, Lan, Maria Chiara Tosi, Mirna Zordan, Caterina Villani, Silvia Maroso, Alex Pellizer, Aldo Aymonino, and Gianni Talamini (2017). *Walkable Cities in High Density China*. Shanghai: Tongji University Press.

World Bank, and Development Research Center of the State Council, the People's Republic of China (2014). *Urban China: Toward Efficient, Inclusive, and Sustainable Urbanization*. Washington, DC: World Bank.

Yang, Yong, and Ana V. Diez-Roux (2012). "Walking Distance by Trip Purpose and Population Subgroups." *American Journal of Preventive Medicine* 43 (1): 11–19.

10 Urban and regional differences in healthcare service delivery in South Korea

Seunghyun Lee

Introduction

One of the major and recurring questions in urban studies is the relationship between geographies of the urban and the non-urban. This question was raised again during discussions about the formulation of the Sustainable Development Goals (SDGs), especially the debates over the inclusion of a stand-alone goal for sustainable cities, which ultimately became SDG 11. Some in the development community pushed back against the urban goal out of concern that the issue of the sustainability of non-urban areas would become marginalized, neglected, or even erased by the prioritization of the urban.

The concern over inequity and inequality is similarly at play in core questions of urban governance and how networks of governance are structured from national to regional to local levels. With the transition from statist development approaches to neoliberal governance, with its decentralized and devolved approach, the importance of cities within governance and the delivery of services and resources appears to have increased throughout Asia. One underlying assumption in this transition is that cities offer geographic advantages for governance, whereby their demographic densities allow for governance efficiencies when compared to more dispersed populations. Along with the benefits of demographic density, the assumption is that cities enjoy high levels of social capital that generate societal benefits, such as a high number of medical doctors per capita. The elevation of the urban within governance models, however, needs to address the significant inequities and inequalities that persist in the relationship between the urban and the non-urban. This chapter presents a case study of the South Korean healthcare system, which offers a cautionary tale of the ways that a structural bias toward the urban – in the context of the ascendance of the urban within Asian approaches to governance – can result in undesirable inequity and inequality.

The South Korean healthcare system is characterized by two key trends: the dominance of the private sector, both for-profit and not-for-profit hospitals, over the public sector and its urban-based geography of services (Kwon, 2003; Peabody et al., 1995; Yang, 1996). Private sector dominance results in increased inequity on access to healthcare among and within regions, as well as service dependency on a few hospitals in metropolitan areas; the healthcare system also falters in terms of providing services to South Korea's aging population. At the same time, the urban bias leads to shortfalls in medical services in rural areas. With limited resources, public healthcare services are unable to compensate for market shortcomings, which limits the system's ability to provide local residents in non-urban areas with fair access to quality healthcare.

Utilizing government reports, academic research, and publicly available statistics, this chapter examines the asymmetry of healthcare among and within regions and the way this asymmetry limits the state's ability to address policy problems both in the public and private sector; it then suggests a governance-based model as a policy alternative for South Korea's healthcare service delivery. The governance-based approach leverages the role of diverse stakeholders – including different levels of government, healthcare providers, politicians, and civil society – in addressing the market-driven geographic inequities in South Korea's healthcare system.

Healthcare and medical institutions in South Korea

For both public and private sector operators, healthcare and medical institutions in South Korea are classified according to the Medical Service Act by level of services provided. There are five levels: (1) clinics; (2) midwifery clinics; (3) hospitals, which includes hospitals, dental hospitals, and oriental (traditional medicine) hospitals; (4) intermediate care hospitals; and (5) general hospitals. The Ministry of Health and Welfare (MOHW) can designate as a "superior" general hospital one that is "specialized in providing medical services requiring high level of expertise for treating serious" health issues (The Medical Service Act, Article 3, 3–4). The designation can be made for a general hospital that satisfies requirements such as having at least 20 specialized departments and medical specialists or a training program for doctors who intend to become medical specialists. A superior general hospital is thus the highest medical facility status in South Korea. The MOHW evaluates superior general hospitals every three years and may re-designate or revoke the designation depending on the result.

Asymmetric healthcare resources in metropolitan regions and other regions

Despite having a universal public healthcare system, the services available to citizens differ both among and within regions. General hospitals in urban areas are equipped with state-of-the-art diagnostic and surgical equipment, and they attract and retain competent physicians. The MOHW designated 42 general hospitals as superior general hospitals in the period 2018–2020. Apart from three hospitals in Seoul, all the other superior general hospitals are university-affiliated hospitals. Among the 42 superior general hospitals, 21 are located in the Seoul metropolitan region including Seoul, Incheon metropolitan city, and Gyeonggi Province (Do). The other 21 are located throughout the country, mostly in urban areas, including 10 that are affiliated to the national university. Those national university-affiliated hospitals serve local residents who need high-quality healthcare services. The result of this concentration of good-quality hospitals in urban areas is that healthcare resources in non-urban areas are insufficient to meet the needs of local patients. A study examining regional disparity of medical service use found that patients living in non-urban areas will travel hundreds of kilometers to see doctors in hospitals in the Seoul metropolitan area or other urban areas, particularly if they have doubts about a serious disease that requires a specialized medical exam for proper diagnosis or if they need advanced-level surgery (Park, 2012).

Human resources in health and medical services also suffer from an asymmetric geographic distribution between metropolitan and other regions. According to the National Health Insurance Service's statistics on healthcare human resources, 52.7% of physicians in South Korea work in the Seoul metropolitan area, as do 63.3% of hospital interns and residents. The number of doctors who choose to work in the Seoul metropolitan area after doing their internship and residence in another region is expected to increase, especially among those who are originally from the Seoul area. The ratio of physicians per capita illustrates the differences among regions. The average number of physicians per 1,000 people is 1.9 at the national level. However, the number of physicians per 1,000 people in Seoul is 2.8, whereas in Gyeongbuk Do[1] the figure is just 1.3. The majority of Dos are rural, and in most of them the ratio of physicians to population is lower than the national average. There is also a lack of physicians in agricultural and fishing Guns, whereas hospitals in the newly constructed cities have a higher ratio of physicians. There is thus a lack of equity and equality in access to quality healthcare resources, with areas such as Gangwon Do, Gyeongbuk Do, and many others in need of policy intervention to increase the number of physicians (Oh, 2012).

There is, however, another side to this inequity, as illustrated by statistics that show that in Seoul metropolitan area the number of hospital beds is actually below the national average. The city has 35.8% of the total hospital beds in South Korea, while 27% of beds are in other cities, and 37.2% are located in small and medium-sized cities and towns (Si and Gun). Although the ratio of physicians to population is high in the Seoul metropolitan area, the ratio of hospital beds to population is the third lowest among 17 metropolitan cities and Dos (MOHW and Korea Institute for Health and Social Affairs, 2017). These numbers imply that hospitals in the Seoul metropolitan area experience difficulties providing in-patient healthcare services for those who need to be hospitalized unexpectedly due to acute disease or urgent surgery. Table 10.1 gives an overview of statistics relating to healthcare institutions and resources.

Disadvantaged populations in rural areas

Since a significant portion (approximately 50%) of South Korea's total population lives in the Seoul metropolitan area, some observers may take its concentration of healthcare resources for granted. However, given the population structure in Korea, this concentration can be framed as a policy challenge of caring for an

Table 10.1 Healthcare resources and the elderly population across the regions

		Public and Private Healthcare and Medical Institutions*				Public Healthcare and Medical Institutions**				Population
		Number of physicians	Physicians per 1,000 people	Number of hospital beds	Hospital beds per 1,000 people	Number of public hospitals	Public hospital (% of total)	Number of physicians	Number of hospital beds	Age 65 and above (% of total)***
Metropolitan City	Seoul	28,189	2.8	86,630	8.7	21	4.2%	3,027	8,553	13.3%
	Busan	7,637	2.2	71,129	20.3	10	2.5%	785	4,117	15.7%
	Daegu	5,495	2.2	36,653	14.8	9	4.3%	802	3,669	13.7%
	Incheon	4,469	1.5	32,093	10.9	7	4.2%	100	1,196	11.4%
	Gwangju	3,434	2.3	39,228	26.7	9	3.5%	609	2,951	11.9%
	Daejeon	3,455	2.3	23,427	15.5	7	6.2%	608	3,179	11.5%
	Ulsan	1,702	1.5	15,378	13.1	1	1.0%	2	100	9.6%
Special Self-Governing City	Sejong	180	0.7	1,249	5.1	0	0.0%	0	0	9.2%
Do	Gyeonggi	18,846	1.5	129,320	10.2	30	4.2%	1,516	9,547	11.1%
	Gangwon	2,575	1.7	18,475	11.9	20	19.8%	491	4,162	17.6%
	Chungbuk	2,389	1.5	21,252	13.4	10	9.6%	415	2,838	15.2%
	Chungnam	2,995	1.4	27,710	13.2	14	8.9%	165	3,587	16.3%
	Jeonbuk	3,522	1.9	39,067	20.9	12	5.7%	541	3,508	18.5%
	Jeonnam	3,042	1.6	40,908	21.5	22	9.6%	378	4,933	21.5%
	Gyeongbuk	3,515	1.3	43,913	16.3	23	10.0%	220	4,670	18.4%
	Gyeongnam	5,221	1.5	60,858	18	22	7.0%	999	6,437	14.4%
	Jeju	1,047	1.6	5,055	7.9	5	20.0%	270	1,288	14.1%
Total		97,713	1.9	692,345	13.4	221	5.8%	10,928	64,735	13.8%

Sources:

* MOHW and Korea Institute for Health and Social Affairs (2017).

** MOHW and National Medical Center (2017).

*** As of 2017; Statistics Korea at: www.kostat.kr

aging society. The population of 65 years and over in metropolitan cities, where quality healthcare services are available, is between seven and 14 per cent, which is within the normal range of an aging society. By comparison, people aged 65 and above in Jeonnam Do represent over 20 per cent of the general population (see Table 10.1).

The problem of access to healthcare becomes even more apparent when scaling the population statistics down to Si and Gun level. In 16 Sis and 70 Guns, over 20 per cent of the total population is aged 65 and over, which indicates that those Sis and Guns have a much higher than normal elderly population (Ministry of the Interior and Safety, 2018). With the exception of Hwasun Gun, where the Chonnam National University Hwasun Hospital is located, these Sis and Guns do not have a superior general hospital within their jurisdiction; consequently, their elderly people have to travel to other regions to receive quality healthcare services. Patients have the choice of visiting a university-affiliated hospital within their Do, a superior general hospital outside their Do, or a hospital in a metropolitan city. Park (2012) shows that the higher the ratio of the elderly to the general population in a jurisdiction, the higher the use of medical services outside of the home jurisdiction. This inequity in services will continue to increase as South Korea's population grows older and has more need of quality healthcare.

As their name suggests, superior general hospitals are literally superior to other hospitals when measured by their holdings of medical equipment. According to the Health Insurance Review and Assessment Service (HIRA), 42 superior general hospitals, which represent just 0.06% of the total number of hospitals (69,808), have 159 magnetic resonance imaging (MRI) scanners and 253 computerized tomography (CT) scanners; they accounted for 10.6% and 12.9% of total MRI scanners and CT scanners in South Korea in 2017 (HIRA, 2018). Additionally, expensive medical equipment such as the Gamma Knife and Cyber Knife are widely available in superior general hospitals but in only a few general hospitals (ibid.). HIRA's annual assessment of the quality of healthcare services since 2006 illustrates that superior general hospitals carry out more surgical procedures than other types of hospitals when a disease is acute and the results of surgery determine the survival of patients. For example, in the case of stomach cancer, 43 superior general hospitals carried out 17,697 surgeries in 2015, which accounted for 73.3 per cent of total surgeries that year (HIRA, 2017).

The geographic asymmetry in regional healthcare services also applies with respect to childbirth. The fertility rate in South Korea in 2016 was 1.2, which was the lowest of the OECD countries.[2] This low fertility rate is contributing to the increase in the ratio of elderly in South Korea. Although the government has introduced policies to increase fertility rates, those policies do not necessarily have the desired effect in rural regions where pregnant women experience inconvenience and obstacles in accessing healthcare services, such as finding an obstetrician available for regular check-ups and finding a doctor in their jurisdiction when giving birth. Statistics from the Korea Institute for Health and Social Affairs demonstrates that pregnant women in Seoul metropolitan area travel 1.1 km, and women in Sis travel 4.8 km to see an obstetrician who can deliver a baby by Cesarean section, whereas pregnant women in Guns travel 24.1 km (Lee, 2015). In terms of the ratio of obstetricians to the population, Seoul has over twice the number of obstetricians – 1.97 per 10,000 people – when compared to rural areas: Gyeongbuk has 0.81, Chungbuk has 0.91, Gyeongnam has 0.94, and Chungnam has 0.97 per 10,000 (Kim, 2016). The government's pro-fertility demographic policy appears to be undermined by the lack of geographically accessible healthcare services for pregnant women and their newborn babies.

The geographic accessibility of healthcare services is critical to people of all ages, and it should not matter where they live. People living in towns lacking hospitals with emergency rooms are exposed to risks that people living in urban centers do not have to face, as they cannot assess emergency treatment, especially for life-threatening medical situations. This geographic inequity is especially pertinent during man-made or natural disaster events, when people without emergency services need to be transported to locations with services or face a situation of self-care. Although all citizens have the legal right to receive emergency medical treatment – South Korea's Emergency Medical Service Act establishes the right to services without discrimination on the basis of sex, age, ethnicity, religion, social status, and economic conditions – non-urban people experience difficulties accessing such emergency treatment. In South Korea, governments at different levels can designate existing institutions as emergency medical institutions, giving the state the capacity to address the geographic inequity and structural denial of rights. The Minister of Health and Welfare, for example, has the authority to designate the National Emergency Medical Center, regional emergency medical centers, and specialized emergency medical centers. Additionally, the mayor of a metropolitan city or the governor of a Do can designate local emergency medical centers, and a mayor of a Si/Gun/Gu can designate local emergency medical institutions in their jurisdictions. Despite the state's capacity to rectify the situation, however, 43 Guns do not have local emergency medical institutions, while 93 Si/Gun/Gus do not have an emergency physician (Oh, 2013).

Traveling in search of quality healthcare: is it worth it?

With healthcare services concentrated in superior general hospitals located in the Seoul metropolitan area, patients experience accessibility barriers to well-known hospitals. It is especially difficult for non-urban patients who rarely have informal networks in urban regions or the medical field to make an appointment to see a physician. On average, patients have to wait two to three months to see a physician. Moreover, due to a shortage of post-surgery beds, patients are often required to wait a further two to three months for surgery (Hong and Song, 2011; Kang, 2014). Patients with appointments wait an average of 1 hour in the hospital before seeing their doctor, although the treatment itself might be very quick: "1 hour of waiting and 3 minutes of treatment" is a tacit understanding among patients seeking treatment at a superior general hospital. Some diseases, such as cancers, have long waiting times, which aggravates symptoms and may impact patients' recovery or life expectancy. Long waiting times increase opportunity costs. Patients and their families deploy strategies to navigate the obstacles, such as leveraging informal networks to find someone who knows the doctor they want to visit in order to ask for an earlier appointment. This can be much harder for non-locals, so that geographical inequities lead to asymmetries in degrees of patient social capital, which in turn influence outcomes for when a patient can see a physician, when they can get diagnosed, and when they can receive treatment.

The South Korean government tries to encourage residents in rural areas to trust in local hospitals through a system of government-approved hospitals. For example, the government designates central medical institutions for areas lacking medical services. These central medical institutions are expected to have the facilities, personnel, and equipment necessary to provide adequate health and medical services (Public Health and Medical Services Act Article 13). Moreover, the government has designated 23 general hospitals as specialized public medical centers for children and seniors, especially those with respiratory diseases and degenerative arthritis.

Nevertheless, despite the cost and inconvenience, many people prefer to travel to metropolitan cities to see a renowned doctor in a superior general hospital, because trust in rural hospitals is low. If a superior general hospital is not available, patients can visit a general hospital in their Si or Gun or a neighboring jurisdiction or a superior general hospital within their Do. According to a patient survey conducted by the Seoul National University Hospital on medical services and health policies at a university-affiliated hospital (Kim, 2018), 48.8% of people visit a university-affiliated hospital based on their own or their family's judgment and not on a physician's referral. Among them, 24.2% of respondents chose university-affiliated hospitals because of their facilities and medical equipment, while other responses pointed to subjective reasons such as low trust in a clinic or hospital-level medical institution and high trust in a university-affiliated hospital. The knowledge and awareness of patients and their families influences their provider selection decisions, especially if they pick a nearby general hospital or a superior general hospital in an urban area.

Superior general hospitals in the Seoul metropolitan area are supposed to be equipped with quantitatively and qualitatively better healthcare resources. We can look at the hospital evaluation and accreditation process to see the advantages of the urban superior general hospitals. The MOHW evaluates general hospitals every three years to designate superior general hospitals. Following the Medical Service Act, Article 58, the Korea Institute for Healthcare Accreditation (KOIHA), a non-profit corporation entrusted by the MOHW, performs the accreditation program by evaluating hospital-level health institutions, although it does not necessarily guarantee the quality of healthcare services. Hospital-level institutions can voluntarily apply for the accreditation program, but it is compulsory for intermediate care hospitals and mental health institutions. Only four hospitals that voluntarily applied for accreditation failed their reviews in the first seven years of the accreditation program. However, in 2017, four newborn babies died at the Ewha Woman's University Mokdong Hospital (hereafter, the Ewha

Mokdong Hospital) as the result of an infection that occurred during preparation for injections. The Ewha Mokdong Hospital was one of the superior general hospitals in the period 2015–2017 and had received the highest level of evaluation (Park, 2017). It had already submitted an application to be designated as a superior general hospital for 2018–2020, but when forensic results confirmed that it had breached anti-infection guidelines by using contaminated injectors on the premature babies, the Ewha Mokdong Hospital withdrew its application.

Inadequate public healthcare to overcome market failures

Most public health and preventive measures are public goods that are non-exclusive (there are no grounds for denying access to anyone) and non-rival in consumption (consumption by one person does not affect the availability of the good to others) (Binder et al., 2008; Moon, 2007). If healthcare services were to follow the rule of neoclassical economic theory, by which all patients would pay directly for the services they used, market failures would seriously damage the national public health system (Moon, 2007). Costs of serious illness could result in large financial losses for patients, and consumers of an unregulated private insurance market could suffer from adverse selection with limited knowledge about their health status and health insurance plans (Hsiao, 1995). Health and medical services provided by the public sector are designed to guard against such market failures and soften the impact when they happen.

South Korean law protects against geographic inequities in access to public health and medical services; Article 2-1 of the Public Health and Medical Services Act holds that the state shall "ensure all citizens equal access to medical services and to protect and promote their health, irrespective of which region they live in". As market-based healthcare services for people in rural areas are limited, they have to be supplemented by public health and medical services. In 2017, there were 221 public health and medical institutions (see Table 10.1) involving local governments as well as ministries at the national level, such as the Ministry of Education, the Ministry of National Defense (MND), the MOHW, and the Ministry of Employment and Labor. The Ministry of Education is associated with the largest number of public health and medical institutions – 23 out of the total of 221. This is because national university-affiliated hospitals are established by the designation of the Minister of Education. The national university-affiliated hospitals, with specialized departments and medical specialists, are located in all Dos. Including national university-affiliated hospitals, 62 public health and medical institutions are classified as general or superior general hospitals. Furthermore, a local government can establish local medical institutions. The establishment of a local medical center requires prior consultation with the MOHW (Act on the Establishment and Management of Local Medical Centers); provincial and municipal hospitals can be established by local governments under a municipal ordinance.

Some public health and medical institutions specialize in diagnosis and treatment for medical conditions such as cancer, mental health, and dental care or in particular types of patients such as the elderly, police officers, military, and those suffering from the misfortune of industrial accidents. For example, with the exception of three hospitals, public health and medical institutions in Gyeongbuk specialize in long-term care; hospitals under the auspices of the MND are accessible only to the military, and one hospital in Gyeonggi has responsibility for local emergency medical services.

The proportion of public health and medical institutions to the total number in South Korea is relatively small, accounting for just 5.8% of the country's 3,803 hospital-level medical institutions (MOHW and National Medical Center, 2017). Yet, relatively speaking, public health and medical institutions are equipped with more beds than private (both for-profit and not-for-profit) hospitals. Hospital beds in public health and medical institutions number 64,735, which is 10.54 per cent of the total number of 614,123 hospital beds in hospital-level medical institutions in South Korea. However, not all facilities are open to the public. For example, in Gangwon Do, there are 20 public health and medical institutions among 101 hospital-level medical institutions, which is a high ratio of public institutions (MOHW and National Medical Center, 2017), but eight of them are established for specific patients such as industrial disaster patients or soldiers. Since the territory of some jurisdictions in Gangwon Do is adjacent to the Military Demarcation Line between South and North Korea, which makes them military zones, there are five military hospitals under the MND, which cannot be used by non-military patients.

It is clear that in the current public health delivery system, South Korea does not ensure "equal access to medical services" to all citizens. The numbers of public facilities and physicians are not enough to meet the nation's healthcare needs – such as childbirth and emergency medical services in rural areas – and to solve its problems, such as an aging population. The domination of private sector healthcare services has exacerbated the concentration of services in a small number of superior general hospitals and the resulting opportunity costs and information asymmetries among patients. In order to begin attracting people to use their local facilities, the state needs to develop a level of public trust in public health and medical institutions that is equal to the public's trust in private hospitals.

Governance-based healthcare: an opportunity for success

South Korea's market-oriented healthcare system has failed to ensure equity in access to healthcare. Given John Rawls' concept of distributive justice (Rawls, 1971), all people should be valued equally. Therefore, each person has an equal right to achieve his/her optimal health status, without distinction based on inherent social backgrounds such as geography, affiliations, and socio-economic resources (Braveman et al., 2011). Privatized healthcare in South Korea led to a maldistribution of healthcare, resulting in asymmetries of information among patients and generating opportunity costs. The market-orientated approach does not provide rural residents with equitable access to healthcare resources. To address the inequity, public health and medical institutions can supplement services where the market fails; however, the South Korean government has not taken appropriate measures to fill the gap.

Yet, addressing health inequities requires steps beyond enhancing market- or state-led policy approaches. What is needed, instead, is a redefinition of governance that enhances the role of civil society, especially its ability to augment public and private sector accountability. Civil society can build citizen coalitions through collective actions that work with the public and private sector to forge greater equity and equality within the healthcare system (Marmot et al., 2008). Including different stakeholders from a range of civil society actors, this collective action approach to governance-based healthcare systems can be an alternative way to solve government and market failures (Hwang, 2013). There are several reasons why the governance-based approach promotes healthcare for all.

First of all, healthcare is a complex policy area in which diverse social problems are entangled. The governance-based approach is best equipped to deal with this complexity. The South Korean government, as discussed earlier, is confronting health, welfare, and economic challenges with particular sectors, such as the elderly population, but also with demographic trends like low fertility rates. To ensure that everyone, from the youngest to the oldest, urban and rural residents alike, has a fair opportunity to access good-quality healthcare, the governance-based model enables politicians to deliver their campaign promises through stronger collaborations between civil society and state officials. After local elections in June 2018, for example, elected governors sought to fulfill their electoral commitments to strengthen the public health system in their Do. The elected governor of Gangwon promised that he would establish seven obstetricians/ gynecologists in Gangwon. The elected governor of Gyeonggi promised that he would designate six provincial hospitals as central medical institutions for areas lacking medical services. Such electoral pledges reflect public demands for greater access to public health. To deliver on their promises, politicians need to work with government officials at the national and local level and listen to the public and health workers.

Moreover, by allowing different stakeholders to be engaged, the governance-based model in healthcare can promote increased information and knowledge exchanges among healthcare providers, healthcare researchers, and government officials. For example, MOHW and the National Medical Center held the 4th Public Health Forum on 13 December 2017, the topic of which was "building collaborative governance for the development of public healthcare". Over 300 people from health and medical institutions, the government sector, and research institutes and universities participated in the forum. They exchanged ideas about how healthcare governance can overcome the limitations of the current public healthcare system in South Korea. Presenters emphasized the role of the national university-affiliated hospitals, collaboration among ministries, health insurance structures, demographic trends, and the problem of physician shortages in areas lacking medical services. Through such opportunities, stakeholders can learn how people in different sectors view the healthcare service delivery system, what kinds of health-related data are available, and how they can contribute to solving problems in the healthcare service delivery system. Although the work to bring the governance-based approach to address inequities in healthcare is at an early discussion stage, it is gaining traction through gatherings like the 4th Public Health Forum.

The governance-based model has several potential benefits. One such benefit is that it can help to reduce the high demand for services in the system's superior general hospitals. The governance-based model promotes formal networks among superior general hospitals and the system's other hospitals, both public and private, through a formalized referral system as well as a patient transport system. Such networking can mitigate excessive demand for superior general hospitals in the Seoul metropolitan area by enabling physicians to refer patients to local hospitals across the country. The Seoul National University Hospital's survey on medical service use and health policy shows that 87.8% of people would be willing to transfer to a nearby clinic or hospital if their physician at a university-affiliated hospital advised them to do so (Kim, 2018). Superior general hospitals are currently building a partnership with local clinics and hospitals to facilitate treatments and post-treatment plans for patients with severe diseases such as cancers and cerebrovascular diseases. However, fragmented information on those partnerships makes it difficult for patients to find who's who in the network. If superior general hospitals work together to build an integrated online system to open their partnership information to the public and if patients and their families share their experience of using those partnership services in a local healthcare and medical institution, enhanced networks can also more fairly distribute information to the general public about healthcare services, such as which public and local hospitals have experts for particular medical issues. Information asymmetries can also be overcome by the governance-based approach by promoting the quality of these services in order to combat public bias and misperceptions about services. It can also encourage network participation among private hospitals that normally have little profit incentive to join networks.

Finally, the governance-based approach can improve the monitoring of the quality of healthcare, which can in turn generate improved services. When diverse stakeholders participate in monitoring and evaluating the quality of healthcare services, health and medical institutions will comply with the government's guidelines and standards. The governance-based approach can bring such monitoring to the private healthcare sector, where quality of care is neither protected nor guaranteed by the free market system (Yang, 1996). MOHW, for example, has delegated the Evaluation and the Accreditation Program to the KOIHA for the purpose of increasing patient safety and quality of patient care. The KOIHA is supposed to involve diverse stakeholders in its evaluation committee (Suk, 2013). However, critics point out that this oversight mechanism is not working in its assessment function because it includes too many interest groups mainly related to health and medical institutions such as the Korean Hospital Association, Korean Medical Association, the Korean Dental Hospital Association, and the Korean Medicine Hospitals' Association (Park, 2017). The governance-based approach can help to limit the way that some hospitals game the system by satisfying the criteria of the accreditation program only for the evaluation period. We know that only four hospitals have failed to pass accreditation reviews during recent years; we also know that the hospital with the highest level of evaluation, Ewha Mokdong Hospital, was implicated in the deaths of four newborn babies through infection. The governance-based model can address such limitations within the monitoring and assessment mechanism by increasing transparency and by allowing diverse stakeholders outside health and medical institutions, such as patient groups, to monitor and evaluate the quality of care in hospitals.

The governance-based model can help to leverage existing legal frameworks to increase the opportunities for stakeholder engagement. To realize this objective, the approach calls for the composition of governing boards to be reformed, reducing the inclusion of a range of healthcare stakeholders. While local medical centers have a degree of civil society representation, university-affiliated hospitals do not allow civil society to be involved in their operation even though many of them serve more patients than local medical centers and are designated as superior general hospitals. According to the Act on the Establishment and Management of Local Medical Centers, local medical centers shall take into consideration the sex ratio and maintain balance among directors. Local medical centers should have at least two local government officials but also at least six directors from the following sectors: one recommended by the local council, one expert in the field of health and medical service, one recommended by the non-profit and non-governmental organization sector, and one representative chosen by local residents. On the other hand, the Act on the Establishment of National University-Affiliated Hospitals specifies that the directorship of university-affiliated hospitals should consist of the president of the university-affiliated hospital itself; the dean of the dental college; the president of the relevant dental hospital; one individual nominated by the Minister of Strategy and Finance; and one person nominated by the Minister of Education from among Grade III public officials, the vice mayor or vice governor of a metropolitan city or a Do. The only space that the legal framework of the university-affiliated hospitals allows for civil society is "at least one external person who has good knowledge and experience in hospital management". Most university-affiliated hospitals have one or two directors who do not have a hospital management-related career, but many of those directors are not representatives of civil society but have legal or financial knowledge as lawyers or financial experts. The governance-based approach proposes that, for their board of directors, the university-affiliated hospitals have directors recommended by the non-profit and non-governmental organization sector and local residents in order not to focus only on managerial aspects but to listen to the public with regard to their service needs.

Notes

1 The Local Autonomy Act of July 2017 classified local governments into the following two categories: (1) high-level local government, which includes Special Metropolitan City, Metropolitan City, Metropolitan Autonomous City, Do, and Special Self-Governing Province; (2) low-level local governance, including Si, Gun, and Gu.
2 According to the OECD website (OECD.org).

References

Binder, Sue, Lola Adigun, Courtenay Dusenbury, Allison Greenspan, and Paula Tan-huanpää (2008). "National Public Health Institutes: Contributing to the Public Good." *Journal of Public Health Policy* 29 (1): 3–21.

Braveman, Paula A., Shiriki Kumanyika, Jonathan Fielding, Thomas LaVeist, Luisa N. Borrell, Ron Manderscheid, and Adewale Troutman (2011). "Health Disparities and Health Equity: The Issue Is Justice." *American Journal of Public Health* 101 (Supplement 1): S149–S155.

HIRA (2017). "The Result of the Quality Assessment of Stomach Cancer in 2006." Gangwon-Do: Health Insurance Review and Assessment Service.

HIRA (2018). *2017 Health Insurance Review & Assessment.* Gangwon-do: Health Insurance Review and Assessment Service.

Hong, Du Pyo, and Jaeki Song (2011). "The Effective Distribution System for the Concentration of Patients to Extra-large Hospitals." *Journal of the Korean Surgical Society* 20: 373–383.

Hsiao, William C. (1995). "Abnormal Economics in the Health Sector." *Health Policy* 32 (1–3): 125–139.

Hwang, S.K. (2013). "A Study on the Modeling of Local Healthcare Governance." *The Korean Journal of Local Government Studies* 16 (4): 137–161 (in Korean).

Kang, H.J. (2014). "Policy Direction for Decreasing the Concentration of Patients to Extra-large Hospitals." *Health and Welfare Policy Forum* 4 (210): 65–76 (in Korean).

Kim, B.K. (2016). "Regional Gaps in the Number of Physicians per Population. Gyeongbuk Has Less Than Half of Physicians per Population in Seoul." *Yonhap-news*, 7 February. www.yna.co.kr/view/AKR20160204185300017 (in Korean).

Kim, S.H. (2018). "9 Out of 10 People Is Favorable to Transfer to Local Clinics After Treatment at National University-affiliated Hospitals." *Medifonews*, 1 February (in Korean).

Kwon, Soonman (2003). "Payment System Reform for Healthcare Providers in Korea." *Health Policy and Planning* 18 (1): 84–92.

Lee, S.Y. (2015). *Equity of Pregnancy, Delivery and Infancy Infrastructure and Policy Implication.* Yeongi-gun: Korea Institute for Health and Social Affairs (in Korean).

Marmot, Michael, Sharon Friel, Ruth Bell, Tanja A. Houweling, Sebastian Taylor, and Commission on Social Determinants of Health (2008). "Closing the Gap in a Generation: Health Equity Through Action on the Social Determinants of Health." *The Lancet* 372 (9650): 1661–1669.

Ministry of the Interior and Safety (2018). "51.78 Million of Total Population in 2017. 80,000 Increase in a Year." Seoul: Ministry of the Interior and Safety, 10 January. www.mois.go.kr/frt/bbs/type010/commonSelectBoardArticle.do?bbsId=BBSMSTR_000000000008&nttId=61421 (in Korean).

MOHW and Korea Institute for Health and Social Affairs (2017). "Social Security Factbook 2017." Sejong: Ministry of Health and Welfare; Yeongi-gun: Korea Institute for Health and Social Affairs.

MOHW and National Medical Center (2017). "National Statistics: 2016 Public Health and Medical Institutions." Sejong: Ministry of Health and Welfare and the National Emergency Medical Center.

Moon, S.H. (2007). "Healthcare Policy and Governance." *Journal of Governance Studies* 2 (1): 163–196 (in Korean).

Oh, Y.H. (2012). *An Analysis of National Public Healthcare Study in 2011: The Quality Assessment of Healthcare Human Resources and Its Asymmetry by Specialties, Regions, and Types of Hospitals.* Sejong: Ministry of Health and Welfare; Yeongi-gun: Korea Institute for Health and Social Affairs (in Korean).

Oh, Y.H. (2013). "Public Health and Medical Service Policy in Korea." *Korea Institute for Health and Social Affairs Issue & Focus 2013* (33): 1–8 (in Korean).

Park, K.D. (2012). "A Study on Regional Disparities in Healthcare Utilization: Using Spatial Dependence." *Korean Policy Studies Review* 21 (3): 388–415 (in Korean).

Park, K.Y. (2017). "The Hospital-associated Organization Gave the Ewha Mokdong Hospital the Highest Level of Accreditation." *The Hankyoreh*, 26 December. www.hani.co.kr/arti/society/health/825046.html#csidx0a2cc3ef54eb9b38d5bae060f36ac02 (in Korean).

Peabody, John W., Sung-Woo Lee, and Stephen R. Bickel (1995). "Health for All in the Republic of Korea: One Country's Experience With Implementing Universal Health Care." *Health Policy* 31 (1): 29–42.

Rawls, John A. (1971). *Theory of Justice.* Cambridge, MA: Belknap/Harvard University Press.

Suk, S.H. (2013). "Improvement Plans of Accreditation Program for Healthcare Organizations in Korea." *Health and Welfare Policy Forum 2013* 8 (202): 39–47 (written in Korean).

Yang, Bong-Min (1996). "The Role of Health Insurance in the Growth of the Private Health Sector in Korea." *The International Journal of Health Planning and Management* 11 (3): 231–252.

11 Governance of government middle schools in urban China and India

Comparative analysis of supportive accountability and teacher perceptions

Yifei Yan

Introduction

Effective governance that ensures proper management and utilization of various resources is increasingly emphasized as a key to achieving quality and inclusiveness in the basic education sector. This chapter contributes to the understanding of education governance in urban settings of two of the largest – yet still relatively under-explored – public education systems in the world, namely China and India, with a particular focus on their arrangement of teachers' in-service training and career advancement as supportive accountability mechanisms. While in rural areas and less advanced regions the main priority may still lie with ensuring adequate resources, in urban areas issues of governance and accountability are more relevant and urgent: better resources and capacity levels make it imperative that their effective management and utilization be guaranteed so as to achieve desirable education outcomes. Government middle schools in the two capital cities thus serve as good starting points from which to meaningfully explore the role of supportive accountability practices.

Using a unique teacher survey as its main tool of exploration, this chapter reveals that Beijing's frequent "low-stake" training centered at the school level, as well as a horizontal career advancement path, are more likely to match stakeholder incentives and promote professionalism compared to measures undertaken in Delhi. While a deeper understanding of how and to what extent this affects education outcomes still awaits further research, insights generated by this chapter can nevertheless shed some preliminary light on the role of supportive mechanisms as essential complements to the more traditional accountability measures of discipline and control.

Governance matters in a changing context

The importance of basic education in economic and human development has been widely recognized in policy research and practice across the globe. Behind this imperative, the universally agreed goal of basic education has undergone several changes in the last few decades. Whereas earlier education policy put more emphasis on expanding school access and enrollment, the current focus has shifted toward ensuring quality and inclusiveness of education. This is aptly illustrated in the Sustainable Development Goals (SDGs) specified in the United Nations 2030 agenda, among which SDG 4 commits nations to "ensure inclusive and equitable quality education and promote lifelong learning opportunities for all".[1]

This updated goal in turn requires a change in policy instruments to achieve it. Whereas finance and infrastructure played a key role in the universalization efforts of many developing countries to expand access, existing evidence shows that input-based interventions *alone* are inadequate in improving education quality and inclusiveness in both developing and developed countries (e.g., Elmore and Fuhrman, 2001; Evans and Popova, 2016; Mbiti, 2016). India's Sarva Shiksha Abhiyan and the Right to Education (RTE) Act, for instance, have codified various input-related aspects from the number of classrooms and toilets per school to student–teacher ratios, which are duly monitored by administrators. However, despite the progress in enrollment, levels of learning remain poor (Aiyar and Bhattacharya, 2015).

In addition to the input-based approach, another policy instrument increasingly summoned for use in the basic education sector, as in many other sectors, is privatization and marketization: paying from their own pockets offers a strong incentive for education service recipients (students and their parents) to monitor and demand value for the money they pay. A closer pay–performance link and more autonomy and ownership of teaching may also drive teachers and principals to be more motivated. However, from the perspective of society overall, such effectiveness is at best partial: private basic education is still largely unaffordable to the have-nots of society. Hence in most developing countries, including India and China, government schools remain the predominant provider of basic education (Bhatty and Saraf, 2016: 5; Hao and Yu, 2015). Put differently, while private basic education serves as a healthy supplement to the public education system, it would be dangerous to view the former as a substitute for the latter.

While recognizing the limits of input-based interventions, it is increasingly acknowledged that the proper use and channeling of various fiscal, physical, and human resources – that is, the effective governance of the education sector – matters in improving the learning outcomes of all students. And contrary to the implicit assumptions made by advocates of privatization that government is no longer relevant and can even be harmful, effective education governance still needs government to play a pivotal role in providing stewardship (Yan, 2019).

Governance, accountability, and support

Within the emerging literature on governance from bodies such as the World Health Organization, the World Bank, UNDP, etc., the notion of accountability is increasingly highlighted as a key to achieving good governance (see also Erkkila, 2007). While this observation also applies to basic education, much of the recent empirical literature in the field has left this central term undefined (Bruns et al., 2011). A basic definition can nevertheless be retrieved from early educa-tion studies or public administration literature (e.g., Ranson, 1986; Romzek and Dubnick, 1987), both of which recognize accountability as a social relationship between the "accountors" and the "accountees". Within this relationship, the accountors need to be answerable to the accountees for certain actions (or inac-tion) in exchange for the latter's sanctioning of their performance.

To further extend the understanding and theorization of accountability, one part of the literature has come up with several typologies of accountability (see World Bank, 2003). Another approach that is particularly common to the study of educational accountability is to treat accountability as a set of distinctive *mech-anisms*, from school-based management (SBM) and exit exams to information disclosure and so on, each with its own theoretical predictions of how it will lead to strengthened accountability and ultimately improved student learning.

Nevertheless, whether and to what extent these mechanisms are effective remains largely inconclusive even amongst systematic reviews (Evans and Popova, 2016), depending, among others factors, on their design and implementation specifics. More fundamentally, current research on accountability mechanisms emphasizes discipline and control, either from societal actors (SBM, information disclosure) or upper-level government activities (inspections, exit exams). The equally important aspect of support and recognition is relatively under-explored, although the definition of the accountability relationship has never excluded it as an element of the "sanctions". Where supportive measures are studied in the literature, this tends to be limited to short-term supportive measures (such as year-end bonuses, one-off material inputs) rather than long-term supportive interventions such as more institutionalized[2] training and career development including promotion, awards, and recognition.

Methodology notes on case selection, sampling, and fieldwork

This chapter complements and extends the literature by zooming in on two supportive accountability mechanisms, namely teachers' in-service training and their career development, with the rationales justified in the previous section. It aims to compare the governance arrangements and manifestations of these two mechanisms within the contexts of government middle schools in China and India in the urban settings of Delhi and Beijing. These locations are considered suitable for the exploratory goal of the study not only because they are both capital cities and have similar administrative status and set-up. More importantly, existing studies on various accountability mechanisms in the two countries have largely focused on either rural areas or remote and least-advanced regions (e.g., for China, see Loyalka et al., 2013, 2016, 2017; Zhang et al., 2013; for India, see Banerjee et al., 2010; Muralidharan and Sundararaman, 2010, 2011, 2013; PROBE Team, 1999).[3] Although these areas with less optimistic education out-comes certainly deserve serious academic and practical attention, their top priority may still lie in filling the gaps of inadequate resources, rendering the governance issue, albeit important, a lower priority. In contrast, the actual layout of governance and accountability is a much more relevant topic for basic education in urban settings where demand for and aspirations of education are higher and resource constraints relatively low. Furthermore, single-teacher schools (where the mechanisms studied here can hardly apply) and enrollment in these schools are negligible in Delhi, whereas in other states the practice could still be common given lack of resources (e.g., Batra, 2013). It is very difficult to find such schools even in least-advanced regions in China nowadays.

The public middle schools of Beijing and the roughly equivalent government upper-primary/secondary schools in Delhi are compared in this study because they cover the last stage of basic education in the two countries.[4] Given the lack of comparable outcome criteria on which random sampling can be performed (and also the time and budget constraints for the doctoral dissertation on which this chapter is based),[5] the selection of sample districts follows a purposive sampling approach. Fengtai (Beijing) and North Delhi (Delhi) are chosen as two "average" districts (as contrasted to New Delhi/Xicheng on one hand and northeast/suburban districts on the other), which are varied enough for the study to explore whether, in what manner, and to what extent their accountability practices differ. In total, 150 teachers from 33 government middle schools in Delhi and 80 teachers from 22 schools in Beijing were surveyed to better understand the effectiveness of supportive arrangements, especially from the perspectives of teachers as their direct recipients. A breakdown of the sample is presented in Table 11.1. The survey is complemented with on-the-spot follow-up interviews as well as semi-structured interviews with education officials, experts, and NGO workers. All fieldwork was done between September 2016 and December 2017.

Table 11.1 Sample breakdown

Type	Delhi (N=150) (%)	Beijing (N=80) (%)
By Gender		
Male	84 (56)	23 (28.8)
Female	66 (44)	57 (71.3)
By Professional Ranking and Years of Experience		
TGT/Middle School 1–3	20 (13.3)	18 (22.5)
TGT/Middle School 4–10	30 (20)	25 (31.3)
TGT/Middle School 11+	47 (31.3)	27 (33.8)
PGT/High school	21 (14)	10 (12.5)
Guest Teachers	32 (21.3)	0
By Education Level		
Bachelor's/Undergrad	19 (12.7)	62 (77.5)
Master's/Post-grad	120 (80)	18 (22.5)
PhD	5 (3.3)	0
Other or Unspecified	6 (4)	0

Note: TGT = trained graduate teacher; PGT = post-graduate teacher

Supportive accountability and teacher perceptions: a comparative analysis

Analyzing the results from the survey and complementary methods, this section systematically compares supportive accountability as practiced in government middle schools in Beijing and Delhi along three dimensions: coverage, format, and teacher perception.

Coverage and exclusion

In terms of overall training coverage, results of the teacher survey in Delhi reveal that in-service training is almost completely lacking for guest teachers (also known as contract teachers). More than 60% of the 32 surveyed guest teachers had not received training of any type during the survey period. Even among regular teachers, 30 (more than 25%) had not received any training during the same period. Among these 30, 11 had joined the school within the previous year. For the rest, reasons cited for the lack of training included "no trainings ever happened" and "training was planned but later canceled". There are also those who cited personal reasons, such as the need to take another exam or go back to their hometown or simply not feeling well. In contrast, there was near-universal training coverage in Beijing although, as will be shown later, training on different topics can vary substantially in terms of frequency and duration. Overall, 79 of the 80 teacher respondents in Beijing had participated in in-service training during the survey period.

As well as facing neglect in in-service training, guest teachers in Delhi are not eligible for promotion. Overall, 43.3% of the respondents in Delhi have received at least one promotion in their career so far; the figure for Beijing is 52.5%. But none of the guest teachers in the Delhi sample has been promoted, as the career system is exclusively open to regular teachers.

These differences in terms of capacity-building coverage between regular and guest teachers contrast sharply with the lack of substantial differences when it comes to performing teaching and other tasks (Table 11.2). This does not go unnoticed by the guest teachers: not only do they have fewer opportunities for training and career advancement, but they also reported significantly more negative feelings toward such (lack of) support.

Table 11.2 Summary of teaching and non-teaching burdens, Delhi

	No. of subjects taught	No. of standards taught	No. of sections taught	% being class teachers	Average teaching hours spent weekly
GT	1.4	3.2	4.2	62.5	22.4
Regular TGT	1.2	3.4	4.3	73.2	23.8
Regular PGT	1.5	2.6	3.9	57.1	21

Note: TGT = trained graduate teacher; PGT = post-graduate teacher; GT = guest teacher

There is no such dualism in the training and career advancement system in Beijing, as all teachers within the sample schools are regular teachers. Furthermore, differences along other dimensions (such as teaching middle school versus teaching high school, higher versus lower professional ranking) did not seem to have any significant impact on receiving capacity-building support on the one hand and the teachers' feelings toward these arrangements on the other.[6]

Differing formats of provision

Frequency, duration, and providers of in-service training

For those who have participated in in-service training, the total duration of training for recipients in Delhi was estimated at nearly 33 hours on average over the survey period. The training received by respondents in Beijing was estimated at an average of 60 hours. Bearing in mind the inaccuracies of self-reporting, these figures are indicative at best. Yet potential recall bias cannot entirely account for such a stark contrast between Beijing and Delhi, as it is hard to justify why biased estimations from the two groups of teachers would not move in the same direction.

A more plausible explanation for the difference may come from the format in which the training sessions are organized. In Delhi, training programs are mainly concentrated during the (summer) break, with four to six days of six to eight hours each being typical. Training during the vacations was also mentioned by the respondents in Beijing, but this is far from being the main format. The most common types of training in Beijing are instead embedded throughout the semesters. Training sessions on academic content and pedagogy, in particular, are held on a regular basis at a fixed and designated time each week. Even the less frequent training on student management would normally still happen on a monthly basis.

This higher frequency and regularity of training in Beijing is closely related to its "decentralized style of provision". In the comprehensive provision structure in Beijing, the municipal government plays a major role in teacher in-service training primarily for expert teachers at the high end and those from "weak schools" at the low end. Most other training programs are organized instead by the district and the schools themselves. This decentralized pattern is also reflected in the teacher survey. Whereas most training programs mentioned by respondents in Beijing are provided by the district and the schools, the major provider in Delhi is still the state education authorities. There, the role of district-level training providers and the schools is negligible.

Timing and types of promotion

In terms of career advancement, the survey records the time of the latest promotion (month and year) for those respondents who have received a promotion in their career so far. The interval between the promotion time and the time of filling in the questionnaire can therefore be calculated.

The "promotion interval" for respondents in Beijing is around 33 months. In other words, for those who have been promoted, the last promotion happened fewer than three years before the survey. Yet for their counterparts in Delhi, the interval is more than 79 months for current TGTs (trained graduate teachers) and 49 months for current PGTs (post-graduate teachers). In other words, the average PGT has not received any promotion for more than four years, and the average TGT for approximately six and a half years.

There are also differences between the two sample cities in terms of the types of promotion awarded. In Beijing, the survey found 19 instances of teachers being promoted to a higher professional ranking, 17 within-ranking promotions, and 14 promotions to intermediate management positions such as grade head, director of the political education department, etc. In Delhi, among the 65 teachers who have been promoted at least once, only nine (13.8%) have been promoted "to higher professional ranking within the same subject". There are 24 respondents (36.9%) whose latest promotions are "to same ranking but with higher pay scale (grade pay of Modified Assured Career Promotion, or MACP)". Yet the most common type of promotion, experienced by 32 (or nearly 50%) of the promoted respondents, is "to higher professional ranking in a different subject".

The last type can be divided into two scenarios, both of which are closely related to Delhi's (or for that matter India's) teacher promotion structure, which can be described as "the vertical path" (Figure 11.1, left panel). The first possibility is the promotion from PRT (primary teacher), who needs to teach all subjects to primary-level students, to TGT, who mostly teaches a main subject. The second and trickier possibility is to be promoted from TGT of one subject to PGT of another. The survey results uncovered six such cases – for example, teachers promoted from TGT math to PGT English, from TGT science to PGT economics or PGT English, or from TGT English to PGT commerce or political science. Follow-up interviews with these teachers as well as discussions with principals and other teachers suggest that this is sometimes an opportunistic move as the subjects they are promoted into (i.e., promotion-destination subjects) have a better chance of promotion than others, including the subjects in which they were originally teaching. Meanwhile, the possibility of getting a master's degree in the promotion-destination subject may also be made easier by, for instance, the wide availability of correspondence courses. Although the number of instances may not seem substantial so far as the survey is concerned, the repercussions of this type of promotion for current training and career advancement schemes are nevertheless worth attention, which will be further elaborated in the discussion on teacher perceptions later.

In contrast, career development in Beijing's school system is essentially a "horizontal path" (Figure 11.1, right panel). For government teachers in Beijing, promotion occurs independently within each level of teaching (i.e., within primary school from level III to senior; within secondary school from level III to senior). To the extent that both the teaching content and the psychology of students differ substantially across grades and levels of teaching, the horizontal path seems better suited to retaining teachers' expertise within their levels.

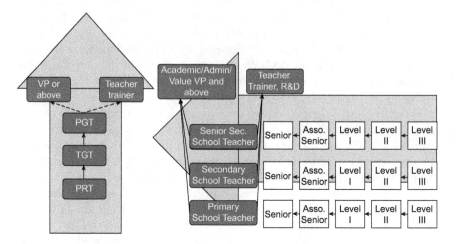

Figure 11.1 Career path of government school teachers in Delhi (left panel) and Beijing (right panel)

Teacher perceptions

On in-service training

According to the teacher survey in Delhi, 144 respondents (96%) indicated that current training arrangements do not match their needs or expectations. This is less surprising when one considers that only 14.9% of respondents who received training confirmed that they were consulted in advance regarding training needs and expectations.

Using a scale from 1 (least satisfied) to 5 (most satisfied), the overall satisfaction with teacher in-service training in the Delhi sample averaged 3.2, with no single item exceeding a score of 4. Training that roughly matched with teacher needs, i.e., on subject content and on teaching methods, enjoyed relatively high satisfaction levels of 3.53 and 3.44 respectively. In both cases, the three common reasons for dissatisfaction among those who were dissatisfied were "quality too low", "content does not match expectation", and "is not useful for solving real-world problems" (Figure 11.2).

Complaints about the low quality of training mainly focused on the lack of experience and expertise of the trainers (known as "resource persons"), who were seen, for example, as "not well qualified". A more serious consequence of this qualification and experience deficit is perhaps reflected in the ineffectiveness of training in solving real-world issues – a problem that occurred most often when the resource persons came from universities and colleges not associated with schools and with little experience of school-level teaching. Respondents commented that conceptualizations by external trainers of curricula and of how a class should be may not be entirely convincing and relevant.

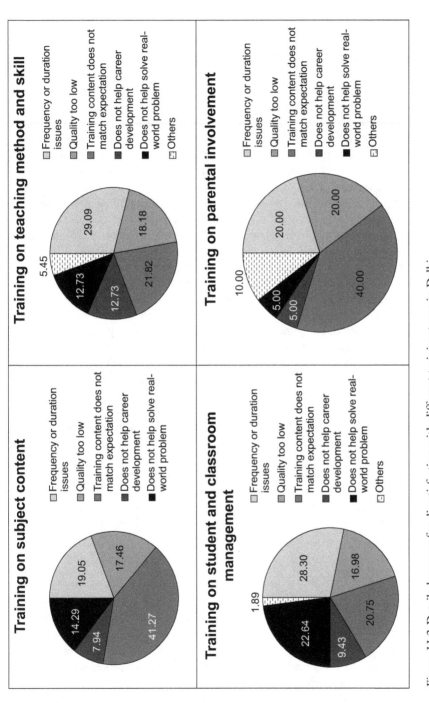

Figure 11.2 Detailed reasons for dissatisfaction with different training types in Delhi

Source: For upper-left sub-figure, n=63; for upper-right, n=56; lower-left, n=53; lower-right, n=20; numbers inside the figures are percentages.

In Beijing, 31.6% of respondents who had received training reported that they were consulted in advance regarding their training needs and preferences. Consultation was mentioned for both school-level and district-level training programs, in the format of survey questionnaires, seminars, or focus-group discussions. The rest of the sample, i.e., nearly 70%, had received no prior consultation as such. One teacher commented that "[training providers] still regard themselves as superior upper-level organizations rather than service providers. Even when they did design some questionnaires [for consultation], they were too complicated and cumbersome to fill in". One respondent used the term "consultative imposition" (征询式安排) to mock the fact that training is still largely imposed top-down despite the intention to look more consultative. Even among those who said they had been consulted, it may still be the case that "school leadership is just consulting us regarding the very broad directions of the training at the very initial stage, without touching upon more detailed aspects" or that implementation was still not satisfactory despite the consultation. Interestingly, there are also teachers who regard consultation with teachers as unnecessary and feel that "only notification would suffice". Despite this, more than 50% of the respondents in Beijing felt that the existing training arrangements matched their needs and preferences.

Teachers' overall satisfaction with in-service training programs in Beijing averaged 4.2 out of 5, one full point higher than the score given by their counterparts in Delhi. Given the generally low incidences of dissatisfaction, reasons cannot be mapped out in as much detail as was done for the responses from Delhi in Figure 11.2. Responses from Beijing are aggregated along two categories of training: those on textbook, academic content, and teaching skills; and the rest, which includes student and classroom management, parental involvement, action research, and so forth (Figure 11.3). Even so, the sub-sample of reasons of dissatisfaction is still very small for training on academic and pedagogical matters (n=15). That for training on "the rest" is larger (n=50). As shown in Figure 11.3, dissatisfaction over either category of training is rarely about the quality, nor is it concerned with training not being helpful for career development. A slightly higher percentage of respondents (13%) felt dissatisfied because the training did not match expectations, while the two major concerns were that training sessions are too infrequent or too short – especially those on student management and parental involvement – and that training is sometimes unhelpful in resolving real-world issues.

On career advancement

According to the teacher survey, measuring satisfaction on the same scale from 1 (least satisfied) to 5 (most satisfied), the average level for respondents in Delhi toward the promotion system is 3. The principal reason for feeling satisfied with the promotion system is the same both for those who have been promoted and those who have not and concerns the "transparency of promotion criteria", rather than fairness or effectiveness in rewarding teaching performance. In fact, the latter only ranks as the third most common reason for satisfaction for both

Training on academic content and teaching skills
(n=15)

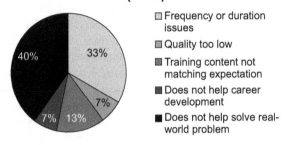

☐ Frequency or duration issues

▨ Quality too low

▩ Training content not matching expectation

■ Does not help career development

■ Does not help solve real-world problem

Training on rest of contents (n=50)

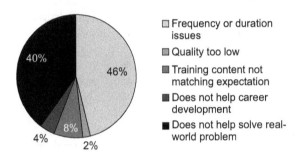

☐ Frequency or duration issues

▨ Quality too low

▩ Training content not matching expectation

■ Does not help career development

■ Does not help solve real-world problem

Figure 11.3 Detailed reasons for dissatisfaction with different training types in Beijing

groups of respondents. In between these two, the second most common reason for satisfaction is different between the two groups: 19% of those not promoted but feeling satisfied with the career system attribute their satisfaction to "optimism about next promotion". Among the 65 respondents who have been promoted, "time to get promoted being reasonable" is the second most picked reason for satisfaction.

Interestingly, the most cited reason for dissatisfaction is the same regardless of whether the respondent has been promoted or not. Taken together, among the 79 respondents who expressed dissatisfaction, 78.5% think that the time to getting promoted is too long. The exclusion of guest teachers from the career scheme is understandably the second most frequently mentioned source of dissatisfaction, applying to 43.4% of those who have never been promoted and feel dissatisfied. In the same subcategory, 39.6% feel dissatisfied because they think promotion is based on factors other than teaching performance, although, among those who have been promoted but are dissatisfied, only 34.6% attribute their dissatisfaction to this reason.

For respondents from Beijing, the average satisfaction level with the promotion system is 3.8. Regarding reasons for satisfaction, "promotion criteria rewarding teacher performance" ranks equally with the time taken to get promoted being reasonable. Close behind these two reasons is satisfaction about "promotion criteria being transparent". Even for those who feel dissatisfied with the promotion system, "promotion criteria not [being] transparent" is rarely the major concern. The most frequently mentioned reason for dissatisfaction is the time to get promoted being too long. The second major concern raised by those feeling dissatisfied, whether they have been promoted or not, is that the "promotion process [is] too competitive and stressful". Several respondents further commented that, even when criteria are transparent and have been fulfilled, promotion might still not happen as there are many other eligible candidates, and the quota – the maximum number of teachers that can be promoted – is limited. Nor is the ultimate decision as transparent to teachers as the criteria per se.

Discussion and concluding remarks

Supportive accountability, especially in the institutionalized formats of teacher in-service training and career advancement, has been relatively less studied, as the education governance and accountability literature is primarily interested in disciplinary and control measures. This chapter constitutes an original attempt to see how support is actually provided in the relatively advanced urban settings of two of the world's largest basic education systems, especially from the viewpoints of teachers who are meant to be the recipients of such support.

While the purpose of the comparison is not to judge which system is superior in this largely exploratory study of how supportive accountability mechanisms are being practiced, it seems clear that some lessons could be learned from the different experiences highlighted in the survey. In terms of Delhi's vertical career development path, for instance, while those who are promoted can still opt for "business as usual", those who are more comfortable retaining their expertise and teaching at the same standard(s) should also be allowed to choose this path, while still getting a salary raise and all the other benefits of promotion. Such flexibility of promotion could be an interim approach toward the full development of separate and independent expertise.

Apart from illuminating potential reform directions, the chapter has also highlighted several common problems that plague the two systems, neither of which is perfect. The two cities sharing information on ongoing reform initiatives designed to make training more relevant or the promotion process less stressful could provide both with timely material for reflection and inspiration for strengthening supportive accountability and, ultimately, promoting high-quality and inclusive student learning.

Notes

1 https://sustainabledevelopment.un.org/post2015/transformingourworld; https://sustainabledevelopment.un.org/sdg4 (accessed 5 October 2019)
2 Institutionalization is slightly different from standardization. In fact, for training as an accountability mechanism to work, it should cater in a systematic manner to different teachers with different needs related to their existing experience.

3 Shanghai is an important exception here, whose top performance in PISA 2009 and 2012 has attracted much international attention. See, e.g., OECD (2011).
4 Hereafter, schools are referred to collectively as middle schools.
5 The dissertation is available online: https://scholarbank.nus.edu.sg/handle/10635/156058 accessed 4 November 2019.
6 Tables of teaching burden and significance tests for the Beijing sample are omitted here to save space but are available from the author upon request (yifei.yan@u.nus.edu).

References

Aiyar, Yamini, and Shrayana Bhattacharya (2015). "As the Example of Education Shows, India's Bureaucratic Reforms Are Falling Short of Maximising Governance." www.caravanmagazine.in/perspectives/post-office-state-education-bureaucratic (accessed 8 October 2017).
Banerjee, Abhijit V., Rukmini Banerji, Esther Duflo, Rachel Glennerster, and Stuti Khemani (2010). "Pitfalls of Participatory Programs: Evidence From a Randomized Evaluation in Education in India." *American Economic Journal: Economic Policy* 2 (1): 1–30.
Batra, Poonam (2013). "Positioning Teachers in the Emerging Education Landscape of Contemporary India." In *India Infrastructure Report*, edited by IDFC Foundation, 219–231. New Delhi and London: Routledge.
Bhatty, Kiran, and Radhika Saraf (2016). "Does Government's Monitoring of Schools Work? A Study of the Frontline Education Bureaucracy in India." PAGE Working Paper No. 28. New Delhi: Center for Policy Research.
Bruns, Barbara, Deon Filmer, and Harry A. Patrinos (2011). *Making Schools Work: New Evidence on Accountability Reforms.* Washington, DC: World Bank Publications.
Elmore, Richard F., and Susan H. Fuhrman (2001). "Holding Schools Accountable: Is It Working?" *Phi Delta Kappan* 83 (1): 67–72.
Erkkilä, Tero (2007). "Governance and Accountability: A Shift in Conceptualisation." *Public Administration Quarterly* 31 (1): 481–518.
Evans, David K., and Anna Popova (2016). "What Really Works to Improve Learning in Developing Countries? An Analysis of Divergent Findings in Systematic Reviews." *The World Bank Research Observer* 31 (2): 242–270.
Hao, Lingxin, and Xiao Yu (2015). "Rural – Urban Migration and Children's Access to Education: China in Comparative Perspective." Background paper for the EFA Global Monitoring Report 2015. https://pdfs.semanticscholar.org/348a/1834ea1c828dd7ae1217bc41600831d5f890.pdf.
Loyalka, Prashant Kumar, Chengfang Liu, Yingquan Song, Hongmei Yi, Xiaoting Huang, Jianguo Wei, Linxiu Zhang, Yaojiang Shi, James Chu, and Scott Rozelle (2013). "Can Information and Counseling Help Students from Poor Rural Areas Go to High School? Evidence From China." *Journal of Comparative Economics* 41 (4): 1012–1025.
Loyalka, Prashant Kumar, Anna Popova, Guirong Li, Chengfang Liu, and Henry Shi (2017). "Unpacking Teacher Professional Development." REAP Working Paper 314. Stanford, CA: Rural Education Action Program.
Loyalka, Prashant Kumar, Sean Sylvia, Chengfang Liu, James Chu, and Yaojiang Shi (2016). "Pay by Design: Teacher Performance Pay Design and the Distribution of Student Achievement." SCID Working Paper No. 533. Stanford, CA: Stanford Centre for International Development.

Mbiti, Isaac M. (2016). "The Need for Accountability in Education in Developing Countries." *The Journal of Economic Perspectives* 30 (3): 109–132.

Muralidharan, Karthik, and Venkatesh Sundararaman (2010). "The Impact of Diagnostic Feedback to Teachers on Student Learning: Experimental Evidence From India." *The Economic Journal* 120 (546): F187–F203.

Muralidharan, Karthik, and Venkatesh Sundararaman (2011). "Teacher Performance Pay: Experimental Evidence From India." *Journal of Political Economy* 119 (1): 39–77.

Muralidharan, Karthik, and Venkatesh Sundararaman (2013). "Contract Teachers: Experimental Evidence From India." NBER Working Paper No. 19440. Cambridge, MA: National Bureau of Economic Research.

OECD (2011). *Lessons From PISA for the United States: Strong Performers and Successful Reformers in Education*. Paris: OECD Publishing.

PROBE Team (1999). *Public Report on Basic Education in India*. New Delhi: Oxford University Press. www.undp.org/content/dam/india/docs/public_report_basic_education_india.pdf.

Ranson, Stewart (1986). "Towards a Political Theory of Public Accountability in Education." *Local Government Studies* 12 (4): 77–98.

Romzek, Barbara S., and Melvin J. Dubnick (1987). "Accountability in the Public Sector: Lessons From the Challenger Tragedy." *Public Administration Review* 47 (3): 227–238.

World Bank (2003). *World Development Report 2004: Making Services Work for Poor People*. Washington, DC: World Bank. https://openknowledge.worldbank.org/handle/10986/5986License:CCBY3.0IGO.

Yan, Yifei (2019). "Making Accountability Work in Basic Education: Reforms, Challenges and the Role of the Government." *Policy Design and Practice* 2 (1): 90–102.

Zhang, Linxiu, Fang Lai, Xiaopeng Pang, Hongmei Yi, and Scott Rozelle (2013). "The Impact of Teacher Training on Teacher and Student Outcomes: Evidence From a Randomised Experiment in Beijing Migrant Schools." *Journal of Development Effectiveness* 5 (3): 339–358.

Part 3
Toward sustainable futures

12 Muddling through the garbage

Household recycling in newly developed Asian cities

Jingru Zhang and Kris Hartley

Introduction

Waste management is an increasingly urgent issue in the rapidly growing megacities of Asia. Waste takes up valuable space in already crowded settings, becoming a nuisance, contributing to the spread of disease, and threatening longer-term public health. The mismanagement of waste can also cause irreversible environmental damage through polluted soil, water, and air. Many Asian cities fail to adequately prioritize waste management. Even in cities of newly industrialized Asian countries, where economic growth has raised living standards and environmental protection has garnered public and policy attention, waste problems are inadequately addressed. Household recycling, a crucial point in the overall waste management chain, is enjoying increased popularity among policymakers as a means to reduce environmental impacts and budgetary burdens.

However, policy challenges linger. The means of recycling common across many Asian cities – informal collection and sorting of garbage by unaffiliated workers – are becoming less common. This implies that fewer people are subject to dangerous working conditions but also raises the need to fill capacity losses. Additionally, most residents live in densely populated apartment buildings with shared garbage bins or chutes, making compulsory recycling costly and difficult to implement. While more recycling responsibilities have been shifted to the government and citizens, participation in recycling programs is low; incentives through vouchers and coupons are neither compelling nor fiscally sustainable. Few of the standard recycling policies enjoy public support, requiring policymakers to take cautious incremental steps in introducing new policies. Against this backdrop, this chapter examines household recycling in two Asian cities where such recycling is not yet widespread. The issues discussed in the chapter are: (1) the seemingly paradoxical situation in which residents of wealthier cities are environmentally aware but at the same time reticent to embrace recycling; (2) the reluctance in some cities to adopt mandatory recycling; (3) the current situation regarding household recycling uptake; and (4) policy options. Although this chapter focuses only on cities that have already committed to waste management efforts that are relatively technologically advanced, policy challenges now being faced by these cities (including so-called wicked problems having no clear cause or solution, such as low individual uptake of recycling) can help illustrate to other cities how to better understand the urgency of waste management and policy alternatives.

In most cases, the opportunity for policy action on improving waste management has been motivated by challenges associated with the use of landfills. Principal among these challenges is land scarcity, leading to tensions among localities – and in some cases countries – about who bears the responsibility for metabolizing waste. Additional tensions emerge from the claim that the right to pollute is tantamount to the right to develop – similar to the reasoning behind debates about carbon emission at global-level negotiations. However, household recycling and waste sorting is one aspect of waste management that does not significantly conflict with economic development in the standard measurable ways. Revenues can be generated from the utilization and treatment of recyclables. Costs include transporting waste from residential facilities, extra labor imposed on individuals (assumed to be constant across socio-economic class, although this issue deserves further attention beyond this chapter), and the transaction cost of compelling individuals to undertake this labor. If the process is undertaken smartly and diligently, net environmental and economic gains can be achieved, in addition to political and civic branding benefits that attend the cultivation of a responsible and green image. Recycling and sorting within households can be feasible and effective environmental protection options. As such, the question for urban policymakers is simple: how can people be encouraged to sort and recycle at home? The solutions, however, are complicated and multi-dimensional. This chapter explores these issues in the context of policy interventions that facilitate household recycling.

The puzzle of incentivizing households to embrace recycling efforts relates to fundamental questions about the nature of public policy, including the ability of governments not only to regulate behavior forcefully but also to inspire individual action in a persuasive way. Examining all actors across the policy development process is essential for addressing such questions. The academic literature has already placed considerable focus on policy subsystems and how coalitions or elites formulate and develop policies (see Baumgartner and Jones, 1991; Howlett et al., 2009; Weible, 2008). Scholars have also explored the role of frontline workers and "street-level" bureaucrats who implement policies, emerging from work done by Lipsky (1971). This chapter acknowledges this mature line of scholarship on the governance side and thus turns to the behavior of individuals – the governed – and the compromises among policy acceptability, effectiveness, and transaction costs of implementation. To situate these ideas within a case context, the chapter investigates household recycling in Shanghai and Singapore, cities that have entered a middle or late-middle stage of development during which tensions are evident between old and new models of waste management. These models respectively include informal versus formal, closed versus open-loop, and thriftiness (individual efforts to restrict usage) versus profligacy (induced by belief in the power of modern waste management to eliminate existential problems that over-consumption has caused).

In Shanghai and Singapore, the long-standing tradition of consumer thriftiness is fading away with rising incomes, but new regulations or self-reinforcing social norms have not been established to the degree that would facilitate transformational change in how individuals view their role in waste management. The argument is not that recycling in these cities is a more urgent issue than it is anywhere else. Indeed, in many places, waste management challenges are far more pressing. However, the economic development of these two cities has enabled the emergence of policy priorities, procedures, and infrastructures that enable a shift in how waste management is approached (e.g., toward systems based on technology). These cities have formal municipal waste collection systems, mature markets for recyclables, and technology-based treatment facilities (e.g., incineration-based power plants and sanitary landfills for items not easily recycled). The two cities have also promoted recycling for many years. In this sense, the prospect of devoting individual effort to recycling is feasible because such efforts would be complemented by existing institutional and technological systems. However, the challenges now facing Shanghai and Singapore will likely be confronted by developing countries in the future, so there is value in examining these cases as canaries-in-the-mine. The chapter proceeds by briefly exploring the necessity for household recycling, before examining recycling programs in Shanghai and Singapore, the feasibility of voluntary recycling and efforts to promote it, and future implications for public policy.

Necessity for household recycling

According to the World Bank (2019), cities worldwide generated 2.01 billion tons of waste in 2016, and the figure is projected to increase to 3.4 billion per year by 2050. Waste authorities often focus on residential waste, among all sources, because it is difficult to manage. Collection from residential premises tends to be more expensive and less efficient compared to collection from industrial premises; residential communities have a relatively higher number of individual waste streams, and collection points are more scattered. Additionally, residential waste is voluminous, accounting for up to half of all municipal solid waste (Hoornweg and Bhada-Tata, 2012).

Source separation and recycling at the household level ensure more efficient collection and utilization of waste. As the first stages of the waste management chain, sorting and recycling are given clear priority in the waste-processing hierarchy in countries around the world (Sakai et al., 2011). As summarized by Cossu (2014), there are six waste management objectives[1] serving three general functions: pollution reduction, energy recovery, and cost saving (see Table 12.1).

Sorting at the household level is encouraged for additional reasons (Table 12.2). One major concern is that household waste usually contains organic waste with high moisture content, mainly from food. Wet components of household refuse, if not removed in advance, can mix with and pollute dry recyclables (e.g., paper and cardboard) during the collection process. Such contamination is irreversible, with cross-contaminated waste ending up in incineration plants or landfills

Table 12.1 Objectives for waste management

| Objectives | Functions | | |
	Curbing pollution	Generating Energy	Saving cost
1 Waste minimization	√		
2 Prolong the lifespan of the landfill			√
3 Recover non-renewable material		√	√
4 Reduce waste management costs			√
5 Decrease pollution from traditional waste management (e.g., leachate from landfill)	√		
6 Reduce carbon emission	√		

Source: Adapted from Cossu (2014)

Table 12.2 Benefits of household source segregation and separation collection

Dimensions	Benefits	Sources
Environmental	Decrease contamination and increase the quality of recyclables for better recovery	Xu et al. (2018); Zhuang et al. (2008)
Economic	Minimize labor inputs in the downstream processes	Murray (1999); Capel (2008)
Social	Bring about positive spillovers: – Environmentally friendly consumption habits – Energy saving – Waste prevention	Sintov et al. (2019); Xu et al. (2018); Thøgersen (1999, 2003)

regardless of its recyclability. This contamination is a potential source of environmental degradation. Another reason for promoting household-level action is that waste separation at later stages can be unduly labor-intensive and therefore costly. Waste separation is often accompanied by some level of manual sorting, even in systems that utilize machine-based sorting (Capel, 2008).

Recycling promotion in Shanghai and Singapore

Shanghai

Shanghai is one of China's four directly administered municipalities and among the nation's most populous cities with 24.3 million residents. Located in the Yangtze River Delta, it has an area of 6,340 km² and serves as a global financial center and transportation hub. The development of household waste sorting and recycling programs in Shanghai has occurred in four stages. The initial stage involved a city-wide experiment with community waste sorting at a small scale. In 1995, the first pilot community waste-sorting project took place in the

Number 7 Neighborhood Committee of Caoyang Village. In 1998, recycling campaigns targeted specified waste streams such as those of batteries and glass.

In the second stage, Shanghai was selected by China's Ministry of Housing and Urban–Rural Development in 2000 as one of eight pilot cities to implement sorting of residential waste. As part of an official government agenda, waste sorting was also included in the city's Three-Year Action Plan for Environmental Protection (Huang et al., 2014). The adoption of waste-sorting programs began to blossom; in the same year, 100 communities introduced waste sorting (Zhang et al., 2012). By August 2003, waste sorting was promoted in 1,294 residential communities (Shanghai Local Chronicles Office, 2003), increasing to 3,700 by the end of 2006.

In the third stage, the government made efforts to ensure broader coverage through new sorting methods. In the previous stage, incineration was considered a suitable alternative for diverting waste from landfills. In subsequent years, however, waste-sorting methods were altered. In 2007, parallel sorting methods were adopted in Shanghai: one for districts with incineration and the other for those without. In preparation for the 2010 World Expo, districts adjacent to the exhibition site aimed for 100% coverage of waste sorting (Zhang et al., 2012). In addition, the idea of a "green account" was introduced in selected communities as an incentive; residents were entitled to redeem cash, vouchers, or daily necessities using points gained from participation in waste-sorting activities (Chen, 2018).

In Shanghai's fourth and final stage, waste sorting was promoted through intensive education and awareness campaigns utilizing social media and other marketing platforms. The flagship initiative during this period was the "Low Carbon Practice for Millions, Starting with Waste Sorting" project introduced in 2011. Previous sorting methods were replaced by a simplified program in which residents are encouraged to sort waste into wet (mainly kitchen waste) and dry wastes. Dedicated collection is provided for selected waste streams such as glass, textiles, and e-waste. Despite Shanghai's producer-focused trade-in services for e-waste, a similar program does not exist for other types of waste streams (The State Council, 2016). Therefore, residents shoulder a majority of the responsibility for waste sorting and recycling while not being held directly accountable due to the voluntary nature of policies. This condition contributes to an overall lack of participation.

Singapore

Singapore is a prosperous island nation located at the southern tip of the Malaysian peninsula, with 5.6 million inhabitants occupying a relatively compact area of 719 km^2. In 2018, Singapore's GDP per capita was USD 64,582, ranking among the highest in the world. Singapore's National Environment Agency (NEA), in its first Zero-Waste Masterplan, aims to extend producer responsibility for e-waste by 2021 and for packaging and plastics by 2025 (NEA, 2019a). According to the OECD (2001), policies addressing extended producer responsibility require producers to take financial and physical responsibility for the life of products after consumption, whether through treatment or disposal. Singapore has already made efforts to address waste and recycling. For example, the Singapore Packaging Agreement, first launched in 2007, encourages voluntary adoption of cost-effective solutions to reduce packaging waste, which accounts for one-third of residential waste (NEA, 2018a). Nevertheless, the household is the scale at which most of Singapore's policies seek to address waste management. The city's strategies have been documented in several guidebooks and include three broad areas: pest control, hygiene, and waste minimization and recycling. The guidelines and guidebooks are prepared by the Singapore Environment Institute (SEI), a division of the NEA responsible for training and knowledge-transfer. Among the guides most directly related to recycling are "A Guide to 3R Practices for Households" – the "3Rs" being reducing, reusing, and recycling (SEI, n.d.); "Guidebook on Setting Up Structured Waste Recycling Programme in Condominiums and Private Apartments" (SEI, 2018); and "Love Your Food: A Handy Guide to Reducing Food Wastage and Saving Money" (SEI, 2016). The 3R guidebook applies to all household-based practices and covers three main topics: the recycling situation in Singapore, tips about how to practice 3R, and places where recycled waste is ultimately stored. The guidebook is designed in the form of a small pictorial booklet for convenient dissemination and easy comprehension.

Food waste in Singapore accounts for approximately 10% of overall municipal solid waste. The recycling rate for food waste remains at 16% (NEA, 2018b); the balance of food waste is incinerated for energy production. As a large share of household waste comes from food waste in Singapore, a special guidebook about reducing food waste has been introduced (SEI, 2016). The 39-page document, provides vivid and detailed illustrations about how to reduce food waste under multiple scenarios covering activities at home, in the office, restaurant dining, and grocery shopping. Singapore also launched the "Save Food Cut the Waste" campaign in November 2012 to educate individuals, organizations, and companies about how to achieve food waste reduction.

The "Guidebook on Setting up Structured Waste Recycling Programme in Condominiums and Private Apartments" (SEI, 2018) is another example of the city's efforts to shape how household waste is managed. As the name implies, the guide pertains only to condominiums and private apartments, not to public housing or landed properties. The latter are already covered in the National Recycling Programme launched by NEA in 2001, while the former are managed by the respective management corporations (MCs) and managing agents (MAs) who have the right to determine locations for recycling facilities within a given estate. Unlike the 3R practices guide for households, which targets residents, SEI (2018) serves as a detailed and informative reference for MCs and MAs to comply with Singapore's Environmental Public Health Act (EPHA). For example, the guide specifies that "the daily recyclables output shall then be computed to be either an additional 30% by volume of the daily refuse output estimated above or 240L/d of recyclables, whichever is higher" (ibid.: 3). Examples of the collection and storage systems of various types of recyclables are also provided, including drop-off bin systems, drop-off multiple intermediate recycling bin systems, door-to-door collection of recyclables through the use of recycling bags, recycling bag systems with designated main collection points or recycling corners, and recyclable chute systems. The roles and responsibilities of all parties are also specified, including those of MCs or MAs and their cleaning contractors, residents, and recycling and cleaning companies.

In both Shanghai and Singapore, governments appear to acknowledge the urgency for improved and widely adopted recycling practices at the household level. Each city has introduced laws and regulations targeting behavior changes at the individual level, along with softer approaches to nudge behavior through marketing campaigns and usage guides. Nevertheless, changing the behaviors of individuals and households is arguably a more difficult task than changing that of producers and businesses. The latter are easier to monitor and regulate and behave predictably in the face of punishments, incentives, and nudges. By contrast, households are more numerous and thus more difficult to collectively monitor, their behavior is less transparent, and they do not always react to even the most coercive policy measures. If participation by households in recycling and conservation efforts is as important as that of producers, it is crucial that governments understand the nature of this divergence in behavior patterns. The remainder of this chapter explores the behavioral dynamics of voluntary recycling in these contexts, including explanations and possible policy solutions.

The perils of voluntary recycling

Recycling has not been widely adopted where related legal structures and institutions are lacking (Glance and Huberman, 1994; Kimura and Shinoki, 2007). Lagging levels of household recycling can be seen as both a "wicked" problem – as mentioned earlier – and a collective action dilemma in which rationally self-interested individuals act without regard to collective welfare unless compelled to do so by coercion or incentives (Hardin, 1971; Olson, 1965). However, Ostrom (2000) views this assumption as untenable; while free-riding is common, there is also extensive empirical evidence of voluntary cooperative behavior. Thus, closer scrutiny of the institutional arrangements that support cooperative behavior would yield a more nuanced understanding about why individuals choose to recycle or otherwise. The attitudes and characteristics of individuals, along with situational factors defining the context of such behaviors, including the influence of family, neighborhood, community, and other institutions built around social bonds, can be as important and relevant to research as the policy instruments adopted. Duroy (2005) empirically determines that an individual's environmental awareness is directly impacted by "subjective well-being" and factors defining her immediate surroundings including levels of urbanization and income inequality; determinants of environmental behavior included education, population pressure, and happiness. According to Hori et al. (2013), in a comparative study of Asian cities, energy-saving behavior (a form of conservation action that could be analogized in intention to recycling behavior) is determined by global warming consciousness and social interaction, among other factors.

Despite their high levels of education, income, and general exposure to global ideas about sustainability, household recycling and waste sorting is not yet a widely embraced norm in either city. In 2017, Shanghai and Singapore generated 7.7 million and 27 million tons of waste respectively. The mandate to execute waste management effectively and efficiently will continue to grow based on the sheer amount of waste generated. Furthermore, evidence from Asian countries indicates that waste generation is positively associated with economic status as measured by GDP per capita (Shekdar, 2009); on this basis, yearly growth in waste generation adds further policy urgency for Shanghai, Singapore, and other rapidly growing cities in the region.

Lagging adoption of household recycling and waste-sorting programs persists despite the levels of environmental awareness (as understood by modern scientific notions of sustainability) that are relatively higher than those found in less economically developed cities. In Shanghai, a city-wide recycling pilot program called "Carbon Reduction through Waste Sorting by One Million Households" was introduced in 2011, and the number of households included in the program doubled by the end of 2015. The goal of the project is to reduce household waste generation by 5% each year based on the 2010 amount. Under the program, households should sort according to five types: kitchen waste (brown bin), hazardous waste (red bin), recyclables (blue bin), glass (green bin), and residual waste (black bin). New recycling bins continue to be placed in various communities, with sporadic recycling campaigns occurring at the neighborhood, district, and city levels. In selected neighborhoods, residents are provided with free recycling bags for kitchen waste and other recyclables, occasionally receiving small monetary rewards or shopping vouchers for participating.

More than 90% of residents are aware of the waste-sorting policy, but only 20% participate (Shanghai Municipal Government, 2018). Based on a 2018 survey of 2,000 residents by the Public Opinion Survey Center of the Shanghai Statistics Bureau, approximately 80% expressed support for recycling (China Environmental Protection Alliance, 2018). However, this percentage dramatically declines when measuring behavior. In a survey of 3,603 residents in 16 districts conducted by the Shanghai Quality Management Association, around one-third of residents in communities hosting pilot recycling programs reported having developed a habit of recycling, while only 16.8% regarded recycling as a norm in their neighborhood. In non-pilot communities, the percentage of voluntary recyclers was only 10% (Luo, 2018).

In Singapore, despite the fact that residents are required only to place recyclables into a co-mingled blue bin, the residential recycling rate has remained at approximately 20% since 2012 – 11 years after the introduction of the National Recycling Program (NEA, 2019b). Both the government and waste management companies have undertaken numerous efforts to promote and ensure the convenience of recycling, including door-to-door collection during the initial stage of the program, education campaigns, and the continued addition of recycling bins (one bin is provided for each city block to shorten travel distance). Singapore's low uptake of residential recycling relative to what might be expected for a city of its wealth arguably undermines its efforts to self-brand as a "city in a garden" and to align with other images of sustainability. Indeed, Singapore suffers from a weak culture of recycling compared with Western countries and Asian cities such as Tokyo and Taipei (Wong, 2018). However, Singapore has shown the ability to influence public perception; one example is NEWater, the city's wastewater-recycling program. Through awareness campaigns, demonstration projects, and education, the government has made progress in mainstreaming this idea.[2]

In both the Shanghai and Singapore cases, it is clear that levels of recycling uptake at the household level are not changing in proportion to awareness and nudging efforts. Differences in collective versus individual rationality may be the culprit: simply put, individuals may not go out of their way to embrace a behavior that might be collectively rational. This phenomenon can be seen through three lenses: the assumption that recycling will not make a significant difference, the reticence to inconvenience oneself when others make no similar sacrifice, and the absence of an immediate consequence for lack of effort or compliance. The first two are largely the domains of social psychology, behavioral economics, and other fields; the third is most directly relevant to the ambit of public policy, and related options are elaborated in the following section.

Policy options

Compulsory recycling

One cause of stubbornly low household recycling rates is the voluntary nature of programs for waste sorting and related recycling activities. Among countries that have achieved a high level of public participation in waste-sorting and recycling programs, most have taken a compulsory approach. This assumes that market mechanisms can induce the recycling behavior where coercive mechanisms cannot, that participants in these mechanisms are rational and will act on the option that they calculate to provide the greatest net benefit individually (if not collectively), and that a "compulsory" market mechanism (i.e., one that does not naturally emerge in response to some need) will function durably and effectively absent government intervention and market distortions such as subsidized pay-offs. The "pay-as-you-throw" principle has been introduced through unit-based waste fee systems in European countries, the UK, Japan, South Korea, Taiwan, and some US cities. The system has been supported by regulations against illegal dumping (Dijkgraaf and Gradus, 2009; Scott and Watson, 2006). Evidence indicates that unit pricing is effective in boosting recycling rates, leading in the Netherlands to a 21% increase in the recycling rate and a 50% reduction in mixed waste and in Sweden to a 140% increase in the recycling rate and a 20% reduction in waste generation within two years of program introduction (Welivita et al., 2015). Panel data across Japanese cities show that a unit-based waste-charging system has both a long-run (eight years) and short-run effect on recycling rates (Usui and Takeuchi, 2014). Compulsory household waste-sorting schemes have been introduced in selected cities in recent years, even in countries such as

Malaysia that have rudimentary or under-developed waste-management systems relative to those in wealthier countries. Under Malaysia's scheme, introduced in January 2016, households failing to comply with sorting rules receive warning notices and potentially a fine of up to RM 1,000. Although the policy has generated heated debate and is not sufficiently implemented in most cities, it has been modestly successful in Putrajaya and Kuala Lumpur (Edward, 2016; Moh and Abd Manaf, 2017). A unit-pricing pilot in Olongapo City, Philippines, has also led to greater gains in social welfare compared to those resulting from the traditional flat-rate fee system (Bennagen and Altez, 2004).

It is fair to ask, then, why Shanghai and Singapore have not adopted compulsory waste-sorting schemes. There are several possible reasons. The first is political; governments of both have a history of intervening decisively and directly in policy matters but are now increasingly reorienting their policy styles on some issues toward more distributed models of self-regulation (a lagging expression of the legacy of market-making as a policy solution favored by neoliberalism and new institutionalism). Singapore's penchant for long-term planning and paternalistic foresight compelled it to address environmental issues as a consequence of development. For example, under the Corrective Work Orders program, introduced in 1992 to address public littering, repeat violators were punitively enlisted in forced public service activities such as cleaning up a specified location (Ferris, 1993). However, the program is no longer implemented as it failed to fully achieve its desired goals and came under critical scrutiny. A similarly coercive program targeting waste sorting appears not to have been considered. Plans by the NEA to implement a "pay-as-you-throw" system lacked public support, possibly suggesting that Singapore's citizens may have reached a threshold for coercive or extractive policies. In place of such coercive initiatives, the Singaporean government seems to have assumed a more cooperative tone in encouraging residents to embrace the concept of "city in a garden" as a guide for personal behavior in working collaboratively toward that vision. The Shanghai Municipal government has also adopted a more cooperative than coercive approach to achieving environmental goals. Examples previously mentioned include efforts to make recycling more convenient through placement of receptacles and provision of recycling bags, along with modest monetary inducements.

The second explanation for why Shanghai and Singapore have not embraced compulsory schemes is that some participation does occur through informal channels. While participation in the formal municipal recycling programs remains low, "rag-and-bone" merchants (those who take possession of waste items and seek to sell them elsewhere) play an important role as waste collectors, dealers, and middlemen between residents and recycling companies (Neo, 2010). The drawback of this practice is that only the most valuable components of waste are recycled. For example, paper, plastic (polyethylene terephthalate – or PET) bottles, and metal are frequently recycled items, but no informal channel exists for recycling kitchen waste, glass, and low-grade plastics. This also implies that recycling uptake and intensity are vulnerable to fluctuations in the market prices of recyclable goods. Nevertheless, the formalization of informal practices is difficult given that cultural factors underlying such practices can be slow to change. Part of the strategy for formalization is to convince the public that things currently being done through informal channels can be done more efficiently and effectively through formal ones.

Finally, city-specific factors also explain why compulsory schemes have not been adopted. In Singapore, overall waste management is already relatively efficient, limiting the visibility or urgency of recycling among citizens. Effective waste management can perpetuate the illusion that household waste sorting and recycling are not crucial public agenda items. Second, the garbage collection system does not incentivize recycling. Roughly 80% of all housing in Singapore is public housing, known as HDB (Housing Development Board) units. In most HDB buildings, floor-level disposal chutes offer residents a convenient method to dispose of waste, most often only meters from their front doors if not within the units themselves. Recycling bins, on the other hand, are placed on the ground floor. This design feature adds to inconvenience and personal cost, arguably disincentivizing people from sorting waste into recyclable materials and complicating the process of monitoring to apply punitive measures for non-compliance. Furthermore, lack of understanding among Singapore residents about what should and should not be recycled limits the effectiveness and efficiency of recycling systems and has become enough of a problem to garner media attention (see, e.g., Razali, 2019).

In Shanghai, current methods of waste treatment do not require more sophisticated waste sorting. Three treatment options for municipal solid waste have been used: landfills, incineration, and biochemical treatment. Landfills, the most common method in both sanitary and unsanitary form, do not require meaningful levels of waste sorting; only hazardous waste (e.g., batteries) is removed while nearly everything else is eligible for disposal. Pre-sorting is required for Shanghai's two other less common treatment techniques. Incineration has been embraced as a means of reducing the volume of landfill waste only in recent years. In this process, it is necessary to remove waste with high water content in order to maximize heat value and minimize the emission of harmful gases. For biochemical treatment, pre-sorting is necessary as only the organic components of waste can be utilized. Nevertheless, the latter two methods do not constitute a significant share of Shanghai's waste treatment portfolio, thus the current need for sorting capabilities remains limited.

From the view of policy process theory (see Sabatier and Weible, 2014), the failure of household waste management policies often occurs at the implementation stage. The issue of concern is the reticence of individuals to sort waste at home despite the presence of recycling policies. Two perspectives can be applied to this issue, both based on the expected relationship between the governing and the governed. One perspective has a low expectation of the altruistic will of the governed and regards lax participation in recycling programs as a compliance problem. This implies that the implementation challenge is primarily a matter of compelling people to follow rules, potentially by reducing barriers to compliance, enhancing monitoring effectiveness, and strengthening punitive measures, among other approaches. The other perspective regards people as agents capable and willing to co-produce public goods and services with the government. This perspective emerges from neoliberal approaches that conceptualize citizenship in the context of competitive markets rather than collective or "public" societies. As such, the adoption of recycling by such agents reflects a rationally motivated behavior to maximize self-interest, with the benefit of generating a collectively rational outcome as well (e.g., sustainability). This perspective reflects Alford and Speed's (2006) argument about the client-centered orientation of the public sector; that is, an individual's propensity to comply with a policy is a function of factors other than the fear of punishment. Under the model of co-production (Poocharoen and Ting, 2015; Whitaker, 1980), citizens are not passive recipients of public services but active participants; the implication is that the role of policy is to create an environment where co-production emerges as an endogenous force based on the rational motivations of individuals. The current structures of the resolutely neoliberal political economy may need revision in this context (e.g., inducements to adopt a collective altruistic outlook), as the implication of using markets to encourage recycling still assumes that individuals act only on individual rationality. Based on a systematic review by Voorberg et al. (2015), most co-production initiatives occur at relatively small scales, with empirical studies typically focusing on the education and healthcare sectors.

Although the perspectives of compliance and co-production feature divergent ideas about policy design and differing implementation contexts, they do not necessarily represent starkly contrasting approaches. Compliance can be classified into four types based on willingness to comply (Gibbins and Newton, 1994): (1) routine action (action perceived by the actor to be obviously appropriate); (2) uninformed compliance (action about which the actor has no preference or concern); (3) grudging compliance (action accompanied by frustration or concern but with defensiveness or no change in attitude); (4) adjusted compliance (action accompanied by an attitude shift in the direction of the rule-maker's preference). Based on these classifications, co-production can be seen as "routine action" to which actors effectively have no objection. While most voluntary recycling schemes ultimately wish to achieve this type of compliance, tensions linger around the expectations of individual benefit when one opts-in to a system designed primarily for collective benefit – this tension is inherent in neoliberal and marketizing models for public goods provision. The policy aim can plausibly be seen as an effort to change non-compliance into grudging or uninformed compliance and finally to routine action as manifest in co-production.

Readiness for bolder steps

In an interview of 40 respondents in Singapore and 48 in Shanghai conducted for this study and focusing on the acceptability of policies about recycling, three explanatory characteristics of respondents emerged: household role, gender, and housing type. Household role types were determined as students, working adults, homemakers, and retirees, with roles corresponding to particular life routines, dining habits, environmental attitudes, time management, and recycling habits. The study found that most respondents consider recycling to be a relatively low priority for most residents of Shanghai and Singapore and that current recycling schemes are not working well. Roughly half of the respondents were supportive of compulsory schemes and unit pricing, although opt-in, as documented earlier, remains low – again underscoring the folly of expecting collectively beneficial behavior by rational actors. Indeed, this may represent a phenomenon in which a resident supports recycling – for everyone but themselves. However, when focusing on various specific arguments underlying broad areas of debate, opinions that originally appeared to be contradictory were found to be consensus in disguise. For example, rather than fearing that harsh policies would harm individual interests, those expressing opposition worried more about the difficulty of monitoring and implementation. Additionally, respondents in Shanghai appeared to be more supportive of punitive measures than did those in Singapore. This finding can be explained in part by the long-held opinion in Shanghai that recycling cannot be implemented absent an effective legal framework.

One challenge with current recycling policies in Shanghai and Singapore is that, without policy incentives or sanctions, people are assumed to recycle only under the following scenarios: (1) they derive a virtuous sentiment from performing moral deeds on behalf of society and contributing to the environment or (2) they feel a sense of personal responsibility. Whether residents will embrace recycling if it is made equally convenient to other methods of waste disposal is difficult to know at the macro-level, as that degree of convenience has not been achieved or mainstreamed outside of pilot programs. According to Gibbins and Newton's (1994) typology of compliant behavior, voluntary policy aims to achieve routine action that is considered appropriate ("no problem") or adjusted compliance in which attitudes change in accordance with changes in the opinions of others ("maybe the boss has a point"). A positive personal orientation toward recycling must exist ex ante or be developed as a result of influence by policy, information, or the input and behavior of others. In other words, this type of recycling behavior cannot be changed without a shift in attitude.

However, attitudinal change is not necessarily a prerequisite for changes in compliant behavior. Based on the survey, few respondents consider current recycling to be absolutely appropriate (despite the receptiveness toward many recycling policies), perhaps because they question its effectiveness in achieving the promised collective outcomes due to operational breakdowns in the system (e.g., "why recycle if the waste will end up in the landfill anyway?"). As such, routine action should not be the only type of compliance sought by governments aiming to advance recycling programs. Compliance can be achieved when the actor has no preference (e.g., "if that is what they want, I will just do it"); this is referred to in the aforementioned typology as uninformed compliance. This type of compliance is exemplified by Singapore respondents, who largely abide by government expectations and believe that people will comply if requested to do so. Recycling-system designs that minimize inconvenience can increase the attractiveness of recycling among those exhibiting a tendency toward this type of willingness to comply. As another option, grudging compliance (e.g., "I don't like it, but I must do it") – which is characterized by frustration and concern – is linked to mandatory recycling as people comply out of fear of sanctions. Apart from fines, social sanctions are also observed through normative pressure, which can have a higher social and administrative cost than voluntary recycling but a lower cost than fines.[3]

As such, a unit-based waste-pricing system may be among the most feasible policy alternatives. This method helps activate legal norms because it signals that household recycling is taken seriously and can be implemented in conjunction with a moderate and politically feasible incentive policy. These incentives, which can be either positive or negative, can be used to "induce people to translate any felt obligation into recycling action" (Hage et al., 2009: 155). While introducing a "polluter pays" approach (tantamount to an individual-targeted version of a Pigouvian tax) through unit-based fees represents a negative incentive, monetary rewards can be a positive incentive. Lessons can be learned from the volume-based waste-fee system in South Korea, in which individuals are charged for general waste services but can throw away recycled items at no cost. Such a case deserves further research through the lens of this chapter's analysis.

Conclusion

This chapter has examined the dynamics of policy action encouraging individual and household adoption of recycling. Through a case comparison between Shanghai and Singapore and a brief survey interpreted through the theoretical lens of compliance types, the chapter has outlined challenges and opportunities in recycling policy. Ultimately, it is argued that direct government intervention through regulations and coercion are only partially effective in altering individual recycling behavior. In closing, it is helpful to take a broader view of the recycling issue. Much research and policy reflection has been devoted to influencing individual recycling behaviors. Such efforts, which have been made across policy domains, are fallaciously rooted in what can be seen as the core problem of the modern (Western) epistemic: the assumption that individuals working in their own best interest lead to the collective best interest. This is the logic behind free markets, with the aggregate decisions of individuals leading to a production system that is efficient, serves the needs of consumers, and leaves (in theory) no value deficit or surplus on either the producer or consumer side. Neoliberalism and new public management brought the tenets of free, efficient markets into the logic of public policymaking – arguably to its peril. In recycling, as in many activities that have a collective component, self-interest is neither always collectively rational nor even individually rational (in cases of limited information or limited processing capability). This can lead to unrealized collective action and a "tragedy of the commons" (overuse of public goods). This breakdown confounds policy and behavioral models built on assumptions about the predictability of human behavior, including those that believe adoption of recycling can be achieved with the proper policy approaches (inducements) and settings (levels of benefit or punishment).

Given the limitations of policies focusing on behavior, it is necessary to look more broadly, including at the starting point of waste generation, the production process. Pursuing a "circular economy" approach is one example of how this broader perspective can be manifested in public policy. Kirchherr et al. (2017: 229) define the circular economy as "an economic system that replaces the 'end-of-life' concept with reducing, alternatively reusing, recycling and recovering materials in production/distribution and consumption processes". This implies that the old model of produce–consume–dispose is linear, leading to unused outputs that accumulate unproductively and generate negative environmental outcomes. Further, efforts to reward recycling behavior in a market model can lead to more of the type of consumption that continues to overburden waste-management systems. One example is Shanghai's "green account" program, introduced in selected communities as an incentive to recycle. Residents are entitled to redeem cash, vouchers, or daily necessities using points gained from participation in waste-sorting activities (Chen, 2018). Arguably, this leads to more consumption and more waste; it is internally contradictory. If rewards systems like this are used to induce recycling behavior, individuals will use those rewards as they rationally choose. This underscores that market mechanisms cannot substitute for fundamental changes in mindset on matters related to recycling and sustainability.

The modern epistemic of society is rooted in the Cartesian culture–nature split; the former is rational, modern, and instrumental, while the latter is to be controlled and tamed according to the same logic. This way of thinking manifested itself in those high-modernist urban-planning and policymaking practices of the mid-20th century that sought to tame wicked problems with seemingly rational constructs like markets (and, where those failed, command-and-control systems). As a final task in this chapter, it is necessary to ponder to what extent the epistemic underlying recycling itself – a way to limit the negative effects of a linear and consumption-based society – is an example of instrumentalist reasoning. By this argument, recycling incentivizes behaviors that lead to its own demand while masking the urgency of the problem and excusing society from confronting harder questions about the structure of a production system long designed to incentivize "throwing things away" (see McDonough and Braungart, 2010). Until policymakers and society view the waste challenge for its wicked and complex nature – rooted in unsustainable systems of thinking, being, and behaving – policies and the behavioral and market models they rely on will continue to fail and recycling will be the only – but incomplete – solution to the problem.

Notes

1 These objectives are not mutually exclusive, but they approach related challenges from multiple angles.
2 For further background and analysis, see Tortajada et al. (2013) and Ching (2010).
3 See Tan and Low (2011) for a discussion about social norms and the fallacy of economic incentives regarding individual behavior in Singapore.

References

Alford, John, and Richard Speed (2006). "Client Focus in Regulatory Agencies: Oxymoron or Opportunity?" *Public Management Review* 8 (2): 313–331.

Baumgartner, Frank R., and Bryan D. Jones (1991). "Agenda Dynamics and Policy Subsystems." *The Journal of Politics* 53 (4): 1044–1074.

Bennagen, Eugenia C., and Vincent Altez (2004). *Impacts of Unit Pricing of Solid Waste Collection and Disposal in Olongapo City, Philippines.* Singapore: EEPSEA, IDRC Regional Office for Southeast and East Asia.

Capel, Claudine (2008). "Waste Sorting: A Look at the Separation and Sorting Techniques in Today's European Market." *Waste Management World*, 1 July. https://waste-management-world.com/a/waste-sorting-a-look-at-the-separation-and-sorting-techniques-in-todays-european-market.

Chen, L. (2018). "Waste Minimization Is the Key to Waste Sorting." *The Paper.* www.thepaper.cn/newsDetail_forward_2040108 (in Chinese).

China Environmental Protection Alliance (2018). "Shanghai Green and Urban Appearance Bureau: Towards an Integrated Waste Sorting System." www.sohu.com/a/251541572_357509 (in Chinese).

Ching, Leong (2010). "Eliminating 'Yuck': A Simple Exposition of Media and Social Change in Water Reuse Policies." *International Journal of Water Resources Development* 26 (1): 111–124.

Cossu, Raffaello (2014). "Collection of Recyclables Does Not Need Demagoguery." *Waste Management* 34 (9): 1561–1563.

Dijkgraaf, Elbert, and Raymond Gradus (2009). "Environmental Activism and Dynamics of Unit-based Pricing Systems." *Resource and Energy Economics* 31 (1): 13–23.

Duroy, Quentin M. (2005). "The Determinants of Environmental Awareness and Behavior." Rensselaer Working Papers in Economics. www.economics.rpi.edu/workingpapers/rpi0501.pdf.

Edward, Jonathan (2016). "Waste Segregation Enforcement Starts Today." *Malay Mail*, 1 June. www.malaymail.com/news/malaysia/2016/06/01/waste-segregation-enforcement-starts-today/1131527.

Ferris, R.J. (1993). "Aspiration and Reality in Taiwan, Hong Kong, South Korea, and Singapore: An Introduction to the Environmental Regulatory Systems of Asia's Four New Dragons." *Duke Journal of Comparative & International Law* 4: 125.

Gibbins, Michael, and James D. Newton (1994). "An Empirical Exploration of Complex Accountability in Public Accounting." *Journal of Accounting Research* 32 (2): 165–186.

Glance, Natalie S., and Bernardo A. Huberman (1994). "The Dynamics of Social Dilemmas." *Scientific American* 270 (3): 76–81.

Hage, Olle, Patrik Söderholm, and Christer Berglund (2009). "Norms and Economic Motivation in Household Recycling: Empirical Evidence From Sweden." *Resources, Conservation and Recycling* 53 (3): 155–165.

Hardin, Russell (1971). "Collective Action as an Agreeable N-prisoners' Dilemma." *Behavioral Science* 16 (5): 472–481.

Hoornweg, Daniel, and Perinaz Bhada-Tata (2012). "What a Waste: A Global Review of Solid Waste Management." Urban Development Series, Knowledge Papers No. 15. World Bank, Washington, DC.

Hori, Shiro, Kayoko Kondo, Daisuke Nogata, and Han Ben (2013). "The Determinants of Household Energy-saving Behavior: Survey and Comparison in Five Major Asian Cities." *Energy Policy* 52: 354–362.

Howlett, Michael, M. Ramesh, and Anthony Perl (2009). *Studying Public Policy: Policy Cycles and Policy Subsystems*. Oxford: Oxford University Press.

Huang, Wenfang, Jie Wang, Xingyi Dai, Mingran Li, and Marie K. Harder (2014). "More than Financial Investment Is Needed: Food Waste Recycling Pilots in Shanghai, China." *Journal of Cleaner Production* 67: 107–116.

Kimura, Kunihiro, and Mikiko Shinoki (2007). "Decision and Justification in the Social Dilemma of Recycling. I." *Sociological Theory and Methods* 22 (1): 31–48.

Kirchherr, Julian, Denise Reike, and Marko Hekkert (2017). "Conceptualizing the Circular Economy: An Analysis of 114 Definitions." *Resources, Conservation and Recycling* 127: 221–232.

Lipsky, Michael (1971). "Street-level Bureaucracy and the Analysis of Urban Reform." *Urban Affairs Quarterly* 6 (4): 391–409.

Luo, S. (2018). "Only a Third of Residents Have Formed the Habit of Recycling." *Xinmin Evening News*, 20 August. http://m.gmw.cn/2018-08/20/content_30656679.htm (in Chinese).

McDonough, William and Michael Braungart (2010). *Cradle to Cradle: Remaking the Way We Make Things*. New York: North Point Press.

Moh, YiingChiee, and Latifah Abd Manaf (2017). "Solid Waste Management Transformation and Future Challenges of Source Separation and Recycling Practice in Malaysia." *Resources, Conservation and Recycling* 116: 1–14.

Murray, Robin (1999). *Creating Wealth From Waste*. London: Demos.

NEA (2018a). "Singapore Packing Agreement." Singapore: National Environment Agency. www.nea.gov.sg/programmes-grants/schemes/singapore-packaging-agreement.

NEA (2018b). "Food Waste Management." Singapore: National Environment Agency. www.nea.gov.sg/our-services/waste-management/3r-programmes-and-resources/food-waste-management.

NEA (2019a). "Zero-Waste Masterplan." Singapore: National Environment Agency. www.towardszerowaste.sg/images/zero_waste_masterplan.pdf.

NEA (2019b). "Waste Statistics and Overall Recycling." National Environment Agency. www.nea.gov.sg/our-services/waste-management/waste-statistics-and-overall-recycling.

Neo, Harvey (2010). "The Potential of Large-scale Urban Waste Recycling: A Case Study of the National Recycling Programme in Singapore." *Society and Natural Resources* 23 (9): 872–887.

OECD (2001). *Extended Producer Responsibility: A Guidance Manual for Governments*. Paris: Organization for Economic Cooperation and Development.

Olson, Mancur (1965). *Logic of Collective Action: Public Goods and the Theory of Groups*. Cambridge, MA: Harvard University Press.

Ostrom, Elinor (2000). "Collective Action and the Evolution of Social Norms." *Journal of Economic Perspectives* 14 (3): 137–158.

Poocharoen, Ora-orn, and Bernard Ting (2015). "Collaboration, Co-production, Networks: Convergence of Theories." *Public Management Review* 17 (4): 587–614.

Razali, Nazurah (2019). "Commentary: Recycling Bins are for Recyclables, Not Junk." *Channel NewsAsia*, 9 August. www.channelnewsasia.com/news/commentary/ikea-sponsored-recycling-bins-for-recyclables-not-junk-singapore-11788898.

Sabatier, Paul A., and Christopher M. Weible (Eds.) (2014). *Theories of the Policy Process*. Boulder, CO: Westview Press.

Sakai, Shin-ichi, Hideto Yoshida, Yasuhiro Hirai, Misuzu Asari, Hidetaka Takigami, Shin Takahashi, Keijirou Tomoda, Maria Victoria Peeler, Jakub Wejchert, Thomas

Schmid-Unterseh, Aldo Ravazzi Douvan, Roy Hathaway, Lars D. Hylander, Christian Fischer, Gil Jong Oh, Li Jinhui, and Ngo Kim Chi (2011). "International Comparative Study of 3R and Waste Management Policy Developments." *Journal of Material Cycles and Waste Management* 13 (2): 86–102.

Scott, Sue, and Dorothy Watson. (2006). "Cost-benefit Analysis of the Introduction of Weight-based Charges for Domestic Waste: West Cork's Experience." ESRI Working Paper, No. 335.

SEI (2016). "Love Your Food: A Handy Guide to Reducing Food Wastage and Saving Money." Singapore: National Environment Agency. www.nea.gov.sg/docs/default-source/resource/fwrguideb40cf0039f4c4940b03d4546b0a91567.pdf.

SEI (2018). "Guidebook on Setting Up Structured Waste Recycling Programme in Condominiums and Private Apartments." Singapore: National Environment Agency. www.nea.gov.sg/docs/default-source/our-services/recyclingguidebook condos.pdf.

SEI (n.d.). "A Guide to 3R Practices for Households." Singapore: National Environment Agency. www.nea.gov.sg/docs/default-source/resource/a-guide-to-3r-practices-for-households.pdf.

Shanghai Local Chronicles Office (2003). "Urban Sanitation Management." 20 August. www.shtong.gov.cn/Newsite/node2/node19828/node63991/node64051/node64168/userobject1ai57205.html (in Chinese).

Shanghai Municipal Government (2018)." Barriers for Implementing the Waste Sorting Policy." http://hpq.sh.gov.cn/xw/001009/20180621/8d26892f-ead5-478e-8912-61dad38b3f58.html (in Chinese).

Shekdar, Ashok V. (2009). "Sustainable Solid Waste Management: An Integrated Approach for Asian Countries." *Waste Management* 29 (4): 1438–1448.

Sintov, Nicole, Sally Geislar, and Lee V. White (2019). "Cognitive Accessibility as a New Factor in Pro-environmental Spillover: Results From a Field Study of Household Food Waste Management." *Environment and Behavior* 51 (1): 50–80.

The State Council (2016). "Notification on the Implementation Plan of the Extended Producer Responsibility System." www.gov.cn/zhengce/content/2017-01/03/content_5156043.htm (in Chinese).

Tan, Charmaine and Donald Low (2011). "Incentives, Norms and Public Policy." In *Behavioural Economics and Public Policy: Examples From Singapore*, edited by Donald Low, 35–49. Singapore: World Scientific Publishing.

Thøgersen, John (1999). "Spillover Processes in the Development of a Sustainable Consumption Pattern." *Journal of Economic Psychology* 20 (1): 53–81.

Thøgersen, John (2003). "Monetary Incentives and Recycling: Behavioural and Psychological Reactions to a Performance-dependent Garbage Fee." *Journal of Consumer Policy* 26 (2): 197–228.

Tortajada, Cecilia, Yugal Joshi, and Asit K. Biswas (2013). *The Singapore Water Story: Sustainable Development in an Urban City State*. London and New York: Routledge.

Usui, Takehiro, and Kenji Takeuchi (2014). "Evaluating Unit-based Pricing of Residential Solid Waste: A Panel Data Analysis." *Environmental and Resource Economics* 58 (2): 245–271.

Voorberg, W.H., V.J.J.M. Bekkers, and L.G. Tummers (2015). "A Systematic Review of Co-creation and Co-production: Embarking on the Social Innovation Journey." *Public Management Review* 17 (9): 1333–1357.

Weible, Christopher M. (2008). "Expert-based Information and Policy Subsystems: A Review and Synthesis." *Policy Studies Journal* 36 (4): 615–635.

Welivita, Indunee, Premachandra Wattage, and Prasanthi Gunawardena (2015). "Review of Household Solid Waste Charges for Developing Countries: A Focus on Quantity-based Charge Methods." *Waste Management* 46: 637–645.

Whitaker, Gordon P. (1980). "Coproduction: Citizen Participation in Service Delivery." *Public Administration Review* 40 (3): 240–246.

Wong, Kai Yi (2018). "Gone to Waste: A Hard Look at Our Recycling Effort." *The Business Times*, 18 August. www.businesstimes.com.sg/brunch/gone-to-waste-a-hard-look-at-our-recycling-effort.

World Bank (2019). "Solid Waste Management." World Bank Brief. www.worldbank.org/en/topic/urbandevelopment/brief/solid-waste-management (accessed 23 July 2019).

Xu, Lin, Xiaoling Zhang, and Maoliang Ling (2018). "Spillover Effects of Household Waste Separation Policy on Electricity Consumption: Evidence From Hangzhou, China." *Resources, Conservation and Recycling* 129: 219–231.

Zhang, Weiqian, Yue Che, Kai Yang, Xiangyu Ren, and Jun Tai (2012). "Public Opinion About the Source Separation of Municipal Solid Waste in Shanghai, China." *Waste Management and Research* 30 (12): 1261–1271.

Zhuang, Ying, Song-Wei Wu, Yun-Long Wang, Wei-Xiang Wu, and Ying-Xu Chen (2008). "Source Separation of Household Waste: A Case Study in China." *Waste Management* 28 (10): 2022–2030.

13 Environmental governance in China

Three cases of central–local interactions

Lili Li

Introduction

Anthropogenic activities in urban areas are a major source of greenhouse gas (GHG) emissions as well as air pollutants such as sulphur dioxide (SO_2), nitrogen oxides (NOx), and atmospheric particulate matter ($PM_{2.5}$). At the same time, cities are threatened by the same problems they are helping to create: climate change and severe air pollution. Urban environmental efforts are therefore crucial for making substantive progress on emissions reduction. As environmental protection has the characteristic of a public good, collective actions are needed in both urban and rural areas to tackle climate change and pollution issues. In general, however, policymakers within city governments tend to discount the future, valuing immediate consumption over long-term sustainability and giving greater weight to the costs of near-term emissions reduction than to the potential future loss resulting from catastrophic environmental damage (Levin et al., 2012). Enforcement of environmental measures at the local level faces challenges, as environmental actions often run counter to the short-term interests of local elites (Heilmann, 2008b). How, then, might national governments oversee local implementation of environmental policy instruments[1] that consider the societal interest? This chapter aims to address this research question by investigating three policy instruments in China: the pollutant discharge fee (*pai wu fei*), the environmental target system (*mu biao ze ren zhi*), and policy experimentation with carbon dioxide emission trading schemes (CO_2 ETS, *tan pai fang quan jiao yi*).

China has been employing command-and-control policy instruments and trying out alternative policy instruments to reduce emissions and enhance urban environmental quality. Command-and-control policy instruments are suitable for managing "first-generation" environmental issues that can easily identify pollution sources and install monitoring facilities (Kostka, 2016). But issues such as CO_2 emissions mitigation may need more flexible policy instruments such as ETS or a CO_2 tax. The Chinese government has formulated a complex policy mix including diverse types of policy instruments; this not only leads to horizontal interactions between the policy instruments themselves but also involves dynamic central–local government interactions at the implementation stage. This chapter contributes to the literature by investigating central–local interactions in the implementation of three different policy instruments in China's policy mix.

Analyzing central–local government interactions is relevant to understanding and enhancing China's environmental governance and environmental policy implementation. Recent literature in favor of environmental authoritarianism argues that authoritarian leaders have the capacity to enforce the right set of environmental policy instruments for the promotion of societal welfare (Beeson, 2010; Kostka, 2016). At the city level, municipal governments may lack the incentive to actively reduce emissions (for instance by shutting down small polluting industrial units) for a number of reasons. For example, there is a risk that enforcing stringent environmental regulations may slow down economic growth; furthermore, emissions such as SO_2 or CO_2 travel across jurisdictions, and the city may bear the cost of emissions reduction while the benefit is shared more widely (Wong and Karplus, 2017). Authoritarian states have sharper policy instruments at hand to push urban environmental efforts.

China's sub-national government operates at a number of levels – national, provincial, municipal, and county (see Figure 13.1). Municipal-level government

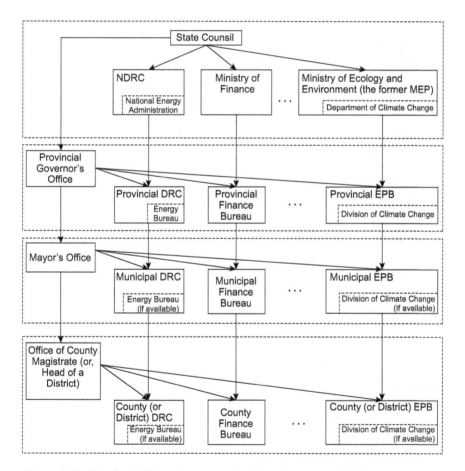

Figure 13.1 China's administrative system in the environmental field

Note: adapted from Tsang and Kolk (2010).

is an important node of this command chain. However, even for an authoritarian regime like China, it is challenging for the government to control environmental policy implementation in the large number of cities,[2] resulting in a gap between national policy plans and local implementation activity. City governments may not strictly enforce environmental policy instruments because of concerns over possible negative effects on economic growth, while the central government struggles to control and verify policy implementation at local level (Lo, 2015). This dynamic central–local interaction is crucial to understanding the environmental implementation gap in China's urban areas.

This chapter takes a case study approach, focusing on three policy cases to highlight the gap between central government policy and local implementation and to explore how central government exerts controls over local policy implementation. It is based on information collected from an extensive review of literature and government policy documents.

Pollutant discharge fee

The pollutant discharge fee (also called emission charge) was one of the earliest policy instruments employed by China for the purpose of emissions control. It is also a prevalent environmental policy instrument worldwide, following the principle of "polluter pays" and levying a fee on each unit of pollutant emitted into the environment in order to internalize the environmental externality of emissions (Watkins et al., 2015). Implementing the pollutant discharge fee increases the operating costs of regulated firms and incentivizes them to change their polluting behavior in order to reduce their emission fees (Ren et al., 2018; Xie et al., 2017). The rate charged is key to the effectiveness of the policy instrument: if emission abatement measures costs more than the emission fees charged by the government, polluters may choose to pay the fees rather than reducing their emissions.

In China, the pollutant discharge fee was adopted in 1982, when the State Council, the main administrative body of the Chinese government, issued the Interim Measures on the Collection of Pollutant Discharge Fee.[3] Initially, polluting firms were charged only when they exceeded concentration-based emissions limits, and the main target was particulate matter (PM) emissions.[4] In 1992, the State Environmental Protection Administration (SEPA)[5] launched pilots in several cities and provinces[6] by which the environmental department of a city or provincial government could impose charges on SO_2 emissions (SEPA et al., 1992). In those pilots, polluters were required to pay for every unit of SO_2 emitted into the environment at the rate of no more than 0.2 yuan/kg.

In 1998, the State Council and SEPA set up two "control zones" – the acid rain control zone and the SO_2 emission control zone – which accounted for about 11.4% of the total area of China and required all jurisdictions covered by the two zones to impose the pollutant discharge fee on SO_2 emissions (SEPA et al., 1998; State Council of China, 1998). In most parts of the two control zones, the charge on SO_2 emission was 0.2 yuan/kg, but provincial-level governments could adjust the charge to a higher rate conditional on the approval of central government. For instance, Beijing changed the rate on SO_2 emissions to 0.5 yuan/kg if emissions were from low-sulphur coal combustion and 1.2 yuan/kg if emissions were from high-sulphur coal combustion.

In 2003, the scope of the SO_2 discharge fee was extended beyond the two control zones, and the rate was increased to 0.6 yuan/pollutant equivalent (PE),[7] and from July 2004 the policy instrument was also applied to NOx emissions at the rate of 0.6 yuan/PE. In 2014, the National Development and Reform Commission (NDRC), Ministry of Finance (MOF), and Ministry of Environmental Protection (MEP) increased the SO_2 charging rate and the NOx charging rate to at least 1.2 yuan/PE (NDRC et al., 2014). Thus, between 1982 and 2018, the national government had calibrated and patched the policy instrument several times to improve implementation effectiveness. Expansion in the scope of implementation and increases in rates of the pollutant discharge fee reflect a trend of growing policy stringency over the years.

After implementing the pollutant discharge fee for more than 30 years, the national government introduced the environmental tax to replace it; the Environmental Tax Law (*huan jing bao hu shui fa*) came into effect in 2018. The current environmental tax rate for air pollutants is between 1.2 and 12 yuan/PE (Standing Committee of the NPCSC, 2018), which places it close to the lower bound of the estimated marginal abatement cost of SO_2 emissions according to the literature (He and Ou, 2017; Lee and Wang, 2019; Yuan et al., 2013). Provincial governments can decide on the exact tax rate according to local contexts (Wang et al., 2019).

As a policy instrument, the pollutant discharge fee has been affected by serious implementation issues. One barrier to implementation is local protectionism in some regions, which has impeded collection of the pollutant discharge fee. Some local governments introduced additional policy instruments to reduce the emission charges imposed on local firms (Zheng et al., 2016). To mitigate local protectionism, the central government imposed more procedural constraints on how local municipal Environmental Protection Bureaus (EPBs) levy the pollutant discharge fee in different circumstances. Nonetheless, environmental concerns continued to give way to economic development when environmental policy enforcement conflicted with development projects supported by other local government agencies (Francesch-Huidobro et al., 2012). This relates to the fact that municipal governments determine the financial resources allocated to municipal EPBs, as well as EPBs' personnel appointments. Other agencies of the municipal government that represent economic interests, such as Development and Reform Commissions (DRCs), may lobby against stricter environmental policy enforcement and further influence the municipal governments' decisions about EPB staffing.

The second major implementation issue is the improper use of pollutant discharge fees that were collected by municipal EPBs. The collected fees were supposed to finance environmental actions and should not have been used for other purposes. However, improper use of the fees was not uncommon. On 23 August 2005, a TV show called *Focus Report (jiao dian fang tan)* reported a local government's arbitrary use of power when spending the revenues from the pollutant discharge fee (e.g., using the money for medical expenses of employees), which aroused attention from both the central government and the citizens. As a result, on the same day, the SEPA issued a notice asking all levels of local governments to strictly implement the "double-track" system, which meant separating the collected fees from expenditure of the environmental government departments. According to the double-track system, about 10% of the discharge fees collected by local EPBs should be given to central government (i.e., the Ministry of Finance), and the remaining 90% should go to the financial departments of the municipal governments, so that municipal EPBs are financed by the financial departments of the municipal governments.

Table 13.1 compares the major policy elements of the pollutant discharge fee and the environmental tax. The change from fee to tax in 2018 was intended to further enforce the charges on emissions. The environmental tax is administered by the tax department, which has experience in tax collection and management. Wang et al. (2019) estimate that the policy change from the pollutant discharge fee to the environmental tax will decrease emission intensities (i.e., emission per unit of total output) by 1.42% on average. The implementation effectiveness

Table 13.1 Policy features of pollutant discharge fee and environmental tax in China

Policy elements	Pollutant discharge fee	Environmental tax
Rate	SO_2, >1.2 yuan/PE; NOx, >1.2 yuan/PE; soot (*yan chen*), 0.6 yuan/PE; dust (*fen chen*), 0.6 yuan/PE	SO_2, NOx, soot and dust: all at rate of 1.2–12 yuan/PE
Collection	Collected by environmental department of all levels of government, monthly or seasonally	Collected by tax department of all levels of government, seasonally
Use of collected fees/taxes	Collected fees go to the local financial budget account and the national financial budget account; the money should be used for environmental protection purposes	Collected taxes go to the tax department of local governments; the money becomes a part of the public finance budget, under unified management
Monitoring and verification	Absence of a strict monitoring and verification mechanism	Under the unified monitoring and verification mechanism of the tax department
Enforcement	Weaker enforcement than that of tax[8]	Enforcement under legislation

Source: Adapted from Zheng et al. (2016); policy documents including *Environmental Tax Law* (2018), *Issues about Adjusting the Rates of Pollutant Discharge Fee* (2014), and *Regulation on the Collection, Use and Management of Pollutant Discharge Fee* (2003).

of the environmental tax, however, is likely to be influenced by the tax rate, the horizontal coordination between the environment department and the tax department, the policy enforcement measures employed by the city government, and the seriousness of its intent in collecting the tax (Wu et al., 2018).

Environmental target system

The environmental target system (*mu biao ze ren zhi*) is a policy instrument targeting local governments of cities (or provinces or counties), aiming to push them to take active policy measures for urban environmental management. This policy instrument adopts a numerical, result-oriented performance management approach, in which compliance with environmental targets, such as SO_2 emissions reduction, becomes an integral part of the indicators in China's cadre evaluation system to assess the performance of city government officials, affecting their career prospects and bonuses (Gao, 2015). The environmental target system was implemented against the background that in many cases sub-national governments valued economic growth above all else and disregarded the environmental damage caused by rapid economic development. The policy instrument thus aims to provide a political incentive for city government officials to give priority to emissions control (Kostka, 2016).

The environmental target system has been added to China's pre-existing nomenklatura-based cadre system. In China, the central government controls local governments (provincial, municipal, county, and township) through the nomenklatura public personnel management system whereby civil servants' career paths are determined by their immediate supervisors (Burns, 1994; Liang and Langbein, 2015). This is complemented by the target responsibility system: the central government signs performance contracts with provincial governments to specify performance targets at the beginning of the year and then evaluates their performance according to the signed performance contracts at the end of the year. Provincial governments, in turn, assign targets to municipal governments, evaluate their performance based on how well those targets are accomplished, and decide accordingly on personnel changes under the nomenklatura system (Chan and Gao, 2009; Gao, 2009). The performance targets are not treated equally. For instance, among a set of targets that a municipal government promises to achieve, some targets are prioritized and carry a veto power, which means that failure to meet these priority targets would jeopardize the municipal officials' prospects (Chan and Gao, 2009).

China's 10th Five Year Plan (FYP), for 2001–2005, set a national target of reducing annual SO_2 emissions by 20% by 2005, relative to the 2000 level. The burden of SO_2 emissions reduction was shared by sub-national jurisdictions (i.e., provinces, cities, counties, and districts). Local governments had to meet emission abatement targets, but target compliance was not yet linked to performance of local government officials.

In 2002, the SEPA implemented the "10th FYP for Preventing Acid Rain and SO_2 Pollution in the Two Control Zones", which introduced the idea of linking environmental target compliance to performance evaluation of local government officials for the first time. However, details on how the environmental target system should be implemented, such as the method of performance evaluation, were not discussed further until the 11th FYP period (2006–2010) (Schreifels et al., 2012; X. Zhang, 2017).

The 11th FYP set the national target of reducing annual SO_2 emissions and annual NOx emissions by 10% by 2010, compared to the 2005 level. MEP and NDRC held negotiations with provincial-level governments to set clear provincial targets, and contracts were then signed by provincial vice governors who committed to reaching those targets (Xu, 2011). The burden of meeting the targets was further disaggregated and shared by municipal governments and eventually polluting firms.

In May 2007, the State Council issued the Comprehensive Work Plan for Energy Conservation and Emission Reduction, which emphasized that local government leaders should be held accountable for emissions reduction in their jurisdictions (State Council of China, 2007b). Moreover, accomplishing emission reduction targets carried veto power, which explicitly links to personnel decisions. In jurisdictions failing to attain emissions reduction targets, local government officials would face penalties such as salary cuts, deployment to a remote locality, expulsion, or being disqualified from promotion or bonuses (Eaton and Kostka, 2014).

In November 2007, the SEPA stated that SO_2 was the major air pollutant that all levels of governments should try to mitigate and that performance of local governments would be evaluated based on the following performance measures: (1) how well they attained the target of SO_2 emission reduction, (2) how well they enforced environmental technologies and policy instruments to reduce emissions (e.g., forced closure of small polluting industrial plants), and (3) how well they monitored and verified progress in emissions reduction (SEPA, 2007). In November 2007, the 11th FYP for the Environmental Protection of China further emphasized the use of the environmental target system to incentivize local governments collectively to protect the environment: progress toward reaching environmental targets would be assessed, ranked, and published every six months; a mid-term assessment and a final assessment would be conducted at the end of 2008 and the end of 2010, respectively, to see how well local environmental targets had been achieved; and the assessment results would affect cadre evaluation of local officials (State Council of China, 2007a).

Since 2008, the SEPA has established six sub-national supervision centers (*huan bao du cha zhong xin*)[9] as representatives of the national government to oversee local governments' enforcement of environmental policies and has developed a department for enforcing quantity-based emissions control (*zong liang kong zhi si*) and a department for environmental monitoring (*huan jing jian ce si*) (Huan, 2011; Schreifels et al., 2012).

More pollutants have been added to environmental target-setting since the 11th FYP. In 2011, the 12th FYP (2011–2015) set the national target of reducing SO_2 emission by 8% and reducing NOx emission by 10% by 2015, compared to 2010 level; it also added the national target of reducing CO_2 emissions per unit of GDP (i.e., emission intensity) by 17%.[10] The recent 13th FYP (2016–2020) established environmental targets to reduce SO_2 emission by 8% below the 2015 level, reduce NOx emission by 10% below the 2015 level, and reduce CO_2 emission intensity by 17% below the 2015 level. The environmental target system is an integral part of the portfolio of policy instruments that the central government employs to achieve these targets for emissions reductions.

The environmental target system follows a top-down approach and faces many implementation hurdles, such as target allocation, limitation of the central government's capacity to verify local environmental performance, and pernicious gaming strategies adopted by local governments (Gao, 2015; Kostka, 2016; Wong and Karplus, 2017; X. Zhang, 2017). Targets' lack of flexibility to local contexts is a major implementation challenge. Local governments may find the environmental targets too difficult to achieve or inconsistent with other policy targets. With the pressure of meeting the targets, there have been cases of local governments temporarily cutting off the electricity supply to reduce emissions in a short period of time (A. Wang, 2013). Under the environmental target system, local officials are inclined to focus on short-term accountability while discounting long-term sustainability (Chan and Gao, 2009).

Difficulty in monitoring and verifying local environmental data is another major implementation challenge. In many cases, local governments fake achievements in emissions reductions, while there is no effective way to detect dishonest reporting of environmental data (Gao, 2015). Meanwhile, the six regional environmental supervision bureaus have spent a lot of resources on monitoring and overseeing local governments' environmental performance.

Policy experimentation

Policy experimentation is a governance model that is frequently used by the central government of China. Local officials try out innovative solutions to reach certain targets or to cope with challenges that emerge during the experimentation activity (Heilmann, 2008b). It is a purposeful and organized process rather than a freewheeling trial. Policy experimentation facilitates institutional innovation while avoiding reformist leaps in the dark, injecting local knowledge into the centralized policy process and stimulating policy learning (ibid.). This experiment-based policymaking is distinguished from other methods employed to inform policymaking, such as theoretical analyses or observational studies (Mosteller and Mosteller, 2006: 487). Policy experimentation can include small-scale and incremental experiments as well as large-scale and transformative experiments (Heilmann, 2008b; Mosteller and Mosteller, 2006: 492–494).

Policy experimentation in the environmental field resonates with the movement toward adaptive environmental management, which values the use of experimentation to search for knowledge, to reduce uncertainty, and to adapt future policy goals and actions (Norton, 2002; Norton and Steinemann, 2001).

But policy experiments discussed in these adaptive environmental management studies are limited to small-scale experiments with iterative and reversible trial measures and pre-selected treatment groups, rarely involving substantial policy process. The policy experimentation concept used in this chapter adopts Hellmann's conceptualization, particularly focusing on policy experimentation that establishes pilot programs in a specific policy field to inform policymaking and that involves dynamic central–local government interaction.

In China, policy experimentation plays a significant role in accelerating policy innovation, institutional changes, and economic gains while avoiding the risk of system breakdown, even in an authoritarian regime (Cao et al., 1999; Miao and Lang, 2015; Rawski, 2018). Policy makers only have a limited degree of freedom to alter status quo; they cannot freely adopt any policy instrument in any circumstance; even if a government has the capacity to initiate large scale institutional changes, its policy decisions are constrained by existing institutions (Capano, 2018; Howlett et al., 2015). In this situation, policy experimentations, which may or may not be scaled up, become pragmatic in terms of mitigating controversies, building up political support, and leading to adaptable policy designs (Heilmann, 2008b; Howlett and Rayner, 2013). Policy experimentation has been used in many policy domains in China, such as the environmental sector, economic reforms, and the health sector (Montinola et al., 1995). In the context of China's authoritarian regime, Chinese-style experiment-based policymaking is characterized as implementation preceding legislation, which is distinct from experiment-based policymaking in other federal systems where legislation precedes implementation. Upscaling of policy experiments happens only with the support of higher administrative-level governments. Heilmann (2008a, 2008b) uses the term "experimentation under the hierarchy" to describe the uniquely Chinese central–local dynamic interaction in experimentation activity, which combines both top-down and bottom-up policy processes: it involves local experimentation, central leadership and interventions during experimentation, identification of successful local experiments by higher-level policy patrons, and finally the selective integration of local experiences into national policymaking. At the local level, successfully conducting policy experimentation can be recorded as an achievement of the relevant local government officials, which may bring them improved career prospects, preferential treatment from central government, and advantages in jurisdictional competition (Montinola et al., 1995).

As an exemplary case, a few cities and provinces have experimented with the policy instrument of emission trading schemes (ETS) for CO_2 mitigation purpose, with approval from the central government. An ETS limits the aggregate emission level of ETS-regulated firms, with each firm allowed to emit up to a certain level. If an ETS-regulated firm emits more than its emission allowance, it can buy emission allowances from firms that have not used their full allocation. Firms face penalties for non-compliance. Therefore, as with the pollutant discharge fee, ETS imposes a cost on emissions, but the price of emissions depends on the demand and supply of emission allowances in the ETS market.

In 2011, China's NDRC issued a policy document, Notice on Piloting CO_2 ETS, to designate DRCs in Beijing, Chongqing, Guangdong, Hubei, Shanghai, Shenzhen, and Tianjin to make implementation plans for CO_2 ETS and to establish Emission Exchanges as the platforms for firm-to-firm trading of emission allowances. Shenzhen established the first CO_2 ETS in June 2013, following by Shanghai ETS (November 2013), Beijing ETS (November 2013), Guangdong ETS (December 2013), Tianjin ETS (December 2013), Hubei ETS (April 2014), and Chongqing ETS (June 2014). The city and provincial governments tried out what worked on the ground, designing and implementing CO_2 ETS with adaptations to local contexts (e.g., political context, economic structure, and marketization level) (Ren et al., 2018). For instance, there are variations among the seven pilot CO_2 ETS in terms of the industrial sectors covered by ETS, allocation methods for emission allowances, reporting and verification procedures, the penalties for non-compliance, and the availability of policy documents guiding policy implementation. Many studies have summarized the design of the seven ETS pilots (Chang et al., 2017; Li, 2018; Munnings et al., 2016; D. Zhang et al., 2014; M. Zhang et al., 2017). The pilots have provided important experiences of designing and implementing the policy instrument; some additional cities or provinces, such as Fujian, established CO_2 ETS after 2015. Learning from the sub-national policy experiments, the central government is considering building a national level CO_2 ETS. However, little is yet known about the design details of the national ETS based on publicly available information (Stoerk et al., 2019).

Sub-national experimentation with CO_2 ETS in China has revealed many implementation issues. First, the CO_2 price is far less than the social cost of CO_2 emissions and displays high volatility in all the sub-national policy pilots (Li, 2018). Second, there is a problem with weak enforcement. The CO_2 ETS pilots have not yet strictly implemented the punitive measures for non-compliance. Lax enforcement has led to limited demand for emission allowances from the regulated firms because they do not take ETS seriously or they have an oversupply of emission allowances, leading to low market liquidity. Governments in some of the pilot schemes (e.g., Beijing) are better at enforcing compliance than others (Deng et al., 2018). Tianjin and Chongqing's ETS have been criticized for their weak policy enforcement, inactive transactions, and limited market liquidity (Dong et al., 2016; Li, 2018; Tan and Wang, 2017; Z. Zhang, 2015); a survey revealed that about 30% of ETS-regulated firms in Chongqing have surplus allowances (Deng et al., 2018). Third, monitoring, reporting, and verification (MRV)[11] of firms' emission data are also critical implementation issues. MRV procedures are intended to ensure the reliability of emission data. Even though all pilots have made MRV rules, the MRV requirements are ambiguous and not strictly implemented (Deng et al., 2018; Tang et al., 2018).

Policy experimentation in China combines logics of bottom-up and top-down approaches to policy implementation, mobilizing bottom-up initiatives and informing national policymakers. It has been an important instrument, helping to bringing about transformational changes in the process of China's economic development;

however, sub-national policy experiments might not lead to an enhanced provision of public goods such as environmental protection given the inclination of local governments to prioritize economic development (Ba et al., 2018; Heilmann, 2008b). Good societal supervision and central government control are key to the success of sub-national environmental policy experiments in China.

Discussion

This chapter has explored three policy instruments implemented mainly in China's urban areas: the pollutant discharge fee, environmental target system, and policy experimentation of CO_2 ETS. Table 13.2 summarizes characteristics of the three policy instruments, which reflect three different types of central–local government interactions.

The pollutant discharge fee was introduced and enforced by the central government to regulate polluting firms, while governments of cities, provinces, or counties were responsible for collecting the emission fees. But local governments do not necessarily implement the policy instrument as intended: they may not strictly impose emission fees on polluting firms, in order to seek fast economic growth, or they may arbitrarily spend the collected fees on non-environmental purposes. To enhance control of local policy implementation, the central government imposed more complex procedural requirements to manage collection and usage of pollution fees and mandated environmental information disclosure of polluting firms to mitigate information asymmetry. Eventually it enacted the Environmental Tax Law to replace the discharge fee with an environmental tax.

The environmental target system was enforced by the central government to motivate local governments of cities/provinces/counties to reduce emissions. City governments sign contracts with the central government and promise to meet binding environmental targets; they are motivated by political incentives to reach the targets but may fake their environmental achievements (Gao, 2015). To cope with the information problem, the central government of China has enhanced the administrative-level regional environmental supervision teams who have been given more power and resources to conduct occasional inspection tours to check on urban environmental performance. This has had a range of effects: it has shifted the focus from checking on emission quantity data to checking on environmental quality, as the former is easier to manipulate than the latter;[12] it has changed the status of local environmental monitoring stations to state-owned so that city governments have less chance to manipulate the environmental data; it has mandated large polluting firms to disclose their emissions to enhance public supervision; and it has increased penalties on data fraud by firms and local governments. These measures have enhanced the quality of data (about pollutants that are easier to monitor, such as SO_2 and NOx), enabling better evaluation of urban environmental performance, conducive to the effective implementation of the environmental target system as well as the environmental tax.

Policy experimentation is often initiated by the central government and then implemented by the local governments who seek central government approval.

Table 13.2 Comparison of the three policy instruments

Policy elements	Pollutant discharge fee	Environmental target system	Policy experimentation: CO₂ ETS
Target emission	Major pollutants: SO₂ emission, NOₓ, COD	CO₂ emission, SO₂ emission, NOₓ, COD	CO₂ emission
Target group	Polluting firms	Local governments [1]	Polluting firms
Mechanism	Pricing emissions	Linking target compliance to cadre evaluation	Pricing emissions
Timing of implementation	1982–2018	2007–	2013–
Implementation approach	Top-down	Top-down	Top-down and bottom-up
Regulator at central level	MEP (1982–2018), State Taxation Administration (2018–)	MEP (2007–2018), Ministry of Ecology and Environment [2] (2018–)	NDRC (2013–2017), Ministry of Ecology and Environment (2018–)
Local implementers	EPBs (1982–2018), local taxation bureaus (2018–)	EPBs (2007–)	DRC (2013–2017), EPBs (2018–)
Implementation scope	National	National	A few cities and provinces
Common implementation issue	Monitoring and verification of emission data	Monitoring and verification of emission data	Monitoring and verification of emission data
Implementation issue specific to the policy instrument	Misappropriation of collected fees; local protectionism	Faking environmental achievements	Limited market liquidity; laxer enforcement
Central government's control	Imposing procedural tools to manage collection and usage of pollution fees; mandating environmental information disclosure of polluting firms; changing from "fee" to "tax", and enacting *Environmental Tax Law*	Moving away from using self-reporting data to real-time environmental quality data, changing ownership of local environmental monitoring stations to be state-owned, mandating environmental information disclosure of polluting firms, enhancing penalties on data fraud, establishing regional environmental supervision bureaus to conduct occasional inspection tours	Selecting of piloting location, MRV guidelines, requiring a third party to verify firms' emission reports, selective integration of piloting experiences into national policymaking

Note: 1) municipal governments further distribute the burden of reaching the binding environmental targets to lower administrative level governments (e.g., urban district level) and major polluting firms. 2) The former Ministry of Environmental Protection incorporated environmental duties dispersed in other government agencies and became the current Ministry of Ecology and Environment in 2018. Information is collected from literature and government policy documents.

The city governments who conduct the policy experimentation have a certain degree of discretion regarding policy implementation. Based on experience and knowledge accumulated during the policy experimentation, the central government might consider upscaling the experimental policy (e.g., CO_2 ETS) to a national policy, if there are policy patrons. However, policy experimentation in the environmental field has not necessarily led to an enhanced provision of public goods, especially when city governments perceive that enforcing environmental policies could limit economic development. Lax enforcement by local officials, passive participation of firms, and difficulty in monitoring and verifying self-reported emissions data are key challenges of CO_2 ETS policy experimentation. In order to encourage local policy innovation, the central government has less direct involvement in policy experimentation than in the other two policy instruments, although, to enhance monitoring and verification of emission data, it provides MRV guidelines and requires that local officials have firms' emissions reports verified by a third party.

Conclusion

Since the 1980s, China has formulated a complex mix of policy instruments to enhance urban environmental quality. Given that environmental issues such as climate change and urban air pollution have characteristics of wicked problems, a mix of policy instruments is more suitable than a single policy instrument to address the varied challenges involved. The central government has adopted various types of environmental policy instruments using the authority and financial and organizational resources at its disposal for environmental governance. In spite of the central government's green agenda, however, effective local implementation remains a challenge. This chapter has taken a case study approach, investigating the implementation of three policy instruments: the pollutant discharge fee (a finance-based policy instrument), the environmental target system (an authority-based policy instrument), and policy experimentation of CO_2 ETS (a finance-based policy instrument). The chapter has demonstrated how local governments implement these policy instruments and how the central government attempts to control the implementation process.

The analysis shows that each policy instrument has its local implementation barriers. Even in an authoritarian country like China, which employs command-and-control policy instruments, city governments have some freedom with regard to implementation, which can affect the ultimate policy outcomes. The central government has weak control over the behavior of city governments at the policy implementation stage, leading some to argue that China's command-and-control policy instruments are actually more like "command-without-control" (Kostka, 2016; Lo, 2015). China has also tried out innovative market-based policy instruments like ETS, but monitoring and verifying emissions data continues to be a major implementation issue. In all three policy instruments, information asymmetry is one of the common implementation barriers. The implication here is that China's environmental governance should not only focus on the choice of the right policy instruments but also on the need to address local implementation obstacles such as data monitoring and verification of various emissions.

China's environmental governance continues to progress and improve, exemplified by the switch from the pollutant discharge fee to environmental tax, the enhancement of environmental information collection and disclosure, and the experimental practices of policy instruments such as ETS. Improved environmental data collection and identification of major pollutants (e.g., SO_2) have mitigated some of the shortcomings of implementation. Further gains could be made by measures such as improving the legal status of MRV regulations and compliance rules to enhance the implementation effectiveness of CO_2 ETS (Tang et al., 2018) and strengthening public supervision to help overcome the barriers to monitoring and verifying environmental performance (X. Zhang, 2017).

Notes

1 Policy instruments, also known as policy tools or policy measures, are the concrete means or devices that are chosen to implement or give effect to public policies (Howlett et al., 2009).
2 China has three types of cities, including six provincial-level cities (four municipalities and two special administrative regions), 293 prefecture-level cities and 375 county-level cities, totaling 674 cities. Data can be found at the website of China's National Bureau of Statistics: http://data.stats.gov.cn/english/easy query.htm?cn=C01
3 This was superseded by the Regulation on the Collection, Use and Management of Pollutant Discharge Fees (issued by the State Council) 2003. The latter has more detailed stipulations about the methods and procedures for imposing the pollutant discharge fee, the use of the collected discharge fees, and the legal consequences of non-compliance.
4 Referring to soot (*yan chen*) and dust (*fen chen*), but without specifying the PM diameter.
5 In 1988, the SEPA was established as a vice-ministerial level government agency, working directly under the State Council. It was upgraded to ministerial level in 1998 and upgraded again to become the Ministry of Environmental Protection (cabinet level) in 2008. It was reorganized and renamed the Ministry of Ecology and Environment in 2018.
6 Pilots included Guizhou province, Guangdong province, Changsha city, Chongqing city, Guilin city, Hangzhou city, Liuzhou city, Nanning city, Qingdao city, Yibin city, and Yichang city.
7 1 pollutant equivalent (PE) = 0.95 kg SO_2 emission; 1 PE = 0.95 kg NOx emission; 1 PE = 4 kg soot; 1 PE = 2.18 kg dust.
8 The pollution discharge fee was supported by the administrative regulation issued by the State Council and had less legal authority.
9 In November 2011, these were renamed regional supervision bureaus (*qu yu du cha ju*) and given greater administrative powers to supervise local governments.
10 Constraining CO_2 emission intensity rather than the total amount of CO_2 emissions saves emission space for new business entrants, and future production increases.
11 Examples of MRV issues include monitoring plans, reporting emissions, verifying emissions of firms, and management of parties that are qualified to verify emission data.
12 This is to tackle cases where data reported by cities show big improvements in emission abatement but the environmental quality does not become better.

References

Ba, Feng, Paul R. Thiers, and Yonggong Liu (2018). "The Evolution of China's Emission Trading Mechanisms: From International Offset Market to Domestic Emission Trading Scheme." *Environment and Planning C: Politics and Space* 36 (7): 1214–1233. https://doi.org/10.1177/2399654417751928.

Beeson, Mark (2010). "The Coming of Environmental Authoritarianism." *Environmental Politics* 19 (2): 276–294. https://doi.org/10.1080/09644010903576918.

Burns, John P. (1994). "Strengthening Central CCP Control of Leadership Selection: The 1990 Nomenklatura." *The China Quarterly* (138), June: 458–491.

Cao, Yuanzheng, Yingyi Qian, and Barry R. Weingast (1999). "From Federalism, Chinese Style to Privatization, Chinese Style." *Economics of Transition* 7 (1): 103–131.

Capano, Giliberto (2018). "Policy Design Spaces in Reforming Governance in Higher Education: The Dynamics in Italy and the Netherlands." *Higher Education* 75 (4): 675–694. https://doi.org/10.1007/s10734-017-0158-5.

Chan, Hon S., and Jie Gao (2009). "Putting the Cart Before the Horse: Accountability or Performance?" *Australian Journal of Public Administration* 68 (Supplment 1): 51–61. https://doi.org/10.1111/j.1467-8500.2009.00621.x.

Chang, Kai, Ping Pei, Chao Zhang, and Xin Wu (2017). "Exploring the Price Dynamics of CO_2 Emissions Allowances in China's Emissions Trading Scheme Pilots." *Energy Economics* 67: 213–223. https://doi.org/10.1016/j.eneco.2017.07.006.

Deng, Zhe, Dongya Li, Tao Pang, and Maosheng Duan (2018). "Effectiveness of Pilot Carbon Emissions Trading Systems in China." *Climate Policy* 18 (8): 992–1011. https://doi.org/10.1080/14693062.2018.1438245.

Dong, Jun, Yu Ma, and Hongxing Sun (2016). "From Pilot to the National Emissions Trading Scheme in China: International Practice and Domestic Experiences." *Sustainability (Switzerland)* 8 (6): 17pp. https://doi.org/10.3390/su8060522.

Eaton, Sarah, and Genia Kostka (2014). "Authoritarian Environmentalism Undermined? Local Leaders' Time Horizons and Environmental Policy Implementation in China." *China Quarterly* 218 (1): 359–380. https://doi.org/10.1017/S0305741014000356.

Francesch-Huidobro, Maria, Carlos Wing Hung Lo, and Shui Yan Tang (2012). "The Local Environmental Regulatory Regime in China: Changes in Pro-Environment Orientation, Institutional Capacity, and External Political Support in Guangzhou." *Environment and Planning A* 44 (10): 2493–2511. https://doi.org/10.1068/a44504.

Gao, Jie (2009). "Governing by Goals and Numbers: A Case Study in the Use of Performance Measurement to Build State Capacity in China." *Public Administration and Development* 29 (1): 21–31. https://doi.org/10.1002/pad.514.

Gao, Jie (2015). "Pernicious Manipulation of Performance Measures in China's Cadre Evaluation System." *China Quarterly* 223 (July): 618–637. https://doi.org/10.1017/S0305741015000806.

He, Ling Yun, and Jia Jia Ou (2017). "Pollution Emissions, Environmental Policy, and Marginal Abatement Costs." *International Journal of Environmental Research and Public Health* 14 (12). https://doi.org/10.3390/ijerph14121509.

Heilmann, Sebastian (2008a). "From Local Experiments to National Policy: The Origins of China's Distinctive Policy Process." *The China Journal* 59: 1–30.

Heilmann, Sebastian (2008b). "Policy Experimentation in China's Economic Rise." *Studies in Comparative International Development* 43 (1): 1–26. https://doi.org/10.1007/s12116-007-9014-4.

Howlett, Michael, Ishani Mukherjee, and Jun Jie Woo (2015). "From Tools to Tool-kits in Policy Design Studies: The New Design Orientation Towards Policy Formulation Research." *Policy and Politics* 43 (2): 291–311. https://doi.org/10.1332/147084414X13992869118596.

Howlett, Michael, M. Ramesh, and Anthony Perl (2009). *Studying Public Policy: Policy Cycles & Policy Subsystems*, 3rd ed. Oxford: Oxford University Press.

Howlett, Michael, and Jeremy Rayner (2013). "Patching vs Packaging in Policy Formulation: Assessing Policy Portfolio Design." *Politics and Governance* 1 (2): 170–182. https://doi.org/10.12924/pag2013.01020170.

Huan, Qingzhi (2011). "Regional Supervision Centres for Environmental Protection in China: Functions and Limitations." *Journal of Current Chinese Affairs* 40 (3): 139–162. https://doi.org/10.1177/186810261104000306.

Kostka, Genia (2016). "Command Without Control: The Case of China's Environmental Target System." *Regulation and Governance* 10 (1): 58–74. https://doi.org/10.1111/rego.12082.

Lee, Chia Yen, and Ke Wang (2019). "Nash Marginal Abatement Cost Estimation of Air Pollutant Emissions Using the Stochastic Semi-Nonparametric Frontier." *European Journal of Operational Research* 273 (1): 390–400. https://doi.org/10.1016/j.ejor.2018.08.016.

Levin, Kelly, Benjamin Cashore, Steven Bernstein, and Graeme Auld (2012). "Overcoming the Tragedy of Super Wicked Problems: Constraining Our Future Selves to Ameliorate Global Climate Change." *Policy Sciences* 45: 123–152. https://doi.org/10.1007/s11077-012-9151-0.

Li, Lili (2018). "Assessing the Implementation of Local Emission Trading Schemes in China: Econometric Analysis of Market Data." *China Policy Journal* 1 (1): 27–55. https://doi.org/10.18278/cpj.1.1.2.

Liang, Jiaqi, and Laura Langbein (2015). "Performance Management, High-Powered Incentives, and Environmental Policies in China." *International Public Management Journal* 18 (3): 346–385. https://doi.org/10.1080/10967494.2015.1043167.

Lo, Kevin (2015). "How Authoritarian Is the Environmental Governance of China?" *Environmental Science and Policy* 54: 152–159. https://doi.org/10.1016/j.envsci.2015.06.001.

Miao, Bo, and Graeme Lang (2015). "A Tale of Two Eco-Cities: Experimentation under Hierarchy in Shanghai and Tianjin." *Urban Policy and Research* 33 (2): 247–263. https://doi.org/10.1080/08111146.2014.967390.

Montinola, Gabriella, Yingyi Qian, and Barry R. Weingast (1995). "Federalism, Chinese Style: The Political Basis for Economic Success in China." *World Politics* 48 (1): 50–81.

Mosteller, Frederick, and Gale Mosteller (2006). "New Statistical Methods in Public Policy. Part I: Experimentation." In *Selected Papers of Frederick Mosteller*, edited by Rederick Mosteller, Stephen E. Fienberg, and David C. Hoaglin. New York City: Springer.

Munnings, Clayton, Richard D. Morgenstern, Zhongmin Wang, and Xu Liu (2016). "Assessing the Design of Three Carbon Trading Pilot Programs in China." *Energy Policy* 96: 688–699. https://doi.org/10.1016/j.enpol.2016.06.015.

National Development and Reform Commission, Ministry of Finance, and Ministry of Environmental Protection (2014). "Issues About Adjusting the Rates of Pollutant Discharge Fee. 国家发展和改革委员会、财政部、环境保护部关于调整排污费征收标准等有关问题的通知." Beijing, China: National Development and

Reform Commission; Ministry of Finance; Ministry of Environmental Protection. www.ndrc.gov.cn/gzdt/201409/t20140905_624993.html.

Norton, Bryan G. (2002). "Pragmatism, Adaptive Management, and Sustainability." In *Searching for Sustainability: Interdisciplinary Essays in the Philosophy of Conservation Biology*, edited by Bryan G. Norton. Cambridge: Cambridge University Press.

Norton, Bryan G., and Anne C. Steinemann (2001). "Environmental Values and Adaptive Management." *Environmental Values* 10 (4): 473–506. https://doi.org/10.3197/096327101129340921.

Rawski, Thomas G. (2018). "Implications of China's Reform Experience." *The China Quarterly*, 144: 1150–1173.

Ren, Shenggang, Xiaolei Li, Baolong Yuan, Dayuan Li, and Xiaohong Chen (2018). "The Effects of Three Types of Environmental Regulation on Eco-Efficiency: A Cross-Region Analysis in China." *Journal of Cleaner Production* 173: 245–255. https://doi.org/10.1016/j.jclepro.2016.08.113.

Schreifels, Jeremy J., Yale Fu, and Elizabeth J. Wilson (2012). "Sulfur Dioxide Control in China: Policy Evolution During the 10th and 11th Five-Year Plans and Lessons for the Future." *Energy Policy* 48: 779–789. https://doi.org/10.1016/j.enpol.2012.06.015.

Standing Committee of the National People's Congress (NPCSC) of China (2018). "Environmental Tax Law. 中华人民共和国环境保护税法." Beijing, China. www.chinatax.gov.cn/n810341/n810755/c3348910/content.html.

State Council of China (1998). "The State Council's Reply to the Issues About Acid Rain Control Zone and SO$_2$ Emission Control Zone. 国务院关于酸雨控制区和二氧化硫污染控制区有关问题的批复. 国函[1998]5号." Beijing, China: The State Council of China.

State Council of China (2007a). "11th FYP for the Environmental Protection of China. 国务院关于印发国家环境保护'十一五'规划的通知. 国发[2007]37号." Beijing, China: State Environmental Protection Administration of China. http://ghs.ndrc.gov.cn/ghwb/gjjgh/200806/P020080616561998751580.pdf.

State Council of China (2007b). "Comprehensive Work Plan for Energy Conservation and Emission Reduction. 国务院关于印发节能减排综合性工作方案的通知. 国发[2007]15号." Beijing, China: The State Council of China.

State Environmental Protection Administration (2007). "The 11th FYP Interim Assessment Measures for the Performance of Reducing the Total Amount of Major Pollutants. '十一五'主要污染物总量减排考核办法（暂行). 环发[2007]124号." Beijing, China: State Environmental Protection Administration of China. www.gov.cn/gongbao/content/2008/content_961664.htm.

State Environmental Protection Administration, Ministry of Finance, State Administration of Commodity Prices, and Trade and Economic Office of the State Council (1992). "Launching the Pilots of Levying Discharge Fees on Sulfur Dioxide from Industrial Coal Combustion. 国家环境保护局、国家物价局、财政部、国务院经贸办关于开展征收工业燃煤二氧化硫排污费试点工作的通知（环监[1992]361号)." Beijing, China: State Environmental Protection Administration; Ministry of Finance; State Administration of Commodity Prices; Trade and Economic Office of the State Council. www.gov.cn/zhengce/content/2010-11/22/content_5206.htm.

State Environmental Protection Administration, Ministry of Finance, State Planning Commission, and State Economic and Trade Commission (1998). "Expanding the Piloting SO$_2$ Discharge Fee Projects to the Acid Rain Control Zone and SO$_2$

Emission Control Zone. 国家环境保护总局、国家计委、财政部、国家经贸委关于在酸雨控制区和二氧化硫污染控制区开展征收二氧化硫排污费扩大试点的通知. 环发[1998]6号." Beijing, China: State Environmental Protection Administration; Ministry of Finance; State Planning Commission; State Economic and Trade Commission.

Stoerk, Thomas, Daniel J. Dudek, and Jia Yang (2019). "China's National Carbon Emissions Trading Scheme: Lessons From the Pilot Emission Trading Schemes, Academic Literature, and Known Policy Details." *Climate Policy* 19 (4): 472–486. https://doi.org/10.1080/14693062.2019.1568959.

Tan, Xueping, and Xinyu Wang (2017). "The Market Performance of Carbon Trading in China: A Theoretical Framework of Structure-Conduct-Performance." *Journal of Cleaner Production* 159: 410–424. https://doi.org/10.1016/j.jclepro.2017.05.019.

Tang, Renhu, Wei Guo, Machtelt Oudenes, Peng Li, Jun Wang, Jin Tang, Le Wang, and Haijun Wang (2018). "Key Challenges for the Establishment of the Monitoring, Reporting and Verification (MRV) System in China's National Carbon Emissions Trading Market." *Climate Policy* 18 (Supplement 1): 106–121. https://doi.org/10.1080/14693062.2018.1454882.

Tsang, Stephen, and Ans Kolk (2010). "The Evolution of Chinese Policies and Governance Structures on Environment, Energy and Climate." *Environmental Policy and Governance* 20 (3): 180–196. https://doi.org/10.1002/eet.540.

Wang, Alex (2013). "The Search for Sustainable Legitimacy: Environmental Law and Bureaucracy in China." *Harvard Environmental Law Review* 37: 365–440. https://doi.org/10.2139/ssrn.2128167.

Wang, Jiayu, Ke Wang, Xunpeng Shi, and Yi Ming Wei (2019). "Spatial Heterogeneity and Driving Forces of Environmental Productivity Growth in China: Would It Help to Switch Pollutant Discharge Fees to Environmental Taxes?" *Journal of Cleaner Production* 223: 36–44. https://doi.org/10.1016/j.jclepro.2019.03.045.

Watkins, Emma, S. Withana, and ten Brink Patrick (2015). "Capacity Building for Environmental Tax Reform – Background Report for a Conference by the European Commission (07.027729/2015/718767/SER/ENV.F.1) and Hosted by the Committee of the Regions (5 October 2017). Based on the Study by IEEP, DCE Aarhus University, ENT Environment and Management, Eunomia, Green Budget Europe, IVM, PBL, Cambridge Econometrics, Denkstatt, Galovic Savjetovanje, SEI, Ekokonsultacijos, Janis Brizga, Katja Kavcic Sonnenschein and Prof. Th." Brussels/London: Institute for European Environmental Policy.

Wong, Christine, and Valerie J. Karplus (2017). "China's War on Air Pollution: Can Existing Governance Structures Support New Ambitions?" *China Quarterly* 231 (August): 662–684. https://doi.org/10.1017/S0305741017000947.

Wu, Jian, Qing Chen, and Alon Tal (2018). "From Pollution Fee to Environmental Protection Tax: The Potential and Limitations of the New Environmental Tax in China." *Journal of Comparative Policy Analysis: Research and Practice* 20 (2): 223–236. https://doi.org/doi.org/10.1080/13876988.2017.1361597.

Xie, Rong-hui, Yi-jun Yuan, and Jing-jing Huang (2017). "Different Types of Environmental Regulations and Heterogeneous Influence on 'Green' Productivity: Evidence From China." *Ecological Economics* 132: 104–112. https://doi.org/10.1016/j.ecolecon.2016.10.019.

Xu, Yuan (2011). "The Use of a Goal for SO_2 Mitigation Planning and Management in China's 11th Five-Year Plan." *Journal of Environmental Planning and Management* 54 (6): 769–783. https://doi.org/10.1080/09640568.2010.528944.

Yuan, Xueliang, Mi Mi, Ruimin Mu, and Jian Zu (2013). "Strategic Route Map of Sulphur Dioxide Reduction in China." *Energy Policy* 60: 844–851. https://doi. org/10.1016/j.enpol.2013.05.072.

Zhang, Da, Valerie J. Karplus, Cyril Cassisa, and Xiliang Zhang (2014). "Emissions Trading in China: Progress and Prospects." *Energy Policy* 75: 9–16. https://doi. org/10.1016/j.enpol.2014.01.022.

Zhang, Mengya, Yong Liu, and Yunpeng Su (2017). "Comparison of Carbon Emission Trading Schemes in the European Union and China." *Climate* 5 (3): 70. https://doi.org/10.3390/cli5030070.

Zhang, Xuehua (2017). "Implementation of Pollution Control Targets in China: Has a Centralized Enforcement Approach Worked?" *China Quarterly* 231 (August): 749–774. https://doi.org/10.1017/S0305741017000959.

Zhang, Zhongxiang (2015). "Carbon Emissions Trading in China: The Evolution From Pilots to a Nationwide Scheme." *Climate Policy* 15: 104–126. https://doi. org/10.1080/14693062.2015.1096231.

Zheng, Yinger, Haixia Zheng, and Xinyue Ye (2016). "Using Machine Learning in Environmental Tax Reform Assessment for Sustainable Development: A Case Study of Hubei Province, China." *Sustainability* 8 (11): 1124. https://doi. org/10.3390/su8111124.

14 Failed healthcare in India

Looking behind the urban-focused narrative

Rumit Singh Kakar and Kris Hartley

Currently the world's second most populous country, India is home to 1.3 billion people (15% of the world population), and its growth rate will make it the world's most populous by 2050. The urgent need for quality healthcare is increasing at an even faster pace. India has one of the world's largest public healthcare systems but has failed to provide adequate healthcare to a majority of its citizens. This chapter examines the causes of declining public health outcomes across both urban and rural India, utilizing existing research, government documents, and other published materials. It concludes with an analysis of India's healthcare challenges through the lens of policy capacity, focusing on the importance of analytical and individual-level capacities for both core and periphery regions of the country.

Healthcare gaps and deficiencies

Quality public healthcare is rooted in equal access to public hospitals staffed with capable professionals and modern equipment. India falls short on both counts, with a public healthcare system that is lagging behind international standards and a private system that is largely inaccessible to the many who need care. According to Bali and Ramesh (2015: 301), the private sector dominates India's healthcare provision while "the skeletal network of public hospitals, understaffed and ill-equipped to deal with current demand for health care services, is choked with patients who are unable to afford private care". The physician-to-patient ratio in India's urban and suburban areas is approximately 0.7 per 1,000 and even worse in rural areas. This ratio is considerably lower than the World Health Organization's minimum recommendation of one doctor per 1,000 patients, with healthcare described as "available but maldistributed and inefficient" (Kumar and Pal, 2018: n.p.). This is a substantial policy challenge given that the majority of India's population resides in rural areas, where primary care centers are often difficult to access due to geographical limitations. These centers also suffer operational limitations including inadequately trained staff, poor supply of essential medicines, and insufficient technologies for effective and timely diagnosis.

Much of India's rural population works for daily wages, and missing a day of work for healthcare reasons can present a significant financial hardship in terms of lost wages. Therefore, the availability of fast and efficient healthcare is vital to maintaining livelihoods. Not seeking healthcare until there is an undeniable medical emergency is a common practice in rural areas, and emergency situations often cannot be handled at primary care centers – even those that are relatively well-equipped. In such cases, patients are typically referred to a public tertiary care facility in the closest major city. This often generates a flood of rural emergency patients into urban tertiary care hospitals that must already care for local residents, presenting an excessive burden.

India's extremely low physician-to-patient ratio likewise compromises the quality of healthcare. Common problems in public hospitals include long waiting times, scarcity of sufficient and sanitary hospital beds, maintenance problems with medical equipment due to overuse, and disillusionment among healthcare staff including doctors, nurses, and maintenance workers. Delays in the procurement and maintenance of medical equipment and other facilities are reflective of logistical and bureaucratic bottlenecks, further increasing waiting times and adding to workplace stress for physicians and staff who are already overworked. An unfortunate but common scene in the general wards of public hospitals is for two or more patients sharing a twin bed in unsanitary circumstances – a precarious situation given the potential presence of communicable diseases and infections. This compounds the frustration of patients and healthcare staff alike.

Due to widespread knowledge about these and other poor conditions, many individuals from urban areas avoid public or government-aided hospitals and medical facilities, instead favoring private hospitals where the quality of care is considered superior in terms of sanitation, staff competence, and equipment. The cost of private medical services is either an out-of-pocket expense or funded through medical insurance. However, insurance coverage is held by less than 20% of the population and disproportionately in states with higher levels of literacy. Those with insurance are generally covered by one of several schemes: the Rashtriya Swasthya Bima Yojana (RSBY) scheme, mandatory social health insurance (SHI) scheme and government insurance scheme, or voluntary private health insurance (VHI) schemes. The tax-funded RSBY scheme covers the highest percentage of those with insurance (77%), followed by the SHI (16%) and VHI (7%). Utilization of public sector facilities is minimal (6%) among those enrolled in private insurance (Prinja et al., 2019).

Choosing among various insurance options is no trivial task in India. Depending on the type of insurance held, individuals may or may not be able to receive adequate care at a facility suitable to their needs. Although government hospitals generally accept public insurance schemes, individuals with financial means typically opt for private hospitals, many of which have agreements with insurance providers for processing cashless transactions. Nevertheless, cashless transaction and insurance reimbursement systems are not without flaws, including unduly long delays in payment approval, clerical inefficiency, and restrictions by insurance companies that effectively minimize payouts. Insurance companies are not solely implicated in these challenges, as the internal operational systems of private hospitals are known for many of the same types of problems. While insurance companies are often faulted for providing low value relative to high premiums, private hospitals have been known to exaggerate the costs of treatment in order to receive higher payments from insurance companies – a common problem in many countries with private health insurance systems.

India's healthcare system suffers from a variety of structural challenges that affect the quality and cost of healthcare for a majority of the population, insured or uninsured. This is not surprising, given that the system is overburdened and under-funded. In India's case, a large population, wide gaps in local fiscal capacity, and continuing socio-economic disparity have yielded a public health crisis in which people struggle to obtain care that meets their needs. Without the time and money to seek preventive care, many patients wait until circumstances are extreme before seeking treatment. The factors behind this crisis are numerous, interrelated, and complex; they include individual preferences and behaviors, management of hospitals, and policy visions at the national level. These and other governance challenges are addressed in the second half of this chapter. The next section describes environmental conditions that exacerbate public health challenges in India.

Health stressors: environmental pollution

A disorganized and under-resourced healthcare system is not the only explanation for India's poor public health outcomes. Increasing exposure to atmospheric and environmental pollutants, in combination with a shortage of access to basic necessities such as clean water, air, and sanitation, are also contributors. Environmental pollution is rising at a rapid pace in India, exacerbated by increased industrial activity, vehicle emissions, and auxiliary open burning, among other factors.

As India's second largest urban region by population – and among the world's largest overall – Delhi routinely records levels of airborne particulate matter more than three to four times the national average and close to 13 times the maximum safe levels laid down in World Health Organization (WHO) guidelines (Guttikunda and Goel, 2013). Safe levels recommended by WHO guidelines are intended to limit or eliminate the possibility of adverse health effects such as acute and chronic bronchitis, asthma, cardiovascular disorders, skin and lung cancers, and death from continued over-exposure. The population living in the Delhi urban region is at high risk for such diseases and disorders. According to reports, in the first decade of this century, mortality rose by 20–24% due to cardiovascular and respiratory disorders associated with air pollution (ibid.). Growing industrial activity in and around Delhi, increases in the number of private and commercial vehicles, and ongoing construction to support population growth are among the major contributors to air pollution.

Other cities in India face similar challenges. In a study of Mumbai, Patankar and Trivedi (2011) report high correlations between airborne particulate matter and cardiovascular and respiratory diseases, also attributing premature mortality rates to airborne particulate matter and nitrogen dioxide in the city. Not only does this have a negative impact on the well-being of pollution victims and their families, it is also responsible for millions of dollars in monetary burdens to the state. With a population of over 12 million, Mumbai has experienced rapidly increasing demand for space. Like Delhi, Mumbai has moved industrial facilities to surrounding areas and expanded housing and related infrastructure on the urban periphery. Industrial clusters in these previously rural areas contribute to air, water, and soil pollution at the urban edge, compounding the effects of rapid population growth and urbanization in the same areas. Even in steady-state circumstances, governments struggle to appropriate the necessary funds for healthcare; in Mumbai's case, the challenge is further deepened by the associated challenges of unrestrained urbanization.

Like many regions in developing countries, rural India also suffers from high levels of air pollution. In these areas, pollutants from industry and vehicle emissions are not necessarily as concentrated as those in cities. However, 80–95% of fuel used by India's domestic households is biomass (wood or animal dung), which emits large amounts of smoke and air pollutants. Outdoor pollution is particularly high in the winter months, when such burning is used for warmth in India's colder regions. At the same time, toxic pollutants from burning biomass indoors, where ventilation is poor and conditions crowded, can also lead to detrimental health effects. High rates of acute and chronic respiratory diseases such as COPD, asthma, and lung cancer have been reported among women, children, and adolescents, the population most acutely affected (Padhi and Padhy, 2008). Furthermore, tobacco use in both active and passive forms compounds health risks, complicates existing lung diseases, and is one of the leading causes of mortality in India. According to Gupta et al. (2005) the variety of uses of tobacco (including smokeless usage) is likely responsible for a higher share of disease and death in India than would be estimated on the basis of global data. In spite of all this evidence, India's exceptionally high levels of air pollution are not being addressed by any major policy measure or any meaningful ground-level initiatives. As the country's health situation worsens, an already fiscally constrained healthcare system is put under further pressure.

Health stressors: caring for vulnerable populations

Daily wage workers

Increasing rural-to-urban migration is another source of strain on healthcare facilities and resources. Many such migrants live in the slums of major cities like Delhi and Mumbai and work in labor-intensive jobs for daily wages.[1] These workers typically lack health insurance and associated benefits through their employers. With little or no economic security, they often struggle to support their families and assume substantial risks to their health and well-being after migrating to India's urban environments.

In India's vast and unplanned urban slums, home to large numbers of rural migrants, living conditions and sanitation facilities are deficient. Although often located in the center of major metropolitan areas and surrounded by well-planned neighborhoods with modern amenities, these slums lack access to clean drinking water and proper waste management. A majority of slum residents rely on community toilets that are rarely cleaned, and for drinking water they rely on decrepit municipal infrastructure, neither of which are sufficient for meeting basic human needs. Slum dwellers often have no choice but to drink water regardless of its condition. Slums are therefore affected by infectious and communicable diseases at higher rates than are more developed areas of cities, adding to an already dizzying array of health stressors for disadvantaged residents. Lack of access to sources of good-quality food further increases vulnerability to disease and infection, and slum dwellers endure lengthier recovery times that could be shortened with balanced diets and healthier lifestyles. Malnutrition and poverty are correlated, and both are closely associated with higher incidence of disease and mortality.

Even in their workplaces, wage workers are unable to escape environmental threats to their health. These workers are often employed in manual and physically stressful jobs with disproportionately high exposure to hazardous pollutants. Even with protective measures such as face masks and safety suits, few factories and work sites strictly enforce standards, as stipulated by the Ministry of Labour and Employment's (2010) National Policy on Safety, Health and Environment at Work Place. Pollutants commonly found at such workplaces can affect internal organs, and consistent exposure over time can lead to health problems such as bronchitis. The impacts of pollutant exposure are often delayed and thus difficult to measure; the absence of immediate and apparent adverse impacts lowers the urgency for policy intervention.

Many daily wage workers seek treatment only if the severity of the condition prevents them from performing their jobs. Even when they have the opportunity and wherewithal to seek medical help, they often face hours of waiting at government hospitals and are thus disincentivized to do so. This can lead to the further accumulation of negative health effects, more difficult treatment at later stages, and longer recovery time. Avoiding treatment due to lack of time and resources can cause life-long medical problems and the risk of premature mortality, threatening families with lost livelihoods. This vicious cycle imposes its own physical and mental stresses on both workers and their families. As reflected in these conditions, it is evident that India's healthcare programs are failing to meet the needs of the public and further contributing to declines in health outcomes. A variety of peripheral factors related to social and economic marginalization exacerbate this problem.

Finally, in addition to environmental pollutants in residences and workplaces and lack of sufficient access to healthcare, a growing addiction to drugs and alcohol is also compromising health among India's migrant workers. According to the National Mental Health Survey of India 2015–2016, roughly 22% of India's population suffers from mental and behavioral health problems due to psychoactive substance abuse, with mental morbidity reaching 13.7% (Gururaj et al., 2016). Males were reported to be most affected by alcohol abuse while females suffered more with depressive disorders. The profile of the population affected by mental health conditions due to substance abuse is growing younger over time, with the aforementioned report showing the prevalence of morbidity among adolescents to be nearly 7%. The report also shows a substantial treatment gap for all mental disorders due to lack of resources, awareness, and government support. Such mental health challenges are, for many individuals, a further burden added to the negative impacts of substance abuse. While physiological challenges are discussed frequently, mental health disorders and underlying complications are rarely spoken of in India due to cultural stigmatization.

Maternal health

Maternal health and related morbidity and mortality also present significant challenges in India. According to the WHO, India was responsible for over 25% of global deaths related to maternal health complications in 2000 (WHO, 2004). While levels of mortality vary by region, India's outcomes overall are lagging and show little sign of improvement. According to a more recent report by the WHO, maternal mortality rates declined in 2015 to 174 per 100,000 live births, an improvement over previous periods but still unduly high (WHO, 2018). Vora et al. (2009) list several causes for maternal deaths in India, including post-partum hemorrhage, sepsis, hypertension, and obstructed labor, as well as abortion and iron deficiency anemia.

The post-partum experience in India can be burdensome and unsatisfactory, even after a healthy, problem-free delivery. Inadequate provision for health check-ups, essential drugs, and wellness and prevention programs compromise efforts to maintain and improve post-partum health, and adherence to religious and non-scientific mindsets at the cost of health can predispose mothers to higher risk of life-threatening diseases and disorders. This in turn can have detrimental effects on the physiological and mental health of newborns. Most causes of low maternal health outcomes are preventable through better access to resources and information among expecting mothers and the population overall. While health challenges related to environmental pathogens and socio-economic inequality require often complex policy efforts, inadequate pre- and post-partum care, high illiteracy rates among females, and scarcity of primary and secondary healthcare centers are some limiting factors that could be modified through direct government intervention.

Theoretical application

Policy background

As the population of India continues to grow, the demand for better health policies becomes increasingly urgent. Since India's independence in 1947, multiple policies have been proposed and some approved, but implementation has been lacking. The country's first detailed primary healthcare plan was introduced in 1948 through the Sir Joseph Bhore Committee report; this plan helped formulate India's National Health Service. Provisions of the plan included curative and preventative care, accessibility of healthcare centers with special attention to vulnerable populations like children and mothers, inter-professional medical consultation for holistic care, and a vision for a generally healthy living environment – all without imposing an undue financial burden on patients. The report also highlighted the disparity between rural and urban healthcare resources and proposed measures to bridge the gap.

India's Planning Commission is responsible for developing five-year plans that include healthcare. Since the Bhore report, multiple five-year plans have been approved with the aim of improving the country's healthcare system. Although these plans are crucial in continuing to provide citizens with facilities and care, a fundamental restructuring of the health system is needed to address emerging and accumulating challenges. This requires measures that include substantial allocations of financial resources along with a feasible plan to achieve the goal of improving access to basic healthcare across geographies, socio-economic status, and health conditions. Duggal (2007: 386) summarizes the challenges of India's healthcare thus:

> the proportion of public resources committed to healthcare in India is one of the lowest in the world . . . India has large-scale poverty and yet the main source of financing healthcare is out-of-pocket expenditure. This is a cause of the huge inequities we see in access to healthcare.

As the share of private provision in healthcare increases, access among low-income families is becoming an increasing hardship. Extensive dialogues and some policy steps have been undertaken concerning implementation of and modifications to various healthcare plans, but, more than seven decades after the Bhore report, the vision of quality and access has not materialized. Gangolli et al. (2005) argue for a larger societal and governmental shift from minimal policies and prioritization of capitalist development to a more social approach via structural changes in governance. Endemic challenges in India's healthcare system require a transformative mindset beyond mere tinkering at the margins of policy and operations.

Analysis of policy efforts

This chapter has thus far argued that India's public health challenges are due in large part to deficiencies in governance and ineffective policy design and implementation. The remainder of this chapter explores these deficiencies through the theoretical lens of policy capacity. Policy capacity is defined by Wu et al. (2015: 166) as "the set of skills and resources – or competences and capabilities – necessary to perform policy functions". According to Bali et al. (2019), capacity is one of the two fundamental elements of policy effectiveness, the other being instrumentality – that is, "the intrinsic ability of the policy tool to address the problem at hand" (ibid.: 6). These conceptualizations offer a systematic and exhaustive lens through which to examine India's healthcare governance.

Governance failures have been ascribed to a number of causes, including insufficient expertise and capabilities in the public sector, fiscal limitations, weak coordination across departments, corruption and malfeasance, and poorly designed policies. In the context of India and other developing countries, an additional explanation is that policy design elements (e.g., instruments and tools) are mismatched with government capacities (Mukherjee and Howlett, 2016). One example is India's premature and poorly planned adoption of non-hierarchical (decentralized) governance for healthcare, favoring markets or networks as alternative channels for service delivery. In the new public management reform era of the 1980s (Hood, 1995), such approaches gained political currency as cost-effective ways to improve service delivery while hollowing-out a supposedly sluggish and under-performing public sector and generating new market opportunities for the private sector. The effects of these reforms were deep and lasting, with impacts evident to this day in the under-resourced public sectors of many countries. The ideologies that supported – and were supported by – new public management also persist in various manifestations of anti- or small-government political rhetoric.

In a study about the adoption of non-hierarchical governance for healthcare in India, Ramesh et al. (2015) argue that health outcomes have been constrained not only by the government's persistently low health expenditures (as a percentage of GDP) but also by its continuing commitment to privatization of health services. According to Maurya (2019), India has undergone three generations of governance reform in healthcare, from hierarchy to market-based and back to a rough hybrid of the two; across these three generations, certain systemic faults remained constant including low governance capacity and lack of attention to service quality and performance (requiring patching and layering as ad hoc quick-fixes). Ramesh et al. (2015) further argue that India's government-funded programs to improve rural health outcomes, including the Ministry of Health's introduction of the National Rural Health Mission (NRHM) in 2005, fell to the responsibility of state governments that lacked the necessary fiscal and administrative capacity to implement them:

> [The Indian] government's small role in providing and financing health care leaves it largely to private providers to shape the market in their own interest with little concern for the financial implications of their actions on users or the society as a whole.

(ibid.: 355)

The transferal to the private sector of responsibility for public services that are fundamental to the lives of individuals and to the broader functionality of society has exposed India to the predictable risk of applying market mechanisms to provision of public welfare: the prioritization of profit over social outcomes.

Under the guise of non-hierarchical governance, India's reliance on privatization has arguably compromised the imperative for government bodies at all levels (national, state, and local) to develop the analytical capacities needed to understand and address persistently low health outcomes. The chronic under-development of these capacities generates a negative feedback loop in which the poor performance of the public sector supports political arguments favoring privatization, leading to declining fiscal support for the public sector and additional declines in performance as a consequence. Hybrid arrangements have been proposed with the aim of capturing both the purported efficiencies of the private sector and the legal authority, political legitimacy, and reach of the public sector. According to Howlett and Ramesh (2016: 301),

> many key sectors from health to education and others now feature elements of either or both hierarchical approaches – regulation, bureaucratic oversight, and service delivery – as well as both market and network-based non-hierarchical approaches, such as co-pays and exchanges, voluntary organizations, and, increasingly, co-production.

These arrangements themselves require their own type of capacity, that of managing networks and guiding them in a strategic direction; this model is embodied by the concept of "steering not rowing" popularized during the so-called reinventing government era of the early 1990s (Osborne and Gaebler, 1992). Alternative models have since emerged that place outcomes (rather than economic efficiency) closer to the center of governance models, including new public service (Denhardt and Denhardt, 2000), public value management (Moore, 1995; O'Flynn, 2007), and others generally characterized as reactions to new public management.[2]

Operational reforms to models of governance can be responsible for lower performance across publicly funded sectors. For example, efforts to undertake decentralization – often with the purpose of streamlining policymaking processes and improving local accountability – can leave substantial levels of responsibility in the hands of unprepared and under-resourced local governments in rural areas. This is an acute problem for healthcare in India. According to Bali and Ramesh (2015: 308), "disparity in terms of administrative capacity and fiscal resources across Indian states is vast and aggravated with decentralisation, which affected the [health] sector's performance". Such capacities and resources are not always appropriately allocated to local governments in support of increased expectations and levels of autonomy. At the same time, decentralized directives also rely on capacities beyond the effective control of the public sector, particularly where there is a history of capable private providers or a lack of public service provision. Such circumstances require a boost in the capacities of public healthcare facilities as a means to equalize access, not only by improving facilities but also by recruiting capable medical staff. According to Strasser et al. (2016: 407), "Capacity building must occur to make rural health care and lifestyle attractive and to encourage students and health workers to practice in rural settings".

The failures of sectoral models (including government, market, and hybrid) are often offset with additional public expenditures, worsening fiscal gaps and raising the prospect of perverse incentives and gaming among public officials and private contractors. For example, in cases where the private sector is incapable of providing a market-based public good of acceptable accessibility and quality or where it produces public or private goods resulting in undue externalities, governments often provide subsidies in an attempt to fill capacity gaps or distort markets to achieve desired welfare outcomes (Howlett and Ramesh, 2016). While this may be a tenable model for well-resourced governments, those that struggle with fiscal constraints (e.g., in India) are unable to sustain such models and may either appropriate insufficient levels of funds or fall into debt. As such, it is evident that the potential of such models to respond to immediate challenges is often unmatched by their longer-term feasibility and durability.

Health governance and policy capacity

In systematizing the analysis of public sector capabilities, Wu et al. (2015) introduce a policy capacity matrix that overlays three types of skills and competences (analytical, operational-managerial, and political) with three levels of analysis (the individual person, the organization such as an agency or policy unit, and the system in reference to national and sometimes global contexts). Analytical competence refers to the ability to develop technical soundness of policies through research and insight about problems, contexts, and solutions. Operational-managerial competence refers to the ability to marshal resources in support of developing and implementing policy initiatives, often in the context of public organization-building and leadership. Political competence refers to the ability to successfully elicit popular legitimacy and connect interest groups and coalitions through aligned interests. The term "matrix" implies that these two groups of three elements apiece can be combined to yield nine types of capacities (individual analytical, individual managerial, etc.). Building from this model, Howlett and Ramesh (2016) outline critical competences and capabilities across four types of governance modes (legal, market, corporatist, and network), arguing that the critical capacity element for market modes is policy analytical capacity and for network modes managerial expertise capacity. Disaggregating the concept of capacity in these ways enables scholars and other analysts to identify capacity weaknesses in otherwise complex and unwieldy governance systems such as India's.

In applying the concept of policy capacity to the case of India's healthcare governance, it is possible to analyze failings across all nine combinations within the Wu et al. (2015) matrix. For example, breakdowns in operational-managerial capacity are highlighted by the ineffectiveness with which many of India's state governments have implemented national-level healthcare directives, as explored in the previously cited studies and numerous others. This chapter concludes by examining the relevance of one type of competence (analytical) and one level of analysis (individual).

First, analytical capacities at all three levels are crucial for understanding the complex determinants of healthcare in any context but especially in those with numerous confounding factors like poverty, social marginalization, geographic isolation, and others. Among Riddell's (1998) eight components of policy analytical capacity are the ability to undertake theoretical, statistical, and applied research, engage in program design and evaluation, and connect research with broader organizational and political contexts and needs. In many countries, substantial efforts have been applied to improving analytical capacities across all levels of government, including investments in monitoring technologies, procedural reforms that mandate inter-agency information sharing, and training and education programs for bureaucrats and government leaders. These and other efforts ostensibly serve to strengthen the ability of governments to bring objectivity, transparency, and rationality to decision-making processes, at once improving the quality of policies and fostering political credibility and legitimacy. Furthermore, governance reforms themselves, such as new public management, have advocated concepts like evidence-based policymaking as a mechanism to countervail older styles of governance that could be seen as opaque, arbitrary, and based on political patronage. Analytical capacity, by this and other names, has been a useful and fundamental component in "good governance" movements.

Contestation over data and analytical methods is another emerging issue in policymaking. In the words of Ramesh and Wu (2008: 182),

> without a bureaucracy with the capacity to analyse policy problems, governments will be unavoidably swayed by factors other than evidence . . . likely to resort to reform fads and formula responses, which over the last few decades have consistently favoured privatization and deregulation.

The underpinnings of policymaking continue to be deeply rooted in supposedly objective empiricism, instrumental rationality, and high-modern totalization in the pursuit of well-defined solutions; nevertheless, this epistemological legacy is struggling to reckon with increasingly synchronous, interconnected, and wicked problems (Hartley et al., 2019). With the emergence of populist and ethno-nationalist movements in some countries, challenges to the legitimacy and authority of governments and policymaking itself are becoming bolder. As such, analytical capacity is under pressure not only to demonstrate its value internally but also to validate its relevance in bringing material solutions to long-standing social problems such as healthcare. Public trust and analytical capacity, seemingly odd bedfellows, are intertwined with one another when examined in practice; the best analysis carries little or no political credibility when divorced from the interests and perceptions of the public. This puzzle is fertile ground for further research.

The second capacity dimension through which complex governance challenges like healthcare in India can be examined is through individual capacity across all three types of skills and competences. Although policy capacity has been conceptualized in multiple ways, the contribution of the Wu et al. framework is the clearer recognition of individual-level capacities as building blocks for and determinants of higher-level capacities. Individual capacity appears to receive only modest attention and is the least theorized among all types in both the academic literature and in empirical measurement undertaken by various global organizations through governance indices. In a study of governance indices including the Worldwide Governance Indicators, KPMG Change Readiness Index, Sustainable Governance Indicators, Global Innovation Policy Index, and Bertelsmann Transformation Index, Hartley and Zhang (2017) find that individual-level capacity – across analytical, operational-managerial, and political competences – receives the least mention and measurement. Individual analytical capacity in particular can be seen as crucial not only for bureaucrats in jobs requiring analysis but indeed among all public servants. According to Howlett (2015: 175), individual policy analytical capacity is "knowledge of policy substance and analytical techniques and communication skills at the individual level". With the devolution of responsibility for implementation of healthcare initiatives from the central to local governments, as seen to various degrees in India and other countries, individual capacities are potentially a significant determinant of success and of differences in outcomes from one sub-national jurisdiction to another. At the ground level and on the public service "frontline", under-resourced rural states are less likely to have public servants proficient in various skill dimensions, from analytical to operational and political. While these states may have such capacities higher up in their administrative hierarchies, the contribution of capable public sector line-workers is crucial for making policies work. According to Howlett (2015), governments function best when bureaucrats at all levels of their given organizations have at least some degree of policy capacity in the form of the ability to apply certain analytical techniques. This capacity is all the more crucial as it is the "street-level bureaucrats" (Lipsky, 1971) that are the eyes and ears of government, able to monitor conditions and observe policies as they are implemented.

Conclusion

The prevailing narrative about the health pathologies of city life fails to recognize systemic problems that compromise public health in all corners of India, urban and rural. This has important implications for the distribution of resources and core–periphery (urban–rural) relationships within the country. The current circumstances demand decisive intervention, including strategic re-prioritization, organizational reform and restructuring where needed, and an overall change in policy mindset that places individual health outcomes as the guiding principle. There may be some potential for longer-term improvement in India's healthcare outcomes with programs like NRHM and RSBY, reducing the need for out-of-pocket expenditures (Bali and Ramesh, 2015) and improving the accessibility of primary care centers (Husain, 2011). From reforms in policies to implementation at the ground level, each step in the reform process should be approached prudently and critically, with an eye toward realistic appraisals of policy capacity and efforts to build needed capacities across analytical, operational-managerial, and political skill sets. Until such measures are taken, the future of healthcare in India will – like the air – continue to be shrouded in haze and uncertainty.

Notes

1 For an in-depth analysis of India's internal migration patterns, see Parida and Raman (2018).
2 See Christensen (2012) for an overview of such models in practice.

References

Bali, Azad Sing, Gilberto Capano, and M. Ramesh (2019). "Anticipating and Designing for Policy Effectiveness." *Policy and Society* 38 (1): 1–13.
Bali, Azad Sing, and M. Ramesh (2015). "Health Care Reforms in India: Getting It Wrong." *Public Policy and Administration* 30 (3–4): 300–319.
Christensen, Tom (2012). "Post-NPM and Changing Public Governance." *Meiji Journal of Political Science and Economics* 1 (1): 1–11.
Denhardt, Robert B., and Janet V. Denhardt (2000). "The New Public Service: Serving Rather Than Steering." *Public Administration Review* 60 (6): 549–559.
Duggal, Ravi (2007). "Healthcare in India: Changing the Financing Strategy." *Social Policy & Administration* 4 (4): 386–394.
Gangolli, Leena V., Ravi Duggal, and Abhay Shukla (2005). *Review of Healthcare in India*. Mumbai: Centre for Enquiry into Health and Allied Themes. www.cehat.org/go/uploads/Hhr/rhci.pdf.
Gupta, Prakash C., Mangesh S. Pednekar, D.M. Parkin, and R. Sankaranarayanan (2005). "Tobacco Associated Mortality in Mumbai (Bombay) India. Results of the Bombay Cohort Study." *International Journal of Epidemiology* 34 (6): 1395–1402.
Pradeep, Banandur S., Gopalkrishna Gururaj, Mathew Varghese, Vivek Benegal, Girish N. Rao, Gautham M. Sukumar, Senthil Amudhan, Banavaram Arvind, Satish Girimaji, K. Thennarasu, P. Marimuthu, Kommu John Vijayasagar, Binukumar Bhaskarapillai, Jagadisha Thirthalli, Santosh Loganathan, Naveen Kumar, Paulomi Sudhir, Veena A. Sathyanarayana, Kangkan Pathak, Lokesh Kumar Singh, Ritambhara Y. Mehta, Daya Ram, T.M. Shibukumar, Arun Kokane, R.K. Lenin Singh, B.S. Chavan, Pradeep Sharma, C. Ramasubramanian, P.K. Dalal, Pradeep Kumar Saha, Sonia Pereira Deuri, Anjan Kumar Giri, Abhay Bhaskar Kavishvar, Vinod K. Sinha, Jayakrishnan Thavody, Rajni Chatterji, Brogen Singh Akoijam, Subhash Das, Amita Kashyap, Sathish R.V., M. Selvi, S.K. Singh, Vivek Agarwal, and Raghunath Misra (2016). *National Mental Health Survey of India, 2015–16: Summary*. Bengaluru: National Institute of Mental Health and Neurosciences.
Guttikunda, Sarath K., and Rahul Goel (2013). "Health Impacts of Particulate Pollution in a Megacity: Delhi, India." *Environmental Development* 6: 8–20.
Hartley, Kris, Glen Kuecker, and J.J. Woo (2019). "Practicing Public Policy in an Age of Disruption." *Policy Design and Practice* 2 (2): 163–181.
Hartley, Kris, and Jingru Zhang (2017). "Measuring Policy Capacity Through Governance Indices." In *Policy Capacity and Governance: Assessing Governmental Competences and Capabilities in Theory and Practice*, edited by X. Wu, M. Howlett, and M. Ramesh, 67–97. London: Palgrave Macmillan.
Hood, Christopher (1995). "The 'New Public Management' in the 1980s: Variations on a Theme." *Accounting, Organizations and Society* 20 (2–3): 93–109.
Howlett, Michael (2015). "Policy Analytical Capacity: The Supply and Demand for Policy Analysis in Government." *Policy and Society* 34 (3–4): 173–182.

Howlett, Michael, and M. Ramesh (2016). "Achilles' Heels of Governance: Critical Capacity Deficits and Their Role in Governance Failures." *Regulation & Governance* 10 (4): 301–313.

Husain, Zakir (2011). "Health of the National Rural Health Mission." *Economic and Political Weekly* 46 (4): 53–60.

Kumar, Raman, and Ranabir Pal (2018). "India Achieves WHO Recommended Doctor Population Ratio: A Call for Paradigm Shift in Public Health Discourse!" *Journal of Family Medicine and Primary Care* 7 (5): 841–844.

Lipsky, Michael (1971). "Street-level Bureaucracy and the Analysis of Urban Reform." *Urban Affairs Quarterly* 6 (4): 391–409.

Maurya, Dayashankar (2019). "Understanding Public Health Insurance in India: A Design Perspective." *The International Journal of Health Planning and Management*. https://doi.org/10.1002/hpm.2856.

Ministry of Labour and Employment (India) (2010). "National Policy on Safety, Health and Environment at Work Place." www.indiaenvironmentportal.org.in/content/305027/national-policy-on-safety-health-and-environment-at-work-place/.

Moore, Mark H. (1995). *Creating Public Value: Strategic Management in Government*. Cambridge, MA: Harvard University Press.

Mukherjee, Ishani, and Michael Howlett (2016). "An Asian Perspective on Policy Instruments: Policy Styles, Governance Modes and Critical Capacity Challenges." *Asia Pacific Journal of Public Administration* 38 (1): 24–42.

O'Flynn, Janine (2007). "From New Public Management to Public Value: Paradigmatic Change and Managerial Implications." *Australian Journal of Public Administration* 66 (3): 353–366.

Osborne, David, and Ted Gaebler (1992). *Reinventing Government: How the Entrepreneurial Spirit Is Transforming the Public Sector*. Reading, MA: Addison-Wesley.

Padhi, Bijaya Kumar, and Pratap Kumar Padhy (2008). "Domestic Fuels, Indoor Air Pollution, and Children's Health." *Annals of the New York Academy of Sciences* 1140 (1): 209–217.

Parida, Jajati K., and K. Ravi Raman (2018). "India: Rising Trends of International and Internal Migration." In *Handbook of Migration and Globalisation*, edited by A. Triandafyllidou, 226–246. Cheltenham and Massachusetts, MA: Edward Elgar.

Patankar, A.M., and P.L. Trivedi (2011). "Monetary Burden of Health Impacts of Air Pollution in Mumbai, India: Implications for Public Health Policy." *Public Health* 125: 157–164.

Prinja, Shankar, Pankaj Bahuguna, Indrani Gupta, Samik Chowdhury, and Mayur Trivedi (2019). "Role of Insurance in Determining Utilization of Healthcare and Financial Risk Protection in India." *PloS One* 14 (2): e0211793. https://doi.org/10.1371/journal.pone.0211793.

Ramesh, M., and Xun Wu (2008). "Realigning Public and Private Health Care in Southeast Asia." *The Pacific Review* 21 (2): 171–187.

Ramesh, M., Xun Wu, and Michael Howlett (2015). "Second Best Governance? Governments and Governance in the Imperfect World of Health Care Delivery in China, India and Thailand in Comparative Perspective." *Journal of Comparative Policy Analysis: Research and Practice* 17 (4): 342–358.

Riddell, N. (1998). *Policy Research Capacity in the Federal Government*. Ottawa: Policy Research Initiative.

Strasser, Roger, Sophia M. Kam, and Sophie M. Regalado (2016). "Rural Health Care Access and Policy in Developing Countries." *Annual Review of Public Health* 37: 395–412.

Vora, K.S., D.V. Mavalankar, K.V. Ramani, M. Upadhyaya, B. Sharma, S. Iyengar, et al. (2009). "Maternal Health Situation in India: A Case Study." *Journal of Health, Population and Nutrition* 27 (2): 184–201.

WHO (2004). *Maternal Mortality in 2000: Estimates Developed by UNICEF and UNFPA*. Geneva: World Health Organization.

WHO (2018). *Country Cooperative Strategy at a Glance: India*. Geneva: World Health Organization. https://apps.who.int/iris/bitstream/handle/10665/136895/ccsbrief_ind_en.pdf.

Wu, Xun, M Ramesh, and Michael Howlett (2015). "Policy Capacity: A Conceptual Framework for Understanding Policy Competences and Capabilities." *Policy and Society* 34 (3–4): 165–171.

15 The technocratic delusion
India's Smart Cities Mission

Glen Kuecker, Tristan Stamets, and Farukh Sarkulov

Indian Prime Minister Narendra Modi has an ambitious plan to build 100 smart cities by 2022. Announced in 2014 and launched in 2015, the plan is the centerpiece for India's great transformation, which finds the convergence of population growth and urbanization driving the nation toward a bifurcation point of realizing either the promise of modernity or a dystopia of inequity and inequality. Understanding the 100 smart cities agenda invites consideration of key questions about 21st-century Asian cities, especially an analysis of how three forces converge to legitimize modernist approaches to social problems: policymaking, the role of cities within national development agendas, and the systems of thought underlying grand, "winning the future" policies. This chapter explores India's Smart Cities Mission in order to reveal the limitations of its utopian vision. The chapter concludes that smart cities are a 21st-century mechanism of capitalist reproduction that valorizes technocratic solutions to social problems. Far from being the bridge to a utopian urban future, smart cities promise to reproduce inequity and inequality.

India's bifurcation point

The June 2015 "Smart Cities Mission Statement and Guidelines" from the Indian Ministry of Urban Development opens with the declaration, "cities are engines of growth for the economy of every nation, including India" (Government of India, 2015: 5). The potential for growth is in India's transition from a rural to an urban population, as upwards of 400 million rural inhabitants are expected to migrate to Indian cities by the middle of this century (Deloitte, 2017: 15). According to India's 2011 census, the urban population that year constituted 30–31% of the nation's total while contributing 63% of gross domestic product (GDP). By mid-century, according to the Deloitte report, urban population is projected to grow to 40% and contribute 75% of GDP. The Ministry of Urban Development maintains that cities need

> comprehensive development of physical, institutional, social and economic infrastructure. All are important in improving the quality of life and attracting people and investments to the City, setting in motion a virtuous cycle

of growth and development. Development of Smart Cities is a step in that direction.

(Government of India, 2015: 5)

Meanwhile, a 2015 United Kingdom Trade and Investment report asserts that India has "an active demand for 'smart city' approaches to solve challenges of urbanisation, which if not met threaten to strangle city life" (UKTI, 2015: 7).

India, however, is building its smart cities upon a troubled urban legacy. With the country's population growing dramatically since the 1950s, the second half of the 20th century featured mass urban migration (Tumbe, 2016). Cities grew without the resources and basic infrastructure to sate the needs of their growing populations. Hundreds of millions of urban dwellers still do not have access to toilets, potable water, sanitary waste collection, or reliable access to health, education, transportation, or work. In an arguable understatement, the Deloitte report declares that "rapid urbanization will put tremendous pressure on existing city services" (Deloitte, 2017: 15). Adding to this pressure is the very real specter of the caste system's ongoing legacy, perpetuating spatial segregation and class clashes that disrupt the urban fabric and hinder social cohesion. Massive economic inequalities resulting from the imbalance in opportunity between favorable and unfavorable castes further concentrates wealth and power amongst the privileged. This half-century's additional 400 million urbanites will compound these trends and portend Mike Davis' dystopian view of 21st century urbanism as articulated in *Planet of Slums* (2007).

The dystopian narrative co-exists with an optimistic vision that is based on India's recent economic success (Rizvi, 2007: 757). Gurcharan Das captures this optimism in his *India Unbound*:

> India, thus, enters the twenty-first century on the brink of the biggest transformation in its history. The changes are more fundamental than anything that the country has seen, and they hold the potential to transform it into an innovative, energetic economy of the twenty-first century.

(Das, 2000: online)

India is the world's second fastest growing economy; its middle class has expanded to 600 million people since the start of the 21st century, and private investment has grown in tandem (Fernandes, 2006; Karnik, 2016). The Modi government hopes to continue India's economic success and envisions bringing the country to the status of a global power. To achieve greater clout in global international politics, India strives to show that it has arrived, and one such demonstration is the Smart Cities Mission. India is at a bifurcation point between an urban dystopia and the promise of modernity, and the nation has placed a major wager that smart cities are the way forward.

The underlying context for India's bifurcation point is the reform of urban policies that started in the early 1990s. These reforms shifted policy from a state-directed economy that favored the rural sector to a neoliberal approach that privileged the private sector and the city as a setting for growth. That process began with the 1991 New Economic Policy, which allowed transnational financial institutions such as the World Bank to become active players in developing India's urban policies. The constitutional reform of 1992 formalized the retreat of the state, which became public policy in a series of anti-poverty measures that matured in 2006 with the Jawaharlal Nehru National Urban Renewal Mission (JNNURM). The JNNURM was replaced in 2015 by the Atal Mission for Rejuvenation and Urban Transformation (AMRUT), a program that aims to bring renewal to 500 cities. In this narrative of ascending neoliberal urbanism, JNNURM was the antecedent to the Smart City Mission, as it focused India's urban policy on an aggressive agenda of synchronizing "the disproportionately fast pace of urban growth and urban infrastructural development" (Banerjee-Guha, 2009: 97). JNNURM aimed to develop 63 "world class" cities through infrastructure development undertaken by private–public partnerships in which the state provides the legal, administrative, and financial framework for a corporate and consultancy-led private sector tasked with implementation (ibid.). The Smart Cities Mission was the logical next step in the trajectory of India's neoliberal urbanization.

Urban corridors constitute the bridge between JNNURM and the Smart Cities Mission. Urban corridors leverage linkages between cities by enhancing transport infrastructure that serves industrialization, urban renewal, and employment growth (De and Iyengar, 2014; Hildyard and Sol, 2017; Khanna, 2016). With at least six currently in development, corridors are an important element of India's plan to win the future. The Delhi–Mumbai Industrial Corridor (DMIC) is the largest and most advanced – and with a USD 100 billion price tag, the most expensive – project in India (Ghosh, 2012). The Indian Institute for Human Settlements (2015: 6) explains the DMIC's importance: it "marks the emergence of new types of actors through special purpose vehicles, private and international consultants, and public–private partnerships, which are playing increasingly critical roles in urban, industrial, and economic development". These new actors feature foreign partners that provide experience and expertise with corridor development; the DMIC is partnered with the Japanese government. A key feature of the DMIC, as Ayona Datta's (2015a, 2015b, 2016) research shows, is smart cities. The CEO of the DMIC project, Amitabh Kant, who previously headed the "Make in India" campaign, has advocated building smart cities entirely from scratch. He stated,

> today's cities not only have to be interconnected, transit oriented, walkable and cycle-able, they have to be the smart cities of the future. . . . It means India can make a quantum leap into the future . . . it means you can drive urbanisation through the back of your mobile phone.
>
> (quoted in Datta, 2016: 59)

The technocratic delusion

Indian elites believe that the convergence of information technology (IT) and urban planning presents an opportunity to solve the country's wide range of wicked problems. The Ministry of Urban Development states that the objective of the Smart Cities Mission "is to promote cities that provide core infrastructure and give a decent quality of life to its citizens" (Government of India, 2015: 5). It holds the promise of "sustainable and inclusive development" in "a replicable model which will act like a light house to other aspiring cities" (ibid.). The faith in technology resembles a delusional urban utopian fantasy in which the smart city acts as a "magic wand" to fix India's woes. The Ministry of Urban Development spins the technocratic delusion this way:

> Application of Smart Solutions will enable cities to use technology, information and data to improve infrastructure and services. Comprehensive development in this way will improve quality of life, create employment and enhance incomes for all, especially the poor and the disadvantaged, leading to inclusive Cities.
>
> (ibid.)

India's smart city technocratic delusion has deep epistemic roots within the modernist conviction that the rule of reason can triumph over any obstacle. There is no darkness too great for the light of rationality, and faith in progress is greater than the reality of wicked problems. This idea has formed the basis for over half a century of public policymaking (Hartley et al., 2019). Smart cities are the 21st-century iteration of the Cartesian mindset, especially its instrumental rationality, where an end is achieved by the most efficient, cost-effective means, without due consideration of the value of the end or recognition of the socially and culturally constructed meanings of what constitutes "efficient" or "cost-effective". The smart city's instrumental reasoning presumes that with enough big data and proper analytics, the right public policy emerges. Rob Kitchin states,

> The drive towards managing and regulating the city via information and analytic systems promotes a technocratic mode of urban governance which presumes that all aspects of a city can be measured and monitored and treated as technical problems which can be addressed through technical solutions.
>
> (Kitchin, 2014: 9)

Kitchin reminds us that

> technocratic forms of governance are highly narrow in scope and reductionist and functionalist in approach, based on a limited set of particular kinds of data and failing to take account of the wider effects of culture, politics, policy, governance and capital that shape city life and how it unfolds.
>
> (ibid.)

The smart city's reductionist logic will not "solve the deep rooted structural problems in cities as they do not address their root causes" (ibid.). In "Why India Cannot Plan its Cities", Ananya Roy (2009) argues that urban forms have idioms, which are particular social and cultural practices that form the deeper logic of everyday life that constitutes the urban. Roy maintains that informality is India's urban idiom and that the idiom of informality is India's true urban planning. Two starkly contrasting idioms – informality and smart city – reflect realities that are in a contradictory and unsustainable co-existence. To perpetuate this contradiction is the technocratic delusion of India's Smart Cities Mission.

The technocratic delusion is also inherent to neoliberal reforms that valorize the authority of narrowly trained experts whose legitimacy is constituted by their specialized knowledge in the triad of public policy: management, administration, and planning. Expert knowledge produces the power to define the problems that need to be solved, and the solutions advanced by the experts in turn generate further expert knowledge. McKinsey Global Institute's 2010 report, *India's Urban Awakening: Building Inclusive Cities, Sustaining Economic Growth* (Shirish Sankhe et al., 2010) illustrates this point. The consultancy played a seminal role in the ascendance of India's neoliberal urbanism. The report's technocratic authority derives from McKinsey's superior reputation that empowers it to mobilize a broad spectrum of technocratic expertise. Research for the report "engaged in discussions with more than 100 Indian and international urban experts and economists, and with officials in state and local governments" (ibid.: 5). Technocratic power exists when the technocrats reference themselves as the experts but also when their knowledge production leads to policy formation and implementation – and beyond – in successive cycles of problem framing, research, reports, and policy recommendations.

Programs like India's Smart Cities Mission, building from the technocratic authority of policies like JNNURM, become the platform for the next power–knowledge feedback cycle, while bringing together the authority of the policy expert with technology's multiple forms of expertise. The digital expertise of the coder joins the problem-solving authority of public policy in generating the smart city discourse.

The smart city idiom is fundamentally driven by the power–knowledge relationship and technocratic authority. Numerous actors are involved in shaping related policy discourses, including the public and private sectors, global development and aid organizations, and research bodies such as think tanks and universities (Rappoport, 2014). As shown in Arundhati Roy's *Capitalism: A Ghost Story* (2014), neoliberal reforms have created a fertile space for close interactions among corporations, foundations, and state actors; Indian capitalists have benefited correspondingly. Private actors have the distinct advantage of being familiar with public tendering processes and can leverage global networks to secure needed capital. Furthermore, they have the connections and resources to call upon the world's most highly regarded experts and consultancies to legitimize their initiatives. Bloomberg Philanthropies, for example, played a key role in Prime Minister Modi's embrace of the smart city idiom, which was partly the outcome of his meeting with the billionaire and former mayor of New York City – and founder of the transnational C40 group – Michael Bloomberg. Bloomberg Philanthropies pitches itself as the "official knowledge partner" of the Smart Cities Mission, facilitating webinars, publishing newsletters, and maintaining websites that promote related best practices and capacity-building (Bloomberg Philanthropies, 2015). The power–knowledge cycle is thus reproduced as India continues to pursue the opportunity to be a global player.

The technocratic delusion empowers large private corporations to be the drivers of the Smart Cities Mission, as they have the necessary advantages in technology, social capital, and finance. Major Indian corporations, including powerhouses like Tata Group and Reliance Industries Limited, have secured contracts while smaller entrepreneurs are left to tussle over the remnants of larger opportunities. One informant for this study, a principal at an internet hardware provider in Bangalore, explained that these companies, in monopolistic fashion, use their financial resources to tender low bids, as they are willing to take short-term financial losses in order to drive out smaller competitors and dominate the market in the long run.[1]

The Smart Cities Mission represents high potential for profit, but the underlying logic of its technocratic urbanism is fallaciously predicated upon the hope of modernity's totalizing agenda. The Mission represents a technocratic delusion that is out of sync with India's demographically driven bifurcation point and is already yielding to this reality; only a few projects, such as Dholera, are full-scale cities from scratch, leaving the majority of projects dedicated to the humbler task of retooling and refurbishing existing cities with a digital magic wand. The totalizing delusion of the technocratic solution, however, persists as even the more modest enterprise of retooling and refurbishing outpaces India's capacity to provide the required financial and social capital.

Plug-and-play urbanism

The Smart Cities Mission's technocratic delusion results in partial measures, incomplete implementation, and improvised efforts. One informant explained that, in Bangalore, it was not possible to put digital cables underground due to the city's relentless traffic. As such, cables are hung from tree to tree and routers nested in branches, ironically and inadvertently proving Roy's thesis: informality is India's urban planning. This phenomenon reflects the Indian concept of *jugaad*, in which necessary frugality leads to intelligent solutions or hacked innovations. Another result is a plug-and-play strategy that emphasizes fully completing at least one project instead of developing many in piecemeal fashion. This approach has the benefit of not committing to a large-scale system whose outcome and impacts are unknown. Also, negative externalities from implementation are limited in scope. By partitioning a more holistic development of smart cities, plug-and-play minimizes potential challenges associated with a rapidly developed, large-scale project. Nevertheless, the slow pace of India's plug-and-play projects calls into question the country's ability to achieve the ambitious goal of 100 smart cities by the 2022 target date or even by the time 400 million more Indians become urban. Informants at ICLEI South Asia maintained that plug-and-play also stymies technocratic approaches due to lack of readiness and capacity for smart technology at the municipal level.[2] Three years after inception, only 5% of projects have been completed while 72% are still in proposal development stage (Jadhav, 2018).

Plug-and-play risks generating what Graham and Marvin (2001) call "smart enclaves" in which the digital divide benefits the rich while further marginalizing the poor (also see Harrison, 2017; Shelton and Clark, 2016). The development authority in Jaipur, for example, has embarked on a smart city initiative that targets tourism. It aims to enhance tourist safety through video monitoring, information at digital kiosks, and free Wi-Fi at certain locations. The plan also calls for the installation of smart traffic metering and traffic light regulation to improve traffic efficiency. With support from the state of Rajasthan, Jaipur's smart city plan was launched before the Smart City Mission was created and maintains independence from the national plan. Jaipur's approach, however, still relies on the private sector; Cisco Systems and Larsen & Toubro dominate the project, providing hardware and expertise. Jaipur leads many other cities in smart city development due to state government involvement and autonomy from the national government; this has allowed Jaipur to stay independent of the tendering process while avoiding competition with other cities for resources. Jaipur's smart city plan, however, is not meant to benefit the majority of Jaipur's three million residents, as it is focused on ensuring tourist safety and satisfaction. Residential areas will not receive free Wi-Fi.

The potential for smart enclaves that marginalize large segments of the urban population points to the social justice consequences of the Smart Cities Mission's technocratic delusion. Human and Land Rights Network (HLRN) notes how most graphic depictions of smart cities (e.g., for promotional purposes) feature skyscrapers, highways, and commercial centers, without a trace of evidence concerning their benefits to economically disadvantaged people (HLRN, 2017). Shivani Chaudhury, executive director of HLRN, articulates the tragic hypocrisy of the smart cities endeavor: "If the predominant visual of the smart city is one in which there is no space for the poor, who are these cities being created for?" (HLRN, 2017: iii). The erasure of those at or below the poverty line sets a dangerous precedent for the Smart Cities Mission. One of India's goals in announcing the Mission was to cement the nation as an international superpower, economically and technologically. The existence of slums and the institutionalized poverty they represent severely compromises this aim, a visible reminder of India's deficit of human welfare. Ultimately, the Indian smart city is an elitist proposition, further stratifying Indian society rather than dissolving persistent class barriers. As Suresh Panigrahi, a slum-dweller rights advocate, notes, "They want to build a new class – a city within a city" (quoted in Jaiswal, 2017: n.p.). T.N. Behra, a 45-year-old from a slum in Bhubaneswar, a city of one million people, explains, "I hear about the plan when they say: 'Oh, they're demolishing something for Smart City.' That's all I know" (quoted in Jaiswal, ibid.). The distillation of the smart city into smart enclaves of "haves" and "have-nots" portends a dystopian future in which only part of the population can access the benefits of smart urbanism while a majority enjoy no improvement in their economic and social mobility.

The specter of capitalist reproduction

Cities play a central role in the reproduction of capital, and in the 21st century it is increasingly clear that smart cities are a leading mechanism for finance capital to find lucrative markets in creating urban infrastructure. United Kingdom Trade and Investment – the government agency that promotes British businesses globally – states that smart cities represent a USD 1.5 trillion opportunity, of which it intends to capture 10%. Raving about the "sheer scale" of the program (UKTI, 2015: 4), the agency sees India's Smart Cities Mission as a strategic point for market capture. The Indian government is keenly aware not only of the market opportunity but also of the role smart cities can play in developing the nation's capitalist system. A government report states:

> Smart Cities are those that are able to attract investments. Good quality infrastructure, simple and transparent online processes that make it easy to establish an enterprise and run it efficiently are important features of an investor friendly city. Availability of the required skills in the labour force and adequate availability of electricity, water, etc. are important features of a Smart City.
>
> (Quoted in Datta, 2016: 55)

K.C. Smitha confirms UKTI's assessment, seeing the Smart Cities Mission as part of the "process" of global South urbanism that "integrate[s]" India's growing cities into "world/global circuits" of neoliberal capitalism (Smitha, 2016: 1). This integration, following David Harvey's ideas about Marxist geography, is part of capitalist reproduction through the production of space, in this case the digitalization of the urban form. Datta's analyses (2015a, 2015b, 2016) of the smart city project of Dholera make it clear that, under neoliberalism, India's urban form has increasingly become an "urban entrepreneurialism" in which the city is a mechanism for competition and innovation through public–private partnerships and speculative, high-profile projects. Again following Harvey, Datta argues that India's smart city neoliberal urbanism is a process of accumulation through dispossession, whereby the poor in rural areas and peri-urban zones are displaced from their land under the logic of neoliberal urban development. She states, "I conclude that land is the final frontier of smart urbanism in India" (Datta, 2016: 53). Datta's analysis finds continuity between her thesis and a study by Goldman (2011) on Bangalore's emergence in the 1990s as India's "silicon valley" and the way it was driven by speculative land transactions that reproduce global capitalism.

The twin forces of speculative capital and the aspirational vision of entrepreneurial capital establish the underlying mechanisms for India's Smart Cities Mission; they are emblematic of how 21st-century urbanism drives the reproduction of capitalism. Additionally, capitalism is increasingly finding markets in the "perfect storm" of 21st-century crises such as climate change (Kuecker, 2014), a thesis suggested by Naomi Klein's *This Changes Everything* (2014). From this perspective, India's Smart City Mission is part of a global response in which 21st-century urbanism is a focal point. Facing the mounting crises of planetary urbanization (see Lefebvre, 2003 [1970]), the global community's response to the perfect storm was UN Habitat's New Urban Agenda, launched in 2016 (see UN, 2017). The agenda is aspirational, a wildly ambitious set of goals that seek to create inclusive and sustainable urbanism by 2036. The agenda originally did not establish how the goals might be implemented, a task the planners left for the 9th World Urban Forum in 2018. At that gathering it became clear that the implementation plan centered on the logic of smart cities (Kuecker and Hartley, 2018, 2019).

Conclusion: why India and why now?

In 2015, the journal *Dialogues in Human Geography* published a special issue about India's Smart Cities Mission that included essays responding to Datta's pioneering research about Dholera. Among the essays, Greenfield (2015: 43) asked: "But why this particular confluence of ideas, why India, why now?" Greenfield's questions surfaced within the field research conducted for this chapter, as informants shared a common pattern in their replies. They discussed the Smart Cities Mission with a tone of suspended disbelief, as if they were willing to play along with its utopian promise. Invariably, a moment arrived when informants commented on the absurdity of project timelines and, more profoundly, the absurdity of building smart cities when 300 million Indians lack toilets. Such moments revealed a skeptical, slightly angry, but also slightly playful disdain for the undertaking. Nested within respondents' Smart City Mission narratives were misallocated resources, the reproduction of marginalization, the continued enrichment of the super-wealthy, the failure to come to terms with the severity of the country's challenges – in short, the idea of the project as a fool's errand. These moments present a riddle: given the obvious flaws of the smart city concept, why has India bet so heavily on it?

Greenfield's answer rests within India's IT fetish and how it "is understood to be desirable for its connotations of efficiency, effortlessness, logic, clean-room sterility and sheer modernity" (Greenfield, 2015: 43). Datta (2015b: 50) builds from Greenfield's lead, referencing Fernandes' (2006) newer generation of the risen middle class. For Datta, it is the "aspirations of technocratic nationalists" in which "smart cities are part of the dreams . . . of 'success' of a young urban population"; for this generation, "to be patriotic is to believe in the power of technology" (Datta, 2015b: 50). The Center for Financial Accountability has referenced aspirations as well, with the director describing the undertaking as "an attempt at getting into the rich man's club" of wealthy developed nations that are at the table for G20 summits.[3] Researchers at India's National Institute of Urban Affairs find the Smart Cities Mission to be an incremental yet significant step in India's development, the logical outcome of the integration between neoliberalism's decentralization and citizen engagement into a holistic approach – a confounding conjoining of strange bedfellows. Indeed, ICLEI South Asia embraced the "test-bed" urbanism perspective in which good policy passes through an initial stage of capacity building and multiple dead-ends and failures before deeper social learning occurs. This chapter finds validity in each of these smart city narratives and places them in the context of urbanism's role in capitalist reproduction and the technocratic delusion driving the utopian aspirations of the smart city solution to 21st-century crises.

Notes

1 Siddarth Shastry, interview, 9 January 2018.
2 Emani Kumar and Ashise Rao Ghoparde, interview, 19 January 2018.
3 Joe Athialy, interview, 16 January 2018.

References

Banerjee-Guha, Swapna (2009). "Neoliberalising the 'Urban': New Geographies of Power and Injustice in Indian Cities." *Economic and Political Weekly* 44 (22): 95–107.

Bloomberg Philanthropies (2015). "Bloomberg Philanthropies Partners with the Government of India to Encourage Smarter Urban Development that Improves People's Lives." Press release 25 June. www.bloomberg.org/press/releases/bloomberg-philanthropies-partners-with-the-government-on-india-to-encourage-smarter-urban-development-that-improves-peoples-lives/.

Das, Gurcharan (2000). *India Unbound: From Independence to the Global Information Age.* New Delhi: Viking Penguin.

Datta, Ayona (2015a). "New Urban Utopias of Postcolonial India: 'Entrepreneurial Urbanization' in Dholera Smart City, Gujarat." *Dialogues in Human Geography* 5 (1): 3–22.

Datta, Ayona (2015b). "A 100 Smart Cities, a 100 Utopias." *Dialogues in Human Geography* 5 (1): 49–53.

Datta, Ayona (2016). "The Smart Entrepreneurial City: Dholera and 100 Other Utopias in India." In *Smart Urbanism: Utopian Vision or False Dawn?* edited by S. Marvin, A. Luque-Ayala, and C. McFarlane, 52–70. New York: Routledge.

Davis, Mike (2007). *Planet of Slums.* New York: Verso.

De, Prabir, and Kavita Iyengar (2014). *Developing Economic Corridors in South Asia.* Manila: Asian Development Bank.

Deloitte (2017). "Smart City/Smart Nation: Client Stories in Action." www2.deloitte.com/content/dam/Deloitte/us/Documents/process-and-operations/us-cons-smart-cities-client-stories-in-action.pdf.

Fernandes, Leela (2006). *India's New Middle Class: Democratic Politics in an Era of Economic Reform.* Minneapolis, MN: University of Minnesota Press.

Ghosh, Swarnabh (2012). "DMIC." Extrastatecraft. http://extrastatecraft.net/Projects/DMIC.

Goldman, Michael (2011). "Speculative Urbanism and the Making of the Next World City: Speculative Urbanism in Bangalore." *International Journal of Urban and Regional Research* 35 (3): 555–581.

Government of India (2015). "Smart Cities: Mission Statement and Guidelines." New Delhi: Ministry of Urban Development. http://smartcities.gov.in/upload/uploadfiles/files/SmartCityGuidelines(1).pdf.

Graham, Steve, and Simon Marvin (2001). *Splintering Urbanism: Networked Infrastructures, Technological Mobilities and the Urban Condition*. New York: Routledge.

Greenfield, Adam (2015). "Zeroville-on-Khambhat, or: The Clean Slate's Cost." *Dialogues in Human Geography* 5 (1): 40–44.

Harrison, Katherine (2017). "Who Is the Assumed User in the Smart City?" In *Designing, Developing, and Facilitating Smart Cities*, edited by V. Angelakis, E. Tragos, H. C. Pöhls, A. Kapovits, and A. Bassi, 17–32. Cham: Springer International Publishing.

Hartley, Kris, Glen Kuecker, and J.J. Woo (2019). "Practicing Public Policy in an Age of Disruption." *Policy Design and Practice* 2 (2): 163–181. https://doi.org/10.1080/25741292.2019.1622276.

Hildyard, N., and X. Sol (2017). "How Infrastructure is Shaping the World: A Critical Introduction to Infrastructure Mega-corridors." *Counter Balance*, December. www.counter-balance.org/wp-content/uploads/2017/12/Mega-Corridors.online.final_pdf.

HLRN (2017). *India's Smart Cities Mission: Smart for Whom? Cities for Whom?* New Delhi: Housing and Land Rights Network.

Indian Institute for Human Settlements (2015). "Urban Corridors: Strategies for Economic and Urban Development." IGC Working Paper C-35117-INC-1. London: International Growth Center.

Jadhav, Radheshyam (2018). "2.5 Years Into Smart City Plan, Only 5% of Projects Finished." *The Times of India*, 10 January. timesofindia.indiatimes.com/india/2-5-years-into-smart-city-plan-only-5-of-projects-finished/articleshow/62436408.cms.

Jaiswal, Nimisha (2017). "India's 'Smart City' Plan Stumbles Over Slums." *New Internationalist*, 19 September. newint.org/features/2017/06/01/smart-city-plan-stumbles-over-slums.

Karnik, Mahura (2016). "600 Million People Are Now Part of India's Middle Class – Including Your Local Carpenter." *Quartz*, 28 July. qz.com/742986/600-million-people-are-now-part-of-indias-middle-class-including-your-local-carpenter/.

Khanna, Parag (2016). *Connectography: Mapping the Future of Global Civilization*. New York: Random House.

Kitchin, Rob (2014). "The Real-time City? Big Data and Smart Urbanism." *GeoJournal* 79 (1): 1–14.

Klein, Naomi (2014). *This Changes Everything: Capitalism vs. the Climate*. New York: Simon & Schuster.

Kuecker, Glen D. (2014). "The Perfect Storm: Catastrophic Collapse in the 21st Century." In *Transitions to Sustainability: Theoretical Debates for a Changing Planet*, edited by D. Humphreys and S. Stober, 89–105. Champaign, IL: Common Ground Publishing.

Kuecker, Glen D., and Kris Hartley (2018). "No Silver Bullet: The New Urban Agenda and Smart Cities." *Fair Observer*, 13 March. www.fairobserver.com/more/global_change/new-urban-agenda-smart-cities-sustainable-development-climate-news-65431/.

Kuecker, Glen D., and Kris Hartley (2019). "How Smart Cities Became the Urban Norm: Power and Knowledge in New Songdo City." *Annals of the American Association of Geographers*. https://doi.org/10.1080/24694452.2019.1617102.

Lefebvre, Henri (2003 [1970]). *The Urban Revolution*. Minneapolis, MN: University of Minnesota Press.

Rappoport, Elizabeth (2014). "Globalising Sustainable Urbanism: The Role of International Masterplanners." *Area* 47 (2): 110–115.

Rizvi, Gowher (2007). "Emergent India: Globalization, Democracy, and Social Justice." *International Journal* 62 (4): 753–768.

Roy, Ananya (2009). "Why India Cannot Plan Its Cities: Informality, Insurgence and the Idiom of Urbanization." *Planning Theory* 8 (1): 76–87.

Roy, Ananya (2014). *Capitalism: A Ghost Story*. Chicago, IL: Haymarket Books.

Shelton, Taylor, and Jennifer Clark (2016). "Technocratic Values and Uneven Development in the 'Smart City'." *Metropolitics*, 10 May. www.metropolitiques.eu/Technocratic-Values-and-Uneven.html.

Shirish Sankhe, Ireena Vittal, Richard Dobbs, Ajit Mohan, Ankur Gulati, Jonathan Ablett, Shishir Gupta, Alex Kim, Sudipto Paul, Aditya Sanghvi, and Gurpreet Sethy (2010). *India's Urban Awakening: Building Inclusive Cities, Sustaining Economic Growth*. New York City: McKinsey Global Institute.

Smitha, K.C. (2016). "Entrepreneurial Urbanism in India: A Framework." In *Entrepreneurial Urbanism in India: The Politics of Spatial Restructuring and Local Contestation*, edited by K.C. Smitha, 1–34. New York: Springer.

Tumbe, Chinmay (2016). "Urbanisation, Demographic Transition, and the Growth of Cities in India." IGC Working Paper C-35205-INC-1. London: International Growth Center.

UKTI (2015). "India's Smart Cities Programme: The UK Offer to Build Together." London: United Kingdom Trade and Investment. https://assets.publishing.service.gov.uk/government/uploads/system/uploads/attachment_data/file/460151/UKTI_-_The_UK_offer_to_build_together__1_.pdf.

United Nations (2017). *New Urban Agenda*. New York: Habitat III Secretariat.

Conclusion

The future of Asian cities in an age of disruption

The chapters in this volume collectively illustrate the numerous policy challenges and opportunities facing Asia's cities, as expressed through a variety of contexts, policy domains, and normative perspectives. A crucial issue raised throughout the volume is whether and to what extent urban policy solutions are outmatched by the gathering convergence of complex, synchronous, and imminent policy dilemmas. This conclusion synthesizes broad themes of the volume into an argument about the prospects for Asia's urban governance amidst increasingly urgent disruptions to social, economic, and environmental stability.

To contextualize the analysis of themes in the volume, this conclusion presents an argument about the present and potential ability of public policy to manage complexity and disruption. The logic of rationality underlying modern policy solutions is entrenched in assumptions about individual behavior and the serial and deterministic way solutions are conceptualized and implemented. During the past half century, governments lured into the apparent clarity and pragmatism of neoliberal and new public management reforms at national and urban levels have in many cases systematically hollowed-out core public service capacities. Public service capacity is explored in this volume through studies of education in China by Yan and of healthcare in India by Singh and Hartley, South Korea by Lee, and China and Indonesia by Tan and Wang. The partial or sweeping hollowing-out of state capacity has the potential to severely compromise urban social and economic resilience, with troubling implications for access to public goods and democratic influence on urban policy. The resulting environment is one increasingly shaped by contestation and power struggles, a phenomenon observed by Vo and Anderson in their chapter about urban public space in Vietnam.

Building on Lefebvre's concept of the right to the city, Harvey (2003: 941) argues that "the creation of a new urban commons, a public sphere of active democratic participation, requires that we roll back that huge wave of privatization that has been the mantra of a destructive neoliberalism". This argument broadly reflects the first part of this volume, which focuses on the impacts of late 20th-century reform ideas in governance, economics, and state–society relations. While the neoliberal turn can in some instances give rise to a reactionary mobilization of civil society, it operates most efficiently in service to its beneficiaries when it squelches competing narratives perceived as a threat to state authority and corporate viability – in a model requiring top-down coordination resembling authoritarian or totalizing ideals. Left in the smoldering aftermath is an untapped store of citizen capacity, knowledge, and passion – the lost potential of a civil society whose energies are directed more at recovering lost agency than at solving imminent problems. The apotheosis of neoliberalism and its assault on the capacities and resilience of civil society are forces that will shape the ability of cities to weather disruptive crises for decades to come.

A key argument throughout this volume is that the prospects for social, economic, and environmental sustainability in Asia are dependent on the effectiveness and responsiveness of urban governance, reflecting the second theme of the volume: social development and the impact of policy models on the lived experience of urban residents. Understanding how external pressures visit disruption and contradiction on policy systems begins by accounting for path dependencies in the evolution of urban governance. Two related phenomena – globalization and neoliberalism – have precipitated this disruption and contradiction.

Globalization has generated unprecedented opportunities for lower-income countries to enter global production systems, if only at low value-added levels. The mobility of industrial production and investment capital is at once a boon for growth ambitions and its own undoing: jobs and investment are in a constant state of geographical flux, flowing to locations with the highest and most immediate economic returns. Under this long-running globalist system of cost arbitrage, few countries, especially those with developing economies, can rest assured of a durable comparative advantage. With production mobility comes instability in employment – from steel workers in the United States Midwest to garment workers in India. Since the advent of the current populist wave in the early 2010s, many countries are turning inward with implications for trade, global collaboration, and other policy domains. Furthermore, in countries with democratic systems and even in some autocracies, disaffection and distrust among the unemployed and socio-economically marginalized is leading to populist agitation, challenging the legitimacy and logic of legacy governance models now relied on to address complex issues like sustainability, as discussed in the third section of this volume.

Toward urban action and global collaboration

In facing the problems that mobility of production and capital engender, national level governments can avail themselves of a networked system of collective guidance and partnership opportunities. The apparatus of global multilateralism, largely under the auspices of the United Nations, focused throughout the 20th century on economic development but is now bringing countries together around environmental, social, and governance concerns. The United Nations Sustainable Development Goals (SDGs) have an overarching vision of economic growth that avoids depleting resources or denying future generations their own health and happiness; indeed, many of the SDG goals relate to human development and dignity, ecological conditions, and ways of thinking that challenge the get-rich-at-all-costs mentality. This marks an important acknowledgment by the global community that governing in the 21st century must embrace a new governance paradigm.

Nevertheless, in-principle endorsement at the multilateral level and disciplined commitment within countries themselves are different things. With constraints such as limited fiscal space, corporate pushback, and tepid political will, some countries appear to have dim prospects for fully embracing the SDGs in national policy – a matter directly and indirectly explored throughout this volume. As governance structures are sodden with neoliberal ideals, contestation over access to policy influence and individual opportunity has exposed parallel and competing epistemological frames – one public-centered and democratic, the other elite and performatively technocratic. Neoliberalism's effort to either marginalize civil society or shape it in economically productive ways has arguably gutted civil society of its pluck and counterbalancing potential, giving governments effective impunity in generating policy and supportive narratives.

Issues concerning the scale of governance – including the well-embraced idea that "all politics is local" (see O'Neill and Hymel, 1994) – underscore the potential of cities to rectify governance failings. Indeed, cities may be the last bastions of hope for achieving an equitable and sustainable future at the global scale. As hubs of economic, social, and political activity – including the exchange of goods, capital, and ideas – cities confront the immediate urgency of global crises on their own doorsteps. Against this backdrop, urban governments must also maintain continuity and quality in service delivery, keeping their visions about sustainability rooted in practical concerns rather than in high political rhetoric. This reality is consistent with Barber's (2013) argument about the pragmatism of urban governments as a model for addressing global challenges and is a topic addressed by Phua's chapter in the context of Singapore's efforts to overcome space and resource constraints to become one of the world's most developed countries. While global-level discussion and national policy buy-in are indispensable for strategic visioning (e.g., the creation of the SDGs), the exigencies of ground-level implementation place cities at the center of the sustainability discussion – and Asia offers instructive cases in first-response. With their dense populations, low-lying and coastal locations, and enduring socio-economic inequalities, Asia's cities are at the forefront of 21st-century governance challenges.

Since the turn of the 21st century, the neoliberal disposition of governance reforms has compelled cities themselves to engage global urban networks (e.g., the C40 Cities Climate Leadership Group, ICLEI – Local Governments for Sustainability, United Cities and Local Governments, Metropolis, and UN Habitat). Participation in these networks provides mayors with opportunities to engage directly with international peers outside the pomp and circumstance of national-level diplomacy (Hartley, 2019). The urban governance community increasingly appears to be establishing and advocating for a global understanding about the unique challenges and needs of cities.

Two purposes served by these networks, among numerous other purposes, are knowledge sharing and political influence. First, cities facing similar challenges thirst for opportunities to compare policy interventions and collectively develop fresh ideas. While high-profile global urban networks are often dominated in membership and influence by large, wealthy cities in developed countries, other networks are emerging around issues more targeted to specific policy issues faced by all types of cities, including environmental management, immigration, low-income housing, and displacement. One example is the Connecting Delta Cities Network, a self-described adaptation implementation initiative involving cities in coastal deltas that are facing sea-level rise and related environmental, social, and economic challenges. Another example is the Indian Institute for Human Settlements, which supports a global network for research and knowledge dissemination about SDG localization and other issues related to sustainability. Localizing the SDGs is one template around which cities can build networking relationships for these and other purposes – indeed, the numerous targets and indicators within each of the 17 SDGs specifies numerous issues directly relevant to cities. A second purpose of urban networks is political influence. By speaking with a collective voice, these networks endeavor to bring global and national attention to pressing urban concerns through the media, summits, and universal declarations.

Toward a policy-based epistemic enlightenment

It is pertinent to conclude this volume by considering the logic of knowledge creation and the missed opportunities to precipitate a paradigm shift in the epistemic foundations of public policy itself. Unprecedented and wicked problems facing cities and the global community challenge society to consider new ways of being, thinking, and doing. Modern policy interventions, while well-meaning, suffer from a limited perspective as they are steeped in the legacy epistemic of problem- and solution-identification. This model is deeply embedded in official governance systems and procedures, as exemplified by multiple chapters in this volume. It is also rooted in how policymakers and political leaders personally conceptualize problems, with individual cognitive biases shaped and perpetuated by mainstream thinking in the education and research efforts of policy and political sciences (Hartley et al., 2019).

This thinking can arguably be traced back to a watershed moment in the history of modern governance: the post-World War II era. In that era, policy challenges were tangible, apparent, and unavoidable: the need to rebuild cities, resuscitate economies, restore alliances, and revive public trust in governance. The emergence of numerous initiatives, such as the formation of multilateral development institutions to manage capital flows and central government programs to restore stability to economic systems, coincided with an unprecedented boost in the technologies of economic measurement and analysis. This lured the field of policymaking into what would become a decades-long infatuation with technocracy, informed in mindset by instrumental rationality and the belief that complex problems can be measured, goals will remain fixed, and solutions tightly calibrated. This has manifested itself in particular visions of urban service delivery, including smart cities as explored in Singapore by Woo and India by Kuecker, Stamets, and Sarkulov.

Locked into a rationalist epistemic, policymaking veered precipitously toward a governance model dominated by elite technocrats and dismissive of alternative forms of knowledge and understanding that fell outside the narrow gaze of quantifiability; this theme is explored in this volume by Hartley and by Kuecker, Stamets, and Sarkulov. Armed with an exclusionary and self-evident perception of its own legitimacy, this problem-solving epistemic produced stately policy interventions resembling in scope and ambition the high-modernist visions of mid-century architects and urban planners.

Taming wicked problems using rational interventions gave the United States the Great Society anti-poverty program, urban renewal and public housing, and an array of government agencies aimed at executing these and other grand plans. The failures of these programs are well-documented, but less is said about how the paternalistic and utopian policy logic underlying these programs lingers to this day in efforts to rationalize nearly every sector of society including education, healthcare, and climate resilience.

This is a moment of reckoning in which society's inability or unwillingness to soberly reflect on the policy failures of the 20th century will shape the way sustainability is defined, problematized, and addressed. The methodical search for and universal application of policy solutions are alluring but suffer structural flaws on account of narrow epistemological scope. While aspirational initiatives like the SDGs bring much-needed attention to these issues – and localization of the SDGs underscores the role of cities within that effort – there is a need to transition from solutions-thinking to a more adaptive predicament-thinking, in which policymaking acknowledges its limited understanding of complex problems and its limited capacity to address them. Furthermore, iteratively and adaptively exploring polity initiatives and their impacts helps policymakers revise their efforts and gives the public and civil society the information to critically assess societal objectives. Participation by civil society will continue to be crucial to legitimizing these complex policy efforts, as argued in Hartley's chapter. Political blowback against high-modern technocracy is an increasing likelihood in an era when many people feel little agency over their own well-being and harbor low certainty about the next generation's welfare.

Coda

Addressing the themes of governance, society, and sustainability, the chapters in this volume collectively raise questions for future research about the ability of Asian cities to confront the unpredictable convergence of wicked problems in the 21st century. More scholarly analysis is needed to better understand how identifying and forging a path toward sustainability is dependent on the flexibility of old policy paradigms to adapt to new ways of thinking and operating.

Efforts to address the many modern challenges of globalism, rapid technological change, an undue focus on short-term goals, and the potential impacts of climate change have been undertaken by institutions at the global and multilateral levels, and some national level governments have individually embraced the sustainability mandate as a lodestar for long-term planning and policymaking.

However, it is at the local level that the impacts of wicked problems are felt most acutely. Urban governments face the challenge of managing these issues while maintaining basic living standards and doing so in a way that recognizes the meaning of history, culture, diversity, and expression of collective ideals in urban space; the combination of these issues is explored by Waschak in the context of Nur-Sultan, Kazakhstan.

Pushed to the margins of society by market forces and exclusionary policies, the hundreds of millions of urban residents around the world who live in poverty are the first exposed to the impacts of climate change. This exposure is exacerbated by persistently bad outcomes in education, public health, and socio-economic mobility. As such, it is clear that the prospects for individual personal fulfilment are dim even without worsening conditions and still less promising under likelier scenarios in which cities are epicenters of runaway inequality and climate change effects. At the same time, a glint of hope in the ashes of neoliberalism can be found in durable and resilient social structures within civil society, those based on trust, reciprocity, and shared experiences. Cities must confront these issues in physical planning, as in the context of street layouts in China by Dai and Frantz, waste management in China and Singapore by Zhang and Hartley, urban public space in Kazakhstan by Waschak and in Vietnam by Vo and Anderson, and in the context of governance quality and reform as explored in the context of Indonesia by Amri and comparatively between Indonesia and the Philippines by Juwono and Cindra.

The best policy ideas of the 21st century are likely to come from cities – first because there are thousands of cities and millions of city dwellers attempting to solve common challenges and at least a few are likely to produce valuable ideas and second because cities are face-to-face with the impacts of 21st-century problems like socio-economic inequality and climate change. As a region with high levels of diversity and creativity to go with deep policy challenges, Asia has the potential to be the cradle of a new global enlightenment – one focused not only on policy models but also on the evolution of consumption-based capitalism to a model that more fully accounts for the true costs of human indulgence, the hubris of rationality, and the moral vacuity of inaction.

References

Barber, Benjamin R. (2013). *If Mayors Ruled the World: Dysfunctional Nations, Rising Cities.* New Haven, CT: Yale University Press.

Hartley, Kris (2019). "Global Goals, Global Cities: Achieving the SDGs through Collective Local Action." The Chicago Council on Global Affairs. www.thechicagocouncil.org/sites/default/files/report_global-goals-global-cities_190923.pdf.

Hartley, Kris, Glen Kuecker, and J.J. Woo (2019). "Practicing Public Policy in an Age of Disruption." *Policy Design and Practice* 2 (2): 163–181.

Harvey, David (2003). "The Right to the City." *International Journal of Urban and Regional Research* 27 (4): 939–941.

O'Neill, Tip, Thomas O'Neill, and Gary Hymel (1994). *All Politics Is Local.* New York: Adams Media.

Index

Note: Page numbers in italics indicate figures; page numbers in bold indicate tables.

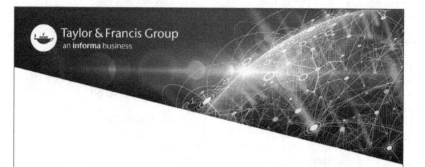